REFORMING INTELLIGENCE

REFORMING INTELLIGENCE

Obstacles to Democratic
Control and Effectiveness

Edited by
THOMAS C. BRUNEAU AND STEVEN C. BORAZ

Foreword by
ROBERT JERVIS

UNIVERSITY OF TEXAS PRESS
Austin

Requests for permission to reproduce material from this work
should be sent to:
Permissions
University of Texas Press
P.O. Box 7819
Austin, TX 78713-7819
www.utexas.edu/utpress/about/bpermission.html

⊗ The paper used in this book meets the minimum requirements
of ANSI/NISO Z39.48-1992 (R1997) (Permanence of Paper).

The views expressed here are those of the authors alone and do not
necessarily represent those of the Department of Navy or the
Department of Defense.

Library of Congress Cataloging-in-Publication Data

Reforming intelligence : obstacles to democratic control and
effectiveness / edited by Thomas C. Bruneau and Steven C. Boraz.
        p.   cm.
Includes bibliographical references and index.
ISBN-13: 978-0-292-71660-5 (cloth : alk. paper)
ISBN-10: 0-292-71660-5 (alk. paper)
1. Intelligence service—Case studies.   2. Civil-military relations—
Case studies.   I. Bruneau, Thomas C.   II. Boraz, Steven C., 1968-
JF1525.I6R44   2007
353.1'72367—dc22
2006102251

CONTENTS

INTELLIGENCE, CIVIL-INTELLIGENCE RELATIONS, AND DEMOCRACY

Robert Jervis

Intelligence and intelligence services are simultaneously necessary for democracy and a threat to it. But this topic is remarkably little developed. There are bookshelves of studies of civil-military relations but almost no counterpart investigations of intelligence. Intelligence failures have fascinated scholars (and exasperated decision makers), but even here our knowledge is thin, and in other areas of intelligence the studies are thinner. This is particularly true for examinations of countries other than the advanced democracies and a few selected dictatorships like Nazi Germany. The essays in this volume are an excellent start to filling these gaps.

INTELLIGENCE: NECESSARY AND DANGEROUS

Intelligence services are vital and troublesome. They are vital because to thrive, or even to survive, the state has to understand its environment and assess actual and potential adversaries. Without good intelligence, a country will thrash about blindly or allow threats to grow without taking countermeasures. It is trite to say that knowledge is power, and perhaps it is more accurate to say that knowledge is needed if power is to be used well. But while we can debate the exact contribution intelligence makes to policy and the extent to which superior intelligence has countered or won wars, it is hard to believe that the role is negligible. Leaders certainly value intelligence; Winston Churchill referred to code breakers as his "hens" because they brought him golden eggs.

Intelligence services also can be troublesome, even leaving aside the problems they can create when they are inadequate. If knowledge contributes to power, then those who have the knowledge are powerful, which is why poorly regulated intelligence services can menace leaders and citizens. This is particularly true when the environment and adversaries that need to be understood are internal as well as external. By its nature, much intelligence is secret and many intelligence-gathering procedures must be kept from public knowledge. This also makes the services dangerous to democracy and difficult to control. Oversight is not easy: some civilian leaders do not want to know what unpleasant methods are being used on their behalf, while many intelligence services resist sharing this information, whether for legitimate security concerns or because of the desire to retain autonomy.

The very fact that intelligence services have such a capacity for secrecy makes them useful for "back channel" communications internationally and domestically. It also means, however, that state leaders may be unsure of the other uses to which intelligence organizations are putting this information, and thus they may have little trust in the service. Such mistrust may then influence those leaders to develop yet more secret, and often informal, organizations to go behind the back of established intelligence services, as Doug Porch, in Chapter 5 of this volume, notes has often been the case in France and was true in the United States under President Richard Nixon.

Of course, most intelligence services have more than information; they have guns as well. This combination multiplies both their threat and their value. In principle, one could completely separate knowledge and force, along the lines of the Directorate of Intelligence and the Directorate of Operations within the U.S. Central Intelligence Agency (CIA). But there is a good reason for keeping them closely knit together, because if force is to be accurately guided, those who wield it need to have direct access to those who supply and process knowledge. Furthermore, to the extent that the information is gathered from sources that are both clandestine and human, in some cases the agents involved in its collection are likely to be the very same people who determine the use of force.

While intelligence services can menace the regime no matter what its nature, the tensions are particularly acute in democracies because this form of government rests on openness, the free flow of information, and unfettered debate. At a minimum, when a democracy requires the extensive use of foreign intelligence and covert operations, the populace cannot be fully informed about its foreign policy and what is being done in the name of the country. It is interesting that many American commentators who are severely critical of covert action talk about "the CIA overthrowing" this or that regime or "the CIA" meddling in the domestic politics of other countries. In fact, the CIA does not operate on its own, and these operations have been authorized and indeed ordered by the president. Thus it would be more accurate to talk about the *United States* overthrowing regimes or meddling in others' politics. But many critics are reluctant to use the more accurate formulation, which would implicate the democratically elected government rather than the shadowy instrument that carried out the policy.

Even if the executive branch keeps the CIA under adequate control, the executive is not the full U.S. government. Congressional oversight continues to be contentious or episodic, and it is far from clear how adequate even better-designed reforms would prove to be. Secrecy requires that information be closely held, which means it cannot be shared with the entire Congress. Even less could questions about specific operations be debated on the floor, although in principle Congress could pass legislation outlining general limits and directions for covert action. Moreover, the danger that the CIA or any intelligence service might act on its own is always present. It is hard to avoid the conclusion that tensions between intelligence and democracy can never be entirely resolved.

Because of their typically hierarchical nature, penchant for order, and links to the military, intelligence services that were established under a former authoritarian regime can represent a particularly potent threat to democratizing countries, which often have weak civilian institutions. These services frequently were used to spy on and intimidate the very individuals and groups that have come to power through democratization. Even if the existing services are willing to give allegiance to a new master, the relationship will be uneasy at best. Even though intelligence services may actually have more rather than less autonomy in democracies than under dictatorships, civilian leaders will have to create and impose new, unfamiliar modes of control, which is never an easy process for either side.

The struggle for control is not simply between the intelligence services and the civil authorities, of course; neither group is a cohesive unit. One intelligence service can seek allies among the civil authorities in its conflicts with other services; even more prevalent are struggles between the executive and legislative branches over how the services are to be supervised and by whom, as Priscila Antunes (Chapter 8) shows happened in Argentina. We usually stress that strengthening state institutional capacity is crucial to the development of a well-functioning democracy, but if the intelligence services are too capable, they can undermine democratic institutions. Indeed, the tendency for other institutions in new democracies to be weak makes it difficult to develop intelligence services that are effective, legitimate, and under control. The fear that intelligence services will be better developed than other parts of the polity can lead civilian officials to render them inefficient, dynamics that Marco Cepik (Chapter 6) shows to be at work in Brazil.

In his study of the Philippines (Chapter 12), Douglas Macdonald describes the series of dilemmas democrats often face when deciding how to reform and rein in intelligence services that had served a previous dictatorial regime. The impulse to be too ambitious and move too quickly (following "blitzkrieg" tactics) is often hard to resist but may be less effective and more dangerous than proceeding incrementally (using "Fabian" tactics) without abandoning far-reaching goals.

The most important general point we can derive from the range of problems and alternative ways of dealing with them that are the subject of many chapters in this book is that while continued success cannot be taken for granted, it is striking that so many new democracies have been able to work out acceptable relations with their intelligence services. Although in some cases, such as Salvador Allende's Chile, domestic intelligence services have joined in overthrowing a democratically elected regime, more recent political transitions have been relatively smooth, and in no cases have the services turned against the new regimes. This is a major achievement whose significance and importance are obscured by the fact that it is a "nonevent"—that is, nothing happened. But the absence of conflict should not be taken for granted, was not inevitable, and might not have occurred if policies had been badly designed. This is not to say that in all cases the arrangements have been optimal, let alone perfect, as many of the chapters make clear. For example, Cris Matei (Chapter 9) describes the way Romania's 1992 Emergency Ordinance solved the Foreign Intelligence Service's funding problem by sacrificing oversight and allowing it to engage in questionable activities. Nevertheless, the worst kinds of breakdown have been avoided, an achievement that is easy to overlook.

There are obvious if diverse interrelations between external intelligence and security on the one hand and internal intelligence and security on the other. Indeed, these links are responsible for many dilemmas. Although among the developed countries, intelligence and security usually are most salient in the external context, this is not true for other countries and is not true for even the developed democracies at all periods of time. Furthermore, internal and external threats are often linked in a variety of ways. Most obviously, internal enemies can seek support from external ones, and vice versa. Terrorist threats are of this kind, and the ties are such that one could not categorize the threat as either internal or external. On other occasions, authorities exaggerate the external menace in order to crack down on internal dissidents or seek foreign adventures in order to reduce internal disagreements and unify the country.

The actual or potential linkages between internal and external enemies create obvious incentives for close ties between internal and external intelligence. But those incentives simultaneously create a dilemma because unifying intelligence services in this way makes them more powerful and increases their potential threat to the regime. We are probably most conscious of this in terms of civil liberties and threats to democracy, but in fact intelligence services can undermine and overthrow dictators as well, something of which they are well aware. It is not surprising that dictators usually try to fragment intelligence services and reward loyalty more than competence, which in turn makes these states less competent and more vulnerable to external, if not to internal, enemies.

There probably are correlations among the level of internal and external threat, the strength of security services, and the viability or absence of democracy. But causation is hard to establish and probably is complex. It is almost a commonplace that democracy is most likely to thrive when internal and external threats are relatively low, and most accounts of democracy's development in the United States and Britain note their privileged international positions. As the American founders were well aware, wars are likely to lead to concentrated and centralized political power and therefore to make tyranny more likely. High internal threat levels foster similar results, in addition to the inherent danger they pose to domestic democratic institutions. One intervening variable is that great threats are likely to lead to the establishment of intrusive security organizations. But these organizations may be more than mere intervening variables; they will seek to justify their own existence by exaggerating if not actually generating threats and, like other organizations, will seek to expand their power and autonomy. Both malign and benign cycles are likely: high-threat environments will call up intrusive security services and make democracy more difficult; a benign environment will allow—although it does not require—restrained services under greater civilian control and will allow greater democracy.

It is often argued, and indeed it might be inferred from the scenarios described above, that there is a trade-off between intelligence effectiveness on the one hand and civilian control on the other. Most obviously, critics have claimed that reforms instituted in the United States in the wake of Watergate and associated scandals concerning abuse of power by the executive significantly harmed American intelligence and even indirectly contributed to the terrorist attacks of 9/11 by reducing the extent to which the Federal Bureau of Investigation (FBI) and the CIA could share information. This correlation is debatable, but even if the critics are correct in this case, I do not think we should be too quick to assume that the general argument holds. I am skeptical that unreformed and unrestrained intelligence services will necessarily do well at ensuring national security. In some cases, legitimate authorities might give intelligence services authorizations and powers that they would not otherwise have. Furthermore and more importantly, reform and oversight can produce efficiencies, force services to cooperate (the CIA-FBI case is instructive here), and limit the fantasies to which such services are prone. By the same token, the gathering and use of intelligence in democratic or democratizing countries over the long run must rest on the consent and indeed support of the citizenry and powerful groups in society. Without significant oversight and at least some public accountability, this support will be very difficult to sustain.

Oversight and civilian control implies politics, with all the good and the bad that this entails. In the American case, many (although not all) of the intelligence failures are linked to politics. Although I doubt whether the CIA would have been able to get the case of the Soviet Union's demise right under any circumstances, constant political pressures made its job more difficult. This was most obvious in military estimates reached during the mid-1970s that led up to the famous—or infamous—Team B exercise. ("Team B" was created in 1976 by the then CIA director George H. W. Bush to reevaluate what he and other hard-liners considered excessively "soft" CIA assessments of the Soviet Union's current condition. Team B declared that the Soviet Union was gaining military and economic strength and posed an increasing threat to the security of the United States. As events proved, even the CIA's conclusions were far too generous, and the Soviet Union was on the verge of economic collapse. See Chris Floyd, "Team Spirit," *Moscow Times*, February 6, 2004, http://www .thetruthseeker.co.uk/article.asp?ID=1503.) Whether the grave over-estimates of Iraq's WMD (weapons of mass destruction) programs in the run-up to the second Iraq war were a result of politicization is still hotly debated. My own feeling is that while this was not one of the major causes of the errors that resulted, the highly charged politi-cal atmosphere in the winter of 2002–2003 made careful and skeptical analysis more difficult. Politics can complicate intelligence in less obvi-ous ways as well. Those with oversight responsibility may choose to reveal secrets to advance their substantive agendas or political careers. Thus in the middle of his (unsuccessful) struggle to retain his Senate seat in 1979, Frank Church chose to announce that U.S. intelligence had "discovered" a Soviet combat brigade in Cuba, and so set off a diplomatic storm that seriously set back Soviet-American relations.

THE ANALOGY OF CIVIL-MILITARY RELATIONS

Much more has been written about civil-military relations than about relations between intelligence services and civilian leaders, and al-though the former still lacks a generally accepted analytical theory, it can nevertheless provide us with some starting points and avenues for exploration of "civil-intelligence relations," as Tom Bruneau and Steve Boraz discuss in this volume's introduction. The two realms present some parallel tensions and dilemmas. To start with, on the one hand both intelligence services and militaries should be strong, efficient, and professionalized, but on the other hand they should not set their own goals and they must respond to civilian authority. The latter re-quirement is not absolute, however. We want the military and intelli-gence to be under civilian control but also to resist illegitimate orders; we need both to guard against the possibility that they will commit unauthorized abuses and to ensure that they will not become an in-strument of abuse even if they are so ordered. In Nazi Germany and most Communist states, intelligence services were under effective and central civilian control (although, especially in the former, efficiency suffered from crippling rivalries). But—or perhaps as a consequence— these services generally performed poorly abroad and were repressive internally. They faithfully followed orders, but as a result their mas-ters failed to gain accurate information about the world and permitted operatives to attack internal opponents (often imagined ones) without restraint. Although the political leaders might have maintained their regimes in the short run, such activities helped bring them down over the longer period.

Nothing so extreme has happened among democracies, but there are paler counterparts. The Vietnam era brought out the tension between obedience and serving the country in both the military and intelligence services. The generals accepted orders, as they should have, but did not give the civilian leaders their unvarnished professional advice and failed to warn that the policy being pursued was not likely to succeed. On the domestic side, the FBI adopted reprehensible and illegal behavior in harassing and oppressing domestic opponents of the war. For obvious reasons, it is difficult to ascertain what if any orders came from the White House, but it seems clear that the FBI's actions were in the spirit of President Nixon's desires. This was a case in which obedience to the current leadership constituted a violation of the fundamental values and principles of the government and country as a whole.

Like the military, intelligence services tend to have a can-do outlook. In part, the reasons are the same: the need to gain favor with the government and its leaders, pride in the service's abilities, a desire to serve. But intelligence officials may feel additional pressure from suspicious civilian leaders who think that the service is disloyal, incompetent, or both. By showing that they are willing and able to do what political leaders ask, members of the service hope to be more valued by them. The obvious danger is that the service will overpromise what it can do and how accurate its estimates will be. Limitations on the declassified record make it impossible for us to reach anything like a definitive judgment, but it is clear that in a number of cases over the years the CIA promised more than it could deliver. Successes like supporting democracy in Italy after World War II and overthrowing regimes in Guatemala and Iran are matched or overmatched by failures in Syria, in Indonesia, and, most spectacularly, at the Bay of Pigs, to take just a few obvious examples.

Turning to threat estimates, the obstacles to accuracy are so great that the errors that litter the record are only to be expected. The problem is not so much that the intelligence professionals greatly overestimate what they can know, but rather that being completely honest with their "customers" (i.e., government officials) could lead the latter to stop buying the product. Leaders want, if not certainty, then at least a good sense of the other country's intentions and capabilities. Although they constantly tell intelligence analysts to give them an honest reading of what the service does and does not know and how great the uncertainties are, the need to act means they must feel certain that the information they have is solid. So the incentive for intelligence services to oversell is matched by the need of consumers to buy too confidently.

These pressures are manifest in current discussions of intelligence reforms within the United States. Leaving aside the question of whether the newly created position of director of national intelligence has much to be said for it, it is noteworthy that those who advocated it imply that it will prevent future terrorist attacks, and many people in Congress and the executive branch seem to accept this wildly overoptimistic assumption. More generally, intelligence consumers always seem surprised by intelligence failures. By definition, the particular failure must be a surprise, but the fact that these failures occur with some regularity should not be. It would be very hard for a leader of an intelligence service to fully explain this to skeptical politicians, however, without raising questions about his competence and the fundamental value of the service.

THE WAR ON TERROR

The present "war" on terror poses special problems for intelligence services and civil-intelligence relations. While I believe that such problems come into especially sharp focus for the United States, they arise in other countries as well.

Most obviously, it is extremely difficult to understand terrorism and predict where terrorist attacks will occur. Although terrorism is an old phenomenon, it has not been subject to careful and dispassionate scholarly study. Governments have tried to keep track of particular terrorist organizations that menace them, but official knowledge too is sharply limited. In fact, it is probably a mistake to speak of "terrorism" as though it were a single entity. Rather than being an "it," terrorism is a "they" — there are lots of different kinds of terrorisms and terrorist groups that vary in capabilities, motives, and methods of operation. Partly for this reason, while every government condemns terrorism in the abstract, the United Nations cannot even agree on a definition, because different countries support or have supported groups that others label as terrorists. Arab countries refuse to see Hamas and Hizbullah as terrorist organizations. The U.S. government apparently is now using Iranian exiles, whom it previously labeled terrorists, for intelligence purposes, while in the 1980s the administration of Ronald Reagan supported the so-called Contras during the cold war, despite well-documented evidence that they employed terrorist tactics against civilians in Nicaragua.

Even if intelligence services had a deep understanding of terrorism, this would not be sufficient to anticipate attacks and disrupt dangerous networks. This sort of information is particularly hard to come by, for reasons with which we are now sadly familiar: the groups mutate rapidly, can be quite small, and are hard to penetrate. Furthermore, the technical means of electronic intercepts and overhead photography upon which advanced intelligence services have come to rely so heavily are of relatively little use against terrorists. Human agents, who can be more useful, are often of questionable reliability in this area, and, even more than in traditional intelligence, it is extraordinarily difficult to separate truth from fiction. During the cold war an agent who claimed that the Soviets were developing mechanical moles that were burrowing under U.S. territory could readily be dismissed; today it is not so easy to say what reports about terrorism should simply be put in the wastebasket.

The problems are of course compounded by the fact that we seek a 100 percent success rate. Stopping 99 percent of the attacks is extraordinarily impressive but pales in light of the 1 percent that succeeds. So the obstacles to accurate intelligence are high, the penalties for failure are severe, and the margin for error is essentially none. Under these circumstances it is natural for intelligence officials to issue a warning even when the evidence is shaky. Crying wolf is costly, but not nearly as costly as failing to sound the alarm in the face of reports that turn out to be accurate. Even when a prudent intelligence analyst might decide against a warning, an elected national leader probably would feel she had to go ahead rather than risk a catastrophic error.

Ironically, some of the pressures being exerted on intelligence are a tribute to it, albeit indirectly. At least in the United States and the United Kingdom, elected officials and the general public expect policies to be supported by realistic intelligence assessments. This in turn means that leaders must argue that their policies are based on the best professional advice. When President George W. Bush and Prime Minister Tony Blair decided to invade Iraq in 2003, they had to be able to justify their policies in terms of what their intelligence services told them about the threat, and this in turn meant that they needed the services to paint a grim picture. This reflects a touching faith in the concept of professionalism and how much can be known about other states. It is not necessarily the only way things could be done, however. A leader might say, "I think Saddam is a terrible menace. This is a political judgment, and I have been elected to make difficult calls like this. Information rarely can be definitive, and while I have consulted widely and listened to our intelligence services and other experts, this is my decision, not theirs." Unfortunately, this is politically very difficult to do, and a policymaker who wants to proceed in the face of ambiguous or discrepant information will be hard-pressed to avoid at least some politicization of intelligence. This is true even though intelligence is often wrong and political judgments right.

Even without this complication, the "war" on terror provides unique challenges to intelligence in a democracy. I use quotation marks because it is far from clear that war is an accurate description of American policy, let alone a wise prescription for it. Although this is not the place to discuss all aspects of this question, the ambiguous nature of the struggle heightens many of the dilemmas, such as the tactics to be used, other values that must be sacrificed for the struggle, and the degree to which we should be willing to accept infringements on civil liberties.

With or without quotation marks, this is a war in which intelligence not only plays a—if not *the*—central role, but also simultaneously makes an extremely heavy demand on it and poses a number of challenges. In fighting terrorism, intelligence is more than an enabler. I do not think it is an exaggeration to say that with good intelligence the problem is relatively easily solved, and that without it even the most potent military force will do little good and actually is likely to do a great deal of harm. But for the reasons noted earlier, gaining good intelligence is particularly difficult. In order to be most effective in this challenging environment, widespread international intelligence cooperation is absolutely necessary. But as we have seen in the United States, it is hard enough simply to get the CIA and FBI to cooperate. National services will never fully share sensitive information, especially about sources. The report of the Senate Select Committee on Intelligence (SSCI) on errors in the assessment of Iraq WMD noted that the infamous (mis)information about Iraq's mobile biological laboratories came from a source being interrogated by a foreign service, while U.S. agents had only extremely limited access to him

("Report on the U.S. Intelligence Community's Prewar Intelligence Assessments on Iraq," U.S. Senate Select Committee on Intelligence, July 9, 2004, http://intelligence.senate.gov/). Furthermore, the very fact that the publicly released SSCI report contained so much detailed information may make foreign services even more hesitant to share information with their U.S. counterparts.

If services are to share information, they must be confident that it will remain secret. My sense is that intelligence services trust each other more than they do their own civilian leaders, let alone leaders of other states. I suspect that the incentives for information sharing at the political level will make services even more careful about the details they provide to their own leaders, both in order to guard against the possibility that politicians will let too much slip out and thereby antagonize peer services, and in order to reduce the danger that any information that intelligence officials have provided will end up on the desks of indiscreet allied politicians. Put another way, there is likely to be a trade-off between the full flow of information among nations' intelligence services and the flow within any country between the service and national leaders.

Along those same lines, the fact that intelligence is now very publicly on the front lines of national defense is likely to increase the services' power domestically and lead them to seek greater power and autonomy. If it is their responsibility to protect the country, they will want the tools to do the job. These include not only funding but also freedom to keep secrets, gather more information, and act on their own professional assessments. All this, of course, places great strains on democratic institutions.

Democratic values may feel the pressure as well. As the Abu Ghraib prison debacle in Iraq and related scandals reveal, pressures to use torture to extract information are hard to resist in a situation where soldiers are under unpredictable terrorist attack. The situation at Abu Ghraib does not seem to be a case in which intelligence services were out of control, however. To the contrary, the basic logic of the "war" on terror indicates what available documents seem to confirm: it was high-level civilians who most strongly felt that information needed to be acquired by whatever means necessary.

I suspect that the conflicting pressures for "results" in the "war" on terror and the need to maintain at least the appearance of democratic values will lead to a familiar implicit, if corrosive, line of policy, in which intelligence services will employ a variety of dirty tricks to which the civilian leaders will turn a blind eye. This will allow the latter to plausibly deny knowledge of illicit activities when they are eventually exposed and will also allow them to spare themselves the psychological discomfort of having to think about those distasteful operations. This of course leaves the services exposed, but many intelligence officials view these tactics necessary, are willing to pay the eventual price, and see such informal arrangements as necessary in a democracy faced by an amorphous threat such as terrorism poses. The unavoidable question, however, is what long-run damage is done to the intelligence service, civil relations, and democracy.

CONCLUSION

Over the past decade the scholarly community has come to realize that intelligence is often the "missing dimension" in our understanding of many particular international conflicts and of international politics in general. But the lack of attention to civil-intelligence relations is even more striking. Our understanding of foreign policy, domestic policy and politics, and institutional arrangements all have suffered for it. The issues are particularly pressing for democratizing countries because their intelligence services usually were a pillar of the old regime. It is striking that most conventional treatments of democratic transitions say so little about how these services are to be pushed, harnessed, and/or won over to the new governing arrangements. The essays in this volume show that the problem is complex, and that solutions are context-dependent rather than following some universal formula.

Many of the same questions and dilemmas arise in established democracies as well and are likely to surface with particular salience during the prolonged "war" on terror in which we now find ourselves. In the United States, these problems are compounded by the enormously complex restructuring of the security and intelligence communities required by recent legislation. Under these conditions, the flow of ideas about dealing with civil-intelligence relations will not— or should not—run simply from the established democracies to the newer ones. The ideas and experiences of those who are trying to lay a new democratic foundation for these relations have a great deal to teach us.

ACKNOWLEDGMENTS

The chapters in this volume are a logical development from the research and teaching programs of the Center for Civil-Military Relations (CCMR) at the Naval Postgraduate School (NPS) in Monterey, California, since the center's founding in 1994. With the support of the executive director of CCMR, Rich Hoffman, who has now succeeded Tom Bruneau as director, a small group of scholars began to develop programs on the topic of intelligence reform. These have resulted in a one-week seminar that is offered abroad, a one-week seminar in residence, and a twelve-week accredited course in the National Security Affairs (NSA) Department at NPS.

In order to update, expand, and enrich the information base of these programs, the United States Defense Security Cooperation Agency provided us with funds to support an international roundtable on intelligence and democracy, organized by CCMR at NPS on August 26–27, 2004. Many of the chapters appearing in this volume were derived from papers delivered as part of the proceedings from that roundtable. Ken Dombroski, lecturer in CCMR, developed the outline for the roundtable, based on the Intelligence and Democracy course he teaches in NSA. Ken also served as co-chair of the roundtable and edited several of the drafts that, in revised form, appear in this volume. Marco Cepik also helped edit several of the early drafts during his appointment as a visiting assistant professor in NSA in the summer and fall of 2004. In addition to the authors who have contributed chapters to this volume, the panel chairs, reviewers, and discussants of the roundtable included Marina Caparini, senior research fellow, the Geneva Centre for the Democratic Control of Armed Forces; Michael Herman, Nuffield College, Oxford; and Mark Kramer, director, Cold War Studies Project, Harvard University. Esther Robinson served as research assistant and was instrumental in keeping the project moving forward. Greta E. Marlatt, head of information services at the Dudley Knox Library of the Naval Postgraduate School, compiled the bibliography and has assisted our research at the Center for Civil-Military Relations for years.

The main intellectual inspiration for the courses, and thus the final book project, was Mr. Terry Johnson, who had spent most of his U.S. Army career in military intelligence, taught courses on Human Intelligence and Counterintelligence in the NSA Department, and provided guidance and insights to the editors so that, at a minimum, we know that there is much to learn in this area. Although he may not actually have used the following phrase, it captures the sense very well: "Those who say don't know, and those who know don't say." It is to Terry, who was forced to give up his work with us after surviving a tragic automobile accident, that we dedicate this book.

INTELLIGENCE REFORM: BALANCING DEMOCRACY AND EFFECTIVENESS

Thomas C. Bruneau and Steven C. Boraz

A FRAMEWORK FOR STUDYING INTELLIGENCE

While there is probably agreement on the importance of the topic of studying intelligence, there is little published material on how to do so. This is paradoxical, because as a category of individuals, it would be difficult to find a more self-critical, analytical, and demanding group of people than intelligence personnel. As a profession, they more closely approximate university professors than any other discipline or calling. We thus find it striking that whereas intelligence officers and the organizations within which they function in the intelligence community (IC) are extremely rigorous methodologically in conducting their work, when we turn to the study of intelligence structures and processes by outsiders and retired intelligence professionals, there is little rigor and virtually no consensus on how to research and analyze the IC. The result is that there has been very little accumulation of public knowledge on intelligence (exceptions include the 9/11 and WMD commission reports). When studies of intelligence are in fact published, some of what passes for data or analysis in the unclassified literature can be wrong, and, unlike academia, there is no public control or competing position to correct the errors. Despite the huge array of books and articles referred to in the bibliography, there is, in fact, very little available analysis, and even less comparative analysis, on the organization of intelligence.[1]

Clearly, the problem in studying the IC is due to the essential, fundamental requirement for secrecy. After all, what intelligence personnel do can be effective only if they do it in secret, and the commitment to maintain secrecy after leaving the community results in minimal exposure and dissemination of information on the IC and its operations. The basic requirement for secrecy drives all other aspects of the profession and the organization of the IC.

Our goal in this introduction is to establish the framework with which intelligence can be analyzed and thus to draw conclusions from the twelve case studies that make up the body of the book. The emphasis here is on a comparative, institutional approach, with its foundation in the way scholars have analyzed civil-military relations (CMR). The relative absence in the literature of analysis of the IC noted above might not be a serious problem if we were concerned with only one or a few relatively open countries, in which case studies might be conducted with slight conceptual clarity, such as in the United States and Canada. Comparative studies are more urgently called for today because, in the contemporary world of global terrorist threats, intelligence must be not only under democratic civilian control but also effective. Thus, in addition to the academic desirability of pursuing the comparative method to achieve analytical results, there is the even more urgent requirement of learning through comparisons. The goal is an understanding of the best practices in organizing intelligence, thereby improving both democratic civilian control and the effectiveness of the IC.

Though political scientists had long eschewed an institutional approach to comparative analysis, we are convinced that institutions remain the core foundations of power in the state and thus provide us a sound basis for analysis. It is through understanding of these institutions that we gain perspective on state organization and can set about identifying effective structural controls to support legitimate and transparent governance.

Our thesis is that intelligence can best be conceptualized as a subfield of civil-military relations. There is substantial and rich literature on CMR, which emphasizes the importance of democratic, civilian control and the clearly identifiable roles and missions that militaries should perform.[2] In similar fashion, intelligence has specific roles and missions, the study of which establishes a way to analyze intelligence community structures and their implications for democratic civilian control and effectiveness. Without this common conceptual framework, it will not be possible to achieve either analytical results or useful recommendations for IC reform globally.

An Institutional Approach

The methodology that guides our inquiries in the right direction is an updated version of Max Weber's classic work on political power and bureaucracy. The approach Weber employed to understand bureaucracies and their locus within state and society leads us to take a closer look at and emphasize the structure of bureaucracy as it relates to CMR, including intelligence. The contemporary version of Weber's approach is known as New Institutionalism. The various subtheories that together loosely constitute New Institutionalism "all seek to elucidate the role that institutions play in the determination of social and political outcomes."[3] In other words, an understanding of the roles of institutions is indispensable to this or any study of how actors manage power relations within a society. As Scott summarizes this approach: "Institutions construct actors and define their available modes of action; they constrain behavior, but they also empower it. Analysis from this perspective is aimed at providing a detailed account of the specifics of institutional forms because they are expected to exert strong effects on individual behavior: structuring agendas, attention, preferences, and modes of acting."[4] Therefore we need to highlight a few of the main elements of this model.

First and most important is the meaning of the term "institution." Peter Hall and Rosemary Taylor describe it as "formal or informal procedures, routines, norms, and conventions embedded in the organizational structure of the polity or political economy."[5] This broad definition is vital to the present volume because it forces us (if we are faithful to the approach) to focus on the institutions that constitute the IC as well as those doing the direction and oversight.

Another key aspect of New Institutionalism is attention to the origins of institutions, which can be understood in two parts. First, we must look to the goals and motivations of the actors involved in creating these institutions, keeping in mind the concept of "unintended consequences." In other words, it is important not to assume initial intent on the part of actors based on the current situation. Second, we must remain cognizant of the fact that, again in the words of Hall and Taylor, we live in "a world replete with institutions."[6] Thus the organizational formats of the IC and the oversight mechanisms, should they be adopted, throughout the democratizing world are roughly similar; the challenge for scholars is to analyze the extent to which a model

3

copied from one country and one context does, in fact, translate into an institution in another country and context.

Finally, it is worth reiterating that the creation and implementation of institutions are all about power, and institutional power relations therefore are a primary concern of New Institutionalism. Some actors have the power to adopt and implement new institutions, while others wield authority to resist this adoption—or more often, implementation. The importance of power relations to the balance between civilian leaders and intelligence organizations cannot be overemphasized. Not only have scholars of New Institutionalism recognized the critical part the creation of institutions plays in structuring relationships of power, but based on the research available, intelligence professionals and their civilian policymakers from around the world also are very much aware of the implications for their own countries. The conditions under which an institution forms will have a strong impact on who determines the rules of the game and how those rules will be implemented. New Institutionalism directs our attention to the centrality of institutions in structuring relations of power, through the conditions of their creation, the interests of those involved in creating them, and the influence of preexisting institutional models.[7]

We posit, then, that we must look to the institutions and the processes whereby information is turned into intelligence and use this as a departure point to then apply our CMR framework to the study of intelligence.

Intelligence as a Subset of Civil-Military Relations

There are several reasons for recommending a CMR-based method to study intelligence, specifically when reviewing a country's intelligence community. Accepting this approach requires us to consider what we mean by CMR. To begin with, we hold that the three fundamental issues of CMR are as follows: democratic civilian control, effectiveness in achieving roles and missions, and efficiency. Democratic control simply means that the military is under the control of the democratically elected, civilian leadership. Effectiveness means that the spectrum of roles and missions—from war to peacekeeping, intelligence, and counterterrorism—are in fact implemented and achieved. And efficiency means that missions are achieved at the least possible cost. It is our argument that these three, this trinity of issues or parameters of CMR, apply to all aspects of CMR. Democratic civilian control can be identified as existing or not. Effectiveness can also be determined, but data are more often available in older democracies than newer ones. It is true, as the IC frequently notes, that intelligence professionals are most effective when their work and successes are not publicly known. On the other hand, incontrovertible proof that the IC was not operating effectively is provided by fiascos such as December 7, 1941; September 11, 2001; March 11, 2004 (Madrid); and September 2004 (Russia). In between, there is partial but sufficient evidence of whether and how well the IC is working, as pointed out by competing sectors of the IC, the media, and nongovernmental organizations (NGOs). In short, effectiveness is an issue or parameter that can be identified and documented.

The same cannot be said of efficiency. How much is intelligence worth? How efficient is it? Given the absence of transparency in intelligence both as a process and with regard to budgets, there is no realistic way in which a cost-benefit analysis can be performed. If IC budgets do become available in the public domain, it may be possible to assess efficiency as well (though, so far, when budgets do become public, they typically do not provide enough data for such analysis). In short, the peculiar characteristics of intelligence limit us to two of the three issues or parameters of CMR. While not optimum, it is still better than any competing analytical alternative with which we are familiar.

There is much more to recommend this CMR-based focus for the study of intelligence beyond the trinity just mentioned. First, in most, if not all, of the newer democracies, intelligence was in fact a monopoly of the military and ultimately led to familiar issues in the civil-military relations literature on transitions and dismantling the military prerogatives continuing from authoritarian regimes.[8] In the Philippines, as demonstrated in Douglas Macdonald's chapter here, intelligence reform is simply a part of civil-military relations and defense reform. In at least one important case that we are very familiar with due to our ongoing programs, that of Romania, the contemporary IC is still militarized despite many proposals to demilitarize it during the last decade and a half of democratic consolidation. (Russia and Moldova are also militarized, but there are no efforts to change that.) In other countries, while the media and NGOs give great attention to reforms leading to new, civilian organizations, we find that military intelligence often remains intact and commonly overlooked. Reforming military intelligence remains a low priority because all attention is given to the civilian organizations, which may or may not have the resources to be able to do their job. We suspect this lack of emphasis is due to a lack of knowledge of and access to military intelligence by the civilians who are supposed to be exercising control.

Even in older and more institutionalized democracies, such as the United States and France, the military still plays a predominant role in intelligence. France has only marginally moved away from complete military dominance of its foreign intelligence organization recently, and in the United States much foreign intelligence was under the control of the military services until the end of the Second World War. Even with the creation of lead agencies under civilian control, as the United States attempted in 1947 with the National Security Act and had to do again recently with the establishment of a director of national intelligence (DNI), the military services still play a key role in intelligence. The congressional debate in late 2004 on the implementation of the recommendations of the 9/11 Commission and the establishment of the DNI showed how important intelligence remains to the military, as evinced by the very high level of political activity to ensure that the reforms would not interfere with the military chain of command and that forces would have timely access to the intelligence product for operations.[9] Further, in the United States some 80 percent of the funds for intelligence have gone to the Defense Intelligence Agency (DIA), the National Security Agency (NSA), the National Reconnaissance Office (NRO), the National Geospatial-Intelligence Agency (NGA), and the intelligence organizations of each of the military services, all military assets. Clearly, these agencies, as part of the Department of Defense, are ultimately responsible to the civilian service secretaries and the secretary of defense, but they have military functions, are often headed by senior officers, either on active-duty or retired, and ultimately serve the military. Finally, maybe the most important argument for a CMR approach to the study of intelligence is that intelligence and the armed forces share the same ultimate goal: to ensure national security.

INTELLIGENCE: MEANING, PURPOSE, AND FUNCTIONS

Before proceeding further, it is necessary to define what is meant by intelligence. Mark Lowenthal, one of the best authors and practitioners in the field, defines intelligence as three different phenomena, which are interrelated and, unless specified, will result in confusion for the novice reader. First, intelligence is a process: "Intelligence can be thought of as the means by which certain types of information are required and requested, collected, analyzed, and disseminated, and as the way in which certain types of covert action are conceived and conducted." Second, it is a product: "Intelligence can be thought of as the product of these processes, that is, as the analyses and intelligence operations themselves." Third, it is the organization: "Intelligence can be thought of as the units that carry out its various functions."[10] Our focus in this book is primarily on this third phenomenon—the combination of organizations that make up a country's intelligence community, or IC. It is our view (following through from our conceptual approach focusing on institutions) that beginning our analysis with the components of the IC, and their interrelationships, will allow us to incorporate the first and second meanings of intelligence described above.

With respect to the mission of intelligence, we assert that intelligence serves two purposes: first and foremost, to inform policy and, second, to support operations, be they military, police, or covert, with the ultimate goal of ensuring state security. There is general consensus that these two missions result in four functions, or roles, of intelligence: collection, analysis, counterintelligence, and covert action. These roles of intelligence are common to most intelligence systems, although many authors and policymakers would prefer to exclude covert action; how they are distributed between and among the intelligence organization differs from state to state.

While we will briefly examine each of these functions individually, it is important to remember that they operate most effectively as part of a process in close conjunction with one another. As Roy Godson points out in the introduction to his book *Intelligence Requirements for the 1980s: Intelligence and Policy:*

> It is difficult to imagine an effective system for collecting intelligence without the analysis that provides effective guidance or "tasking" to collectors. Counterintelligence is necessary to protect collectors from becoming known, neutralized, and exploited by hostile intelligence services. Similarly, a successful program of covert action must be grounded in effective collection, analysis, and counterintelligence. All of this is to say that the nature of intelligence is such that the

several elements of intelligence are parts of a single unified system, whose success depends on all parts working effectively. In short, it must be a "full-service" intelligence system.[11]

Collection

Intelligence organizations collect information. The questions are, what kinds of information do they collect and what means do they employ to collect it? At a minimum, collection is done through signals intelligence, or SIGINT (from intercepts in communications, radar, and telemetry); imagery intelligence, or IMINT (including both overhead and ground imagery); measurement and signatures intelligence, or MASINT (which is technically derived intelligence data other than imagery and SIGINT);[12] and human intelligence, or HUMINT, which is information collected directly by people and includes information provided by ambassadors and defense attachés as part of their normal reporting routines, information obtained at public and social events, and information obtained clandestinely. In addition, intelligence professionals use open sources, sometimes referred to as OSINT, which include periodicals, the World Wide Web, seminars, and conferences. There is an ongoing debate regarding the use of open sources vis-à-vis classified sources since so much information on so many topics is readily available, but the means to collect these data are not planned by intelligence personnel.[13]

Analysis

Raw intelligence information is not very useful without analysis. Analysis, or the anticipation of analysis, also shapes collection requirements. Analysis has always been and will always remain the core skill in and the big challenge of intelligence. The problem is not only with the processing of gigantic quantities of data, but even more with what conclusions to derive from the information. Analysis, in short, is not a simple technical issue but rather includes methods, perceptions, and political preferences. Much of the analytical literature on intelligence in the United States and the former USSR focuses precisely on whether, and to what extent, leaders used the information provided to them by intelligence organizations.[14]

Collection and analysis form the core of intelligence. The process

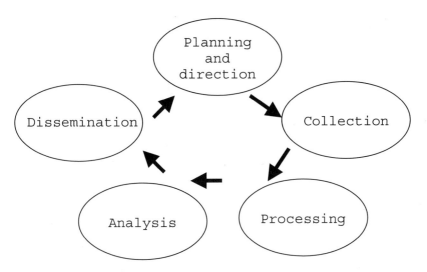

FIGURE 0.1. *The intelligence cycle.*

of putting them together to create reliable, accurate strategic intelligence is dynamic. Often referred to as the intelligence cycle (Figure 1), it begins with the policymaker and his planning staff (for example, in the U.S. case, the president and his National Security Council staff) expressing a need for intelligence information to help them make a national security–related policy decision. Intelligence managers convert these requests into collection plans to acquire the information. The raw data are collected by various intelligence methods, processed, exploited, and given to analysts for integration, evaluation, and analysis for producing finished intelligence products (written reports or oral briefings, for example). These products are disseminated to the consumers (in this example, the president and planners of the NSC), who provide feedback to the intelligence managers for additional or more focused information.

Counterintelligence

At its most basic, the purpose of counterintelligence is to protect the state, and its secrets, from other states or organizations. Seemingly clear and straightforward in these terms, in fact counterintelligence becomes, in the words of the longtime and controversial head of counterintelligence at the CIA James Angleton, " 'the wilderness of mirrors,' where defectors are false, lies are truth, truth lies, and the reflections leave you dazzled and confused."[15] Abram N. Shulsky defines the broad scope of issues involved:

> In its most general terms, counterintelligence refers to information collected and analyzed, and activities undertaken, to protect a nation (including its own intelligence-related activities) against the actions of hostile intelligence services. Under this definition, the scope of counterintelligence is as broad as the scope of intelligence itself, since all manners of hostile intelligence activities must be defended against.[16]

Shulsky, like most American authors on the subject of intelligence, associates counterintelligence primarily with countering foreign threats. In common usage, the term "counterintelligence" also is applied to those intelligence activities aimed at countering internal threats, which British and Commonwealth scholars term "security intelligence." They distinguish these functions from counterintelligence operations aimed at foreign intelligence service activities. Peter Gill defines security intelligence as "the state's gathering of information about any attempts to counter perceived threats to its security deriving from espionage, sabotage, foreign-influenced activities, political violence, and subversion."[17]

Covert Actions

Covert actions—or what the British call special political actions and the Soviets called active measures—are actions intended to influence another state by means that are not identified with the state behind the actions. There are several categories of covert action, ranging from propaganda to paramilitary operations. Mark Lowenthal categorizes them in terms of levels of violence and degree of plausible deniability. The first level, propaganda, includes the utilization of the media in another country to convey a certain message. It is categorized as the least violent means of covert action with the highest degree of plausible deniability. The second level is political activity, which includes funding or other support to government leaders, political parties, unions, religious groups, the armed forces, and the like to follow a certain course of action in another country. Closely linked to this level is economic activity, in which governments use economic weapons, such as destroying crops, influencing markets, and circulating counterfeit currency to destabilize a regime. The final two levels involve much higher degrees of violence and usually provide a lesser degree of plausible deniability. The overthrow of governments by coups, usually through surrogates, may be the final step of other, less violent, methods. Paramilitary operations, which are the most violent method of covert actions, involve the use of force, usually through the employment of indigenous armed elements, to directly attack another state.[18] The larger the paramilitary operation, the less likely it is provide the cover of plausible deniability for the sponsoring state.

Obviously not every country needs, wants, or can afford capabilities in all four functions, or roles, of intelligence organizations, though all countries carry out at least some and have some form of intelligence organization. That these functions exist, that some nations have these capabilities, means that this is the global framework within which intelligence must be understood. If intelligence is created to defend the state, it must defend it within the real context of potential enemies, both other states and nonstate actors, all the while taking into consideration the instruments they have available.

INTELLIGENCE REFORM IN DEMOCRATIC
TRANSITION AND CONSOLIDATION

Since the beginning of the "third wave" of democratic transition with the Portuguese Revolution in April 1974, there has been a general and gradual expansion of democracy to include all regions but for the Middle East. Previously authoritarian regimes collapsed for a variety of reasons, initiating a transition of power to more or less popularly elected civilians.[19] Democratizing countries become consolidated when the new regime's structure and processes become stable. Consolidation is a commonly used concept in comparative politics and is useful because it reflects the idea that the elites and the masses accept democracy[20] as "the only game in town."[21]

TRANSITION FROM THE SECURITY INTELLIGENCE STATES

Although in established democracies it has been domestic security agencies, such as the Federal Bureau of Investigation in the United

States or the Security Service (MI5) in Great Britain, that carry out counterintelligence, this was not the case in authoritarian regimes. There the boundaries and functions of military intelligence and police organizations overlapped or became indistinguishable from each other.

These authoritarian regimes relied on organizations to identify domestic opponents and neutralize their opposition to the government, and they sought, through a variety of means that included a controlled media, to generate at least domestic apathy. In most cases, these organizations were intelligence services. Precisely because of this heavy reliance on these organizations and their centrality to power, the intelligence apparatus grew in size and power, with the result that it was often autonomous, even within authoritarian regimes. In these countries, the role of intelligence was to protect the state's secrets from outsiders, which meant anyone outside the central core of power. And because almost anything could be defined as a state secret, the scope of that which had to be controlled was immense. Although in most instances the intelligence service rhetorically linked internal opposition to putative foreign enemies, the overwhelming focus of the intelligence service in most authoritarian regimes was domestic opposition and not other states.

In general, these security intelligence services functioned more as "political police" than domestic intelligence bureaus. Over time they acquired greater autonomy from policymakers and became insulated from any type of scrutiny. They inevitably gathered political intelligence on tremendous numbers of people, including legislators and judiciary (if any existed), usually unrelated to specific criminal offenses. In several of the countries discussed in this book, such as Argentina, Brazil, Romania, South Africa, and Taiwan, authoritarian intelligence services created what Keller and Gill have called the independent security state—an extreme form of security intelligence organization characterized by a lack of any external controls on intelligence activities.[22]

If the elected government does not control intelligence, it is by definition not a consolidated democracy. We believe that this matters, since democratic consolidation requires both the institutions and the culture of democracy. Central to the culture is legitimacy. Clearly, if a government is monitored—though "blackmailed" probably is a more accurate term—by the intelligence service, then the legitimacy will be restricted. Trust, by the citizens in the institutions of democracy, will never be achieved if the issue of who really rules is not resolved. With an intelligence service left over from the authoritarian regime in fact supervising the government, trust can never be realized. Democratic consolidation is a huge challenge in the best of circumstances. Any handicap, especially one as critical as a lack of legitimacy, is an impediment impossible to overcome.

As demonstrated in the case studies in this book, and clearly epitomized by the almost two decades of frustrated intelligence reform in Argentina, it is a huge task to begin to reform intelligence organizations, with their broad scope and deep penetration in many authoritarian regimes. The challenge of doing so, of promoting democratic consolidation and reform of the intelligence organizations, is exacerbated by the fact that in most countries there is little awareness of intelligence functions and organizations. As highlighted so clearly in the Argentine case, the intelligence organizations resist change, and the legislators know very little about what is involved in intelligence. It fell to a small group of academic advisers to the congress to lobby for reform. Further, in some countries there is real concern that the intelligence apparatus has accumulated, and is still collecting, information that could be used to blackmail elite civilians and politicians. Thus not only is there a lack of information about intelligence organizations, but it is combined with fear, which perpetuates the lack of information. From our work in several regions of the world, it is clear that either the civilian politicians do not know anything about intelligence, or if they do, they simply don't want to deal with it.

ANALYZING INTELLIGENCE REFORM

In the more established democracies, the issues discussed above have been confronted and, for the most part, resolved. (As we will see in France, however, the past lives on, resulting in rather less than optimum effectiveness in intelligence.) For the newer democracies, coming to terms with the legacies of the old regimes and their authoritarian institutions makes intelligence reform that much more difficult.

It is worthwhile, then, to note that reform of the intelligence services means something entirely different for established democracies than it does for countries in democratic transition. In these "older" democracies, reform generally connotes changes in an existing system that already respects control from elected civilian officials. These changes typically *enhance* civilian control and aim to improve effectiveness. In less mature or emerging democracies, reforms are intended to transform an intelligence apparatus that supported the old regime and lacks democratic civilian control. Still, as one reads through this book, striking similarities become apparent between the issues that both established and newer democracies face when trying to reform their intelligence services. Therefore, we return to the two parts of our trinity that provide a means for comparative study: democratic control and the effectiveness of an intelligence community.

Democratic Control of Intelligence

Democratic control of intelligence can probably best be defined as the sum of two parts—*direction* and *oversight*. *Direction* is civilian guidance to a nation's intelligence community with respect to its overall mission. This guidance is typically embodied in some sort of national security strategy as well as the day-to-day feedback an intelligence organization will receive from the civilians it serves. *Oversight* identifies the processes a democratic government has in place to review all aspects of an intelligence community's organization, budget, personnel management, and legal framework for intelligence operations.

The researchers who have contributed to this book—as well as the available, though very limited literature—provide a survey of norms and prescriptions for controlling intelligence in democracies that points to five basic mechanisms: executive, legislative, judicial, internal, and external control. Few democracies, however, have organizations or institutions that span this spectrum of means.

EXECUTIVE CONTROL

Executive control is typically the key variable in ensuring that a state is using its intelligence organizations appropriately, because it is the executive that normally defines the mission of the IC and organizes it, in general terms, to support that mission. Further, the executive branch is the primary consumer of intelligence and therefore provides the greatest direction to the IC on a daily basis. Executive control in established democracies often includes independent oversight of budgetary and personnel matters. Though not ideal, executive oversight alone may establish enough control over a state intelligence apparatus to provide the fulfillment of democratic norms.[23] The main problem of an executive-only control scheme is the danger of the executive using the intelligence apparatus for other than democratic means.

LEGISLATIVE CONTROL

In many of the established and newer democracies, legislatures create the key organizational, budgetary, personnel, and legal oversight mechanisms of an IC, as well as provide balance to the executive branch. Legislatures are charged with ensuring that a country's public resources are spent appropriately and with good accountability, routinely auditing the spending and management policies of intelligence organizations. Additionally, legislatures often ensure that executive direction is both appropriate in terms of national security and in accordance with the rule of law. As will be clear in the first two of the three case studies of the United States, direct legislative oversight is a powerful mechanism for democratic control, though it is important to note that real legislative oversight was not established in the United States until the 1970s, and most new democracies don't really have it.

JUDICIAL CONTROL

Judicial control encompasses an independent judiciary empowered to review and interpret the legal framework for which intelligence operations are conducted. The judiciary can play a large or small role in monitoring intelligence activity, based on its authority within its particular democratic system. In some cases, the control established by the judicial branch resides within the organizations themselves in the form of legal counsel and inspectors general (IGs). These offices provide an internal review of budgetary, personnel, and legal matters. They are also charged with investigating citizen complaints against the organization for which they work. The chapter by Elizabeth Parker and Bryan Pate provides a unique and most comprehensive analysis of judicial oversight in the United States.

INTERNAL CONTROL

Analyzing internal control is a bit more problematic, primarily because each country organizes its intelligence community differently and those organizations have different prerogatives. In general, internal controls feature the aforementioned legal counsels and IGs; a professional ethos and institutional norms; and multiple intelligence organizations, though these organizations usually are developed at the behest of democratically elected officials.

With respect to institutions and professional ethos, we believe that our conceptual approach to CMR is appropriate but must be adapted or tailored to the specific nature of intelligence. In CMR there is a whole set of institutions that societies have designed and developed over the past century or so to control those who hold a monopoly on the means of violence. These range from selective recruitment, professional military education, budgets, officer promotion and retirement, committees in congresses, policy and personnel control in ministries of defense, and finally influence from the media and civil society. The lessons learned and best practices in this domain are readily available and, we believe, transferable to a country's intelligence apparatus, with certain adjustments, globally.[24]

In the specific area of intelligence, multiple intelligence organizations are created as a control mechanism in a "divide and conquer" strategy. By creating multiple intelligence organizations, policymakers seek to prevent any single agency from having a monopoly on intelligence. This is the model in the United States and has been adopted with great vigor in Romania, where there were, as of mid-2006, at least six different intelligence organizations. This proliferation of organizations may or may not be efficient, since the different agencies may battle each other for resources and influence, but it eliminates the potential for any single agency or individual to be the sole source of knowledge and having the power that goes with it—thus creating opportunities for more democratic control. Most countries that are seeking to reform their intelligence structures have moved in this direction.

EXTERNAL CONTROL

External controls in democracies include a free press, private and professional intelligence organizations, independent think tanks, and, in the case of new democracies, foreign-funded nongovernmental organizations (NGOs) that are increasingly expected to monitor intelligence organizations.[25] The contribution of NGOs, especially in new democracies such as Argentina, Guatemala, Indonesia, and Romania, just to mention a few, exerts necessary pressure on the government to pursue intelligence reform.

Intelligence Community Effectiveness

As noted above, virtually everywhere in established democracies there is a separation between different organizations within the IC. Coordinating these agencies is a fundamental challenge democracies face in ensuring the effectiveness of their respective ICs.

The problem is, of course, that there are barriers in coordinating among agencies. Such barriers are due to the normal bureaucratic impediments to interagency coordination, such as protecting turf and fighting for resources. In the specific context of the ICs, these impediments are tremendously magnified and multiplied by their unique characteristics, which all derive from the need to work in secrecy, leading to the concern in providing their product to other organizations that might not safeguard the secrets. An additional factor is the competition among organizations to sell this product to the consumer, which is ultimately the policymaker. The challenge of coordination looms large in the report of the 9/11 Commission, as we shall see in our first chapter on the United States.

More-established democracies have attempted to come to grips with this dilemma by using the multiple agencies to provide peer reviews for finished intelligence products. They have also created a process, termed red-teaming or team B analysis, to challenge established assessments within the intelligence community and offer alternative interpretations, sometimes using organizations outside of the IC. While some of these democracies use this review, or competitive analysis, to arrive at a consensus, other countries capitalize on the process and include alternatives in finished products to ensure that policymakers have more than one side of the story.[26]

Even with the greater emphasis on effectiveness in the more established democracies, there is the continuing concern with democratic, civilian control. It continues to bear repeating that it is simply inherent in the nature of intelligence as a process and organization that these concerns continue. After all, democracy as a system of government is based on accountability of the governors to the governed, requiring transparency, whereas intelligence, in all three meanings of the term, requires secrecy. There is thus an inherent tension, even dilemma, in designing and managing an IC characterized by both democratic civilian control and effectiveness. Learning how to deal with this ongoing dilemma remains the greatest challenge in newer democracies in the area of intelligence. Policymakers in most of these countries appear to suffer from almost pathological problems in understanding that some issues of governmental design, or institutional engineering, are never resolved; they must be continually "worked."

PREVIEW OF OUR WORK

This book is about change in the intelligence institutions of three established and seven newer democracies. Change results in the case of the newer democracies as part of the overall process of democratic consolidation. In the older democracies, change most often occurs due to acute awareness of the lack of effectiveness of the IC in such critical events as 9/11 or the absence of weapons of mass destruction in Iraq rather than any attempts at simply improving the IC.[27] Very likely, effectiveness will increasingly become an issue in the newer democracies as they participate in the global fight against terrorism and face their own internal and external threats.

The chapters that constitute the body of this book were selected for several reasons. First and most importantly, they are case studies of the two fundamental contemporary challenges in intelligence. The United States, Great Britain, and France were chosen as case studies of the difficulty in achieving effectiveness in the roles of the IC. The others, the newer democracies, were chosen to highlight different aspects of the challenge in achieving democratic civilian control over the intelligence apparatuses. There is, however, also a cross-cutting analysis in that two of the chapters on the United States deal with oversight. And at least in the cases of the Philippines, Romania, Russia, and Taiwan, attention is given to achieving effectiveness as well as democratic civilian control. The second criterion for the selection is the geographical diversity. There are case studies from North and South America, Asia, Africa, Western and East-Central Europe, and Russia. The third and last criterion was in some ways the most difficult: to select important countries where we could find either highly developed expertise or a sufficient literature for research on which to base the case studies. We have assembled here a rich set of chapters by true experts. In the case of the United States, Great Britain, France, Romania, Brazil, Argentina, and Russia, the authors have unique experience and insights that allow them to analyze the IC of their respective countries. In the others, the authors are highly regarded experts on either the country or the topic, and in some cases both, such as the authors of the chapters on the Philippines and Taiwan. Access to informed experts on these topics in these countries is no simple matter. All of the authors enjoy privileged access.

It will become obvious, and should come as no surprise to those working in the field of intelligence, that the sources cited in the endnotes of the chapters are very different from one another. Some chapters rely heavily on books and articles, others on the World Wide Web, and yet others on personal interviews. It must be stressed, however, that while the endnotes document the key points in each chapter, in all cases the authors have exposure, insights, and understanding beyond what is found in the endnotes. Indeed, as is generally the case in intelligence, those who know something from a classified source search for published sources to document this information. In short, our authors have documented points known from beyond the sources cited. A final factor of "quality control" for this book is that the editor, and especially the assistant editor, have access to the IC in the United States and possess a broad-based knowledge of intelligence and its role in government through professional knowledge and/or CCMR seminars and longer-term educational programs, now totaling more than five hundred, performed in more than one hundred countries over the last ten years.

The sequence of the chapters that follow has a rationale. We begin with the United States not only because it is the sole remaining superpower, with by far the largest and most comprehensive IC accompanied by obvious challenges of coordination and effectiveness, but also, in the chapters by Steven Boraz and by Elizabeth Parker and Bryan Pate, because of the extensive system of direction and oversight of the IC. Steven Boraz has done a tremendous job of collecting, analyzing, and summarizing the legislation and policies whereby direction and oversight are exercised currently in the United States. Elizabeth Parker and Bryan Pate have drawn on extensive personal experience and research to produce a chapter on a critically important topic, judicial oversight, which has never previously been analyzed so thoroughly. Other countries may want to copy one or more elements of this elaborate and extremely dynamic system of democratic civilian control and oversight. In his chapter, William Lahneman justly highlights the dilemma of combining a vital democratic tradition, the full "rule of law," with all four functions of intelligence. September 11 simply dramatized what has been long known: there is an inherent tension between democracy and intelligence. It is part of the classic tension and trade-off between liberty and security.

In Great Britain there is in intelligence, as in civil-military relations in general, no doubt about civilian control. The elaborate web of institutions and understandings for democratic control is hallowed; whether they can be copied elsewhere is another question. There is in addition, as in the United States, a real question of effectiveness. In the British case, as in France, a professional IC and a long tradition of work in intelligence do not guarantee effectiveness. Whereas Peter Gill calls particular attention to the institutional and political obstacles to accurate intelligence (as product), Douglas Porch highlights the importance of history and culture in impeding the effectiveness of the French intelligence services.

The remaining chapters deal with case studies of intelligence reform as a key element of democratic consolidation. While there was no question but that reform of the intelligence apparatus had to take place as an integral part of democratic consolidation, and did, there is some question as to how well this has worked out. Marco Cepik demonstrates that Brazil has undergone a model reform of the intelligence system. Whether the IC—and especially its central element, the Brazilian Intelligence Agency (ABIN)—is effective or not is an open question. For the outsider, Steven Phillips's study of Taiwan might seem almost too good to be true. Once the government became committed to democracy, intelligence reform had to follow. One can only hope that in other Asian countries, and especially Southeast Asia, the political elites will want to follow the model of Taiwan. Priscila Antunes shows in great detail how intelligence reform in Argentina was brought about by a few members of the congress, and in fact mainly their academic advisers, against the overt resistance of the military intelligence system. Cris Matei provides remarkable detail in documenting the thoroughness of intelligence reform in Romania and highlights the role of the media. If Romania were not a member of the North Atlantic Treaty Organization (NATO) and aspiring to join the European Union in 2007, one might wonder if the reform could have gone so far, so quickly. Kenneth Dombroski documents the model reform of the South African IC, again as part of democratization, and raises the explicit question as to the depth and direction of these reforms. He highlights the central role in the IC of those trained in the former Soviet bloc, thereby raising an issue to which we turn in the book's conclusion. Success in South Africa is extremely critical because the country is important in its own right and as a model for the rest of Africa. If reforms cannot be secured in South Africa, there probably isn't much hope for the rest of the continent.

As Misha Tsypkin demonstrates convincingly in his study of Russia, not only has the democratic state not imposed its values on intelligence, but his detailed analysis leads the reader to question whether there is a democratic state at all, given that the intelligence system has essentially taken it over under Vladimir Putin. As demonstrated in the other chapters, intelligence reform must be a part of democratic consolidation, and it is doubtful whether Russia is heading in that direction. Douglas Macdonald provides an overview of the Philippines, with rich and extensive insights into the historical and cultural obstacles to both democratic civilian control and effectiveness of intelligence. Since it is apparently very difficult to professionalize government service in the Philippines, one despairs of achieving it in the crucial area of intelligence. Macdonald concludes, however, on an optimistic note, which Tsypkin is unable to do.

This book is all about "lessons learned and best practices." Some of the practices may well be considered "worst practices," but even then something can be learned from their dissection. We hope that the framework provided in this introduction, and the rich information conveyed in the twelve chapters, will allow for the accumulation of lessons learned. All of the contributors to this book realize full well that is a tricky topic, an opaque issue to analyze, where much is changing and we know that we can only touch the surface, but it is a topic so critically important for both democratic consolidation and international security that it simply must be treated analytically and comparatively. In the conclusion we will turn to an element that is touched upon in several of the chapters—that is, the education and training of the intelligence professionals—to complement and buttress the institutional reforms analyzed throughout the book. We believe that institutional reforms alone are insufficient to achieve democratic civilian control and effectiveness, unless a cadre of intelligence professionals of adequate size and preparation is put in place to staff these institutions.

NOTES

1. The most notable exceptions include Mark Lowenthal, *Intelligence: From Secrets to Policy* (Washington, DC: Congressional Quarterly Press, 2003); and

Amy B. Zegart, *Flawed by Design: The Evolution of the CIA, JCS, and NSC* (Stanford, CA: Stanford University Press, 1999). For an update, see Amy B. Zegart, "September 11 and the Adaptation Failure of American Intelligence Agencies," *International Security* 29, no. 4 (Spring 2005): 78–111. For a useful argument on comparing intelligence, see Kevin M. O'Connell, "Thinking about Intelligence Comparatively," *Brown Journal of World Affairs* 11, no. 1 (Summer–Fall 2004): 189–199.

2. On roles and missions, see Paul Shemella, "The Spectrum of Roles and Missions of the Armed Forces," in Thomas C. Bruneau and Scott Tollefson, eds., *Who Guards the Guardians and How: Democratic Civil-Military Relations* (Austin: University of Texas Press, 2006), 122–142.

3. Peter A. Hall and Rosemary C. R. Taylor, "Political Science and the Three New Institutionalisms," *Political Studies* 44 (1996): 936.

4. W. Richard Scott, *Institutions and Organizations* (Thousand Oaks, CA: Sage Publications, 1995), 27.

5. Hall and Taylor, "Political Science," 938.

6. Ibid.

7. Further inspiration for the approach here is found in Walter W. Powell and Paul J. DiMaggio, eds., *The New Institutionalism in Organizational Analysis* (Chicago and London: University of Chicago Press, 1991); and W. Richard Scott, *Organization: Rational, Natural, and Open Systems*, 5th ed. (Upper Saddle River, NJ: Prentice Hall, 2003).

8. For an excellent discussion on these issues, see Alfred Stepan, *Rethinking Military Politics: Brazil and the Southern Cone* (Princeton, NJ: Princeton University Press, 1988). It is probably worth noting that the Library of Congress is currently managing a global comparative survey on civil-military relations using Stepan's perspective of prerogatives.

9. For a succinct review of the issues involved, see Richard A. Best Jr., *Intelligence Community Reorganization: Potential Effects on DOD Intelligence Agencies*, CRS Report for Congress (Washington, DC: Congressional Research Service, Library of Congress, updated October 4, 2004).

10. Lowenthal, *Intelligence*, 8.

11. Roy F. Godson, "Intelligence and Policy: An Introduction," in Roy F. Godson, ed., *Intelligence Requirements for the 1980s: Intelligence and Policy* (Lexington, MA: Lexington Books, 1986), 2.

12. Forms of MASINT include acoustic intelligence; radar intelligence; nuclear radiation detection; infrared intelligence; electro-optical intelligence; radio frequency; unintentional radiation; materials, effluent, and debris sampling; and electro-optical and spectroradiometric sources.

13. For abundant open-source intelligence analysis, see, for example, http://www.janes.com, http://www.stratfor.com, and http://www.indigo-net.com/intel.htm.

14. See, for example, Michael I. Handel, ed., *Leaders and Intelligence* (London: Frank Cass, 1989); Christopher Andrew, *For the President's Eyes Only: Secret Intel-*

ligence and the American Presidency from Washington to Bush (New York: Harper Collins, 1995); and Christopher Andrew and Vasili Mitrokhin, *The Sword and the Shield: The Mitrokhin Archive and the Secret History of the KGB* (New York: Basic Books, 1999). For a short and useful discussion of the issues in production and consumption of intelligence, see Mark M. Lowenthal, "Tribal Tongues: Intelligence Consumers, Intelligence Producers," *Washington Quarterly* (Winter 1992): 157–168.

15. Quoted by Peter Wright (with Paul Greengrass), *Spy Catcher: The Candid Autobiography of a Senior Intelligence Officer* (New York: Viking, 1987), 305.

16. Abram N. Shulsky, *Silent Warfare: Understanding the World of Intelligence*, revised by Gary J. Schmitt (Washington, DC: Brassey's, 1993), 111. See also James M. Olson, "The Ten Commandments of Counterintelligence," *Studies in Intelligence*, no. 11 (Fall/Winter, 2001): 81–87. Ken Dombroski was helpful in assisting us to clarify several of the issues involved in counterintelligence as well as covert action.

17. Peter Gill, *Policing Politics: Security Intelligence and the Liberal Democratic State* (Portland, OR: Frank Cass, 1994), 6–7.

18. Lowenthal, *Intelligence*, 129–131.

19. Thus rather than providing explanation, one of the most highly regarded experts of comparative politics comes up with "factors" explaining transitions. See Samuel Huntington, *The Third Wave: Democratization in the Late Twentieth Century* (Norman: University of Oklahoma Press, 1991).

20. Democracy is a system of governance in which rulers are held accountable for their actions in the public realm by citizens, acting indirectly through the competition and cooperation of their elected representatives. See Philippe C. Schmitter and Terry Lynn Karl, "What Democracy Is . . . and Is Not," in Larry Diamond and Marc F. Plattner, eds., *The Global Resurgence of Democracy* (Baltimore: Johns Hopkins University Press, 1993), 40.

21. Among other sources on this approach, see John Higley and Richard Gunther, eds., *Elites and Democratic Consolidation in Latin America and Southern Europe* (Cambridge: Cambridge University Press, 1992), 3–4; and Juan J. Linz and Alfred Stepan, *Problems of Democratic Transition and Consolidation: Southern Europe, South America, and Post-Communist Europe* (Baltimore: Johns Hopkins University Press, 1996), 5–6.

22. See Gill, *Policing Politics*, for the typology of security intelligence organizations, based on W. W. Keller, *The Liberals and J. Edgar Hoover: Rise and Fall of a Domestic Intelligence State* (Princeton, NJ: Princeton University Press, 1989), 13–16, 60–61. Gill categorizes the three types of security intelligence services with respect to levels of autonomy from and penetration of society.

23. Great Britain and France are good examples of established democracies with an executive-only system. In Great Britain, the Intelligence and Security Committee, made up of parliament members, reviews reports on intelligence; however, the committee provides its findings only to the prime minister, and it

does not have full access to all information. In France there is no separate system for overseeing intelligence services. Instead, accountability is provided through the Ministry of the Interior or the Ministry of Defense. See Hans Born and Ian Leigh, *Making Intelligence Accountable: Legal Standards and Best Practice for Oversight of Intelligence Agencies* (Oslo: Publishing House of the Parliament of Norway, 2005); and Peter Chalk and William Rosenau, *Confronting the Enemy Within* (Santa Monica, CA: RAND, 2004).

24. These institutional and other controls are described and analyzed in Bruneau and Tollefson, *Soldiers and Statesmen.*

25. See, for example, http://www.fas.org for information on one of the more active NGOs working in this area of intelligence.

26. Great Britain, until the recent acceptance of the Butler Committee report, was a good example of a consensus intelligence provider. The British system now includes a separate team to challenge assessments and will shortly be appointing a "challenger in chief" to test intelligence material before it is presented to policymakers. See "Cat's Eyes in the Dark," *The Economist*, March 17, 2005. The United States and, to a lesser extent, Australia and Canada are organizations that use the method of competitive intelligence to provide alternative analyses.

27. For a comprehensive survey of earlier reform proposals in the United States, beginning as early as two years after the IC was restructured, see Richard A. Best Jr., *Proposals for Intelligence Reorganization, 1949–2004*, CRS Report for Congress (Washington, DC: Congressional Research Service, Library of Congress, July 29, 2004).

PART ONE

CHALLENGES TO EFFECTIVE INTELLIGENCE IN MODERN DEMOCRACIES

ONE

EXECUTIVE PRIVILEGE

Intelligence Oversight in the United States

Steven C. Boraz

The institutions that have been created to control intelligence in the United States, as elsewhere, reside formally in executive, legislative, judicial, and internal controls as well as informally in public scrutiny of the intelligence community (IC). And although these structures and processes exist, they have been part of the U.S. oversight framework for a relatively short period of time and continue to evolve. This chapter will discuss these procedures, their origins, and the impact of recent changes in oversight stemming from the 9/11 Commission Report, President George W. Bush's August 2004 executive orders (EOs), the Intelligence Reform and Terrorism Prevention Act of 2004 (referred to as the Intelligence Reform Act henceforth), and the creation of the Office of the Director of National Intelligence (ODNI) with John Negroponte at its helm, as well as briefly touching on changes ushered in from the Commission on the Intelligence Capabilities of the United States Regarding Weapons of Mass Destruction (henceforth referred to as the WMD Commission Report).[1]

The U.S. system is one in which the executive and legislative branches have large roles. Since legislative controls became a part of the system of overseeing and controlling intelligence in the United States in the mid-1970s, Congress has taken a continually increasing interest in intelligence and its role in national defense. In fact, the U.S. Congress has probably the most developed mechanisms for reviewing intelligence practices anywhere in the world. Despite the legislative role in intelligence oversight, control of the IC is more concentrated in the executive branch. To illustrate this point, I include a short case study of how executive guidance affects the IC.[2]

ESTABLISHING INTELLIGENCE OVERSIGHT

While the army, the navy, and the State Department all operated intelligence organizations dating back decades, it was not until the National Security Act of 1947 that an "intelligence community" was established. However, in its original form, the act did not provide for legislative oversight. In fact, legislative oversight from 1947 through 1975 was left to the Armed Services Committee in the House of Representatives, a committee that had very little desire to oversee the IC.[3]

Significant change occurred in the mid-1970s amid national reporting of CIA and FBI intelligence operations against members of the antiwar movement within the United States, as well as the CIA's attempts to destabilize or replace existing governments in the international realm. Coupling these developments with the Watergate scandal, Americans demanded greater accountability of their government. Congress responded and set about to investigate the numerous allegations of misconduct within the IC, as well as the executive branch's role as overseers.

One of the first actions Congress took was implementing the Hughes-Ryan Amendment in 1974, requiring the president to "find" that a covert action was important to the national security of the United States and mandating that the president report to Congress in a "timely fashion a description and scope of any operation with the appropriate Committee" in Congress as designated recipients of the finding.[4] Congress now had its first role in establishing oversight, though this role would prove controversial for years to come, as the next chapter, on judicial oversight, highlights.[5]

Congress then established two special committees to investigate the abuses in the IC: the Church Committee in the Senate and the Pike Committee in the House. Both committees investigated a wide range of CIA activities, though Senator Frank Church tended to focus on the activities of the IC and Congressman Otis Pike focused more closely on intelligence failures. The Church Committee published its findings in fourteen reports in 1975 and 1976.[6] Although the Pike Committee report was never officially released (much of it was leaked and found its way into the *Village Voice*), the findings of both committees led to the creation of the Senate Select Committee on Intelligence (SSCI) and the House Permanent Select Committee on Intelligence (HPSCI), both of which are discussed later in this chapter. The Church Committee reports still represent the seminal event in establishing legislative oversight of the IC.

As the Pike and Church Committees were working, the executive branch also sought to investigate intelligence wrongdoing, and President Gerald Ford established a commission on CIA activities, headed by Vice President Nelson Rockefeller. The Rockefeller Commission issued a single report in 1975 delineating some CIA abuses, including mail opening and surveillance of domestic dissident groups, but the report was largely viewed to be soft on the CIA.[7] However, its findings and issuance led President Ford to issue Executive Order (EO) 11905, entitled "United States Foreign Intelligence Activities." This EO created "policies to improve the quality of intelligence needed for national security, to clarify the authority and responsibilities of the intelligence departments and agencies, and to establish effective oversight to assure compliance with law in the management and direction of intelligence agencies and departments of the national government."[8] Ford's order also prohibited political assassinations, reestablished his own cabinet's policies and procedures for establishing national security policy, reaffirmed the central role of the director of central intelligence (DCI), and, for the first time, delineated the roles and missions of the remainder of the intelligence community's agencies.[9]

STANDING OVERSIGHT MECHANISMS

As mentioned earlier in this chapter, the IC is subject to executive, legislative, judicial, internal, and external oversight. The several organizations and mechanisms that carry out said oversight will be detailed here shortly, though this chapter only touches on judicial oversight since that topic is covered in the next chapter.

The executive branch will be dealt with first because its oversight has the greatest impact on intelligence, because of the branch's role in developing and implementing policy. Since the purpose of intelligence is to inform policy and support operations, the IC works for the executive branch or its agencies. And while Congress has had an increasing role in the operations of the IC since the formal establishment of the SSCI and HPSCI, the executive remains the primary consumer of intelligence and has the most contact with IC personnel.[10] In short, the executive branch is a proactive body that drives intelligence, and Congress is reactive.[11]

The Executive Branch

The executive branch has at its disposal three standing oversight bodies: The President's Foreign Intelligence Advisory Board, the Intelligence Oversight Board, and the Office of Management and Budget. In addition, executive oversight of the IC occurs through four important means: executive orders, presidential directives, presidential findings, and daily management.

PRESIDENT'S FOREIGN INTELLIGENCE ADVISORY BOARD

The President's Foreign Intelligence Advisory Board (PFIAB), which was created under the Eisenhower administration and has existed in some form for each president since except for President Jimmy Carter, is an entity within the executive office of the president formed "to assess the quality, quantity, and adequacy" of intelligence collection, analysis, counterintelligence, and other activities of the IC and reports "directly to the President and advises him concerning the objectives, conduct, management and coordination of the various activities of the agencies of the IC."[12] The board is composed of no more than sixteen persons, all from outside government.

INTELLIGENCE OVERSIGHT BOARD

Once a separate organization under the president, the Intelligence Oversight Board (IOB) was made a standing committee of the PFIAB in 1993. The IOB is composed of four members of the PFIAB as appointed by the PFIAB chairman. The IOB conducts independent oversight investigations as required and reviews the oversight practices and procedures of the inspectors general and general counsels of intelligence agencies.[13]

OFFICE OF MANAGEMENT AND BUDGET

The Office of Management and Budget (OMB), as part of the executive office of the president, reviews intelligence budgets in light of presidential policies and priorities, clears proposed testimony, and approves draft intelligence legislation for submission to Congress.[14]

EXECUTIVE ORDERS

Executive orders offer the president a succinct way to give oversight and direction to the IC. As previously noted, President Ford provided the first formal executive order on the IC. President Carter issued his own order on intelligence, and President Ronald Reagan issued EO 12333 in December 1981, which remained the standard for the IC for more than twenty years, until the passage of the 2004 Intelligence Reform Act. In addition to laying out the broad goals of providing the president and the National Security Council with information to support policy development, EO 12333 specified the duties of each component of the IC, highlighting the DCI's role in coordinating intelligence policy and advising the president and the National Security Council; discussed the legal conduct of intelligence activities; and codified the requirement for the IC to provide information to Congress.

In August 2004, President George W. Bush signed four EOs designed to provide guidance to the IC: EO 13353, "Establishing the President's Board on Safeguarding Americans' Civil Liberties"; EO 13354, "The National Counterterrorism Center"; EO 13355, "Strengthened Management of the IC";[15] and EO 13356, "Strengthening the Sharing of Terrorism Information to Protect Americans."[16] These orders were a response to the 9/11 Commission recommendations, as well as a politically expedient move in the middle of the presidential campaign. EO 13355, which was technically an update to the Reagan-era EO 12333, specifically gave the DCI increased powers and set the stage for the role a future director of national intelligence might have. EO 13355 stopped short of creating a new intelligence czar, because the Bush administration insisted that was the job of Congress, but it helped guide legislative debate on how to restructure the IC. In fact, the context of each one of the Bush EOs was incorporated into the Intelligence Reform Act.

PRESIDENTIAL DIRECTIVES

The name of presidential directives has changed over the years from President Kennedy's National Security Action Memorandums to the current National Security Presidential Directives (NSPDs), but the substance always provides executive guidance on the national security goals of the administration.

NATIONAL SECURITY COUNCIL

Although the National Security Act of 1947 mandates the makeup of the National Security Council (NSC), each president since Truman has put his own personal stamp on the council. This is often the first directive the president provides to his cabinet and defines the way the NSC will form policy, thus guiding intelligence. In the current administration, for instance, President Bush has created NSC Policy Co-ordination Committees, among them a committee of intelligence and counterintelligence.[17]

INTELLIGENCE DIRECTIVES

The Bush administration has provided very explicit guidance to the IC, embodied in NSPD 26, which was designed to create "a dynamic process for articulating and reviewing intelligence priorities." Based on the guidance provided in NSPD 26, the director of central intelligence then established a National Intelligence Priorities Framework (NIPF) "as a mechanism to translate the national foreign intelligence objectives and priorities approved by the National Security Council into *specific guidance and resource allocations* for the Intelligence Community" (emphasis added).[18] The importance of this type of executive guidance cannot be overstated, for it drives virtually everything the IC does and is worth examining in more detail, which is done later in this chapter. However, because NSPD 26 and the NIPF are classified, I will examine President Bill Clinton's Presidential Decision Directive on Intelligence (PDD-35) because much of it is available in the public domain. And while NSPD 26 is different from PDD-35, the Clinton directive on intelligence provides insight on how the executive sets the IC's overarching agenda.

PRESIDENTIAL FINDINGS

As discussed previously, in order to carry out a covert operation, the president must prepare a "finding," determine if the action is legal and supportive of policy, and report that finding to Congress in a timely fashion. Congress has the ability to raise concerns to the executive branch about a specific operation, but the executive branch makes the final decision on when to go ahead with an operation. The final authority vested in the president is powerful as an oversight tool and in determining IC activities.

DAILY MANAGEMENT

The executive branch provides the most important and near-continuous feedback on a day-to-day basis. It does so in the form of the National Security Council, and often the president himself providing oversight by giving immediate feedback to the President's Daily Brief and other routine intelligence updates the executive branch receives.

The Legislative Branch

Congress also has a role in oversight, and these functions exist in both the House and the Senate.

THE SENATE SELECT COMMITTEE ON INTELLIGENCE

The Senate Select Committee on Intelligence (SSCI) was established in 1976 under Senate Resolution 400 to

> oversee and make continuing studies of the intelligence activities and programs of the United States Government. . . . In carrying out this purpose, the Select Committee on Intelligence shall . . . assure . . . intelligence necessary for the executive and legislative branches to make sound decisions affecting the security and vital interests of the Nation. It is further the purpose of this resolution to provide vigilant legislative oversight over the intelligence activities of the United States.[19]

Membership in the SSCI has ranged from thirteen to seventeen, with the majority party in Congress having one more member than the minority. Members of the SSCI serve no more than eight-year terms.[20] One majority and one minority member from the Appropriations, Armed Services, Foreign Relations, and Judiciary Committees are required to be a part of the SSCI, with the remaining seats, currently seventeen, to be filled from the Senate at large.[21] Rather than being voted onto the committees, as is the norm in the Senate, the majority and minority leaders within the Senate appoint the SSCI members.

In addition to its role in annually authorizing appropriations for intelligence activities, the SSCI carries out oversight investigations and inquiries as required. It also handles presidential nominations referred to the Senate for the positions of DCI, deputy DCI, and inspector general of CIA, and it reviews treaties referred to the Senate for ratification as necessary to determine the ability of the IC to verify the provisions of the treaty under consideration.[22]

HOUSE PERMANENT SELECT COMMITTEE ON INTELLIGENCE

The House Permanent Select Committee on Intelligence (HPSCI) was established in 1977 under House Rule 48. Like its Senate counterpart, the HPSCI authorizes appropriations annually, receives annual updates from the IC, and conducts oversight investigations as required.

Membership in the HPSCI is currently set at nineteen, with ten majority and nine minority seats. The one-seat majority of the majority party has not always been the standard of the HPSCI. Typically the makeup has reflected partisan numbers within the house. Like the Senate, there is a requirement that members serve on the Appropriations, Armed Services, Foreign Affairs, and Judiciary Committees, and there is term limit, though it is six years in the HPSCI. Unlike the Senate, where majority and minority leadership appoints committee members, the Speaker of the House appoints everyone assigned to the HPSCI.[23]

MULTIPLE AND SEPARATE AGENCIES

Most intelligence communities have different intelligence organizations to ensure that no single organization can control all of the nation's intelligence. The United States is no exception and currently employs sixteen intelligence organizations.[24] This separation allows for specialization within intelligence function, as well as ensuring that no single agency controls all of national intelligence. Although the president, in many cases, has defined the roles and missions of each one of these organizations, it is Congress that is responsible for creating them, as was done in the National Security Act of 1947 and the Intelligence Reform Act of 2004.

ADDITIONAL CONGRESSIONAL OVERSIGHT

In addition to the standing intelligence committees of each chamber, the Defense and Homeland Security Committee, the Senate Armed Services Committee, the House National Security Committee, and both Senate and House Appropriations Committees have some oversight mechanisms in that each of these bodies appropriates and apportions funds to sections of the IC.

Internal Mechanisms

There are also institutions and practices within the IC itself that support oversight. They include inspectors general, a peer-review process often referred to as competitive intelligence, and professional standards.

INSPECTORS GENERAL AND GENERAL COUNSELS

Each element of the IC is subject to the jurisdiction of an inspector general (IG), either within its specific organization or within its parent organization. The CIA's inspector general is statutory, appointed by the president and confirmed by the Senate, and is responsible for investigating any alleged improprieties or program mismanagement within the CIA. The CIA IG submits semiannual reports of her activities to the two congressional intelligence committees and, under certain circumstances, must report directly to these committees.

The Department of Defense also has an IG, required by statute, who reports to the secretary of defense (SECDEF) and whose jurisdiction extends to all of the intelligence elements of the Department of Defense. In addition, each such element (e.g., NSA, the National Geospatial-Intelligence Agency [NGA], the Defense Intelligence Agency [DIA], and National Reconnaissance Office [NRO]) has its own nonstatutory IG, appointed by the head of the agency, who performs oversight.

Non-Defense intelligence elements similarly are subject to oversight by independent IGs. For example, the State Department's Bureau of Intelligence and Research (INR) is subject to oversight by the State Department IG, and the FBI's National Security Division, by the FBI inspector general.

The general counsels of intelligence agencies also perform an oversight function, reviewing proposed and ongoing activities to ensure their compliance with law and policy.[25]

Work in the IG office can come at the direction of Congress, the president, or a cabinet secretary, or it can be initiated internally. The majority of IG work is focused on program fiduciary management, but the office can also investigate personnel management and alleged improprieties, ensuring that the standards of the President's Council on Integrity and Efficiency are upheld.[26]

COMPETITIVE ANALYSIS

Competitive analysis is a process in which the organizations within the IC that produce all-source, or "finished," intelligence (DNI, DIA, CIA, and the State Department's INR) provide analysis to decision makers that has undergone a rigorous peer review and can be separate and distinct from that of the other organizations. A process of "red-teaming," or Team B, analysis also occurs within the IC, and sometimes by outside experts looking at the same data, to challenge established analysis within the IC and offer alternative interpretations. It is common practice, especially in national intelligence estimates (NIEs), to have highlighted "dissenting" views in which alternative analyses to the main findings are provided.

Those who study U.S. intelligence see this as a unique process, one that serves policymakers well and a system that provides a level of oversight and accountability within the IC by providing a peer review of analysis.[27] EO 12333 formally directs this process: "Maximum emphasis should be given to fostering analytical competition among appropriate elements of the IC."[28] The Intelligence Reform Act also instructs the director of national intelligence to support competitive analysis by ensuring "that the elements of the IC regularly conduct competitive analysis of analytic products, whether such products are produced by or disseminated to such elements."[29]

PROFESSIONAL STANDARDS

Each one of the agencies within the IC has a variety of training courses that range from initial intelligence education to intermediate and advanced training in the form of advanced degrees, or through "journeyman training" on new analytical techniques, changing technical capabilities, and the like. In addition, courses are routinely provided on standards of conduct and ethics, organizational policies, and laws regarding the IC. All serve to instill a professional ethos in IC employees, one of the most critical aspects, if not the most crucial, in ensuring that internal oversight is in place.

External Mechanisms

While the media and other watchdog groups have an important role in overseeing intelligence, they "cannot provide the depth of public scrutiny of the IC that they can of other government departments"[30] because of the secrecy inherent in the intelligence business. That said, external sources have proved useful in overseeing the IC, from Seymour Hersh's article on CIA misconduct in 1974, to the 9/11 Commission Report, to, in mid-2006, the NSA's eavesdropping on people inside the United States.[31]

An interesting aspect in the media's role in overseeing intelligence in the United States is what is commonly known as the CNN effect, in reference to twenty-four-hour news operations and their ability to be anywhere rapidly. All too often a media outlet will report an event that the IC was unaware of or where analysis was proven wrong. The conventional view of external actors providing oversight is that they will expose some failure or misconduct. The CNN effect often forces the IC to play catch-up or prove/disprove what is in the news. The impact is that twenty-four-hour news media can actually alter IC collection and analysis, a role heretofore reserved for the DCI and leadership within each intelligence agency.

In addition to the media, there are numerous professional intelligence organizations that primarily serve as advocacy groups for the IC but that also have provided some measure of oversight. These organizations differ distinctly from the media in that their membership is made up of current and former intelligence personnel.[32]

Summary

While separate organs in the U.S. democratic organizations share in the responsibility of overseeing intelligence, one can see that executive control is the most prevalent and most important in ensuring that a state is using its intelligence organizations appropriately. It is the executive that defines the mission of the IC and normally organizes it, in general terms, to support that mission. Further, the executive branch is the primary consumer of intelligence and therefore provides the greatest direction to the IC on a daily basis.

CHANGES IN OVERSIGHT IN THE INTELLIGENCE REFORM ACT

The Intelligence Reform Act was signed into law in December 2004, codifying many of the changes made in the executive orders that President Bush signed in August. Most notably, the Intelligence Reform Act reorganized the IC by creating the office and position of a director of national intelligence (ODNI/DNI) with real personnel and budgetary decision-making authority (see Figure 1.1).[33]

Putting the legislative stamp on IC organization was something that Congress had not really done since the establishment of the IC in the National Security Act. The Reform Act:

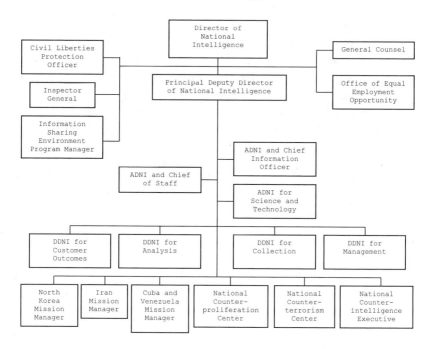

ADNI is Assistant Director of National Intelligence
DDNI is Deputy Director of National Intelligence
   Source: Office of the Director of National Intelligence

FIGURE I.I. *Office of the Director of National Intelligence. Adapted from the ODNI website, http://www.odni.gov.*

1. Identified the DNI as the principal adviser to the president, the NSC, and the Homeland Security Council, effectively demoting the DCI to the role of running the CIA alone. The bill empowered the DNI to determine intelligence requirements and priorities for the entire IC.[34]

2. Restructured the CIA, primarily defining it as a human intelligence and analysis organization. In addition, the bill placed the National Intelligence Councils, which had been under the purview of the CIA, under the DNI.[35]

3. Provided increased budget authority by directing the DNI to develop, coordinate, and monitor the intelligence budget, including the portion of the budget that is coordinated within the Defense

Department. This also provided the DNI with authority to review and approve any transfer of funds within the National Intelligence Program (NIP) and for the SECDEF to transfer funds within the Military Intelligence Program (JMIP). Congress added an oversight requirement to notify the appropriate congressional committees when funds exceeded certain set amounts, ensuring that the transfer would be for "a higher priority intelligence requirement."[36]

4. Authorized the DNI to transfer personnel within intelligence organizations, adding a similar congressional notification requirement to transferring funds. It also directed the DNI to set standards for training, education, and career development within the IC.[37]

In addition to reorganizing the IC with a new lead agency, Congress also reemphasized its role in providing supervision of the IC. The Intelligence Reform Act further

1. Established a National Counterterrorism Center, with the DNI as its titular head, and provided broad guidance so the DNI could establish other national intelligence centers as necessary. The bill also implored the president to ensure that his budget supports these centers.[38]

2. Gave the DNI veto power over any authority other than the president or Congress in selecting directors of various intelligence agencies.[39]

3. Established a Civil Liberties Board as a buffer to any potential IC abuses.[40]

4. Set requirements for improved information sharing within the IC.[41]

5. Emphasized competitive intelligence and red-teaming as an important mechanism in the intelligence process, thus ensuring that no single agency is the keeper of all information.[42]

6. Stressed the importance of analysis as part of the intelligence cycle and the need to improve analysis throughout the IC—as an oversight mechanism designed to improve IC efficacy.[43]

7. Established an Inspector General Office as part of the office of the DNI to function as an internal IC oversight body.[44]

8. Emphasized the importance of the apolitical nature of intelligence and also ensured that the DNI did not reside within the Oval Office.[45]

9. Required the DNI and other IC organizations to report back to Congress on the implementation of various portions of the Intelligence Reform Bill.[46]

10. Established a Joint Intelligence Community Council (JICC), chaired by the DNI and composed of the secretaries of state, treasury, defense, energy, and homeland security, as well as the attorney general, to advise the DNI on establishing requirements, developing budgets, financial management, and monitoring and evaluating the performance of intelligence agencies.[47]

In sum, the Reform Act provided many changes in the organization of the IC, reemphasized the importance of information sharing, civil liberties, cross-governmental intelligence centers, and competitive and accurate analysis. It did not, however, change the basic control process in the U.S. system. In fact, Congress reiterated the importance of the executive office in assigning the position of the director, who is "subject to the authority, direction and control of the President" with a budget "based on intelligence priorities set by the President."[48]

CHANGES IN THE IC STEMMING FROM THE WMD COMMISSION REPORT

After the 2003 U.S. invasion of Iraq and the subsequent failure to find evidence of an active Iraqi program to develop weapons of mass destruction (WMD), President Bush directed the formation of the Commission on the Intelligence Capabilities of the United States Regarding Weapons of Mass Destruction to advise him on ways to improve the intelligence capabilities of the United States, particularly with respect to WMD. The WMD Commission, as it became known, completed its report on March 31, 2005.[49] The Bush administration has endorsed a multitude of the commission's recommendations.[50] The overarching structure of the Office of the Director of National Intelligence (ODNI) is designed to meet some of the weaknesses highlighted in the report. A comprehensive analysis of the WMD Commission report is beyond the scope of this chapter, but the report led to other changes in the IC:

- Establishment of a National Counter Proliferation Center to manage and coordinate the intelligence community's activities related to nuclear, biological, and chemical weapons, as well as their delivery systems.

- Updated information sharing, human resources and technology development policies, and the appointment of key positions within the Office of the Director National Intelligence (ODNI) to carry out these policies.

- Establishment of a National Intelligence University.

- Reinvigoration of oversight mechanisms within the PFIAB and JICC and throughout the IC to ensure that the best collection, analysis, and counterintelligence training, methods, and policies are in place.

THE IMPACT OF EXECUTIVE GUIDANCE

As noted above, it is the executive branch that truly guides the IC, and the current Bush administration NSPD 26, combined with the National Intelligence Priorities Framework (NIPF), is the guide for the intelligence community today. Again, the great preponderance of information on the NIPF remains classified. We do know that the NIPF provides for a "topic manager" for several different subjects of intelligence concern. For example, the former director of the Terrorism Threat Integration Center[51] was the topic manager for terrorism and was responsible for establishing areas of collection emphasis related to terrorism as well as playing a leading role in the analytical process in conjunction with other IC agencies.[52]

Because of the classified nature of the NIPF, this section reviews how the Clinton administration's Presidential Decision Directive on Intelligence (PDD-35) affected U.S. intelligence from its issuance to Clinton's departure from office. PDD-35 defined intelligence collection and analysis requirements and focused intelligence leadership with clear policy goals. It separated intelligence requirements into two broad categories: "hard targets" such as Cuba, Iran, Iraq, Libya, and

North Korea; and transnational issues like weapons proliferation, narcotics, international crime, and terrorism.[53] In addition to the broad categories of hard targets and transnational issues, PDD-35 had two ways of setting priorities. The first was a tier structure of the president's prioritized needs, with upper-tier countries being of higher importance and lower-tier countries being of less interest to the United States. The second type of prioritization was specifically assigning importance to issues, and the Clinton administration stated that support to military operations (SMO) was the top priority for intelligence.[54]

At the time of its issuance, March 1995, the IC was struggling to determine future needs and requirements as the community transitioned from looking at the former Soviet Union to an emerging world in which threats were numerous but there was no enemy with the enormity of the Soviets. What PDD-35 did was to outline requirements and thus shape resources, collection, tasking, analysis, and production at each level of the IC.

Like all governmental agencies, the IC has finite resources, and the requirements laid out in PDD-35 helped intelligence leadership define how it would spend funds in order to support decision makers. The process for spending during the mid-1990s was called the needs process and was derived from PDD-35 and strategic intelligence reviews, which identified the core intelligence issues, priorities, and gaps for various geographic regions and transnational issues, as well as longer-term topics.[55] Planners from the IC, in conjunction with the executive branch, would use these requirements to submit proposals for funding to Congress. Congress, for the most part, would fund the IC based on this budget input.[56] As the intelligence resource managers received funding, they would apportion it according to the requirements laid out in PDD-35.

As the money funneled into intelligence agencies, agency management naturally reallocated their personnel to the hard-target countries and top issues. They also assigned their collection resources to the higher-tier requirements. Although PDD-35 specifically stated that it was not meant to be an exhaustive list of requirements, the result was a lack of collection and analysis on any country or issue not in one of the higher tiers. Indeed, a congressional study remarked:

> When requirements outstrip capability, prioritization obviously is needed. However, PDD-35 . . . in some ways appears to have wors-

ened the problem. Analysts believe the tier system is being imposed too rigidly. As a result, the top five or six requirements receive the great majority of the resources so that we do them exceedingly well, but those below, especially those beneath the top tier level, languish with leftovers at best.[57]

In addition to the tier system, the priority PDD-35 placed on SMO influenced the IC, and managers had to move resources and personnel to provide for military contingencies. This worked well to support military operations in Bosnia, where coverage and analysis were adequate; however, contingencies that emerged in Liberia, Congo, Kenya, East Timor, and Sierra Leone forced managers and planners to surge personnel and often start from scratch.[58] Others lamented the focus because it put long-term analysis on the back burner and led to diminished support to policymakers at the State Department and in the White House. For instance, it has been suggested that SMO was a contributing factor in the failure to provide warning of the Indian nuclear test in May 1998.[59] Combined with the tier system, the concentration on SMO created more worldwide intelligence gaps and ultimately had the effect of putting the cart before the horse: "The Community spends more time gathering intelligence for potential SMO than for monitoring other developments that might help policy makers avert the need to ever have to deploy forces."[60]

In analyzing the impact PDD-35 had, it is important to take a broad view of the context in which it was created—a world with a variety of emerging threats but no monolithic enemy like the Soviet Union. Framing the situation must also take into account that intelligence is a resource with limits on budget and personnel. What PDD-35 did was to define, in pretty clear terms, what the priorities of the consumers of intelligence were and, therefore, told IC management where to put their resources. Countries and issues in upper tiers got looked at; countries in lower tiers didn't.

At its best, PDD-35 provided much-needed focus for the IC in a time of great ambiguity. At worst, the directive pulled resources away from issues of lesser import in an attempt to provide depth while sacrificing breadth. It is interesting and somewhat damning, however, to note that the IC's focus on hard targets did not yield substantive results in some cases. In reviewing PDD-35, a congressional study on intelligence observantly lamented, "The IC cannot base its long-range planning primarily on high-level policy maker–defined requirements because policy makers, by their very nature, tend to concentrate on immediate problems and do not think long-term.[61]

Finally, in comparing the structure of the current NIPF to PDD-35, one could argue that the Bush version is more streamlined than Clinton's policy, with better clarity on specific issues, particularly terrorism, and a lessened emphasis on support to the military. Like PDD-35, the NIPF is the primary means the IC uses to allocate its resources.

CONCLUSION

The oversight practices in the United States, summarized below in Table 1.1, are often described as unique, primarily because of the legislative branch's extensive use of control mechanisms. Former DCI Robert Gates noted, "The result of these realities is that the [IC] today finds itself . . . positioned nearly equidistant between the executive and legislative branches . . . a position unique in American history and the world."[62] Gates's point was that congressional involvement in intelligence made the IC serve two masters. And although Congress has most certainly involved itself in IC business in more ways than any other legislative organization in the world, its purpose remains, in the strictest sense of the terms identified in this book's introduction, to provide oversight rather than control of intelligence.

The recent changes established through the Intelligence Reform Act, in fact, confirm this, with Congress addressing issues of organization, budget, legality, and accountability while looking to the president to provide direction and establish priorities. In short, the executive branch in the United States still holds sway.

Changes in internal oversight are progressing at a rapid and dynamic pace. Impacts stemming from the Reform Act and the 9/11 and WMD Commissions continue to be felt. The DNI and his office are routinely fine-tuning processes as they come to grips with controlling the behemoth that is the U.S. intelligence community.

In sum, the oversight regime in the United States generally conforms to the arrangement of checks and balances between the executive and legislative branches that exist within the U.S. constitutional system. As highlighted by the United States, establishing oversight in democracies can take years to implement and is as evolutionary a process as is consolidating democracy.

TABLE I.I OVERSIGHT REGIME OF THE
UNITED STATES INTELLIGENCE COMMUNITY

Group	Oversight bodies or mechanisms	Oversight role
Executive	PFIAB, PIOB, OMB, executive order, presidential directive, presidential finding, daily feedback	Set requirements; direct and review all facets of IC activity; approve covert action; organize IC to support requirements
Legislative	SSCI, HPSCI, Armed Services, Homeland Defense, and Appropriations Committees	Establish law; apportion and control spending; review IC organizations, management, and accountability; nominations and confirmations; covert operations prior notice; treaty verification
Internal	Inspectors general, competitive analysis, multiple organizations	Legality of management, spending, and operations; peer review; no single agency with all knowledge
External	Media, private intelligence organizations, think tanks	Ensure proper conduct of IC; a growing role in focusing IC collection and analysis

NOTES

1. There have been extensive changes in the oversight mechanisms within the United States since I originally wrote this chapter. I have attempted to capture, at least in summary if not in detail, the most important ones. There will no doubt be more changes in the future.

2. For a more detailed review of the IC and oversight history, see L. Britt Snider, *Sharing Secrets with Lawmakers: Congress as a User of Intelligence* (Washington, DC: Center for the Study of Intelligence, February 1997); and Aspin-Brown Commission, "The Evolution of the U.S. Intelligence Community—An Historical Overview," appendix A in *Preparing for the 21st Century: An Appraisal of U.S. Intelligence*, Report of the Commission on the Roles and Capabilities of the United States Intelligence Community, March 1, 1996, http://www.access.gpo.gov/intelligence/int/into22.html.

3. See Marvin C. Ott, "Partisanship and the Decline of Intelligence Oversight," *International Journal of Intelligence and Counterintelligence* 16, no. 1 (Winter 2003): 74. Ott argues that "oversight hardly existed, and what there was occurred outside the purview of most of the Congress and the public."

4. *Foreign Assistance Act*, sec. 662 (22 *U.S. Code* § 2422).

5. By the end of the 1970s, there were eight "appropriate committees" of Congress, four in each chamber. In 1980, Congress, in agreement with the Carter administration, passed the Intelligence Oversight Act (formalized in sec. 5 of the National Security Act of 1947), reducing the formal recipients of the presidential finding to the Senate and House Committees on Intelligence. The notification system was circumvented during the Iran-Contra affair in 1985–1986. Congress updated the oversight law with the Fiscal Year 1991 Intelligence Authorization Act, which contained a series of new provisions for reporting on covert action. See "Congressional Precedents and Powers," http://www.house.gov/rules/jcoc2ar .htm; and Senate Select Committee on Intelligence, *Legislative Oversight of Intelligence Activities: The U.S. Experience*, report (Washington, DC: U.S. Government Printing Office, 1994): 20–25. With respect to Iran-Contra, see U.S. Congress, *Report of the Congressional Committees Investigating the Iran-Contra Affair*, 100th Cong., 1st sess., 1987, S. Rep. 216, H. Rep. 433; and *Joint Hearings in Executive Session as Declassified before the House Select Committee to Investigate Covert Arms Transactions with Iran and the Senate Select Committee on Secret Military Assistance to Iran and the Nicaraguan Oppositions*, 100th Cong., 1st sess., 1987.

6. The complete texts of all fourteen Church Committee reports are online at http://www.aarclibrary.org/publib/church/reports/contents.htm. For an overview on the Pike Committee, see Gerald K. Haines, "Looking for a Rogue Elephant: The Pike Committee Investigations and the CIA," http://www.cia.gov/csi/ studies/winter98_99/art07.html.

7. See Mark M. Lowenthal, *U.S. Intelligence: Evolution and Anatomy* (Westport, CT: Praeger, 1992), 41. The complete text of the Rockefeller Commission, *Report to the President by the Commission on CIA Activities within the United States* (June 1975), is online at http://www.history-matters.com/archive/church/ rockcomm/contents.htm.

8. Executive Order 11905, February 18, 1976: sec. 1.

9. Ibid.

10. Some scholars advocate that the Congress should play a more active role in oversight, while others lament the loss of executive authority in making national security decisions. For arguments that favor a strong role by the legislature, see Ott, "Partisanship and the Decline of Intelligence Oversight" (though Ott laments the effects of partisan politics on the SSCI and HPSCI); and "Proposed Remarks by Robert M. Gates, Director of Central Intelligence before the World Affairs Council of Boston," in U.S. Senate Select Committee on Intelligence, *Legislative Oversight of Intelligence Activities*, appendix 10. For the counterargument, see Stephen F. Knott, "The Great Republican Transformation of Oversight,"

International Journal of Intelligence and Counterintelligence 13, no. 1 (Spring 2000): 49–63; and Fred F. Manget, "Presidential Powers and Foreign Intelligence Operations," *International Journal of Intelligence and Counterintelligence* 5, no. 2 (Spring 1992): 131–148.

11. This is, admittedly, mild oversimplification. When the Constitution offers clear guidance, such as that related to treaty verification or confirmation procedures, legislators are much more active and help create policy. Dr. Ott confirmed this is the case and also noted that a senator may take a personal interest in an issue and help set the policy agenda, as Senator John Glenn did with U.S. counterproliferation policy. Dr. Marvin Ott, interview with the author, October 18, 2004.

12. Executive Order 12863, President's Foreign Intelligence Advisory Board, September 13, 1993.

13. Ibid.

14. "An Overview of the Intelligence Community," http://www.gpoaccess.gov/int/pdf/into23.pdf.

15. Executive Order 13355 was technically an update of EO 12333.

16. In October 2005, President Bush revoked EO 13356, updating it with an EO entitled "Further Strengthening the Sharing of Terrorism Information to Protect Americans." The theme remained largely unchanged.

17. National Security Presidential Directive 1, February 13, 2001.

18. George Tenet, "Written Statement for the Record of the Director of Central Intelligence before the National Commission on Terrorist Attacks upon the United States, March 24, 2004."

19. S Res. 400, 94th Cong., 2nd sess., sec 1.

20. S Res. 445, which was passed by the Senate on October 9, 2004, included a provision that reduced the membership in the SSCI by two and eliminated the term limit.

21. S Res. 400, Sec 2.

22. "Overview of the Intelligence Community."

23. Rule 48, Permanent Select Committee on Intelligence. The term limit in the House was also repealed by the Intelligence Reform Act.

24. For purposes of this study, the IC consists of the Central Intelligence Agency (CIA); the National Security Agency (NSA) of the Department of Defense (DoD); the DoD's National Geospatial-Intelligence Agency (NGA); the DoD's National Reconnaissance Office (NRO); the DoD's Defense Intelligence Agency (DIA); the intelligence entities of each of the four armed forces (army, navy, air force, and marine corps); the State Department's Bureau of Intelligence and Research (INR); the Treasury Department's Office of Terrorism and Finance Development; the FBI's Directorate of Intelligence, and the Drug Enforcement Administration's Office of National Security Intelligence, both in the Department of Justice; the Department of Energy's Office of Intelligence; and the Directorate of Information Analysis and Infrastructure Protection and the Directorate of Coast Guard Intelligence, both in the Department of Homeland Security. Addi-

tional intelligence collection and analysis capabilities exist across various federal, state, and local law enforcement organizations. The community is led by the director of national intelligence.

25. See "Overview of the Intelligence Community," part 4.

26. Commander Wayne Hugar, Department of Defense IG office, interview with the author, October 4, 2004. The President's Council on Integrity and Efficiency was established in 1981 by Executive Order 12301 under President Reagan and reaffirmed by executive orders from Presidents Bush in 1988 and Clinton in 1992. It is an interagency committee chaired by the Office of Management and Budget's deputy director for management. The mission is to continually identify, review, and discuss areas of weakness in federal programs and operations and their vulnerability to fraud, waste, and abuse. The council also develops plans for coordinated, government-wide activities that address these problems and promote economy and efficiency in federal programs and operations. Available online at http://www.whitehouse.gov/omb/fedreg/pcie-memberlist.pdf.

27. Ott interview. Dr. Ott, a former SSCI staffer, emphasized the importance of competitive analysis as an internal oversight mechanism. He stated that perhaps the strongest argument against having a national intelligence director was that the position would significantly diminish competition and adversely affect the IC. Others argue differently. For example, Gregory Treverton notes that while competitive analysis is always supposed to be part of the process, it is rarely done with vigor: "It is often viewed by analysts as more of a supplemental exercise than an essential component of the analytic process" and is generally used for less critical issues. See Gregory F. Treverton, *Making Sense of Transnational Threats: Workshop Reports* (Santa Monica, CA: RAND, 2005), xi. Philip Davies argues that competitive analysis in the U.S. system is the reason it is so fragmented and most often produces not better, but worse, intelligence. See Philip H. J. Davies, "Intelligence Culture and Intelligence Failure in Britain and the United States," *Cambridge Review of International Affairs* 17, no. 3 (October 2004): 495–520.

28. Executive Order 12333, "United States Intelligence Activities," December 4, 1981: part I(a).

29. Sec. 102(a) of P.L. 108-458.

30. Ott, "Partisanship and the Decline of Intelligence Oversight," 73.

31. See Seymour Hersh, "Huge CIA Operation Reported in U.S. Anti-War Forces, Other Dissidents in Nixon Years," *New York Times*, December 22, 1974; and *The 9/11 Commission Report: Final Report of the National Commission on Terrorist Attacks upon the United States*, http://www.gpoaccess.gov/911/. The commission is better known as the 9/11 Commission. While its mandate was from the Congress, the report—an unclassified exposé of the IC's handling of the attacks of September 11, 2001—became a national best seller and provided the impetus for executive and legislative attempts to change the IC, which is why I categorize it as an external actor. On NSA eavesdropping, see James Risen and Eric Lientblau, "Bush, U.S. Spy on Callers without Courts," *New York Times*, December 16, 2005.

32. A short list of such organizations includes the Association of Former Intelligence Officers, the DIA Alumni Organization, the National Military Intelligence Association, the Armed Forces Communications and Electronics Association, the Military Intelligence Corps Association, Naval Intelligence Professionals, the Marine Corps Intelligence Association, and Retired Air Force Intelligence Personnel.

33. John Negroponte was appointed the first DNI by President Bush and confirmed in April 2005. The standards and oversight procedures of the ODNI are still being formed. Negroponte published the National Intelligence Strategy of the United States of America in October 2005, setting the framework for a more unified, coordinated, and effective IC. The NIS is available at http://dni.gov/publications/NISOctober2005.pdf. The National Intelligence Strategy is a significant internal oversight tool to "guide Intelligence Community policy, planning, collection, analysis, operations, programming, acquisition, budgeting, and execution." See Office of the Director of National Intelligence News Release 4-05, "National Intelligence Strategy," October 26, 2005, http://dni.gov/press_releases/20051025_release.htm.

34. Sec. 102 of P.L. 108-458. EO 13355 identified the senior intelligence official's role the same way.

35. Secs. 102, 104, and 104(a) of P.L. 108-458.

36. See Sec. 102(a) of P.L. 108-458. Whereas Executive Order 12333 gave the DCI authority over the National Foreign Intelligence Program (NFIP—the NIP predecessor), it did not prescribe a role for the DCI in developing funding for the JMIP and the Tactical Intelligence and Related Activities (TIARA) program; instead EO 12333 stated simply that there "should be no unnecessary overlap" between the NFIP and the Defense Department's military spending authority. The NFIP budget controlled funding for the DCI and his staff; the intelligence departments in State, FBI, Treasury, and Energy; and portions of NSA, the National Geospatial-Intelligence Agency (NGA), and Defense Intelligence Agency (NSA, NGA, and DIA are all under control of the Secretary of Defense). TIARA and JMIP apportioned funds to DIA, DoD Airborne sources, the armed forces, and Special Operations Command. See U.S. House Permanent Select Committee on Intelligence, *IC21: The Intelligence Community in the 21st Century*, 104th Cong., 2nd sess., 1996, http://www.access.gpo.gov/congress/house/intel/ic21/ic21_toc.html.

37. Secs. 102 and 102(a) of P.L. 108-458.

38. Ibid. This codified EO 13354 into law.

39. Sec. 1001 of P.L. 108-458.

40. Sec. 1061 of P.L. 108-458. This codified EO 13353 into law.

41. See Sec. 1016 of P.L. 108-458. Many would argue that information sharing had already become not only a priority but was written into law through the USA Patriot Act (P.L. 107-56).

42. Sec. 1017 of P.L. 108-458.

43. Secs. 1017, 1019, 1020, 1041, and 1042 of P.L. 108-458.

44. Sec. 1078 of P.L. 108-458.

45. Secs. 102 and 1020 of P.L. 108-458.

46. The reporting requirements for the IC were extensive in the bill. The DNI, the directors of the CIA and FBI, and the president were required to report back to Congress regarding such varied issues as overall IC transformation, operational coordination between CIA and DoD, information sharing, competitive analysis, product peer review, establishment of a nonproliferation center, linguistic and educational requirements, the use of open-source intelligence, and security clearances. See Subtitle G, Secs. 1011, 1013, 1016, 1017, 1019, 1041, 1052, 1095, 2001, and 3001 of P.L. 108-458.

47. Sec. 1031 of P.L 108-458.

48. Sec. 1011 of P.L. 108-458.

49. The report is available at http://www.wmd.gov/report/.

50. For a complete list of Bush administration responses to the WMD report, see "President Bush Administration Actions to Implement WMD Commission Recommendations," http://www.whitehouse.gov/news/releases/2005/06/20050629-5.html.

51. The establishment of the NCTC disestablished the TTIC, though much of the organization of the TTIC was included in the NCTC.

52. Testimony of John O. Brennan, Director, Terrorist Threat Integration Center, before the 9/11 Commission, April 14, 2004.

53. Mark M. Lowenthal, *Intelligence: From Secrets to Policy*, 2nd ed. (Washington, DC: Congressional Quarterly Press, 2003), 43.

54. See ibid.; and U.S. House, *IC21, parts 3, 11, and 12*.

55. U.S. House, *IC21, part 3*.

56. According to the 9/11 Commission's review of classified appropriations, in the second half of the decade, Congress appropriated some 98 percent of what the administration requested for intelligence programs. The 9/11 Commission Report, 105.

57. U.S. House, *IC21, part 4*.

58. Overviews of military operations from 1991 to the present can be found at http://www.globalsecurity.org/military/ops/recent-ops.htm.

59. Richard A. Best Jr., *Intelligence Community Reorganization: Potential Effects on DOD Intelligence Agencies*, CRS Report for Congress (Washington, DC: Congressional Research Service, Library of Congress, updated October 4, 2004).

60. U.S. House, *IC21, part 3*.

61. U.S. House, *IC21*.

62. Robert M. Gates, "The CIA and American Foreign Policy," *Foreign Affairs* 66, no. 2 (Winter 1987/1988): 224–225.

TWO

RETHINKING JUDICIAL OVERSIGHT OF INTELLIGENCE

Elizabeth Rindskopf Parker and Bryan Pate

THE PARADOX OF FOREIGN INTELLIGENCE OVERSIGHT

To function effectively, all democratic governments must subject their actions to open public debate, review, discussion, and response. These are the essential ingredients of oversight and accountability. Yet, to survive in an often hostile world, these same governments must also be able to collect, analyze, and use foreign and domestic intelligence—information of ongoing value only insofar as its methods of collection and secrecy can be maintained. This is the paradox of intelligence oversight: the need to achieve open review of secret materials and activities without destroying their value.

In the United States, there are many established mechanisms of oversight and accountability, both inside and outside the government. Under the U.S. Constitution, the three separate branches of the federal government—executive, legislative, and judiciary—share power through a system of checks and balances. Each has the obligation and authority to ensure that the other two branches perform their assigned functions appropriately. This tripartite division naturally encourages oversight and accountability between the branches. In addition, each arm of the government provides its own unique internal oversight. Within the executive branch, management reviews are conducted by numerous offices, each of which typically includes an inspector general and a general counsel to ensure that it is complying with the law. Congressional oversight occurs through the appropriations process, congressional audits, and statutory reporting requirements. Judicial review of the legality of actions taken by the two political branches occurs frequently, with judgments rendered on a case-by-case basis. Outside the government, the actions of each branch are subjected to scrutiny by an independent and active press and are ultimately adjudged by the electorate through the democratic process.

Yet, for the national intelligence system, these traditional oversight mechanisms are an awkward fit. Perhaps this is part of the reason why, historically, oversight of intelligence has been uneven in its success. Often, the importance of maintaining secrecy to protect the sources and methods of the intelligence capabilities appears directly opposed to the effective functioning of the existing oversight structures. Moreover, the secrecy surrounding intelligence activities seems to limit the role of the press to reporting on periodic scandals—some real, some not. Some critics argue that the broader goals of oversight—the effectiveness of the overall intelligence system—are inadequately served by the current system.[1]

Secrecy concerns have also restricted the judiciary's role in reviewing intelligence activities. For good reason, court procedures in a democracy do not easily accommodate secrecy. Uncomfortable with secret procedures, the judiciary has been reluctant to engage issues arising from intelligence activities, even when such matters are properly presented to them.[2] There is an important corollary to the concerns of the judiciary: judicial openness is commonly seen by all branches of government as a threat to effective intelligence gathering. Thus, because revealing individual secret facts can threaten the underlying "sources and methods" by which substantial amounts of intelligence are produced, legislated exceptions to public legal review are common where intelligence information is involved. Most notable in this regard is the exception for foreign intelligence contained in the Freedom of Information Act—the primary statute providing accountability through citizen access to government information.[3]

In a few of the areas where intelligence issues inevitably come under the purview of the judiciary, Congress has stepped in to strike the balance between competing concerns. For example, to facilitate the adjudication of criminal trials that involve critical evidence that cannot be made publicly available, Congress has established the Classified Information Procedures Act (CIPA).[4] CIPA is modeled on earlier protective orders fashioned by the judiciary to handle such problems and provides a procedure for the courts to follow in handling classified evidence during a public trial. It is the means Congress has chosen to achieve the dual objectives of protecting national security and ensuring defendants a fair trial.

Procedural provisions like CIPA, however, have not alleviated the fundamental impediment to greater judicial involvement in the review of intelligence activities: an overriding reluctance on the part of the judiciary to become involved with foreign affairs and national security concerns. Is this resistance inevitable and unavoidable? Or are there structures that exist now, or could be devised, that would allow greater oversight by the courts in the overall process of collecting, analyzing, and using intelligence?

These questions are particularly timely as terrorism places the national security structures under increasing pressure to respond in new ways both at home and abroad. With headlines exposing abused detainees, "torture memos," race-based "no-fly lists," and "illegal wiretapping," it is evident that the traditional balance between national security and individual liberty is being challenged, making even more important the courts' role in ensuring that responses to terrorism do not fundamentally degrade personal freedoms and liberties. What role should the courts have in intelligence oversight in a time of terrorism? Before considering this question, we will first review the origins of existing oversight structures; then we will examine the basis for the judiciary's reluctance to participate in national security matters; and finally, we will consider one example of active judicial oversight that may presage future approaches, especially if terrorism continues to pose a credible threat beyond the foreseeable future.

THE ORIGINS OF MODERN INTELLIGENCE OVERSIGHT

The current role of the judiciary in intelligence oversight can be understood only if it is described against the background of the existing oversight structures of the other branches. As we all know and has been described in the previous chapter, the intelligence services are executive-branch organizations that were formed by Congress and receive their funding through Congress. As a result, they are continuously accountable to both the executive and the legislative branches. Whether, and how, the judiciary can improve the current oversight structure will depend on if, and where, the existing framework is failing.

Not surprisingly, just as intelligence is itself secret, so too are many of the means we have developed for controlling it. As a result, detailing the complete history of executive, legislative, and judicial oversight mechanisms is simply not possible. Fortunately, not all intelligence reform has been shrouded in secrecy. The development of legislative control over "covert actions,"[5] for example, can be traced through a series of unclassified investigations and public legislation. The evolution of covert action oversight is particularly important because its reforms have affected almost every other intelligence activity. Moreover, it provides a good illustration of the iterative process that is characteristic of intelligence oversight reform in general. Although controlling covert action is just one aspect of intelligence oversight, studying its development is essential to understanding the current oversight framework.

Although the United States had conducted intelligence activities in every conflict since the War for Independence, organized intelligence collection "on a substantial scale" began with President Franklin Roosevelt's creation of the Office of Strategic Services (OSS) in 1942.[6] After World War II, President Harry Truman disbanded the OSS, replacing it with the Central Intelligence Group. Shortly thereafter, Congress enacted the National Security Act of 1947 (NSA),[7] creating America's first peacetime intelligence organization, the Central Intelligence Agency (CIA).[8]

Creating a peacetime intelligence service through the vehicle of public legislation was a wise choice. Publicly acknowledging the establishment of a governmental intelligence collection capability laid the foundation for ensuring accountability of intelligence activities and, in so doing, distinguished American intelligence from its foreign counterparts for many years. Making the formation of an intelligence service public knowledge was not inevitable. In fact, had the executive been determined to keep the creation of such an organization secret, it could have challenged the formation of the CIA as an inappropriate exercise of Congress's power. Under the separation-of-powers doctrine, one branch of government cannot invade the constitutionally defined province of another branch. Since intelligence is arguably an inherent part of the president's constitutional authority to act as commander in chief, the executive could have challenged the constitutionality of the NSA. Whatever the validity of that position, however, it was not seriously pursued. As a result, the creation of America's most secret organization was no secret at all.

It is evident from the text of the statute that the NSA focused explicitly on creating a *peacetime* intelligence service. It neither expressly authorized the CIA to conduct covert actions nor provided for general congressional oversight of intelligence activities. The latter issue was immediately rectified by the appropriations process. Because Congress authorized the funding for intelligence activities, the lack of an explicit oversight mechanism within the NSA itself did not leave the newly formed intelligence service without any legislative supervision. As we will see, however, Congress did not immediately exercise this authority, and there is little evidence of legislative control over the CIA during its formative years.[9]

Although the NSA has always been a public document, interpretations of the statute have not always been openly disclosed. Perhaps the most controversial interpretation of the NSA was undertaken by the first general counsel of the CIA. Under some pressure from within the government, the general counsel eventually succeeded in construing the text of the statute to authorize covert actions. This interpretation was not made public and thus escaped the debate and accountability mechanisms that would have accompanied such a disclosure. This lack of oversight certainly contributed to the breadth and extent of CIA covert activities leading up to and during the Vietnam War.

In 1974, following a series of revelations about CIA activities in Vietnam and its involvement in the Watergate scandal, Congress took its first meaningful steps to control covert action. In addition, the executive branch reinvigorated and expanded its internal oversight efforts within the intelligence agencies and the branch as a whole. For example, the CIA and the National Security Agency revamped their offices of general counsel and inspector general to create more effective means of internal oversight and review. Similarly, President Gerald Ford established a new structure, the Intelligence Oversight Board, within the office of the president, to further encourage and support an internal watchdog, or intelligence oversight, function.[10]

Congress acted through legislation and investigation. In 1974, as a cautious first step, it passed the Hughes-Ryan Amendment to the Foreign Assistance Act of 1961 (henceforth Hughes-Ryan).[11] This provision did not expressly authorize congressional review of covert actions. Instead, Hughes-Ryan provided that no appropriated funds could be "expended by or on behalf of the Central Intelligence Agency for operations in foreign countries, other than activities intended solely for obtaining necessary intelligence,"[12] unless the president made "findings" that the activity was "important to the national security of the United States." The president was then required to report these findings "in a timely fashion" to a total of eight congressional committees.[13]

Immediately after Congress enacted Hughes-Ryan, the Senate Select Committee to Study Governmental Operations with Respect to Intelligence Activities, led by Senator Frank Church, and the House Select Committee on Intelligence, led by Congressman Otis Pike (the Church and Pike Committees), began investigating domestic and foreign covert CIA activities.[14] These investigations led to the establishment of the Senate Select Committee on Intelligence in 1976 and the House Permanent Select Committee on Intelligence the following year.[15] The recommendations of these two committees on the proper role of the CIA in supporting national security laid the foundation of the Intelligence Authorization Act for Fiscal Year 1981.[16]

The 1981 act amended Hughes-Ryan and added section 501 to the NSA.[17] The amended Hughes-Ryan made a more explicit reference to covert actions[18] and kept its requirement that the president make a finding that such activities were "important to the national security of the United States" before the CIA could expend funds to carry them out. More importantly, section 501 of the NSA now specifically required the "Director of Central Intelligence and the heads of all departments, agencies, and other entities of the United States involved in intelligence activities" to

> keep the Select Committee on Intelligence of the Senate and the Permanent Select Committee on Intelligence of the House of Representatives (hereafter in this section referred to as the "intelligence committees") *fully and currently informed* of all intelligence activities which are the responsibility of . . . any department, agency, or entity of the United States, including any significant anticipated intelligence activity.[19]

For some, the intrusive nature of these oversight requirements raised concerns that the new law might be unconstitutional. To ensure that the Congress had not overstepped its bounds or interfered with the constitutional responsibilities of the president, Congress created three exceptions to this rule.[20] First, the "approval of the intelligence committees" was not to be considered "a condition precedent to the initiation of" an intelligence activity. Second, during "extraordinary circumstances affecting vital interests of the United States," the president could limit reporting his findings to only a few select members of Congress.[21] Finally, the president was allowed to "fully inform the intelligence committees in a *timely fashion* of intelligence operations . . . for which *prior notice was not given.*"[22]

In response to the 1981 act, President Ronald Reagan issued Executive Order 12333.[23] This order further defined the duties and responsibilities of the organizations and individual positions within the intelligence community. Executive Order 12333 authorized the CIA to conduct covert actions (referred to as "special activities") and mandated that it "cooperate with the Congress in the conduct of its responsibilities for oversight of intelligence activities" under the NSA and the amended Hughes-Ryan.[24] As a result, by the end of 1981, the law governing covert action oversight was split into three different documents.

This fragmented system was replaced in its entirety by the provisions contained in the Fiscal Year 1991 Intelligence Authorization Act.[25] The sweeping changes instituted by the 1991 act were the result of congressional investigations into the Iran-Contra covert arms-trading affair.[26] These investigations revealed that the executive branch had aggressively interpreted the existing statutory framework so that the oversight provisions would not apply to an "arms for hostages" program run through the National Security Council. To prevent such a situation from developing again, Congress repealed Hughes-Ryan in its entirety and added section 503 to the NSA.[27] Section 503 defines "covert action" and establishes specific reporting requirements for these activities. Most significantly, the president must submit his findings to the intelligence committees "as soon as possible after such approval and *before* the initiation" of the covert action.[28] Two exceptions were retained: the president can limit disclosure to a small group of congressional leaders, and if the president chooses to withhold prior notification, he is obligated subsequently to report his findings "in a timely fashion."[29]

The story of how Congress, through trial and error, instituted and refined covert action oversight is representative of how such requirements developed within other portions of the intelligence community. To an outside observer, this tedious and lengthy struggle over covert action governance often appeared to be no more obvious than a "wrestling match under a blanket." Yet in the end, a revolution in oversight expectations had occurred. The struggle had resulted in hundreds of briefings annually before congressional intelligence committees supported by a small army of staff. In fact, by the turn of the century, congressional oversight had become so pervasive that on the eve of

9/11, the intelligence community possessed very little information that could be denied to the intelligence oversight committees.

THE ORIGINS OF JUDICIAL RELUCTANCE
IN INTELLIGENCE OVERSIGHT

No elaborate review mechanisms such as those in Congress exist with regard to the judiciary's role in intelligence oversight. Unlike Congress, which responded to perceived intelligence abuses by enacting a series of increasingly restrictive and intricate statutory frameworks, the courts have demonstrated a reluctance to participate actively in matters involving national security, including intelligence collection. As we have noted, the limited role of the judiciary in the history of modern intelligence has its origins in the difficulty that U.S. courts have had in handling secret information. However, the need for secrecy to protect intelligence does not tell the full story of why the courts have not been more actively involved in intelligence oversight.

There is nothing in the Constitution that bars the courts from subjecting the security affairs of our nation to formal judicial review. Were the judiciary so inclined, it certainly could have crafted a way to interject itself into the national security decision-making process. Courts, however, have taken a different approach. Rather than developing a way to expand its jurisdiction to ensure that it possessed final review of foreign policy decisions, the judiciary has created a series of doctrines that allow it to avoid getting involved altogether. The Supreme Court has established a practice of weighing in on national security affairs only where they touch upon the individual rights and constitutional protections due citizens. Only then has it helped to illuminate the boundaries of executive and legislative authority. Otherwise, perhaps wisely, the judiciary has basically allowed national security policy to be formulated by the "political branches" of government without restriction.

The seeds of this deference to the executive and legislative branches were planted early in the nation's history. In 1803, Chief Justice John Marshall created what has come to be known as the "political question doctrine" in his majority opinion in *Marbury v. Madison*.[30] This jurisprudential tool allows the judiciary to express no opinion on matters that it feels are better left to be worked out by the other branches of government. In Marshall's words:

By the Constitution of the United States, the President is invested with certain important political powers, in the exercise of which he is to use his own discretion, and is accountable only to his country in his political character, and to his conscience. . . .

[W]hatever opinion may be entertained of the manner in which executive discretion may be used, still there exists, and can exist, no power to control that discretion. . . . [A]nd being entrusted to the executive, the decision of the executive is conclusive.[31]

Chief Justice Marshall's discussion of the political question doctrine in *Marbury* was later expounded upon in the 1962 case of *Baker v. Carr*.[32] There, Justice William Brennan laid out the six conditions that make an issue unreviewable by a court under the political question doctrine.[33] One of those conditions is the "lack of judicially discoverable and manageable standards for resolving [the issue]."[34] Courts dealing with challenges to national security decisions typically find such "judicially discoverable and manageable standards" lacking. They conclude that the case presents a "political question" that is "nonjusticiable" and incapable of review.[35] Such holdings pass no judgment on the merits of the claim, but simply declare the court's inability to decide the issue.

Beyond the political question doctrine, procedural requirements buttress the courts' ability to avoid reaching the merits of challenges to national security questions. The most common of these is "lack of standing" on the part of the party bringing the action.[36] The standing requirement is difficult to satisfy in cases challenging national security policies because the plaintiffs often cannot demonstrate an appropriate "injury in fact." Courts have consistently found that the injury to a private citizen that was caused by the foreign affairs policy of the United States is too attenuated to satisfy the standing requirements. Nor are legislators spared the need to overcome this injury hurdle.[37] As a threshold procedural requirement, standing must be satisfied before the court can reach "the merits" of the issue at hand. Thus, such cases eliminate the need and the opportunity for judicial review of the underlying issue.

Where the lower courts have found that a private individual or legislator has met the standing requirements (or the courts have declined to decide that issue), the courts have sometimes been able to avoid addressing the merits of the case by holding that the issue is "not ripe." The district court in *Dellums v. Bush*[38] described a ripe case as one where "all the factors necessary for a decision are present then and there" and held that it would not render a decision unless "the dispute before the court [was] truly ripe."[39]

The ripeness doctrine is particularly useful for dispensing with cases brought by legislators seeking to enjoin an action of the president. As Justice Powell pointed out in *Goldwater v. Carter*,[40]

> [the] Judicial Branch should not decide issues affecting the alloca-
> tion of power between the President and Congress until the political
> branches reach a constitutional impasse. Otherwise we would encour-
> age small groups or even individual Members of Congress to seek
> judicial resolution of issues before the normal political process has
> the opportunity to resolve the conflict. . . . If the Congress chooses
> not to confront the President, it is not our task to do so.[41]

The position articulated by Justice Powell in *Goldwater* leaves very few disputes between legislators and the president open to adjudication. It appears that, under the ripeness doctrine, courts will review cases brought by legislators against the president only if he refuses to follow a properly passed law.

The rationale behind the judiciary's reluctance to weigh in on deli-cate decisions of the executive regarding national security has been classically described by Justice George Sutherland in *United States v. Curtiss-Wright Export Corp.*:[42]

> It is important to bear in mind that we are here dealing not alone
> with an authority vested in the President by an exertion of legislative
> power, but with such an authority plus the very delicate, plenary and
> exclusive power of *the President as the sole organ of the federal govern-*
> *ment in the field of international relations.* . . . It is quite apparent that if,
> in the maintenance of our international relations, embarrassment—
> perhaps serious embarrassment—is to be avoided and success for our
> aims achieved, . . . [legislation] must often accord to the President a
> degree of discretion and freedom from statutory restriction which
> would not be admissible were domestic affairs alone involved. More-
> over, *he, not Congress, has the better opportunity of knowing the conditions*
> *which prevail in foreign countries.* . . . He has his confidential sources
> of information. He has his agents. . . . Secrecy in respect of informa-

tion gathered by them may be highly necessary, and the premature disclosure of it productive of harmful results.[43]

In adopting this deferential view toward executive actions involving foreign affairs, the judiciary could be accused of abdicating its responsibility for providing a check on the executive's actions. Most will agree, however, that this "foreign affairs doctrine" has probably been a wise course for the courts to follow throughout most of our history. In many areas of national security, the courts are not well positioned to determine the best policy for the country, nor should they be. The executive branch provides a responsiveness and unity of action that extensive second-guessing by private individuals and minorities of legislators through the courts would impair. By limiting its role to deciding issues of foreign policy only where they involve constitutional claims, the court has avoided interjecting itself into disputes that probably are better dealt with by the political branches.

Although the Supreme Court willingly defers to the president on foreign affairs issues, in domestic cases and situations involving liberty the courts have taken on a more active role. This schism between foreign and domestic affairs is best discussed by the Court in what became known as the steel seizure case.[44] There, just sixteen years after *Curtiss-Wright* was decided, six justices refused to defer to President Truman's invocation of his national security power as justification for the seizure of the vast majority of America's steel mills in support of the Korean War effort. Instead, the Court held that the president lacked the authority to take such actions in the absence of legislation. Although the steel seizure case dealt with a national security policy, the Court's focus was on the constitutional issue of whether the president possesses the authority to take *domestic* action in the absence of legislation. It clearly found that the president does not, even when invoking his powers as commander in chief.

THE OVERSIGHT POTENTIAL OF THE JUDICIARY

To say that the courts have limited their own ability to review national security activities, which of course includes the collection, analysis, and use of intelligence, is not to say that they have played no role. To the contrary, even their limited efforts have had a substantial impact on the way in which intelligence is managed. And, on occasion, judicial intervention has prompted the creation of new structures to guide and control national security policy, particularly with regard to intelligence. Perhaps the most dramatic example of this influence involves wiretapping. The Foreign Intelligence Surveillance Act (FISA)[45] now governs the use of wiretaps to collect foreign intelligence within the United States. It is the result of a series of judicial decisions that framed the contours of the "warrant clause" of the Fourth Amendment.[46]

As background, the Fourth Amendment was added to the Constitution in order to prevent the government from issuing a form of what were known as "general warrants" in England. These warrants did not require a description of the individual or property to be seized and had no geographic limitations. Consequently, they provided government agents with a powerful and immediate means of disrupting the life of any "suspect." By requiring "probable cause" and a description of the "place to be searched, and the persons or things to be seized," the framers intended to remove this intimidating tool from the hands of law enforcement.[47]

As people began to communicate electronically, it was initially unclear whether and how the Fourth Amendment might apply to such communications. In the 1928 case of *Olmstead v. United States*,[48] the Supreme Court declared that intercepting telephone conversations without a warrant did *not* violate the Fourth Amendment, and therefore evidence gathered from such intercepts could be used in a criminal trial. In the *Olmstead* opinion, the Supreme Court invited Congress to pass legislation making such intercepts inadmissible in legal proceedings. Six years later, Congress made it a crime "to intercept and divulge or publish the contents of wire and radio communications."[49] Subsequently, the Supreme Court held that the new law made evidence, and the "fruits of the evidence," obtained through wire and radio intercepts inadmissible in a criminal trial.[50]

The Justice Department, however, did not interpret this decision as requiring a warrant for *all* wiretaps. Instead, it determined that a warrantless interception by the government would be considered unlawful only if the contents of the communications were divulged outside the federal establishment. Consequently, the government continued to conduct warrantless "national security" wiretaps. In the 1967 case of *Katz v. United States*,[51] the Supreme Court overturned the *Olmstead* decision and held that the warrant clause of the Fourth Amendment did apply to electronic surveillance. However, the Court specifically noted that its decision might not be applicable to cases "involving the national security."[52]

Responding to the *Katz* case, Congress enacted the Omnibus Crime Control and Safe Streets Act (Safe Streets Act).[53] Title III of the Safe Streets Act set forth a detailed procedure for obtaining the authorization to conduct electronic surveillance in criminal investigations.[54] At the heart of this procedure was the need to obtain judicial authorization (now known as a Title III warrant). Notably, the act specifically denied placing any limitations on electronic surveillance for national security purposes.

In what became known as the Keith case in 1972,[55] the Supreme Court addressed one issue left open by *Katz* and the Safe Streets Act: the president's power "to authorize electronic surveillance in *internal security matters* without prior judicial approval."[56] Although the Keith court acknowledged the "constitutional basis of the President's domestic security role," it found that "it must be exercised in a manner compatible with the Fourth Amendment."[57] The Court held that the Fourth Amendment "requires an appropriate prior warrant procedure" in cases involving domestic security.[58] As it had in *Katz*, the Supreme Court in the Keith case specifically left open the issue of whether the Fourth Amendment requires a neutral magistrate to issue a warrant before the government can conduct electronic surveillance of "foreign powers and their agents" for national security purposes.[59]

Instead of waiting for the Supreme Court to pass judgment on the unresolved issue of foreign intelligence, Congress enacted FISA, which effectively codified existing law. For electronic surveillance involving national security, FISA provides a procedure for obtaining a warrant through application to the special FISA court (the Foreign Intelligence Surveillance Court).[60] The requirements for such a warrant differ substantially from those required for a Title III warrant.[61] FISA also permits the attorney general to authorize surveillance without a warrant of "the contents of communications transmitted by means of communications used exclusively between or among foreign powers."[62] The Supreme Court has not formally ruled on the constitutionality of FISA, but its willingness to pass up numerous opportunities to modify it over the past twenty-five years evinces a tacit approval of its provisions.

From 1978 through September 2001, FISA worked well and was rarely the subject of controversy. An administrative process evolved over time that allowed surveillance requests to be presented, reviewed, and authorized with no significant problems. From time to time, some questioned the fact that during the first twenty-three years of the FISA court's existence, it approved almost every warrant application that came before it. These critics often fail to appreciate the extensive review that these applications were subjected to by the executive branch prior to submission. This internal screening process is intended to ensure that the FISA court receives only warrant applications that clearly meet FISA's requirements. If the FISA court expresses concern about a provision in an application, then the executive branch agency will revise the application to alleviate the concern. Applications are approved by the FISA court only if they meet the requirements laid out in FISA.

When FISA was enacted in 1978, it required every warrant application to certify that "*the purpose* of the surveillance [was] to obtain foreign intelligence information."[63] As a result of the 1980 case of *United States v. Truong Dinh Hung*,[64] this phrase was interpreted by both the executive and legislative branches to require that the "primary purpose" for seeking a warrant be to obtain foreign intelligence. This interpretation reflected the consensus within all branches of the government that warrants issued pursuant to FISA should not be used for criminal investigations. This understanding lasted for more than two decades.

In the aftermath of 9/11, Congress enacted the Uniting and Strengthening America by Providing Appropriate Tools Required to Intercept and Obstruct Terrorism (USA PATRIOT) Act of 2001.[65] Among the many changes to intelligence gathering introduced by the Patriot Act was the replacement of "the purpose" with the language "a significant purpose" in the FISA section quoted above. This seemingly insignificant change set in motion an unusual course of events that quickly resulted in the first appeal ever taken from a FISA court, the first publication of a FISA court opinion, and the publication of the FISA appeals court decision. These recent developments offer new lessons regarding the evolving role of judicial review in intelligence oversight.

When Congress amended FISA through the Patriot Act, some were concerned that FISA's more flexible standards would now be available for criminal warrants. This could potentially blur the difference between the warrant requirements for criminal investigations and national security collection. In light of this concern, the FISA court chose to proceed with caution. The executive branch, however, still responding to 9/11, was eager to interpret the new standard more aggressively. These opposing views quickly came to a head, leading to the first appeal from a FISA court ruling. The resulting case, known as *In Re: Sealed Case*,[66] produced surprising results. Not only was a new standard endorsed for FISA warrants, but, for the first time, proceedings before the FISA court produced a series of publicly available judicial decisions. In addition, the unusual nature of the FISA court system itself was exposed: it operated in secret, it never issued public opinions or orders, only the government appeared as a litigant, and appeals were thus possible only when the government was denied a request.

In Re: Sealed Case is of particular interest to the evolution of judicial oversight of intelligence activities, not for the controversial decision that it reached, but for what it revealed about judicial review in the FISA application process. Because of *In Re: Sealed Case*, the public was given a window into the development of a jurisprudence of intelligence collection that had previously existed only in secret documents shared between the FISA court, the Congress, and the executive branch. By disclosing the judicial procedures under FISA to the public, *In Re: Sealed Case* exposed what is perhaps the most significant shortcoming of the system: its one-sided nature. How can both sides of a warrant application be considered when only one litigant is involved?

CONCLUSION: EXPAND THE JUDICIARY'S ROLE IN INTELLIGENCE OVERSIGHT

In Re: Sealed Case shows that judicial resistance to reviewing national security policy can be overcome. It also suggests that the judiciary can adapt its traditional review structures so that courts can participate in defining the boundaries of intelligence collection. However, the fact that courts are capable of becoming involved in intelligence oversight does not necessarily mean that they should. What justifies a more active role for the judiciary in intelligence oversight? If an active role is justified, what would it look like, how could it be established, and what are the concerns with increasing the involvement of the judiciary in this field?

One of the judiciary's core functions within the U.S. system of checks and balances is to prevent the executive and legislative branches from encroaching upon freedoms guaranteed by the Constitution. The courts have established a long and consistent history of fulfilling this role in contexts ranging from free speech to freedom of religion to privacy rights. Even in issues involving national security, when the political branches have been willing to curtail liberty in favor of security, the courts have stepped in to sculpt the boundaries of an acceptable policy. Where the government has pushed too far, the courts have exerted their constitutional authority to recast the balance in favor of the individual.

As the U.S. national security strategy is reshaped to meet the threat of terrorism, we are beginning to see that the central challenge to defending U.S. citizens at home lies in finding the balance between liberty and security. Establishing the appropriate relationship between these competing interests is particularly difficult in the domestic intelligence context. Expanding the role of the judiciary in the intelligence oversight process might be the best way to achieve an optimal level of security without sacrificing individual liberties.

FISA provides a good example of how this might be done. The FISA court has been surprisingly successful in managing the domestic use of intrusive technologies to collect foreign intelligence.[67] The role of the FISA court, and the Fourth Amendment jurisprudence that led to its creation, are tangible examples of how courts can influence the balance of security and liberty and then protect that balance once it has been struck. If the threat of terrorism increases, the role of the FISA court in protecting liberty might be expected to grow proportionately. In addition, as new surveillance technologies are developed, some, such as data mining, will require a new analysis of the competing liberty and security concerns. The courts should influence the development of the structures that will govern the use of these technologies and then be placed in the best position to protect the rights of the citizens. Regardless of the purpose of the activity, whenever intelligence collection creates the potential to encroach upon a constitutionally protected freedom, the judiciary will have to provide the essential reassurance that government action accords with the public statutory and constitutional framework.

FISA may be the best example of how the judiciary can provide reassurance when citizen rights and foreign intelligence requirements collide; but it is not the only example. For instance, foreign intelligence is rarely released in response to citizen requests under the Freedom of Information Act;[68] however, public judicial review ensures that administrative information release processes are handled correctly.[69] Moreover, the possibility of such review provides a strong incentive for agency officials to carefully adhere to the law in the first place. Courts have also balanced individual rights and intelligence agency needs in determining when a government employee's obligation to preserve the secrecy of information is overcome by his right to free speech.[70]

Liberty and security will probably remain in tension in America for the foreseeable future. The nature of the terrorist threat—concealable, dispersed groups that can penetrate the nation's borders and cause damage at a strategic level—has blurred historical distinctions between domestic tranquillity and national security. In the aftermath of 9/11, U.S. citizens witnessed a poorly prepared executive branch employ drastic security measures: mass deportations, detentions without trial, race-based profiling, and interrogation methods that could constitute torture. As the political branches adjust to the challenges posed by terrorism, they will likely continue to choose the most expedient means of ensuring security, encroaching on some, if not many, personal liberties.

In 2004 the Supreme Court decided two cases concerning this new security posture. In *Hamdi v. Rumsfeld*,[71] the Court mandated that U.S. citizens detained as "enemy combatants" be allowed to challenge their detention before a neutral magistrate. In *Rasul v. Bush*,[72] the Court granted foreign nationals held at Guantanamo Bay, Cuba, the right to file a petition for habeas corpus in a U.S. federal court. Although these decisions are limited in scope, they show that this Supreme Court was willing to "push back" against Congress and the executive where it saw civil liberties at stake. In so doing, it was shaping the national security policy.

The Court must continue to be engaged in this process and use its authority to recalibrate those security measures that tread unconstitutionally on civil rights. In addition, the judiciary as a whole must contribute to the public discussion and analysis of the security posture. Although legislation will play the major role in forming the legal structure for the national security, statutory mandates are too rigid and politicized to substitute for the balanced and flexible approach offered by judicial review. More importantly, it is the courts that ultimately must be able to articulate the constitutionally grounded doctrine that authorizes the government's chosen response to this very real threat of terrorism.

Although it is clear that the judiciary can make valuable contributions to intelligence oversight, especially in light of the current security situation, it is less clear how this might be accomplished. Once again, we can look to the evolution of FISA for suggestions. For example, the creation of a secret tribunal such as FISA carried with it inherent problems in an open society. However, the publication of *In Re: Sealed Case* demonstrates that the open discussion of law and policy that is essential in a democracy can take place even while the underlying facts are kept secret. A similar approach might be considered in other intelligence arenas.

In this regard, it is important for the United States to keep in mind its enemy's strengths and weaknesses. Unlike the Soviet Union, the terrorists that America now faces do not have the infrastructure necessary to prosecute a wide-ranging counterintelligence effort directed at U.S. intelligence organizations. Consequently, it is worthwhile to reexamine whether the way in which information about the application of rules governing intelligence needs to remain hidden from view. Is there a way for courts wrestling with intelligence issues to disseminate their legal reasoning in such a manner that the benefits of disclosure would offset any potential loss of intelligence information? Such a solution will be needed if the executive branch intends to expand the intrusive collection techniques available under FISA's purview, as some knowledgeable commentators have suggested.[73]

Finally, the benefits of having the judiciary conduct periodic reviews of domestic intelligence activities should be evaluated. Other nations, notably the United Kingdom, have staffed commissions of judges to conduct such reviews, purportedly with much success. These review bodies could be constituted through a judicial branch process that would be devoid of much of the politics involved in congressional investigative committees. They could be permanent organizations, or they could be put together periodically and then disbanded after a term of years. Such judicial review, if made available, might enhance public confidence in the measures being taken in the name of security.

Employing the judiciary in a new manner, however, raises certain problems. The role of the judiciary in the U.S. system of government has been carefully defined by its Constitution and its courts. Article III of the Constitution authorizes the courts to exercise jurisdiction over "cases" and "controversies." It does not expressly authorize the judiciary to create investigative bodies or to review security policies outside of a trial. Based on the language of Article III, the courts have interpreted their constitutional authority narrowly. Perhaps more importantly, courts have historically deferred to the political branches for issues involving national security. These are significant obstacles to

expanding the role of the judiciary in intelligence oversight. Nevertheless, examination should be undertaken to identify ways in which these
obstacles can and should be overcome. The judiciary's independence
and expertise will be vital to formulating a new security doctrine that
strikes the balance between liberty and security in a time of terrorism.

NOTES

1. See William E. Odom, *Fixing Intelligence: For a More Secure America*, 2nd
ed. (New Haven, CT: Yale University Press, 2004), for a discussion of how Congress has failed to understand and correct structural problems of the intelligence
system in its periodic efforts at intelligence reform.

2. An example is the state secrets privilege, which permits a court to refuse
to allow testimony which the government alleges will damage national security.
This provision was recognized by the Supreme Court in *U.S. v. Reynolds*, 345 U.S.
1 (1953).

3. The Freedom of Information Act (FOIA) is codified at 5 *U.S. Code* § 552.
For the provisions excluding review of intelligence documents, see 5 *U.S. Code*
§§ 552(b)(1) and 552(b)(3).

4. 18 *U.S. Code* app. III §§ 1–16.

5. The Fiscal Year 1991 Intelligence Authorization Act provides a lengthy
definition of covert action at 50 *U.S. Code* § 413b(e). In short, a covert action
is a government activity designed to influence political, economic, or military
conditions abroad, where the role of the U.S. government will not be publicly
acknowledged.

6. *Report to the President by the Commission on CIA Activities within the
United States* 45 (June 1975), http://www.history-matters.com/archive/church/
rockcomm/contents.htm.

7. Public Law 80-253, 61 *Stat.* 495–510 (1947).

8. 61 *Stat.* 497. For an in-depth background on the formation of the CIA, see
John Ranelagh, *The Agency: The Rise and Decline of the CIA* (New York: Simon and
Schuster, 1987), 37–111.

9. See Ranelagh, *The Agency*, 479–482 (summarizing unsuccessful efforts to
enhance oversight structures prior to the early 1970s).

10. Executive Order 11905, 41 *Fed. Reg.* 7703.

11. *Foreign Assistance Act of 1974*, Public Law 93-559, §32, 88 *Stat.* 1795, 1804
(1974).

12. 88 *Stat.* 1804. This language was "code" for non-intelligence-gathering activities that we now know as covert action. At the time of this enactment, however,
the term "covert action" was considered too sensitive to mention in legislation.

13. Ibid.

14. See Senate Select Committee to Study Governmental Operations with Respect to Intelligence Activities, *Foreign and Military Intelligence: Final Report of the Select Committee to Study Governmental Operations with Respect to Intelligence Activities*, 94th Cong., 2nd sess., S. Rep. 94-755, April 26, 1976; and House Select Committee on Intelligence, Recommendations of the Final Report of the House Select Committee on Intelligence, 94th Cong., 2nd sess., H. Rep. 94-833, February 11, 1976.

15. The Senate Select Committee on Intelligence was established by Senate Resolution 400; see S. Res. 400, 94th Cong., 2nd sess., 122 *Cong. Rec.* 4755 (1976). The House of Representatives Permanent Select Committee on Intelligence was established by House Resolution 658; see H. Res. 658, 95th Cong., 1st sess., 123 *Cong. Rec.* 22932 (1977).

16. *Intelligence Authorization Act for Fiscal Year 1981*, Public Law 96-450, § 407, 94 *Stat.* 1975, 1981–1982 (1980).

17. Ibid.

18. The amended Hughes-Ryan referred to a class of activities called "significant anticipated intelligence activities," defined as foreign activities undertaken by the CIA that were not "solely for obtaining necessary intelligence." These were covert actions.

19. *50 U.S. Code* § 413(a)(1) (emphasis added).

20. See Marshall Silverberg, "The Separation of Powers and Control of the CIA's Covert Operations," *Texas Law Review* 68 (1990): 575, 600–601.

21. *50 U.S. Code* § 413(a)(1)(B).

22. *50 U.S. Code* §§ 413(a)(1)(B) and 413(c) (emphasis added).

23. *46 Fed. Reg.* 59,941 (1981).

24. Ibid. at 59,952.

25. *Fiscal Year 1991 Intelligence Authorization Act*, Public Law 102-88, 105 *Stat.* 429 (codified at 50 *U.S. Code* §§ 413–413b).

26. For a detailed discussion of the Iran-Contra affair, see Theodore Draper, *A Very Thin Line: The Iran-Contra Affairs* (New York: Simon and Schuster, 1992).

27. *50 U.S. Code* § 413b.

28. Ibid. (emphasis added).

29. *50 U.S. Code* § 413(c)(1)–(3).

30. *Marbury v. Madison*, 5 U.S. (1 Cranch) 137, 177 (1803).

31. 5 U.S. at 165–166.

32. *Baker v. Carr*, 369 U.S. 186 (1962).

33. Justice Brennan listed these as follows: "[A] textually demonstrable constitutional commitment of the issue to a coordinate political department; or a lack of judicially discoverable and manageable standards for resolving it; or the impossibility of deciding without an initial policy determination of a kind clearly for non-judicial discretion; or the impossibility of a court's undertaking independent resolution without expressing lack of respect due coordinate branches of govern-

ment; or an unusual need for unquestioning adherence to a political decision already made; or the potentiality of embarrassment from multifarious pronouncements by various departments on one question" (369 U.S. at 217).

34. Ibid.

35. See, e.g., *Crockett v. Reagan*, 558 F. Supp. 893, 898 (D.C. Cir. 1983); *Mitchell v. Laird*, 488 F.2d 611 (D.C. Cir. 1973).

36. To establish standing, a party must demonstrate (1) "injury in fact" (injury of a legally protected interest); (2) a causal relationship between the injury and the challenged conduct; and (3) that a favorable decision will provide redress. Almost without exception, cases brought by individual citizens, citizen groups, or legislators to challenge national security policies are dismissed for failure to meet these tests. For a complete discussion of standing, see *Northeastern Florida Chapter, General Contractors of America v. City of Jacksonville*, 508 U.S. 656, 663–664 (1993).

37. In fact, according to then judge, now Justice Antonin Scalia, the Supreme Court "has never found standing to resolve, or reached the merits of, an intra- or inter-branch dispute presented by a federal officer whose only asserted injury was the impairment of his governmental powers." *Moore v. United States House of Representatives*, 733 F.2d 946, 960–961 (D.C. Cir. 1984) (Scalia, J., concurring), *cert. denied*, 469 U.S. 1106 (1985).

38. 752 F. Supp. 1141 (1990).

39. 752 F. Supp. at 1149.

40. 444 U.S. 996 (1979).

41. 444 U.S. at 997–998.

42. 299 U.S. 304 (1936).

43. 299 U.S. at 319–320 (emphasis added).

44. *Youngstown Sheet & Tube Co. v. Sawyer*, 343 U.S. 579 (1952).

45. 50 U.S. Code § 1801 et seq. For a thorough discussion of the FISA statute, see Norman Abrams, *Anti-Terrorism and Criminal Enforcement*, unabridged ed. (St. Paul, MN: West Group, 2003), 390–424.

46. The Fourth Amendment provides: "The right of the people to be secure in their persons, houses, papers, and effects, against unreasonable searches and seizures, shall not be violated, and no Warrants shall issue, but upon probable cause, supported by Oath or affirmation, and particularly describing the place to be searched, and the persons or things to be seized."

47. Ibid.

48. 277 U.S. 438 (1928).

49. *Federal Communication Act of 1934*, 48 Stat. 1103.

50. *Nardone v. United States*, 302 U.S. 379 (1937); 308 U.S. 338 (1939).

51. 389 U.S. 347 (1967).

52. 389 U.S. at 358 n.23.

53. 18 *U.S. Code* §§ 2510–2520.

54. 18 *U.S. Code* § 2518.

55. *United States v. United States District Court*, 407 U.S. 297 (1972).

56. 407 U.S. at 299 (emphasis added).

57. 407 U.S. at 320.

58. Ibid.

59. 407 U.S. at 322.

60. See 50 *U.S. Code* §§ 1803, 1805.

61. Cf. 50 *U.S. Code* § 1804(a)(3) and 50 *U.S. Code* § 1805 with 18 *U.S. Code* § 2518. Note the differences in the duration of surveillance, notification, probable cause, and identification requirements.

62. 50 *U.S. Code* § 1802.

63. 50 *U.S. Code* § 1804(a)(7)(B) (amended 2001) (emphasis added).

64. *United States v. Truong Dinh Hung*, 629 F.2d 908 (4th Cir. 1980).

65. Public Law 107-56, 115 *Stat.* 272.

66. *In Re: Sealed Case* No's 02-001, 02-002, 310 F. 3d 717 (2002).

67. Obviously, we do not subscribe to the notion that the FISA court inappropriately rejected collection requests that, if granted, would have prevented the 9/11 attacks.

68. Sections 552(b)(1) and 552(b)(3) of FOIA (5 *U.S. Code* § 552) exclude public review of intelligence documents.

69. See, e.g., *Webster v. CIA*, 486 U.S. 592 (1988), which precludes review of employment termination under the Administrative Procedures Act, 5 *U.S. Code* § 706, although permitting constitutional review.

70. See, e.g., *Snepp v. United States*, 444 U.S. 507 (1980).

71. 124 S. Ct. 2633 (2004).

72. 124 S. Ct. 2686 (2004).

73. For a discussion of the benefit of greater surveillance, particularly of selected international visitors, see Philip B. Heymann, *Terrorism, Freedom, and Secrecy: Winning without War* (Cambridge, MA: MIT Press, 2003), 104–106.

THREE

U.S. INTELLIGENCE PRIOR TO 9/11 AND OBSTACLES TO REFORM

William J. Lahneman

Many factors contributed to the failure of the U.S. intelligence community (IC) to detect the al Qaeda terrorist network's plans to use hijacked commercial aircraft to carry out the suicide attacks against the United States on September 11, 2001. This chapter focuses on those features of IC performance that were affected by the United States' political tradition based on democratic principles that emphasize and protect the individual freedom of each citizen. From the very beginning of the Republic, these democratic principles have been canonized in the Constitution and the Bill of Rights, explicitly limiting the ways in which government can intrude into the private lives of citizens.

This emphasis on individual rights presents obstacles to running an intelligence organization. As described in the introduction, intelligence organizations must rely on secrecy, which clashes with the values of an open society. In addition, intelligence agencies must routinely use techniques such as electronic eavesdropping and espionage, and they must at least consider the use of techniques such as assassination and other forms of paramilitary operations that are clearly illegal in all societies. While most people involved in national security agree that a double standard must be used—one set of practices where foreign countries are concerned and another set for domestic conduct—the exact nature of these standards and how they have been implemented in the U.S. system has already been highlighted in Chapters 1 and 2.

The U.S. IC has experienced a number of events and scandals that have resulted in congressional and blue-ribbon investigations. These panels have produced recommendations that, in many cases, have resulted in laws and executive orders imposing new restrictions or clarifying existing limitations on acceptable IC behavior.[1] A significant share of this guidance came from a desire to protect the civil rights of U.S. citizens, to restrict the IC from engaging in activities that clashed too strongly with U.S. values, and to prevent the IC from becoming a powerful, independent force not properly accountable to the government and the American people.

The 9/11 attacks and subsequent commission report have been the primary impetus for the latest round of intelligence reform.[2] Despite ongoing debates about the efficacy of certain courses of action, significant initiatives already have been implemented, and the U.S. IC has undergone its most sweeping reorganization since the end of World War II. And the reform process is far from over.

This chapter examines one particular dimension of the reform effort: how did the dynamic tension between the legitimate need for a considerable degree of secrecy in intelligence operations and the defense of the American ideal of individual freedom contribute to the 9/11 intelligence failure?

THE 9/11 U.S. INTELLIGENCE FAILURE AND ITS AFTERMATH

The attacks al Qaeda carried out on September 11, 2001, are now familiar history in the United States and throughout the world. The response, the Bush administration's war on terrorism, has placed servicemen and servicewomen from America and many other countries in harm's way in Afghanistan, Iraq, and other parts of the world. And while U.S. leadership has attempted to track down al Qaeda operatives, multiple efforts were initiated to learn why the government had failed to detect al Qaeda's plans for the attacks. The families of those who had lost loved ones in the 9/11 attacks organized into a particularly influential group that kept the American public focused on this issue. The intelligence community experienced the most scrutiny in this regard, since it is responsible for providing indications and warnings about impending attacks and other threats, but many other parts of the federal government received scrutiny as well. Congress, charged with oversight of the IC, opened an investigation into the events surrounding the attacks,[3] and the Congressional Research Service produced unclassified reports periodically to keep Congress informed about the progress of reforms and important issues.[4] Executive-branch agencies that might have played a role in preventing the attacks, including most of the intelligence agencies, conducted their own investigations and studies.[5] Most prominently, the president commissioned a blue-ribbon panel, the National Commission on Terrorist Attacks upon the United States—dubbed the 9/11 Commission—to perform a detailed fact-finding mission and analysis.[6] Its members stressed that they would strive for consensus in their findings to elevate the inquiry above partisan politics. Last but not least, several independent organizations and individuals studied the attacks, reviewed the reports of the official commissions, and issued findings.[7]

To further complicate matters, scholars and practitioners alike have continued to debate whether it is really possible to prevent surprise attacks in the first place.[8] The balance of evidence seems to indicate that, despite best attempts, the nature of the intelligence enterprise guarantees that sooner or later an opponent will be able to perform a successful surprise attack. However, it seems reasonable that even if surprise is inevitable, it is still beneficial to minimize surprise attack by striving for an effective indications and warning apparatus. Not only does this offer the hope of minimizing death and destruction, but political considerations also demand that reforms be attempted following intelligence failures, particularly after a traumatic experience like the 9/11 attacks.

While many studies were still in progress, the government began to act to reduce the chances that terrorists could conduct another surprise attack. The administration published the *National Strategy for Homeland Security* in July 2002[9] and established an Office of Homeland Security within the Executive Office of the President. After Congress passed the Homeland Security Act of 2002,[10] the Office of Homeland Security became the Department of Homeland Security, incorporating many formerly independent federal agencies.[11] In December 2004, Congress enacted the Intelligence Reform and Terrorism Prevention Act of 2004, which included the establishment of the director of national intelligence (DNI).[12] Recently, the DNI issued *The National Intelligence Strategy of the United States of America: Transformation through Integration and Innovation* to showcase his reform strategy.[13]

The fact that intelligence reform initiatives were implemented prior to the completion of many inquiries and studies created a situation ripe for legitimate second-guessing and criticism. In addition to criticism directed toward specific reform initiatives, some critics asserted that political considerations had triumphed over enlightened policies. For example, Richard Posner argued that Congress and the Bush administration's desire to demonstrate progress on intelligence reform during the presidential election campaign resulted in flawed legislation. He added that the government's rush to action was stoked by a strong public relations campaign directed by the members of the 9/11 Commission and the families of 9/11 victims.[14]

FINDINGS OF THE 9/11 COMMISSION RELEVANT TO INTELLIGENCE REFORM

There is wide agreement that the 9/11 Commission Report contains the most thoroughly researched information about the attacks themselves, the immediate response to the attacks, and the history of the U.S. government's actions to detect and prevent the attacks. And while there hasn't been agreement on how to address many of the issues facing the IC, virtually no one would challenge the finding that the IC needs to improve its information sharing. Similarly, no one would dispute that human intelligence about al Qaeda was inadequate prior to 9/11.

After its thorough review of al Qaeda activity prior to the attacks of September 11, 2001, the commission summed up its recommendations for IC improvement with the phrase "achieving unity of effort."[15] It argued for unifying strategic intelligence and operational planning against terrorists across the operational divide, for unifying the IC by instituting a new director of national intelligence, for unifying the many participants in the counterterrorism effort in an information-sharing system, for unifying congressional oversight of the IC and other agencies engaged in counterterrorism and homeland security, and for making the FBI and other organizations that are charged with homeland defense better able to perform their counterterrorism roles.

The commission's general assessment was clear: The IC needed to improve its coordination of collection activities, analysis, distribution, and production.[16] It also needed to invigorate its clandestine operations capability.[17]

INTELLIGENCE AND AMERICAN DEMOCRACY

The commission rendered ten specific findings, based on its examination of all phases of government performance with regard to the attacks. Many of these applied to the IC and will be discussed further.[18] But in what ways did America's democratic tradition emphasizing individual rights and an open society contribute to the failure of intelligence capability and coordination prior to the 9/11 attacks? As a starting point, it is useful to observe that the report's findings were categorized in two ways: conceptual and operational failures. *Conceptual failures* pertained to the "failures of imagination" noted by the report: the failure to give adequate weight to potential threats to nontraditional targets (the U.S. homeland) from nontraditional agents (transnational terrorists) using nontraditional methods (airliners as weapons of mass destruction). *Operational failures* referred to organizational and other structural problems that prevented the IC from learning of plans for the attacks, either by discovering a single piece of crucial information or by assembling bits of seemingly unrelated information from many sources into a coherent indicator of impending attack.

This chapter does not examine conceptual failures, because this type of failure does not appear to be a function of America's democratic political culture. However, the same cannot be said for some of the operational failures. In the case of 9/11, although it is by no means certain that the IC would have detected plans for the attacks even if its various parts had shared and thoroughly analyzed all of the available information, a case can be made that the tension between intelligence activities and American democracy was at least partly responsible for some of the operational failures documented by the 9/11 Commission. For purposes of this analysis, these failures are subdivided into issues of capability and issues of coordination.

Capability Issues

One of the commission's findings stated that the IC was unable to provide the actionable intelligence required by policymakers to enable the United States to mount limited military attacks on Osama bin Laden and al Qaeda. Another finding noted deficiencies in the IC's capabilities to respond to the terrorist threat, most notably the inadequacy of the CIA's ability to conduct two aspects of clandestine operations, HUMINT (human intelligence) and covert (paramilitary) action. Both aspects refer to a lack of necessary capabilities — spies within al Qaeda and sufficiently robust paramilitary capabilities, respectively — for attacking terrorists outside U.S. borders.

These findings are interrelated. A lack of spies in bin Laden's organization, and even in Afghanistan as a whole, greatly increased the difficulty of locating bin Laden and forecasting his future movements. Without this information, there was no "actionable intelligence" for mounting an attack against him. However, even if this information had been available, U.S. covert action capability was inadequate to mount a successful attack. As a result, the United States would need to rely on proxy forces, such as members of the Northern Alliance fighting the Taliban regime in Afghanistan. U.S. policymakers considered that this option would have a lower chance of success and a greater potential for undesirable side effects (e.g., collateral damage) than were acceptable. Thus, they were limited to considering cruise missile strikes that arguably required an even greater degree of accurate intelligence than a covert operation.

THE HUMINT DEFICIT

Theoretically, the IC had three principal channels for collecting information about al Qaeda, the whereabouts of bin Laden, and his intentions: imagery, signal, and human intelligence (IMINT, SIGINT and HUMINT). IMINT potentially offered the capability to provide information about the current location of the al Qaeda leadership, but this was not its principal mission. Rather, IMINT was designed to monitor military activity and to identify and provide information for the analysis of military installations and weapons systems. It therefore was valuable for locating and assessing terrorist training camps, for example, but less helpful for tracking bin Laden's movements. SIGINT offered the capability to provide information about both the current location and the intentions of al Qaeda's leadership—information about bin Laden's future travel plans, for instance. However, it required a cooperative target that communicated via electronic means. Apparently, SIGINT failed to provide the necessary information to make an attack on bin Laden possible. All that remained at the IC's disposal was HUMINT, and, as noted above, U.S. HUMINT capabilities in Afghanistan prior to 9/11 were wholly inadequate.

The weak state of America's HUMINT assets prior to 9/11 was partly due to history, partly a result of the changing nature of the threat environment following the cold war, and partly due to America's democratic tradition. In the 1990s, the IC discovered that agents within it had identified almost all of the U.S. agents operating within the former Soviet Union and Warsaw Pact countries. The Soviets subsequently killed or imprisoned virtually all of these agents. Furthermore, those U.S. agents who remained available following these purges turned out to be double agents who were working for the Soviets and providing disinformation to the IC.[19] Given this historical precedent, it is small wonder that many in the IC considered that deemphasizing HUMINT would be a net gain to the U.S. intelligence effort by reducing a significant source of disinformation.

The changing nature and diversity of the threats to U.S. national security following the cold war also had a negative effect on U.S. HUMINT operations. The new, less identifiable threats made developing a list of plausible espionage targets difficult. Then, once a list of plausible targets for espionage had been identified, it required time to develop spy networks in these regions. Some targeted areas, such as Iraq, North Korea, and Iran, proved very difficult to infiltrate. This lack of success in HUMINT operations also contributed to its overall demise in the IC because it was not getting results.

America's emphasis on human rights and freedom also contributed to the weak state of America's HUMINT assets prior to 9/11. Americans and the U.S. government have always been ambivalent at best about employing spies. In the 1990s, U.S. policymakers operationalized this ambivalence in two ways. First, the development of better and better SIGINT capabilities seemed to make the need for extensive HUMINT capabilities obsolete, which led to a de-emphasis of HUMINT for intelligence collection.[20] Second, for the recruitment of new spies, it set in place standards that were intended to prevent the scandals of the past. This attempt to police the recruitment of foreign agents also had the unforeseen effect of weakening HUMINT capabilities.

Prior to 9/11, CIA case officers operating in foreign countries, who managed spy networks composed of nationals of the host country, were required to ensure that their operatives were not guilty of human rights violations and possessed a series of positive attributes. While specific requirements remain classified, "the guidelines establish[ed] a balancing test that weighs the value, or potential value, of the intelligence gathered against the person's record of human rights abuses."[21] Recruitment of persons who had violated human rights or failed to exhibit the required attributes required high-level approval within the CIA.

In theory, the guidelines were designed to protect the CIA from a recurrence of the scandals of the past. The requirement to obtain permission from headquarters to proceed in the recruitment of agents with dirty hands was designed to protect case officers from becoming scapegoats if an operation went sour, by ensuring concurrence from senior officers in questionable recruitments. It was also believed that the requirements would embolden case officers to recruit agents with bad human rights records who nevertheless might prove extremely useful. In practice, however, the policy backfired. It discouraged case officers from recruiting the type of unsavory characters who didn't meet the requirements but may have made outstanding spies. Case officers perceived that it was less risky from a career standpoint to avoid such dubious recruits altogether because it placed the officers under headquarters' spotlight. The result was a risk-averse climate that weakened U.S. HUMINT capabilities.[22]

COVERT ACTION INADEQUACIES

The existence of a robust covert action capability might have made up for the inability to obtain actionable intelligence through HUMINT by providing an alternative to the limited cruise missile strikes that required such detailed targeting data. SIGINT or IMINT alone might have been sufficient to enable the initiation of a paramilitary covert action that placed a team or teams of covert agents on the ground near where bin Laden was believed to be located. Such an operation might have been able to capture bin Laden rather than kill him, which would have been far more useful.

As noted by the 9/11 Commission, U.S. covert action capabilities were not up to such tasks. Accordingly, covert action was an option only if foreign proxies were used. While the U.S. government pursued this approach, nothing came of it. The leadership of the CIA and the National Security Council thought the chance of success was too low and the risk of collateral damage too high. There also was concern that the U.S. government would suffer heavy criticism if, despite best efforts, bin Laden were killed during the operation, because many would accuse the United States of conducting a thinly veiled assassination plot.[23]

As with HUMINT capabilities, America's democratic political culture had played a role in keeping the CIA's covert action capabilities weak. The 1970s and 1980s were a time of severe criticism of the IC for a number of abuses of power and the use of several covert action methods deemed contrary to respect for human rights and therefore inappropriate in a democracy (as previously documented in Chapters 1 and 2).

Although covert actions require congressional notification rather than congressional approval, "a prudent covert action briefing team will report [congressional concerns] to the executive," according to Mark Lowenthal, a former director of the House Permanent Select Committee on Intelligence. "This should be enough to cause the operation to be reviewed. The executive branch may still decide to go ahead, or it may make changes in the operation to respond to congressional concerns."[24]

Assassination is one type of covert action that the IC cannot employ during peacetime. The ban on assassinations was a significant consideration in the plans for mounting a covert operation against bin Laden prior to 9/11. Initially instituted by President Gerald Ford in Executive Order 11905 of February 18, 1976, the prohibition on assassination was reaffirmed by Presidents Jimmy Carter (Executive Order 12036 of January 24, 1978) and Ronald Reagan (Executive Order 12333 of December 4, 1981).[25] Reagan's order remained in effect on 9/11 because no subsequent president had issued a new executive order on intelligence.[26]

The ban derives from both idealist and pragmatic considerations. On one hand, the Church Commission, which gave rise to the ban, asserted that the "cold-blooded, targeted, intentional killing of an individual foreign leader has no place in the foreign policy of the U.S."[27] Short of war, "assassination is incompatible with American principles, international order, and morality."[28] Thus the ban derived directly from America's democratic tradition.

On the pragmatic side, it is not clear that assassination would improve situations. First, the person who succeeded the assassinated leader might be worse than his predecessor. Second, assassination might fuel rather than deter future attacks. In fact, a successful assassination might beget retaliation in the form of more assassinations.[29] Two aspects of the ban need clarification. First, as noted above, the ban applies to peacetime conditions, which was the situation prior to the 9/11 attacks. Second, under conditions of peace, the only situation in which assassinations are considered legal is when they occur coincident to U.S. military attacks in response to attacks on Americans. Presidents contemplating a military response to an attack on Americans have successfully argued that their powers under the U.S. Constitution as commander in chief and executor of the nation's laws gave them ample authority to strike back at the attackers, even if the strike was likely to kill the head of state or commander who might have authorized the attack.[30]

This was the issue that concerned the Clinton administration in 1998 as it contemplated the covert operation against bin Laden's headquarters in Afghanistan. A covert action to kill bin Laden may have been illegal, but not an operation that attempted to capture him, even if he were killed in the process. Alternatively, cruise missile attacks in response to the terrorist attacks on the U.S. embassies in Africa did not constitute an assassination attempt, even if bin Laden were killed in the attacks.

In the wake of 9/11, U.S. response options have been governed by the joint resolution of Congress authorizing the use of force against the perpetrators of the attacks, the constitutional authority of the president as commander in chief of the U.S. armed forces, and the laws of war—not EO 12333, banning assassination.[31] These changed conditions have reinvigorated the potential of covert paramilitary action as a counterterrorism tool, but only if U.S. policymakers and the American people come to accept this "wartime measure" as compatible with America's democratic tradition.

Coordination Issues

Several of the 9/11 Commission's findings address aspects of intelligence coordination and knowledge sharing:

1. The FBI's limited intelligence collection and strategic analysis capabilities, limited capacity to share information both internally and externally, insufficient training, and perceived legal barriers to sharing information degraded its performance at detecting plans for the 9/11 attacks.

2. Permeable U.S. law enforcement, border, and immigration control agencies failed to share intelligence information that would have improved the chances of identifying and arresting the hijackers, thus preventing or reducing the scale of the attacks.

3. Aviation security failed to use the U.S. TIPOFF watch list that listed two of the hijackers. It also mishandled several of the hijackers identified by the CAPPS [Computer-Assisted Airline Pas-

senger Prescreening System] screening system—searching their checked baggage rather than their persons. This could have been avoided if the IC had uncovered the hijackers' general intentions to use aircraft as weapons and had communicated this knowledge to aviation security organizations.

Some of these coordination failures stemmed from the "failures of imagination" described by the 9/11 Commission. For example, agencies failed to share knowledge partly because of a lack of awareness of the true threat posed by transnational terrorism, a threat that used methods demanding close coordination among the various parts of the U.S. government concerned with counterterrorism.

However, America's democratic tradition was responsible for a significant share of the coordination failure for two main reasons. First, it has influenced to a considerable degree the legal limits placed on the IC to act domestically, which, in turn, affected IC institutions and culture regarding domestic security. Second, it has affected the ways that power has been distributed among the various agencies in the IC. The ramifications have played a major role in determining how the different parts of the IC relate to each other and to all other parts of the U.S. government.

LIMITING THE IC'S POWER TO ACT DOMESTICALLY

As noted above, many intelligence activities are illegal. While the IC arguably must perform these kinds of activities in other countries in the name of national security, it is inappropriate to subject the American people to them because it would violate their civil rights. The U.S. Constitution's Fourth Amendment prohibits "unreasonable searches and seizures," a right that has been interpreted as implying broad rights to privacy—freedom from government intrusion and surveillance—in one's personal affairs (as detailed in Chapter 2). These rights extend to U.S. citizens wherever they might reside and to U.S. persons[32] regardless of their nationality. Failure to apply these controls on intelligence activities conjures visions of a secret police that operates above the law, spying on Americans for reasons unconnected to national security. The world is full of examples of such conduct; preventing it is a legitimate concern.

In the United States, domestic activities related to intelligence traditionally have been lumped into the category of "counterintelligence." The need to perform counterintelligence while protecting the rights of U.S. citizens and persons was institutionalized following World War II by assigning the FBI as the lead counterintelligence agency. The newly created CIA, along with collection agencies such as the NSA (National Security Agency) and the NRO (National Reconnaissance Office), would perform foreign intelligence operations. These organizations were prohibited from performing domestic intelligence collection, law enforcement, and internal security functions. As the years passed, many other law enforcement agencies assumed some counterintelligence functions. These included the Drug Enforcement Administration, the Immigration and Naturalization Service, the Customs Service, the Coast Guard, the Secret Service, and the Bureau of Alcohol, Tobacco, and Firearms. Unlike counterintelligence operations during World War II, which were concerned not only with espionage but with the possibility of sabotage performed against vital infrastructure such as dams, bridges, and power plants, cold war counterintelligence efforts increasingly focused on discovering and coping with espionage by agents of foreign powers living in the United States. Counterintelligence increasingly came to be synonymous with counterespionage.

Counterespionage is inherently complex. Foreign agents could be U.S. citizens or foreign nationals. They could be under either official (representative of a foreign government) or unofficial (posing as a businessperson, a professional, or an academic) cover, with each category having different legal rights. The fact that some of these agents might have penetrated U.S. intelligence agencies further complicated the situation, since a large share of the responsibility for detecting such "moles" resided with the penetrated organizations themselves. Furthermore, domestic counterespionage cases might have overseas connections. Finally, advances in electronic eavesdropping and the explosion in transnational communications have blurred the distinction between what constitutes a domestic eavesdropping operation and a foreign one.

Despite the inherent need for coordination and knowledge sharing among agencies if a counterespionage program is to be effective, the selection of the FBI as America's primary counterintelligence agency made sense at the time and continued to be appropriate during most of the cold war.[33] The FBI's core competencies as a law enforcement agency directly supported its counterespionage mission, since most counterespionage cases resembled domestic law enforcement cases.

U.S. domestic law contains many provisions that seek to protect individuals from government tyranny. The need to protect individual freedom imparts a decidedly procedural bias to law enforcement activities, particularly where the issue of evidence is concerned. Accordingly, law enforcement professionals tend to emphasize the need to build a case deliberately while observing all required procedures. They work to amass a preponderance of evidence to try to assure a conviction when warranted. This approach also imparts a bias toward secrecy in law enforcement operations. Sharing information about a case might reduce the chance of obtaining a conviction and endanger other investigations in progress.

The FBI's biases toward procedural correctness and secrecy supported its counterespionage mission. Once potential spies were identified, the FBI mounted a surveillance effort to confirm suspicions, to learn about other agents and contacts, and to uncover methods. The bureau developed its counterespionage cases in essentially the same way it developed its cases against organized crime and other violators of federal law. This approach required a considerable degree of secrecy, not only from suspects but also from other parts of the U.S. government, to protect evidence and prevent suspects from being tipped off to investigations. Secrecy was paramount if the government intended to start supplying a foreign agent with disinformation or planned to try to turn a spy into a double agent working for the United States.

Saying that the FBI was a good fit as lead counterintelligence agency is not the same as saying that the U.S. counterintelligence effort was particularly effective during the cold war. It was not. As mentioned above, a steady stream of foreign agents who had passed valuable information to the Soviets was discovered working within the IC, and the information they had passed to the Soviets virtually destroyed the U.S. intelligence network in the USSR and compromised U.S. national security in other important ways. However, these problems stemmed from a number of performance problems within various IC agencies. The FBI's practice of developing counterespionage cases in the same way that it developed its law enforcement cases was not particularly responsible for these problems. The bureau's reluctance to share information, a trait it shared with the rest of the IC, was a contributing factor.

Following the cold war, the principal focus of counterintelligence changed. The perceived threat from the spies of foreign powers diminished, while emerging threats from transnational terrorism, transnational criminal networks, and the proliferation of weapons of mass destruction assumed importance. The notion of transnational terrorists conducting an attack on the U.S. homeland using illegally acquired nuclear weapons became the new worst-case scenario. In hindsight, it is clear that, in the mid-1990s, the U.S. counterintelligence mission changed from one that was predominantly focused on counterespionage to one focused on counterterrorism.

Transnational terrorists have used advances in technology and the ongoing process of globalization to develop networked organizations capable of exploiting weaknesses in modern border control, transportation, trade, and financial systems to mount destructive attacks by small numbers of agents. As a result, if U.S. intelligence collection efforts against these networks are to be effective, they must be directed globally. This effort must include collection activities against suspected terrorists living within the United States.

Prohibitions against domestic intelligence collection, coupled with the intelligence-counterintelligence institutional divide that solidified during the cold war, worked against such wide-ranging collection efforts, as well as against the analytic efforts that must accompany them. Prior to 9/11, U.S. law essentially prohibited the CIA, the NSA, and many other members of the IC from collecting intelligence within U.S. borders. The FBI was not staffed to assume a growing counterterrorism intelligence collection mission. It also was not apparent that the FBI could legally spy on Americans outside a law enforcement framework any more than the CIA or the NSA could. In addition, the FBI's organizational culture, with its biases toward procedural correctness and secrecy, was not optimized to deal with the emerging terrorist threat.

The procedural bias means that law enforcement operations are reactive: people are prosecuted for committing crimes. But successful counterterrorism efforts are preventive: alleged terrorists must be apprehended prior to committing a crime. To prevent attacks, authorities must act on evidence that is often scanty, particularly when compared with that needed for a successful legal prosecution.

As noted above, a bias toward secrecy is not limited to the FBI, but extends to all of the IC. While failure to share knowledge was a problem when counterespionage was the principal mission of counterintelligence efforts, it constitutes a huge problem now that counterterrorism occupies center stage. The global, networked nature of the terrorist threat means that several IC agencies might detect intelligence (as opposed to evidence) of an impending attack. Each piece of intelligence might provide only a clue to terrorist plans. Thus, knowing when to share knowledge becomes a critical ingredient in effective counterterrorism efforts.

As the 9/11 Commission Report indicated, steps to adjust to these new realities by developing an effective domestic intelligence collection capability against possible terrorist attacks, instituting effective measures to identify and monitor known and suspected terrorists within the United States, and establishing procedures to encourage appropriate knowledge sharing had not progressed sufficiently by the time of the 9/11 attacks. This should not be a surprise when one considers the strong institutional and legal barriers that had been erected to prevent domestic intelligence collection activities.

However, the commission stopped short of supporting a domestic intelligence agency with the sole purpose of collecting intelligence on domestic threats, similar to the MI5 in Great Britain or France's Directorate of Territorial Security (DST). Again, the history of abuses committed by the FBI in the 1960s and 1970s played a significant role in this recommendation, as did American democracy—a "Big Brother" agency was not palatable even to those trying to fix a broken system.[34]

POWER DISTRIBUTION IN THE INTELLIGENCE COMMUNITY

It would be incomplete to focus solely on the legal barriers and their impact on IC culture and institutions regarding domestic intelligence collection to explain why the IC failed to share knowledge that, in hindsight, pointed to plans for the 9/11 attacks. The fact that the various members of the IC are essentially independent bureaucratic actors within the executive branch of government was reason enough for each agency to guard jealously its exclusively held intelligence information.

The IC is a collection of bureaucracies, each of which has grown in size and complexity since World War II and has been influenced along the way by the changing American-style democracy. As a result, each agency's relationship with the others involves some degree of competition for power, defined both by budget (access to resources) and by degree of influence (access to senior policymakers):

> The inter-organizational side of bureaucratic behavior . . . is easily summarized: All bureaucratic organizations pursue their own purposes, promote their own power, enhance their own position in the governmental hierarchy, and strive to endure. . . . Secrecy is one of

the principal tools that bureaucracies use to gain and preserve power. Bureaucratic agencies seek to minimize interference in and regulation of their operations. To the extent possible, they keep their proceedings secret from potential enemies . . . who might use such knowledge to attack their operations publicly, and they conceal activities that can injure their public image.[35]

The IC's legitimate need to keep much of its work secret further increases the natural bureaucratic tendency toward secrecy, with the result that intelligence agencies are distinctly biased toward hoarding rather than sharing information with each other (as well as with state and local law enforcement agencies). This is the "stovepiping" problem that received wide attention in the 9/11 Commission Report, where it was cited as detracting from the community's "unity of effort."[36] Since agencies in similar lines of work (collection or analysis) view themselves as competitors, they resist sharing information that might improve another agency's performance. As a result, they "sometimes vie with one another to respond to requests for intelligence — largely as a means of assuring continued funding levels — regardless of which [agency] is best suited to provide the required intelligence."[37] They also tend to resist the entrance of new actors, such as private firms that offer alternative methods to collect and analyze data.[38]

The unique development of American democracy has an even greater impact on the "unity of effort," which is hampered by bureaucratic infighting because it is not just a "bottom-up" issue. In fact, power brokers in the IC are sometimes reluctant to use their authority, for a variety of reasons, in order to tighten the unity of effort. For example, the newly created CIA office designed to manage IC HUMINT efforts, the National Clandestine Service (NCS), will have only a limited role, allowing the FBI and the DoD to have significant control of their respective HUMINT apparatuses. Senator Pat Roberts, who chairs the Senate Intelligence Committee, described the changes as "a negotiated settlement" among the various agencies. He said that he would have preferred that Director of National Intelligence John Negroponte exert his authority to "manage human intelligence collection worldwide." Instead, one of the senior officials associated with the new CIA organization noted, "We won't tell the FBI how to do their business, and we don't tell the DoD how to do their business."[39]

BUREAUCRATIC POWER IN CONGRESSIONAL OVERSIGHT

A similar pattern repeats itself in the U.S. Congress, where responsibility for oversight of the IC is spread among a large number of committees and subcommittees. For example, the 9/11 Commission reported: "The leaders of the Department of Homeland Security now appear before 88 committees and subcommittees of Congress. One expert witness . . . told us that this is perhaps the single largest obstacle impeding the department's successful development."[40]

While this probably represents a worst-case scenario because of the department's sweeping mandate, most estimates place the number of committees and subcommittees responsible for various aspects of IC performance in the mid-twenties. The commission went on to say:

> Of all our recommendations, strengthening congressional oversight may be among the most difficult and important. So long as oversight is governed by current congressional rules and resolutions, we believe the American people will not get the security they want and need. The United States needs a strong, stable, and capable congressional committee structure to give America's national intelligence agencies oversight, support, and leadership.[41]

Reform of the cumbersome congressional oversight system is very difficult because each committee and subcommittee is intent on retaining if not increasing its power.

Such politics will exist in large bureaucracies regardless of whether the government is democratic, authoritarian, or even totalitarian. But America's democratic tradition is partly responsible for this state of affairs, and because power is decentralized, reform remains difficult.

INTELLIGENCE REFORM SINCE 9/11

Since 9/11, there have been several reforms and attempts at reform of the IC, aimed at improving its capability to detect plans for another terrorist attack on the U.S. homeland and, more generally, to enable it to deal effectively with the threat posed by transnational terrorism. While detailed analysis of these initiatives is beyond the scope of this chapter, progress to date suggests that the American democratic tradition will play a large role in determining the shape of any subsequent intelligence reforms.

The Intelligence Reform and Terrorism Prevention Act of 2004 is the most recent and visible effort at reform. The act is designed to improve knowledge sharing, unity of effort, and accountability in the IC by changing the community's management structure, though it contains no provisions for changing current congressional oversight arrangements. The act also specifically addresses the need to preserve privacy and civil liberties.[42]

Three other initiatives—the U.S. Patriot Act, the Total Information Awareness (TIA) Program, and the CAPPS II—have been criticized for impinging on the rights of Americans. The Patriot Act has enhanced government powers to monitor Americans as part of the war on terrorism. It remains the most controversial of the three because many feel it has gone too far toward eroding civil liberties. Even at its inception, immediately following the 9/11 attacks, Congress stipulated that sixteen surveillance provisions would expire on December 31, 2005. The Patriot Act was an important issue of debate during the 2004 presidential campaign, and only recently was Congress able to come to a compromise on its continuation.[43]

The TIA Program was discontinued by the DoD less than a year after its inception in 2002 when its intended goal of connecting information from both government and private databases into one unified information network for combating terrorism drew extensive criticism for "spying on Americans."[44]

CAPPS II, the follow-on to CAPPS, was designed to satisfy criticism that its predecessor had violated civil liberties to an unacceptable degree and had been ineffective at its mission of identifying terrorists about to board commercial aircraft. However, CAPPS II has failed to pass muster in the former regard. The Department of Homeland Security, which is responsible for developing a passenger screening system, announced that it was scrapping the initiative and would attempt to develop a better one in cooperation with the Transportation Security Administration. The announcement followed a finding by the Government Accountability Office that CAPPS II had failed to meet seven of eight privacy criteria for an effective system.[45]

CONCLUSION

America's democratic tradition—one that prizes individual rights and the civil liberties that seek to guarantee them—provides part of the explanation for why the U.S. intelligence community failed to detect al Qaeda's plans for the 9/11 attacks. Clearly, myriad other important reasons not associated with America's political tradition also degraded the IC's performance prior to 9/11, and they are documented in the 9/11 Commission Report.

America's democratic tradition is partly responsible for the lack of HUMINT and covert action capabilities within the IC. Better HUMINT could have detected plans for the attacks. A more robust covert action capability could have disrupted plans for the attacks by killing or capturing Osama bin Laden and members of al Qaeda's senior leadership.

America's democratic tradition is partly to blame for the lack of knowledge sharing across the IC prior to the attacks. Improved knowledge sharing might have detected plans for the attacks even in the absence of enhanced HUMINT capabilities. The desire to preserve Americans' civil liberties was almost exclusively responsible for the separation of domestic and foreign intelligence activities within the IC, and the deliberately contentious nature of the American system of governance is partly to blame for the bureaucratic competition in both the IC and the Congress. Both factors discouraged the increased knowledge sharing essential for dealing effectively with the new threats posed by transnational terrorism.

In spite of these negative effects, one must view the restrictions that a desire to preserve civil liberties places on the IC as a welcome constraint. An awareness of these constraints helps policymakers concentrate their attention and imagination on enhancing IC performance for combating transnational terrorism and other threats to international security without unwittingly compromising core principles of American democracy in the process. After all, the U.S. government, with the IC at the core, has as its goal securing the "Blessings of Liberty" as stated in the preamble to the Constitution.

NOTES

1. For a summary of the proposals, see Richard A. Best Jr., "Proposals for Intelligence Reorganization, 1949–2004" (Washington, DC: Library of Congress, Congressional Research Service, July 29, 2004). For an excellent synopsis since 1947, see Phyllis Provost McNeil (Aspin-Brown Commission), "The Evolution of the U.S. Intelligence Community—An Historical Overview," in Loch K. Johnson and James J. Wirtz, eds., *Strategic Intelligence: Windows into a Secret World: An Anthology* (Los Angeles: Roxbury Publishing Co., 2004), 5–20. A partial listing of investigative panels and their reports prior to the 9/11 attacks includes the Dulles-Jackson-Correa Report (1948), the Hoover Commissions (1948 and 1954), the Schlesinger Report (1971), the Rockefeller Commission (1975), the Church Committee (1976), the Pike Committee (1976), the Murphy Commission (1975), the Tower Board (1986), the Jacobs Committee (1989), the Gates Task Forces (1991), and the Vice President's National Performance Review (1993). More recent reports include *The 9/11 Commission Report: Final Report of the National Commission on Terrorist Attacks* (New York: W. W. Norton and Co., July 2004) and *The Commission on the Intelligence Capabilities of the United States Regarding Weapons of Mass Destruction* (Washington, DC: U.S. Government Printing Office, 2005).

2. Notwithstanding reports regarding the intelligence failure to accurately describe Iraq's ability to produce weapons of mass destruction. See Senate Select Committee on Intelligence, *Report of the Select Committee on Intelligence on the U.S. Intelligence Community's Prewar Intelligence Assessments on Iraq*, 108th Cong., 2nd sess., S. Rep. 108-301, July 7, 2004, http://www.gpoaccess.gov/serialset/creports/iraq.html; *The Commission on the Intelligence Capabilities of the United States Regarding Weapons of Mass Destruction; Comprehensive Report of the Special Advisor to the DCI [Director of Central Intelligence] on Iraq's WMD*, March 2005, http://www.cia.gov/cia/reports/iraq_wmd_2004/; and Richard Kerr et al., *Intelligence and Analysis on Iraq: Issues for the Intelligence Community*, Kerr Group Report, part 3, July 29, 2004, http://www.gwu.edu/~nsarchiv/news/20051013/kerr_report.pdf.

3. House Permanent Select Committee on Intelligence and Senate Select Committee on Intelligence, *Report of the Joint Inquiry into the Terrorist Attacks of September 11, 2001*, 107th Cong., 2nd sess., December 2002, S. Rep. 107-351, H. Rep. 107-792 (Washington, DC: Government Printing Office, 2002), http://www.gpoaccess.gov/serialset/creports/911.html.

4. See, for example, Richard A. Best Jr., *Intelligence Issues for Congress*, CRS Issue Brief for Congress (Washington, DC: Congressional Research Service, Library of Congress, updated September 15, 2005).

5. See, for example, Rob Johnson, *Analytic Culture in the U.S. Intelligence Community: An Ethnographic Study* (Washington, D.C.: Government Printing Office, 2005); Robert Jervis, Richard Betts, Melvyn Leffler, and James Wirtz, "Report on CIA Tradecraft, Analysis, and the Iraq WMD," NIE unpublished report for the director of central intelligence, December 13, 2004; and William J. Lahne-

man, ed., *The Future of Intelligence Analysis: A Report for the Assistant Director of National Intelligence for Education and Training* (College Park: Center for International and Security Studies at Maryland, University of Maryland, January 27, 2006), http://www.cissm.umd.edu.

6. 9/11 Commission Report.

7. See, for example, *Protecting America's Freedom in the Information Age: A Report of the Markle Foundation Task Force* (October 2002), http://www.markle taskforce.org/documents/Markle_Report_Part1.pdf; and Gregory F. Treverton, "The Next Steps in Reshaping Intelligence," Rand Occasional Paper (2005), http://www.rand.org/pubs/occasional_papers/2005/RAND_OP152.pdf. Examples of works by individuals include William E. Odom, *Fixing Intelligence for a More Secure America*, 2nd ed. (New Haven, CT: Yale University Press, 2004); Gregory F. Treverton, *Reshaping National Intelligence for an Age of Information* (Cambridge: Cambridge University Press, 2003); Melissa Boyle Mahle, *Denial and Deception: An Insider's View of the CIA from Iran-Contra to 9/11* (New York: Nation Books, 2004); Arthur S. Hulnick, *Keeping Us Safe: Secret Intelligence and Homeland Security* (Westport, CT: Praeger/Greenwood, 2004); Richard A. Posner, *Preventing Surprise Attacks: Intelligence Reform in the Wake of 9/11* (Lanham, MD: Rowman and Littlefield, 2005); and Stansfield Turner, *Burn before Reading: Presidents, CIA Directors, and Secret Intelligence* (New York: Hyperion, 2005).

8. For the seminal work on this topic, see Richard K. Betts, "Analysis, War, and Decision: Why Intelligence Failures Are Inevitable," *World Politics* 31 (October 1978): 61–89. For application to the 9/11 attacks, see Posner, *Preventing Surprise Attacks*. See Jervis et al., "Report," for application to the Iraqi WMD intelligence failure.

9. *The National Strategy for Homeland Security* (Office of Homeland Security, July 2002), http://www.whitehouse.gov/homeland/book/index.html.

10. *Homeland Security Act of 2002*, 107th Cong., 2nd sess., http://www.dhs.gov/interweb/assetlibrary/hr_5005_enr.pdf.

11. See http://www.dhs.gov for information about this new department.

12. *Intelligence Reform and Terrorism Prevention Act of 2004*, Public Law 108-458 (December 17, 2004), http://travel.state.gov/pdf/irtpa2004.pdf.

13. *The National Intelligence Strategy of the United States of America: Transformation through Integration and Innovation* (October 2005), http://www.fas.org/irp/offdocs/nis.pdf.

14. Posner, *Preventing Surprise Attacks*, 4–5.

15. 9/11 Commission Report, 399.

16. A number of other reports, books, and articles advocate this conclusion. See *Report of the Joint Inquiry into the Terrorist Attacks of September 11, 2001;* William J. Lahneman, "Knowledge Sharing in the Intelligence Community after 9/11," *International Journal of Intelligence and Counterintelligence* 17, no. 4 (Winter 2004–2005): 614–633; John Deutch and Jeffrey H. Smith, "Smarter Intelligence," *Foreign Policy* January/February 2002, 64–69; Treverton, *Reshaping National Intel-*

ligence; Arthur S. Hulnick, *Fixing the Spy Machine: Preparing American Intelligence for the Twenty-first Century* (Westport, CT: Praeger, 1999); and Bruce D. Berkowitz and Allen E. Goodman, *Best Truth: Intelligence and Security in the Information Age* (New Haven, CT: Yale University Press, 2000).

17. For a breakdown of the elements of clandestine operations into liaison, espionage, covert action, and counterterrorism, see Treverton, *Reshaping National Intelligence,* 137–138.

18. A summary of the findings can be viewed in *The 9/11 Commission Report Executive Summary,* http://www.9-11commission.gov/report/911Report_Exec.htm.

19. For a description of these notorious events, see Johnson and Wirtz, *Strategic Intelligence,* 16–19; and Frederick L. Wettering, "Counterintelligence: The Broken Triad," in ibid., 327–341.

20. Frank J. Cilluffo, Ronald A. Marks, and George C. Salmoiraghi, "The Use and Limits of U.S. Intelligence," *Washington Quarterly* 25 (Winter 2002): 61.

21. Ibid., 62.

22. Ibid., 64–65.

23. See 9/11 Commission Report, 111–115, for a detailed description of the most ambitious plan to capture bin Laden using Afghan tribal allies in 1998.

24. Mark M. Lowenthal, *Intelligence: From Secrets to Policy,* 2nd ed. (Washington, DC: Congressional Quarterly Press, 2003), 128.

25. Aspin-Brown Commission, "The Evolution of the U.S. Intelligence Community—An Historical Perspective," appendix A in *Preparing for the 21st Century: An Appraisal of U.S. Intelligence, Report of the Commission on the Roles and Capabilities of the United States Intelligence Community,* March 1, 1996 (Washington, DC: U.S. Government Printing Office, 1996), http://www.access.gpo.gov/intelligence/int/into22.html.

26. Frederick P. Hitz, "Unleashing the Rogue Elephant: September 11 and Letting the CIA Be the CIA," *Harvard Journal of Law and Public Policy* 25 (2002): 757.

27. Select Commission to Study Governmental Operations with Respect to Intelligence Activities (known as the Church Commission), *Intelligence Activities and the Rights of Americans,* book 2 of *Final Report of the Select Committee to Study Governmental Operations with Respect to Intelligence Activities,* 94th Cong., 2nd sess., April 26, 1976, S. Rep. 94-755 (Washington, DC: U.S. Government Printing Office, 1976), 6.

28. Ibid.

29. Hitz, "Unleashing the Rogue Elephant," 394.

30. Ibid., 393.

31. Ibid., 393–394.

32. Defined as (1) any individual who is a citizen of the United States, a permanent resident alien of the United States, or a protected individual; (2) any juridical person organized under the laws of the United States or any jurisdiction within

the United States, including foreign branches; and (3) any person in the United States.

33. Other arrangements are possible. For example, in the United Kingdom, counterintelligence is the responsibility of a separate agency, MI5, which, unlike the FBI, does not also perform law enforcement duties.

34. For an elegant and detailed argument for a domestic intelligence agency, see Gregory F. Treverton, "Next Steps"; and Treverton, "Terrorism, Intelligence, and Law Enforcement: Learning the Right Lessons," *Intelligence and National Security* 18, no. 4 (Winter 2003): 121–140.

35. Charles W. Kegley and Eugene R. Wittkopf, *American Foreign Policy*, 5th ed. (New York: St. Martin's Press, 1996), 482–483.

36. 9/11 Commission Report, 407–419.

37. Lowenthal, *Intelligence*, 98.

38. For example, see William J. Lahneman, "Outsourcing the IC's Stovepipes?" *International Journal of Intelligence and Counterintelligence* 16, no. 4 (Winter 2003-2004): 573–593.

39. Quoted in Douglas Jehl, "Little Authority for New Intelligence Post," *New York Times*, October 14, 2005.

40. 9/11 Commission Report, 421.

41. Ibid., 419.

42. For a summary of the Intelligence Reform and Terrorism Prevention Act of 2004, see http://hsgac.senate.gov/_files/ConferenceReportSummary.doc. For a detailed look at several major initiatives, see Lahneman, "Knowledge Sharing."

43. For a summary of these key provisions and the pro and con arguments of each, see Larry Abramson and Maria Godoy, "The Patriot Act: Key Controversies" (National Public Radio, February 24, 2006), http://www.npr.org/news/specials/patriotact/patriotactprovisions.html.

44. Shane Harris, "Lightning Rod," *Government Executive*, July 15, 2004, http://www.govexec.com/features/0704-15/0704-15s3.htm.

45. Greta Wodele, "Panel Urges Passenger-Screening Plan Similar to CAPPS II," *GovExec.com Daily Briefing*, July 28, 2004, http://www.govexec.com/dailyfed/0704/072804tdpm2.htm.

FOUR

KEEPING "EARTHLY AWKWARDNESS"

Failures of Intelligence in the United Kingdom

Peter Gill

The production of intelligence is a process by which knowledge is developed so that it provides support and/or justification for government action—that is, policy. As such, intelligence production represents one particular example of the more general social phenomenon by which knowledge interacts with power. But it is a particularly important example because the consequences of the intelligence/policy nexus can, quite literally, be matters of life and death. During 2003, in those countries of the "coalition of the willing" that invaded Iraq, unprecedented public controversies regarding intelligence and policy developed particularly because of the failure to find the weapons of mass destruction (WMD) that had been the primary justification for the invasion.

Intelligence has always been central to states' efforts to protect themselves, but the new doctrine embraced by the administrations of both U.S. president George W. Bush and British prime minister Tony Blair gave it a new, and, crucially, heightened public significance. Governments of states finding themselves under military attack from outside do not need intelligence to tell them, and their publics would not need persuasion, that defense is required. However, if states are to preempt those who are perceived to threaten them, then intelligence is much more crucial. First, it is central to the process by which the seriousness of the threat is assessed, and second, it will have to provide the basis for some process of convincing skeptical publics that preemptive war is required. In the case of the Iraq invasion, these new circumstances have led in the United Kingdom to hitherto unheard levels of exposure of intelligence and policymaking processes.

This chapter draws on the findings of the four inquiries conducted between June 2003 and July 2004 concerning WMD in Iraq[1] and seeks to place these in a broader context in order to consider more gen-

eral issues of the intelligence process. First, it raises central conceptual issues about the way in which social science discusses information,
power, and their relationship; second, it describes the UK machinery
for national intelligence assessments; third, it discusses key findings of
the inquiries with respect to the analysis and dissemination of intelligence; and finally, it draws conclusions on the relationship between
intelligence and policy that relate to broader themes of the book.

SURVEILLANCE: KNOWLEDGE AND POWER

Surveillance is a core concept in explaining modern governance.
Though discussed in different ways by social theorists such as Dandeker, Giddens, and Foucault,[2] there is a core of similarity in their
definition of surveillance, as constituted by two primary components:
first, the gathering and storing of information and, second, the supervision of people's behavior. In other words, it is concerned with knowledge and power. In contemporary Western social theory, surveillance
is seen as the central aspect both of the establishment of modern "sov-
ereign" state forms and of the more recent decline of sovereignty as
it is replaced by "governance" (or, for Foucault, "governmentality"),[3]
including the concomitant recognition of the significance of private
forms of governance. Furthermore, studies of non-Western societies
show that surveillance is similarly central there: its philosophical basis
may be crucially different (for example, the rejection of individual-
ism), but its core goals—understanding and control—remain.[4] So, not
surprisingly, global surveillance is argued by David Lyon to be an intrinsic part of the general economic restructuring of capitalism that is
referred to as globalization,[5] and post-9/11 developments have served
only to accelerate this already existing trend.[6]

Power operates in, broadly, two ways. In the first, actors seek to
influence, persuade, or coerce others into behaving in ways that they
would not otherwise. This power is zero-sum—the gains of one actor
are balanced by the losses of the other. A "second stream" of power
is less concerned with the power of one actor over another than with
power as an ability to make things happen. This is a non-zero-sum
view of power; it focuses less on specific holders and more on the
strategies and techniques of power.[7] Various theorists have developed
this view of power in which cultural and ideological factors are central
to the construction of consent around particular ways of thinking.[8]

Thus the expertise that derives from a particular form of knowledge can provide the basis for empowerment for some (and disempowerment for others) and is an important adjunct to the (mainstream) power that derives from occupying a position of command.

There is insufficient space here to discuss how information in general interacts with power; the concentration here is on the more specific case of intelligence. Intelligence analysts seek knowledge with a degree of certainty sufficient to satisfy and inform those who wish to act upon it; clearly this knowledge may fall somewhere short of "truth." Assessment is the search for truth. How do you arrange it so that you have the maximum chance of coming near to that elusive ideal, and how do you ensure that if you come near to it, you are listened to?[9]

Hibbert's ideal is certainly elusive, even in principle. The realities of the intelligence process determine not only that "knowledge" may fall far short of "truth" but also that intelligence may not be translated into policy. Indeed, the relationship may be reversed: power may actually determine what is viewed as "knowledge." The following examination of the intelligence fiasco regarding Iraqi WMD demonstrates the need to be alert to these realities.

UNITED KINGDOM: ORGANIZATION OF
ANALYSIS AND ASSESSMENTS

The unitary structure of UK government means that it is relatively straightforward—certainly by comparison with the United States—in providing central coordination of national intelligence assessments. There is a Joint Intelligence Committee (JIC), which consists of the heads of the three intelligence agencies—Security Service, Secret Intelligence Service (SIS), and Government Communications Headquarters (GCHQ)—as well as the intelligence staff at the Foreign Office, the Defense Intelligence Staff (DIS), and senior representatives from the Ministry of Defense (MOD), the Department of Trade and Industry, the Treasury, and the Home Office. And while the separate intelligence agencies themselves originated during the first two decades of the twentieth century, interdepartmental coordination was not attempted before the Second World War. The JIC was created in 1936 to support the military chiefs of staff but succeeded only in occasionally bringing together the intelligence directors of the armed services and, from 1939, a Foreign Office representative. From 1941 onward, under pressure from Winston Churchill, the JIC acquired a staff and began to develop an assessment capability independent of the services and other concerned departments. Technological advances in intelligence collection and the steady postwar subordination of the armed services in the Ministry of Defense (completed in 1963) were accompanied by the development of the JIC as the principal interface between the intelligence agencies and the Foreign Office and Defense Ministry. In 1968 a Joint Intelligence Organization (JIO) was set up in the Cabinet Office to provide assessments staff (on secondment from all the departments represented on the JIC), and the post of intelligence coordinator was established.

Each of the UK agencies conducts its own analysis and may disseminate this to customers or, in some cases, pass on single-source reports as well as forwarding them to JIO. The JIC, located within the Cabinet Office, represents the main instrument for determining collection priorities and providing a national assessment of what is gathered. The JIC meets weekly, and other departments attend the meetings when necessary.

The Butler Inquiry into the intelligence on WMD described the JIC's main function as to provide "Ministers and senior officials with co-ordinated intelligence assessments on a range of issues of immediate and long-term importance to national interests, primarily in the field of security, defense and foreign affairs" (par. 43).[10]

The then-chair of the JIC, John Scarlett, described the basic JIC process to the Hutton Inquiry into the circumstances of the death of Iraq arms expert David Kelly: raw intelligence is issued by the collection agencies together with their evaluation to customers in the policy departments and to relevant JIC assessment staff. The actual work program for staff is set by an interdepartmental group chaired by the chief of the assessment staff responding to requests from policy departments. An initial draft of an assessment would be prepared by the relevant staff officer based on her own expertise and contacts in Whitehall. This would be circulated to interested parties for comments and then go before a formal meeting of an interdepartmental Current Intelligence Group (CIG). Chaired by one of the deputy heads of assessment staff, the CIG would agree to a new draft for recirculation and, after any further changes, presentation to a full meeting of the JIC. After any further changes, which the JIC "almost always" makes, the approved assessment would be circulated.[11] The approved assessment includes text that seeks to answer the questions raised by the sponsors as well as a section for "key judgments" in which the JIC states its formal view on the central questions posed within the broader context of other JIC assessments, open sources, and so on.[12] Some CIG assessments, rather than becoming full JIC papers, may be circulated under the authority of the chief of the assessments staff. Also, "immediate assessments" for more rapid analysis of developing events may be produced for policy departments.[13]

The split between assessment for "intelligence" and "security" purposes was indicated in the UK by the relative autonomy of the Security Service from JIC targeting decisions and the separate committee structure for protective security advice. As we have seen, the post of intelligence coordinator was established in 1968 to attempt to overcome interdepartmental rivalries. The official description of the role remained essentially unchanged until 2001, when the post reflected the shift to a greater concern with "security." When Sir David Omand was appointed as security and intelligence coordinator in the summer of 2003, the status was increased to that of a permanent secretary, and he replaced the cabinet secretary as the senior security adviser to the prime minister (PM). Through the 1990s the same person had chaired the JIC as well as being coordinator; now the roles were separated.

The JIC chair would remain responsible for presenting JIC judgments directly to the prime minister and for advice on assessments but would otherwise be accountable to the coordinator. The Butler Inquiry heard some criticisms of the new arrangements, specifically that the reduced role of the cabinet secretary in security and intelligence matters had contributed to an excess of informality in decision making on Iraq: the relevant cabinet subcommittee did not meet, and decisions, often in unminuted meetings, were made by a small group of ministers, officials, and military officers. In the year leading up to the invasion, the cabinet never discussed policy on the basis of circulated papers but just received oral briefings from the PM or the foreign or defense secretary (pars. 606–611).

The Security Service has always reported to ministers separately from the JIC (and the CIG), but a more precise picture of the terrorism threat process became public only as a result of the Intelligence and Security Committee inquiry into the Bali nightclub bombing of October 2002 in which two hundred people, mainly Australians but including twenty-four Britons, were killed. Although the Security Service was reviewing the adequacy of the threat assessment process after 9/11 and prior to Bali, this did not stop the ISC from being highly critical regarding both assessment and dissemination in the weeks before October 2002. From its examination of the intelligence and warnings in the period before October 2002, the ISC concluded "that there was no action that the UK or its allies could have taken to prevent the attacks," but the committee was highly critical of the Security Service's failure to increase the threat level in Indonesia after violent incidents earlier in the year.[14] The lack of specifics in the report make it difficult to judge whether this was much more than hindsight, but the committee went on to recommend that the warning scale be increased to seven points with at least another level between "significant" and "high."[15] Given that attack warnings are much more of an art than a science, it is not immediately clear how a longer scale would help without some very precise definitions of terms such as "significant" and "high."

Immediately after 9/11, in October 2001 a Counter-Terrorism Analysis Centre (CTAC) had been established by the Security Service.[16] Continuing review of these arrangements was still under way when the Bali bombing occurred, and in June 2003 a Joint Terrorism Analysis Centre (JTAC) started operating, with a greater number of staff from agencies other than the Security Service. They were mainly from the Secret Intelligence Service, GCHQ, and DIS, but also from the Foreign and Commonwealth Office (FCO), the Home Office, the police, the Cabinet Office, the Office of Nuclear Safety, and the Department of Transport's security division (TRANSEC). This arrangement sought to overcome the problems of information sharing normal to "task forces" by ensuring that each representative had access to his or her home database.[17] A year later, the ISC was complimentary of the early performance of JTAC,[18] which was developing a role for all-source security assessments to parallel that of the JIC regarding intelligence.

IRAQ: PROBLEMS WITH COLLECTION AND VALIDATION

In the first chapter of their report, the Butler team do attempt some much needed public education regarding major features of the intelligence process, including the main forms of collection and some of the inherent problems of analysis. Initially they describe the apparently more successful efforts to identify the existence of WMD programs in Iran, Libya, North Korea, and the Khan network based in Pakistan. Turning to Iraq, the inquiry started with the relevant JIC assessments and worked its way back through the intelligence, both accepted and rejected, on which they were based (par. 8).[19] In the period from the end of the first Gulf War until 1998, most of the information came from inspectors with the United Nations Special Commission on Iraq; after their withdrawal, "information sources were sparse," especially on chemical and biological programs (par. 433). After 1998, SIS had five main human sources, two of whom were dominant in terms of quantity and influence of reports but who generally did not have firsthand knowledge of WMD programs. "As a result reports were mainly inferential" and not generally confirmed from other (presumably technical) sources (par. 435).[20]

The Butler Inquiry does not provide us with the raw data of these reports, but the references made to them in the March 15, 2002, JIC assessment illustrate their poverty: "Intelligence on Iraq's weapons of mass destruction (WMD) and ballistic missile programs is sporadic and patchy" (par. 270). "Although there is very little intelligence we continue to judge that Iraq is pursuing a nuclear weapons program" (par. 272). "We continue to judge that Iraq has an offensive chemical warfare (CW) program although there is very little intelligence relating to it" (par. 275).

Butler identified a number of reasons for the paucity of sources and problems with validation: the clear difficulties of recruiting human sources in a regime as repressive as Iraq's; the length of reporting chains, with reports based on second- or thirdhand information; and the pressures to obtain intelligence in the lead-up to the invasion, which had agents being asked to report on fields well beyond their usual ones, and lending more credence to new and untried sources than would normally have been the case. It was also noted that organizational changes within SIS in the late 1990s had weakened internal processes for quality assurance on agents (pars. 440–444).

The Butler Committee report stated:

Validation of human intelligence sources after the war has thrown doubt on a high proportion of those sources and their reports, and hence on the quality of the intelligence assessments received by Ministers and officials in the period from summer 2002 to the outbreak of hostilities. Of the main human intelligence sources described above:

a. One SIS main source reported authoritatively on some issues, but on others was passing on what he had heard within his circle.

b. Reporting from a sub-source to a second SIS main source that was important to JIC assessments on Iraqi possession of chemical and biological weapons must be open to doubt.

c. Reports from a third SIS main source have been withdrawn as unreliable.

d. Reports from two further SIS main sources continue to be regarded as reliable, although it is notable that their reports were less worrying than the rest about Iraqi chemical and biological weapons capabilities.

e. Reports received from a liaison service on Iraqi production of biological agent were seriously flawed, so that the grounds for JIC assessments drawing on those reports that Iraq had recently-produced stocks of biological agent no longer exist (par. 436).

Problems with Analysis

The modern transformation of intelligence by the application of highly sophisticated surveillance and information technology has tended to overshadow the fact that, at its core, it remains an intellectual process. Technology has certainly contributed to analysis[21]—for example, the use of relational software to provide links between disparate data sets and the contemporary development of data warehouses—but the "attribution of meaning" to items of information or linked networks of items requires the application of thought and judgment. The thinking and judgments take place, of course, at a number of different levels within the intelligence process: it is convenient to identify the individual, the small group, and the organization. While intelligence within states is bureaucratized, the role of small work groups and their informal subcultures and the strengths and weaknesses of individual analysts must all be acknowledged if a full picture of analysis and the problems to which it is prone is to be developed.

The Butler Inquiry demonstrates an awareness of some of these— for example, the possibilities of groupthink and "mirror imaging," the role of organizational memory with respect to previous analytical failures, and the dangers of compartmentalization and politicization (pars. 53–58). We shall see in the following discussion the extent to which the Butler Inquiry identified these problems as actually having an impact on the Iraqi intelligence process.

Problems with Assessments

We have already noted the general role carried out by assessments staff, and the Butler team do not provide as detailed a review of their work as they did for the initial source reports and JIC assessments. Specifically, they do not comment on the process by which assessments were produced by the thirty staff members and negotiated through the interaction with the collection agencies and within the CIGs and the JIC itself. However, they do note that assessments staff "were not fully aware of the access and background of key informants" and would therefore have been unable to judge the weight to be given to reports they received (par. 456). Butler's recommendation that the size and the continuing dependence on officials detailed from other agencies be examined echoes the criticism made years ago by Michael Herman that recruitment and organization for all-source analysis in the UK are "too amateurish and hand-to-mouth."[22]

It is in the JIC that the "professional" production of intelligence collides with the broader political concerns of policy managers. The Butler team examined the process by which raw information was converted into assessments, and they concluded that JIC assessments correctly reflected intelligence material; with the exception of the "forty-five minute" claim (see below), they found no evidence of distortion of assessments toward particular policy concerns and concluded that intelligence made good use of available technical expertise (pars. 449–451). They did, however, note that assessments tended to be colored by overreaction to previous errors, that over time the disappearance of caveats from worst-case scenarios led to those scenarios becoming prevailing wisdom, and that assessments were far weaker regarding government and social issues in Iraq (pars. 456–459). The most direct criticism was that of the inclusion of the "forty-five minute" claim in the assessment of September 9, 2002. The earlier inquiry by the ISC had established that assessments staff did not know what munitions the report referred to, nor from and to where those munitions could be moved, but the staff judged that it referred to the time needed to move battlefield chemical and biological munitions from where they were stored to military units (par. 508).[23] Butler criticizes its inclusion in the assessment without the statement of the qualifications (par. 511).

Throughout the intelligence process, the use of language is crucial; indeed it is determinative of what, in the end, is considered to be "knowledge" upon which policy may be based or by which it is rationalized. Intelligence seeks to improve knowledge by reducing uncertainty but, by widely varying degrees in different conditions, is only partially successful. The way in which different national systems seek to convey this uncertainty varies. For example, U.S. National Intelligence Estimates (NIEs) incorporate footnotes recording the dissents of particular agencies from the main conclusions. In the UK the JIC eschews dissenting footnotes, but Butler describes how JIC accommodates uncertainty: when the intelligence is unclear or inadequate, the JIC may report different interpretations as long as the membership agrees they are viable alternatives (par. 45), but it is not the current convention to produce alternative or minority hypotheses (par. 603). So JIC normally attempts to reach a consensus in the assessment, and the section on "key judgments" often will include warnings as to the thinness of evidence. Inevitably this search for consensus "may result in nuanced language," Butler concludes. "Subtleties, such as 'the intelligence indicates' rather than 'the intelligence shows,' may escape the untutored or busy reader. We also came across instances where Key Judgments unhelpfully omitted qualifications about the limitations of the intelligence which were elsewhere in the text" (par. 603).

But if language is nuanced in order to satisfy those who are producing it, the subtleties of what they mean may well escape those who receive it. Butler notes that not even the producers are themselves clear as to the significance of the language: "We have been told that some readers believe that important distinctions are intended between such phrases as 'intelligence indicates . . . ,' 'intelligence demonstrates . . .' and 'intelligence shows . . . ,' or between 'we assess that . . . ,' 'we judge that . . .' and 'we believe that . . .'" "We have also been told that there is in reality no established glossary, and that drafters and JIC members actually employ their natural language" (par. 45 n. 13).

Then what hope is there for the reader? Butler does not suggest any particular way of trying to deal better with this problem—it is indeed inherent in any process involving language—but does recommend that the intelligence community review its conventions (par. 604).

Issue might be taken with Butler's analysis of the political pressures operating on and within the JIC; the conclusions do not always follow the logic of the analysis. There are two criticisms that can be made: one relating to Butler's own logic, the other applying a broader analytical context. The report notes how, since the 1960s, the initial JIC membership of intelligence producers and users (MOD and FCO) has been expanded to include the Treasury, Trade and Industry, and the Home Office (par. 42). While this reflects the shifting parameters of national intelligence over the period, Butler acknowledges the possibility that "the presence of more policy heavy-weights than in the past" may have compromised JIC objectivity (par. 592). Further, even some of the producers on JIC had no analytical background, and so the possibility of JIC "judgments" being influenced by policy concerns seems strong indeed. Yet despite the evidence throughout the report of the distance between the actual information being collected and the judgments based upon it (see Table 4.1, pages 112–114), the limited scope of assessments staff from other agencies to mount challenges to "prevailing wisdom" (pars. 598–599), and the pressures of time and events to search for and validate intelligence (pars. 441–442) that has subsequently proved to be groundless, Butler declares that this objectivity had not been threatened. And why? Because "we have been assured by all witnesses that the tradition of the JIC has prevented policy imperatives from dominating objective assessment in the JIC's deliberations" (par. 596).

If this reference is to all witnesses who were serving on the JIC during 1998–2002, then one might respond: "They would say that, wouldn't they?" If the reference is to all witnesses, including previous JIC members and officials, then we are entitled to doubt that this statement is true: among those interviewed by Butler were former JIC chair Roderic Braithwaite and Michael Herman, both of whom have made strong public criticisms of JIC performance over Iraq. In Braithwaite's view: "[JIC] stepped outside its traditional role. It entered the prime minister's magic circle. It was engulfed in the atmosphere of excitement which surrounds decision-making in a crisis. Whether they realized it or not, its members went beyond assessment to become part of the process of making and advocating policy. That inevitably undermined their objectivity."[24]

On a later occasion, Michael Herman said: "I can only believe that [JIC] got too close to the problem in a sense or too sucked in to the Whitehall consensus that something had to be done about Iraq. I suspect that if the JIC gets too close to the issues, then there is this temptation of providing intelligence to please."[25]

In a broader context, the problem with Butler's conclusion is that it assumes that political power operates only in what may be called the "first stream." Even Lord Hutton, a judge, had grasped the possibility of more "subconscious" — "second stream" — operations of power and influence in his discussion of the relationship between the head of the JIC, John Scarlett, and the head of Blair's press operation, Alistair Campbell.[26] But Butler provides inadequate analysis of the extent to which prior assumptions regarding Iraqi behavior — including worst-case scenarios of the possession and deployment of chemical and biological weapons and deception when combined with political imperatives emanating from the political core of both U.S. and UK administrations — produced "assessments" that were barely supportable at the time and subsequently proved to be significantly inaccurate. The dominant consciousness meant that the JIC never asked the questions it should have. Michael Herman points out that, in light of the failure to develop any firm intelligence after 1988 about the presence or production of WMD in Iraq, the question should have been "Could it be because there are no WMD there at all?"[27]

As we saw above, when concern was expressed by analysts, it was overridden by the very political "heavyweights" by whom Butler was reassured.

"No Good Will Come of This": Problems with Dissemination

As with analysis and assessments, there are a range of potential problems with the dissemination of intelligence that cannot be discussed in the space available, but UK officials cannot claim to have been ignorant of the potential problems. Just a decade earlier, a succession of ministers, officials, and diplomats had given evidence to Lord Justice Scott's inquiry into arms sales to Iraq during and after the Iran-Iraq War when they were supposedly prohibited. Intelligence was just one of a number of issues covered by the Scott inquiry, but one observer noted: "Witness after witness described how crucial intelligence reports were ignored, forgotten about, mislaid, withheld from ministers, or misinterpreted. It was difficult to know whether civil servants responsible for distributing intelligence reports to decision-makers in Whitehall were incompetent buffoons or devious manipulators."[28]

In 2002 the already flawed assessment process was to be compounded by a public dossier falsely claiming authority and certainty that could never have been based on the "information" gathered about

Iraqi WMD in the years preceding the invasion; rather it depended on a series of judgments about the meaning of "absences of information." In summer 2002, conscious that their respective publics were not entirely convinced of the necessity for war against Iraq, the Bush and Blair governments coordinated their strategies, and there are two key points at which they sought to justify invasion: in the autumn of 2002, and early in 2003, as they sought to obtain a second UN Security Council resolution.[29] In September 2002, the UK government produced a dossier entitled *Iraq's Weapons of Mass Destruction*,[30] and on January 30 the UK government published a further dossier, *Iraq: Its Infrastructure of Concealment, Deception, and Intimidation.*[31]

In the UK, it was the September 2002 dossier that would eventually receive the closest attention because of the forty-five-minute claim and the establishment of the Hutton Inquiry, but the January dossier achieved even more rapid notoriety when the finding emerged that most of it had been plagiarized from academic sources.[32] Although it did contain some material from SIS, it had been compiled in Downing Street's communications department and was not cleared by the JIC.[33] It rapidly became known as the "dodgy dossier" and sank from public view. Government embarrassment was compounded by the fact that Colin Powell had approvingly referred to the dossier in his February 5, 2003, presentation to the United Nations. An examination of these public statements makes it clear that, at the very least, the case for the continued and threatening existence of WMD in Iraq was presented at a level of certainty quite unheard-of in intelligence assessments.

At the time of the preparation of the September dossier, concern had been expressed by some DIS staff at the validity of the forty-five-minute claim, and, somewhat unusually, Brian Jones (then head of the Nuclear, Biological, Chemical Technical Intelligence Branch in DIS) expressed these concerns to his chief in writing on September 19.[34] However, the director and deputy director of DIS, neither of whom was from an analytical background (Butler, par. 590), did not take these concerns further with the JIC, partly because they were told of a fresh SIS report issued on September 11 that indicated accelerated production of chemical and biological agents in Iraq and thus tended to confirm the forty-five-minute claim. Jones and his staff were not shown this report. Butler concluded:

[I]t was wrong that a report which was of significance in the drafting of a document of the importance of the dossier was not shown to key experts in the DIS who could have commented on the validity and credibility of the report. We conclude that arrangements should always be sought to ensure that the need for protection of sources should not prevent the exposure of reports on technical matters to the most expert available analysis. (Par. 452)

So the DIS chiefs signed off on the dossier, content that this fresh report justified the certainty with which the forty-five-minute claim was stated. Butler notes that perhaps the pressure of events in the lead-up to the dossier caused more weight to be given to a new source than would normally be the case (pars. 569–578). This judgment can only be stronger since, after the war, SIS withdrew the intelligence from this source as being unreliable (par. 575) and also called into question the report on which the forty-five-minute claim itself was based (par. 512).

In the UK government's dossier published on September 24 there were four references to the forty-five-minute claim—for example, in the executive summary: "As a result of the intelligence we judge that Iraq has . . . military plans for the use of chemical and biological weapons, including against its own Shia population. Some of these weapons are deployable within forty-five minutes of an order to use them."[35]

Speaking to the Commons on the same day, Blair said:

The intelligence picture that they [the intelligence services] paint is one accumulated over the last four years. . . . It is extensive, de-tailed and authoritative. . . . [It] concludes that Iraq has chemical and biological weapons, that Saddam has continued to produce them, *that he has existing and active military plans for the use of chemical and biological weapons, which could be activated within forty-five minutes,* in-cluding against his own Shia population, and that he is actively trying to acquire nuclear weapons capability.[36] (Emphasis added.)

Shortly before political furor erupted in June 2003 when a BBC reporter asserted that the government had included the forty-five-minute claim in the dossier even though knowing it to be probably wrong, the Intelligence and Security Committee had started to inves-tigate the issue of the prewar intelligence. The committee concluded:

The dossier was for public consumption and not for experienced readers of intelligence material. . . . The fact that it was assessed to refer to battlefield chemical and biological munitions and their movement on the battlefield, not to any other form of chemical or biological attack, should have been highlighted in the dossier. *This was unhelpful to an understanding of the issue.*[37] (Emphasis added.)

In its response the government took no responsibility for the "silences" in the dossier. Regarding the ISC criticism that the forty-five-minute claim was "unhelpful," the government merely noted that the dossier did not say that Iraq could deliver chemical or biological weapons by ballistic missiles within forty-five minutes.[38] Although it did not, it was precisely this failure to make clear just what the assessments were that amounted to serious misrepresentation of the nature of the threat from Iraq. In its annual report for 2003–2004, the committee itself expressed its dissatisfaction with the government's response.[39]

The Butler Inquiry reached the same conclusion on the forty-five-minute claim as the ISC and, acknowledging that the publication of the dossier was unprecedented in explicitly deploying JIC assessments, concluded that "it was a serious weakness that the JIC's warnings on the limitations of the intelligence underlying its judgments were not made sufficiently clear in the dossier" (par. 465).[40]

Given the political stakes at the time, this is arguably something of an understatement. Butler acknowledges that the purpose of the dossier was for the advocacy of policy rather than the dispassionate assessments prepared by JIC, but adds:

[T]he language in the dossier may have left with readers the impression that there was fuller and firmer intelligence behind the 'judgments' than was the case: our view, having reviewed all of the material, is that 'judgments' in the dossier went to (although not beyond) the outer limits of the intelligence available. . . . The prime minister's description, in his statement to the House of Commons on the day of publication of the dossier, of the picture painted by the intelligence services in the dossier as *"extensive, detailed and authoritative"* may have reinforced this impression. (Par. 464, emphasis in original.)

It is important to note that Butler's terms of reference were not just the dossier but the intelligence "used by the Government before the conflict" (par. 1), so the committee's brief clearly included ministerial statements as well as documents. With respect to the certainty (or otherwise) of information on Iraqi WMD, the report sets out clearly the difference between the language of JIC's assessment of September 9, 2002, and the September 24, 2002, dossier.[41] As we saw above, Butler was content to conclude that this gap "was a serious weakness" that went to the "outer limits of the intelligence available." If so, then if one looks at the *further* gap between the dossier and the prime minister's statement to the House of Commons, it is simply inadequate to conclude that this *may* just have reinforced the impression that intelligence was firmer than it was. If the dossier went to the "outer limits" of the intelligence, then Blair's statement went *beyond* those limits. The only possible conclusion is that the prime minister misled the House of Commons. At a subsequent appearance before the Commons' Public Administration Select Committee, Butler was criticized for his failure to blame individuals, to which his response was that his team had not found evidence of negligence on the part of any particular individual. However, he also indicated their unwillingness to reach a "political" rather than "legal" conclusion: "On the political issues, we wanted to give people the information but we felt that really the proper place where governments should survive or fall is with parliament and the electorate. . . . It would have been a heavy responsibility and one where it would have been improper for us to say that we think the Government should resign on this issue."[42]

LOST IN TRANSLATION?

Table 4.1 presents the main points of translation by which pieces of (unvalidated, unanalyzed) "information," however obtained, may be processed into intelligence reports and subsequently become part of all-source assessments that provide the basis for or rationalization of public policy. Of course, there is much attrition during the process—not all pieces of information collected are validated or, if so, necessarily passed on by the collectors; not all assessments are formally passed to ministers as JIC papers. Some of this attrition results from sheer lack of resources, but some involves conscious selection and judgments of priorities and significance. Applying this schematic to intelligence with respect to Iraq indicates the extremely tenuous threads by which the UK government's war policy was connected to knowledge of Iraq's weapons capabilities.[43]

TABLE 4.1 LOST IN TRANSLATION?
THE PRODUCTION OF INTELLIGENCE

Process	Function	Product	Iraq WMD examples
Collection	gathers . . .	"information" (picture, drawing, taped conversation, verbal or written account of meeting with source, reports from other agencies or international bodies, e.g., UN Special Commission).	None of the original source reports on which intelligence regarding Iraqi WMD was based has been published.
Validation	evaluates . . .	the degree of certainty that can be ascribed to the information. This may be in terms of the chain through which the information has arrived or the previous record of the source.	"Validation of human intelligence sources after the war has thrown doubt on a high proportion of those sources and of their reports, and hence on the quality of the intelligence assessments received by Ministers and officials in the period from summer 2002 to the outbreak of hostilities" (Butler, par. 436).
Analysis	produces . . .	"intelligence"—attributes meaning to the information. This may relate to the significance of an individual piece of information. "Analysis assembles individual . . . reports into meaningful	"Intelligence on Iraq's weapons of mass destruction . . . and ballistic missile programs is sporadic and patchy." Regarding nuclear weapons, "there is very little intelligence." "[T]here

TABLE 4.1 CONTINUED

Process	Function	Product	Iraq WMD examples
		strands" (Butler, par. 30).	is very little intelligence relating to [Iraq's chemical warfare program]" (JIC, March 15, 2002).
Assessment	provides . . .	broader context for the intelligence by integrating material from all sources (overt and covert) and making not only broader judgments based on what is known but also assumptions as to what is not known. For example, JIC assessments in the UK, and NIEs in the United States.	"Recent intelligence casts light on Iraq's holdings of WMD and on its doctrine for using them. Intelligence remains limited and Saddam's own unpredictability complicates judgments about Iraqi use of these weapons. Much of this paper is necessarily based on judgement and assessment" (JIC, September 9, 2002).
Dissemination	distributes . . .	both single items of intelligence from agencies and all-source assessments to policymakers and executive agencies. Rarely, as in the case of the September 2002 Iraq dossier, assessments may be communicated explicitly to the public.	"As well as the public evidence, however, significant additional information is available to the Government from secret intelligence sources, described in more detail in this paper" (dossier, September 24, 2002).
Ministers governing	provide . . .	policy advocacy.	"What I believe the assessed intelligence has established

TABLE 4.1   CONTINUED

Process	Function	Product	Iraq WMD examples
			beyond doubt is that Saddam has continued to produce chemical and biological weapons. . . . I am in no doubt that the threat is serious and current" (PM's foreword to dossier). "The intelligence picture . . . is extensive, detailed and authoritative" (PM, September 24, 2002).

CONCLUSION: KNOWLEDGE AND POWER REVISITED

The previous discussion has concentrated on the issue of how information was developed into intelligence and disseminated to politicians and whether or not they exaggerated this information in public presentations. This is a significant issue, but there is another approach to the intelligence-policy relationship. Authors differ on the extent to which ministers may become in thrall to secret intelligence. For example, Reginald Hibbert wrote of "a risk in ministers and leaders and top officials becoming absorbed into a culture of secrecy, a culture where secrecy comes to be confused with truth and where, after a time, contact is lost with earthly awkwardness."[44]

Yet, as Hibbert was writing, the events that gave rise to the Scott Inquiry into the sale of arms and equipment to Iraq were unfolding, and a series of ministers who were involved later told Scott just what notice they took of intelligence. David Mellor, a former Home and Foreign Office minister, recalled that intelligence reports did not contain "shattering information about who was doing what to whom. . . . They were significantly less riveting than the novels would have you believe. They weren't as interesting as the metal boxes marked, 'Eat after reading.'"[45]

In similar vein, former Foreign Secretary Geoffrey Howe recalled: "In my early days I was naïve enough to get excited about intelligence reports. Many look, at first sight, to be important and interesting and significant and then when we check them, they are not even straws in the wind. They are cornflakes in the wind."[46]

As we now know, in the case investigated by Scott, the intelligence on Iraq was being "spun down." Had policy *followed* the intelligence that Iraq was using machines imported from the UK for the production of arms, then government policy would have had to change, but ministers did not want to change that policy, and that may be at least part of the explanation of the dismissive comments above. By contrast, in 2002 the intelligence was being "spun up."[47]

However, as noted at the outset, power may determine knowledge as much as vice versa, and so we need to consider the possibility that the accuracy or otherwise of Western intelligence was actually unimportant. Most of the evidence for this possibility concerns the United States rather than the UK. The then Treasury secretary Paul O'Neill reported that the discussion of Iraq at the first National Security Council meeting of the new Bush administration—that is, before 9/11, was about finding a way to overthrow the regime, not about what the intelligence said.[48] Former counterterrorism coordinator Richard Clarke has testified regarding the White House attempt, in the immediate aftermath of 9/11, to pin the blame on Iraq.[49] If so, then why all the fuss about WMD? Former deputy secretary of defense Paul Wolfowitz said that this was for bureaucratic reasons: it was the one reason about which the U.S. cabinet could present a united front.[50] If the removal of Saddam Hussein was to be legitimate multilateral action, then it needed to be carried out under the auspices of the various UN resolutions passed since 1991. They did not refer to the awfulness of the regime or to its alleged links with al Qaeda; the ultimately unsuccessful quest for a specific UN resolution authorizing the invasion could be made only if grounded on WMD.

For his part, Blair insisted to Butler that his concern over the proliferation of WMD was growing, if anything, faster than in the Bush White House and that he had asked the new president about the issue in February 2001. Then "after September 11th it took on a completely different aspect. . . . [W]hat changed for me with September 11th was that I thought then you have to change your mindset. . . . [Y]ou have to go out and get after the different aspects of this threat. . . . [Y]ou have to say, 'Right, we are not going to allow the development of WMD

in breach of the will of the international community to continue'"
(par. 257).

This is not a mind-set that is likely to be receptive to intelligence
that raises doubts or asks questions, and Blair seems to have become
immersed in that culture identified by Hibbert where contact is lost
with "earthly awkwardness."[51] On this reading, the only role for intelligence was to provide support for a policy already determined—knowledge was simply to support power.

As doctrine shifts away from a defensive concept of security intelligence toward a more offensive, preemptive stance, there are major
implications for intelligence agencies, personnel, and their networks.
Intelligence has always had to struggle to be heard, especially if the
"knowledge" it offered was ambiguous or inconsistent with the policy
preferences of those in power. The latter are always more interested
in action and demand answers, not questions. Only the keenest professionalism and energetic oversight can prevent a more general shift
toward "national security" states, where intelligence becomes merely
the handmaiden of "hard" executive power rather than informing
wider debates as to the respective weights of "soft" and "hard" power.

Finally, after the events of the past two years, intelligence personnel
must sincerely wish that their work had not been deployed explicitly in
such a controversial cause, but it is hard to see how governments can
avoid similar exercises in the future. If so, Butler makes some worthy
suggestions as to how they might be improved (pars. 466–468) but
does not address the core of the problem—the assumed right of governments to mislead their publics in the name of national security.
This issue received a full airing before Scott's 1990s inquiry into arms
sales, when Robin Butler himself, then cabinet secretary, endorsed the
official view that ministers could give partial information to Parliament and public without misleading them: "Half the picture can be
true."[52] Yes, it can, but in the case of the Iraqi invasion, ministerial presentations amounted to clear distortion. People were misled, and the
credibility of intelligence, slowly emerging from the cold war cocoon
of secrecy, has been much damaged as a result.

NOTES

1. Controversy erupted in the United Kingdom at the end of May 2003 when
a BBC report accused the government of including material it knew to be wrong in

its September 2002 dossier on Iraqi WMD. The House of Commons Foreign Affairs Committee (hereafter FAC) conducted an immediate inquiry that reported a month later: *The Decision to Go to War in Iraq*, HC 813-I, 2003. The prime minister appointed the Intelligence and Security Committee (hereafter ISC) to investigate, and it reported in September: *Iraqi Weapons of Mass Destruction: Intelligence and Assessments*, Cm. 5972, 2003. When the apparent source of the BBC report committed suicide in July 2003, the prime minister appointed Lord Hutton (a House of Lords judge nearing retirement) to investigate; he reported in January 2004: *Report of the Inquiry into the Circumstances Surrounding the Death of Dr. David Kelly C.M.G*, HC 247. Hutton's report by no means quelled the controversy that had been growing for months with the failure to find WMD in Iraq. The prime minister appointed a group of privy councillors headed by Lord Butler to examine broader issues; their *Review of Intelligence on Weapons of Mass Destruction*, HC 898, was published on July 14, 2004.

2. Christopher Dandeker, *Surveillance, Power, and Modernity: Bureaucracy and Discipline from 1700 to the Present Day* (Cambridge, UK: Polity Press, 1990); Anthony Giddens, *The Nation State and Violence* (Berkeley and Los Angeles: University of California Press, 1985), 181–192; Michael Foucault, "Governmentality," in Graham Burchell, Colin Gordon, and Peter Miller, eds., *The Foucault Effect: Studies in Governmentality* (London: Harvester Wheatsheaf, 1991).

3. Burchell et al., *Foucault Effect*.

4. Adda Bozeman, "Knowledge and Comparative Method in Comparative Intelligence Studies," in Bozeman, *Strategic Intelligence and Statecraft* (Washington DC: Brassey's, 1992), 198–205.

5. David Lyon, *Surveillance Society* (Buckingham, UK: Open University Press, 2001), 103. Also see James Der Derian, *Antidiplomacy: Spies, Terror, Speed, and War* (Oxford: Blackwell, 1992), 46; Reg Whitaker, *The End Of Privacy: How Total Surveillance Is Becoming a Reality* (New York: New Press, 1999).

6. David Lyon, *Surveillance after September 11* (Cambridge, UK: Polity Press, 2003).

7. John Scott, *Power* (Cambridge, UK: Polity Press, 2001), 6–12. See also Stewart Clegg, *Frameworks of Power* (London: Sage, 1989).

8. For example, Foucault; see his "Governmentality." On Gramsci's concept of hegemony, see Quintin Hoare and Geoffrey Nowell Smith, trans. and eds., *Selections from the Prison Notebooks of Antonio Gramsci* (London: Lawrence and Wishart, 1971), 55–60; Steven Lukes, *Power* (Basingstoke, UK: Macmillan, 1974).

9. Hibbert, "Intelligence and Policy," 125–126.

10. Paragraph numbers in parentheses throughout the chapter refer to the so-called Butler Review, *Review of Intelligence on Weapons of Mass Destruction*, HC 898, July 14, 2004.

11. John Scarlett evidence to Hutton, August 26, 2003, secs. 92–96; http://www.the-hutton-inquiry.org.uk/.

12. Ibid., September 23, 2003, secs. 78–79.

13. ISC, *Annual Report for 2003–2004*, Cm. 6240, June 2004, par. 142.

14. ISC, *Inquiry into Intelligence, Assessments, and Advice Prior to the Terrorist Bombings on Bali 12 October 2002*, Cm. 5724, December 2002, pars. 18–21.

15. Ibid., par. 24.

16. Prime Minister, *Government Response to the Intelligence and Security Committee Inquiry into Intelligence, Assessments, and Advice Prior to the Terrorist Bombings on Bali 12 October 2002*, Cm. 5765, February 2003, par. 11.

17. Personal information.

18. ISC, *Annual Report 2003–2004*, pars. 92–99.

19. Inquiries such as this can never be sure they have seen all the documentation they should. This may be because they see only what they ask for; in other cases, not all of the relevant documents will be provided. For example, none of the other three UK inquiries has received everything: the Foreign Affairs Committee, as a select committee, saw only those papers that ministers saw fit to provide; the Intelligence and Security Committee thought they had seen all relevant JIC assessments but later discovered that they had not (*Annual Report 2003–2004*, n. 18, par. 145) and the Butler Inquiry reported that SIS decided in July 2003 that the source of the forty-five-minute claim could not be validated, though the head of SIS did not tell Lord Hutton this when he gave evidence in September 2003.

20. By comparison, during the same period the CIA had four human sources but on non-WMD topics. Senate Select Committee on Intelligence, *Report on the U.S. Intelligence Community's Prewar Intelligence Assessments on Iraq*, July 7, 2004, 260; Bob Woodward, *Plan of Attack* (New York: Simon and Schuster, 2004), 107.

21. The discussion in this section distinguishes analysis from assessment (see also Table 4.1), although the two may often be conflated in practice—for example, Butler, par. 33.

22. Michael Herman, "Intelligence and Policy: A Comment," *Intelligence and National Security* 6, no. 1 (January 1991): 235–237.

23. ISC, *Iraqi Weapons*.

24. "A Fight to the Death," *Panorama*, BBC1, January 21, 2004.

25. "A Failure of Intelligence," *Panorama*, BBC1, July 11, 2004.

26. Hutton Report, par. 228(7).

27. Ibid.

28. Richard Norton-Taylor, *Truth Is a Difficult Concept: Inside the Scott Inquiry* (London: Fourth Estate, 1995), 101. The origin of the quotation in the title of this section is Stella Rimington. When asked whether she would, as Security Service director general, have resisted Blair's request for a dossier, she replied: "I can't say, as I don't know the circumstances . . . but I expect I would have thought: no good will come of this" (Daily Telegraph, June 13, 2004).

29. Butler reports that by March 2002, the UK government was considering two options to achieve Iraqi disarmament: toughening the existing containment, or removing the regime by force (par. 429). Yet Blair told Butler how ridiculous it was that he was being questioned four to five months later about the prospects

for war, and he denied that the September dossier was intended to advocate any particular policy (par. 313). John Scarlett and Jack Straw gave Butler the same view that the object was to get people to take the issue seriously rather than advocate any specific policy (par. 325–326). These claims appear somewhat disingenuous, given that Blair's own foreword to the dossier stated his belief that one of the two options was no longer viable: "It is clear that, despite sanctions, the policy of containment has not worked sufficiently well to prevent Saddam from developing these weapons. I am in no doubt that the threat is serious and current, that he has made progress on WMD, and that he has to be stopped" (*Iraq's Weapons of Mass Destruction: The Assessment of the British Government*, September 24, 2002, http://www.number10.gov.uk/output/Page271.asp).

30. The earlier drafts of the dossier were entitled *Iraq's Programme for WMD*. The various drafts are in the appendices to the Hutton Report and can be read at http://www.the-hutton-inquiry.org.uk/content/report/index.htm.

31. Available at http://www.number-10.gov.uk/output/page1470.asp.

32. Mainly from Ibrahim al-Marashi, "Iraq's Security and Intelligence Network: A Guide and Analysis," *Middle East Review of International Affairs* (September 2002).

33. ISC, *Iraqi Weapons*, pars. 129–135.

34. Reprinted in Hutton Report, n. 2, par. 193. John Morrison, former DIS, spoke of how unusual it would be for someone of Brian Jones's seniority to protest in writing over such an issue in "A Failure of Intelligence," *Panorama*, July 11, 2004.

35. *Iraq's Weapons of Mass Destruction*, n. 33, par. 5.

36. *House of Commons Debates*, September 24, 2002, col. 3.

37. ISC, *Iraqi Weapons*, par. 86.

38. Prime Minister, *Government Response to the ISC Report on Iraqi Weapons of Mass Destruction: Intelligence and Assessments 11 September 2003*, Cm. 6118, February 2004, par. 15.

39. ISC, *Annual Report*, par. 87.

40. Intelligence material had been used before—in October 2001, prior to the Afghanistan invasion, for example—but it did not explicitly acknowledge JIC authorship.

41. See box in Butler, p. 81.

42. *Daily Telegraph*, October 22, 2004.

43. Since the writing of this chapter was completed, this conclusion has been reinforced by further evidence that Blair told Bush in March 2002 that he would support military action to change the Iraqi regime. Also, from summer 2002 onward, bombing of Iraq was increased steadily in the hope of provoking Saddam Hussein into some action that would provide a pretext for war. M. Smith, "Blair Hit by New Lead of Secret War Plan," *Sunday Times*, May 1, 2005; M. Danner, "The Secret Way to War," *New York Review of Books*, June 9, 2005, 70–74. Relevant documents are accessible at http://www.downingstreetmemo.com.

44. Hibbert, "Intelligence and Policy," 125.

45. Cited in Norton-Taylor, *Truth*, 99.

46. Cited in ibid., 99–100.

47. Mark Phythian, "Hutton and Scott: A Tale of Two Inquiries," *Parliamentary Affairs* 58, no. 1 (2005): 124–137.

48. Richard W. Stevenson, "Bush Sought to Oust Hussein from Start, Ex-Official Says," *New York Times*, January 12, 2004.

49. Richard Clarke, *Against All Enemies* (New York: Simon and Schuster, 2004).

50. Todd S. Purdum, *A Time of Our Choosing: America's War in Iraq* (New York: Times Books, Henry Holt and Co., 2003), 261–262.

51. Hibbert, "Intelligence and Policy," 125.

52. Cited in Norton-Taylor, *Truth*, 91.

FIVE

CULTURAL LEGACIES OF
FRENCH INTELLIGENCE

Douglas Porch

Many countries have ambiguous relations with their intelligence services. Even mature democracies find intelligence-state relations to be subjects of some delicacy. Given a history of war, invasion, empire, and on occasion a shaky but ultimately triumphant tradition of republican control of the military, one might logically conclude that, of all countries, intelligence should play a critical, central role for France. But while that role has been central, it has seldom been critical. Why is this so? In France, as elsewhere, part of the explanation lies in bureaucratic mechanisms that translate to a lack of systematic evaluation of intelligence. However, beyond these often personality-driven bureaucratic interactions that impact intelligence-state relations, in France a special intelligence culture has developed from the stormy historical relationship between government and intelligence agencies. To paraphrase Tolstoy's famous observation about families—successful intelligence services resemble each other in that they have managed to master the basics of collection and analysis and their product is trusted by the decision maker. Unhappy intelligence services, however, are all unhappy in their own way. In the French case, it is because a special culture of state-intelligence relations has developed that has caused a particularly dysfunctional relationship to develop between intelligence services and decision makers.

Before sketching a catalog of French intelligence failures, it is perhaps proper to begin by noting French intelligence successes, of which there are at least three. First, in the realm of code breaking, the French services excelled through the First World War. Unfortunately, they failed to keep pace in the era of the mechanical cipher. Nevertheless, French counterintelligence at least played midwife to the cracking of the enigma codes in the 1930s, a second accomplishment, by acquiring the codebooks from a German spy named Hans Thilo Schmidt, and passing them on to Polish code breakers in Warsaw.[1] And even though most French intelligence operatives remained loyal to the Vichy regime between 1940 and 1943, they never revealed to the Germans that the Allies possessed replicas of enigma. Third, the Direction de la Surveillance du Territoire (DST), the equivalent of the British Security Service (MI5), although small, is considered an extremely professional organization.

With that said, all intelligence services operate on two basic levels — collection and analysis. Intelligence is then "packaged" in some form or another for the decision maker, who decides to act, or not, upon the information provided. The French are probably as proficient as most services in collecting and analyzing information, within the limitations imposed by size and lack of technological support; however decision makers' ability to "accept" intelligence is unique to the French case.

Still, analyzing "what did the 'decider' know and when did he know it?" is largely guesswork because it is complicated by a sixty-year restriction of access to intelligence documents. Minutes of cabinet and military staff meetings are fragmentary when they exist at all. French intelligence documents for the 1930s, captured by the Germans, eventually ended up in Moscow and are only gradually being repatriated to Paris. The preference of French politicians for back-channel information, sometimes supplied by private intelligence sources, precisely because they often distrusted official ones, makes information difficult to track. Intelligence bulletins are decidedly unhelpful, because they usually adopt a smorgasbord approach, simply listing snippets of information without prioritizing them. This allows decision makers to select intelligence that accords with their preferred course of action, while giving intelligence services the "out" that they had indicated the risks should the strategy prove disastrous — as in 1940.

The question of "what did the decision maker know and when did he know it?" is also complicated by the tendency of many ex-professionals to rush into print as soon as they reach retirement age. At their best, these memoirs offer interesting glimpses into the workings of French intelligence services and compensate up to a point for the absence of archives.[2] Their strength is that they portray the French secret services, in particular military intelligence, as relatively efficient organizations that managed to gather much useful intelligence on German capabilities in the 1930s. Unfortunately, they ignore the complex relationship—one might say complicity—that exists between intelligence specialists and decision makers. They also make sweeping claims for the strategic as well as the operational value of the intelligence that they produced, claims that are unverifiable and, one suspects, exaggerated. Their memoirs too often portray themselves as Cassandras, intelligence professionals in possession of "truth," ignored or deemed inaccurate by "defeatist" politicians unwilling to take action, or ignored by generals who "mirror image"—dismissing assertions that the Germans were planning to use maneuver warfare in the wooded hills of the Ardennes, because the French generals, who had only reluctantly created armored divisions before 1940, thought the tactic impossible.[3]

Given the turbulent history of modern French politics, it is hardly surprising that many of these ex-professionals have political axes to grind. The underlying theme of the World War II generation of writers, many of whom continued to serve Vichy after 1940 and who paid the price when Charles de Gaulle took power in 1944, is that France had an excellent intelligence organization that was ignored by defeatist Republicans before 1940 and then disorganized and politicized by the Gaullists. Post-1945 French political turbulence has kept this theme a vibrant one in the works of intelligence professionals, who argue that the hostility, indifference, and interference of politicians have kept the French secret services disorganized, abused, and inefficient.[4] Like every myth, this one has a foundation in reality. But intelligence-state relations are an interactive process. Why are they so poor in France? What does this tell us about the intelligence culture there? Might the intelligence services bear some responsibility for this state of affairs? In fact, French politicians have had every reason to be distrustful of their intelligence services since the Dreyfus Affair at the turn of the last century threw French politics into such turmoil. Continued scandals and "dirty tricks" with their origins deep in secret service machinations have meant that French politicians have preferred to keep their secret services at arm's length, open to political patronage, and inefficient because they do not want them to become too powerful. The downside is that the intelligence services are left in a poor position to inform policy.

A final group of writers on intelligence is made up of investigative journalists who, while often well informed, tend to oscillate between two extremes: either the work of the French services amount to little more than the pathetic intrigues of marginal functionaries, or they represent the tip of a vast and powerful conspiracy against the state. The role of spies is given dramatic and exaggerated prominence, and the deeds spun out in cloak-and-dagger fashion.[5] There is little understanding of the political and bureaucratic context in which intelligence services labor, or appreciation of the human factors that limit the impact of information on the decision-making process. In short, their works are often stories told out of context and thus leave the reader to ask why this spy or the network of agents was important. How was the information they gathered used? Did they affect the course of events in any way?

This survey of existing literature suggests that there is room for a study of French intelligence that attempts to resolve some basic questions about its role in France. After all, as a nation living in the shadow of a more powerful neighbor, Germany, intelligence should have supplied an important warning system for France. Was it important? If not, why? What have been the strengths and weaknesses of French intelligence? How did the secret services operate within the context of French political culture? While attempting to answer those questions, my research has integrated approaches developed by scholars of intelligence like Michael Handel, Richard Betts, Roberta Wohlstetter, and John Ferris, who have made important theoretical points about the relationship of intelligence organizations to the decision-making process.[6]

FRENCH INTELLIGENCE SERVICES AND THEIR OVERSIGHT

Before continuing on with this review of French intelligence culture, it is worthwhile to briefly discuss the French intelligence agencies and the very limited oversight that exists within France. The primary French intelligence agencies and a brief description of their missions are as follows:

The Direction Générale de la Sécurité Extérieure (General Directorate for External Security, or DGSE) is responsible for strategic and military intelligence related to external defense and counterintelligence outside of French borders. Its missions include collection and analysis of strategic and technical intelligence and the conduct of covert operations. Its predecessors were the Bureau Central de Renseignement et d'Action (Bureau of Information and Action, known by its French acronym, BCRA) and the External Documentation and

Counterespionage Service (in French, the Service de Documentation Extérieure et du Contre-espionnage, SDECE).

The Direction du Renseignement Militaire (Directorate of Military Intelligence, or DRM) is technically responsible for tactical and operational military intelligence matters but also plays a role in strategic intelligence. Its assets are all military, and there is no covert branch of the DRM.

The Direction de la Protection et de la Sécurite de la Défense (Directorate for Defense Protection and Security, DPSD) is responsible for military counterintelligence operations and information security, as well as political surveillance of the military.

The Direction Centrale Renseignement Généraux (General Information Service, or RG) is an internal security organization with broad working arrangements with the national police. It is primarily responsible for internal intelligence, anything having to do with race issues, and runs human intelligence (HUMINT) sources.

The Direction de la Surveillance du Territoire (Directorate of Territorial Surveillance, or DST) is responsible for internal intelligence and focuses on counterterrorism, counterintelligence, and protecting France's economic and scientific infrastructure.

Oversight and Control

The DGSE, DRM, and DPSD report to the president and prime minister but are directly administered by the Ministry of Defense, which also maintains smaller signal intelligence (SIGINT) and information security intelligence organizations. Both the RG and the DST work for the Ministry of the Interior. There is no system in place for parliamentary oversight,[7] and each intelligence organization acts independently of any coordinating authority, problems which will be highlighted throughout the remainder of the chapter. Interestingly, France does make public the top-line budgets of their intelligence organizations.

THE CHARACTER OF THE FRENCH SECRET SERVICES

The problem of intelligence services generally is that, though founded to reduce uncertainty, either they fail to do this or they often may increase it. In this respect, the French services have conformed to the bureaucratic norm. That said, the generic problems that afflict all intelligence services have been accentuated in France for at least five reasons. First, French intelligence has been influenced, one might even say deformed, by the fact that it has historically served a national policy whose ambitions have outdistanced the capabilities of French diplomacy or military force. Second, France has a history of poor state-intelligence relations going back to the Dreyfus Affair. Third, France is the only major democracy whose foreign intelligence community is primarily dominated by the military. This has complicated attitudes toward intelligence, especially on the left, where distrust of the army has been endemic throughout the twentieth century. Fourth, the French Resistance bequeathed the legacy of a strong "action" culture in the post–World War II era, a culture reinforced by long experience in colonial wars and, as will be argued, by the limitations of French power alluded to in point one above. And finally, French intelligence departs from the "Anglo-Saxon" norm because domestic or counterintelligence is more highly valued than external intelligence within the French political culture. This is because France has a very precise vision of its national identity based on cultural and linguistic integrity of the nation. Any threat to the homogeneity of the community is perceived as a national security issue. Let us examine each of these points in more detail.

The Influence of French Intelligence on Policy

A primary handicap of French intelligence is that it serves a political system whose policymakers and strategists set idiosyncratic, even irrational, priorities beyond France's powers to achieve. Because it was a relatively weak power, intelligence, especially accurate intelligence, was especially vital to France. France required an organization that could serve as a warning—administer a reality check on policymakers, remind military strategists that military plans had to be tailored to the capabilities of French forces. Of course, it was not entirely France's fault that it often has been tempted to overreach itself—one of France's dilemmas since 1871 is that it dwells in the shadow of a powerful Germany. That said, however, many of France's foreign policy problems have been self-inflicted. France has been preoccupied, even obsessed, by its role as a world leader. From 1945 to 1962, it fought a series of bloody wars to retain its colonial empire. And even since 1962, Paris has invested considerable resources to protect "La Francophonie" in

Africa and Quebec. This attempt to exert French global leadership reached astonishing proportions under Charles de Gaulle in the 1960s, when the French president spurned NATO in 1966 and led his country on an ultimately sterile quest to rally Europe beneath the banner of French leadership to throw off what he saw as the tyranny of U.S. influence.

The problem of how an intelligence service informs a government whose foreign policy and strategy are beyond its means is not at all confined to France. The dilemma for all intelligence services is to survive as a viable bureaucracy while preserving the integrity of their product, balancing *veritas* with survival, influence, and the allocation of resources. The general solution is to "go with the flow," to supply intelligence that reflects the assumptions of the policymakers rather than try to challenge them. The contentions of Colonel Paul Paillole to the contrary, to judge by the *bulletins de renseignements*, it appears that the pre-1940 Deuxième Bureau did just that, spreading the information before the decision makers and allowing them to choose that which best accorded with their assumptions and preferred course of action. If the decision maker makes the wrong decision, then the intelligence service can always point out that the "correct" intelligence was supplied, had the decision maker cared to take note of it. The risk, as Richard Betts and Michael Handel have pointed out, is that while the intelligence service may survive, the nation may perish because intelligence becomes irrelevant and strategic surprise almost inevitable. This is clearly the case in 1914 when the breadth and power of the Schlieffen Plan caught the French commander in chief General Joseph Joffre by surprise. Likewise, in 1940, General Maurice Gamelin's Dyle-Breda Plan was shattered by an unexpected German attack through the Ardennes.

How does this theory apply in the French case? The problem for French intelligence was not that the decision makers whom they served willfully ignored their reports charting the strength of the German armed forces. *Au contraire*, French generals were very well informed of the realities of German power before both world wars. The question is, what influence did this intelligence have on policy and strategy? The problem for France was that intelligence became a threat, because it confronted France with the realities of its own weakness. For this reason, intelligence invited despair and demoralization. Bombarded by gloomy reports on German capabilities, French leaders began to think in terms of the worst-case scenario. Despite good intelligence—

indeed, because of good intelligence—in both 1914 and 1940, French commanders displayed an infallible ability to overreach themselves. The problem was psychological. They appeared to have become demoralized by the disparity of the odds against them, to have lost touch with reality, to have been driven to the desperate extremity of a *fuite en avant*—offensives, forward movements, preemptive actions—which set them up for a counterpunch.

In 1914 Joffre knew that the Germans would attack France through Belgium—that much of his intelligence, at least, was accurate. However, the Deuxième Bureau failed to inform him that the younger Moltke planned to integrate reservists into his front-line divisions, therefore extending the Schlieffen Plan west of the Meuse. But would it have made any difference if the Deuxième Bureau had dropped a copy of the Schlieffen Plan on Joffre's desk? Probably not. Why? Because the disparity of the balance of power made intelligence "a threat" to Joffre. It was not that intelligence was ignored. It was simply that for Joffre, an offensive strategy became a form of psychological defense against the reality of the overwhelming nature of German military power. Because Joffre planned to attack, he paid scant attention to the intentions of the enemy. The irony was that the exact same reaction was happening on the other side, where the German General Staff had concluded that a dramatic action was required to break out of their "encirclement." The result was that Plan XVII and the Schlieffen Plan mirrored each other, for each grafted a worst-case strategic scenario onto best-case operational assumptions.

A similar mentality ruled French leaders before 1940. Colonel Paillole is correct when he argues that, in the 1930s, the Service de Renseignements supplied generally reliable intelligence on the growing German might. He maintains that French military intelligence believed the implications of this information on policy should have been to preempt Hitler before German forces became too powerful. However, the result of this intelligence was the opposite—it simply confirmed for politicians like Edouard Daladier the wisdom of a policy of appeasement. But while the government adopted a cautious policy, intelligence helped to persuade Gamelin to adopt a military strategy that bore great risks. The French commander decided that his best option in the face of superior German strength was to gain a line as far forward as possible in Belgium and Holland in 1940. This caused him to squander his strategic reserve and opened him to the counterthrust of the Manstein Plan. Paillole claims to have reaped the most promising indication of German intentions when in April 1940 he received one of his double agents, a Polish ex-priest named Paul Schlokoff, who told him that he had been ordered by the Abwehr to reconnoiter the roads and bridges between the Ardennes and the mouth of the Somme. However, when Paillole conveyed information to the commander of the Northwest Theater, General Alphonse Georges, he was told that this contradicted information that predicted an attack farther north. He was thanked for his information and shown the door.[8] Paillole's contention to the contrary, there is no archival evidence that French intelligence ever penetrated the Manstein Plan, any more than they had that of Schlieffen. These must count as critical failures of French intelligence.[9]

Then again, what if the Deuxième Bureau had found out these German plans? Would Gamelin have altered his strategy, any more than had Joffre? Probably not, for the reason mentioned above. The realities of French weakness seemed to necessitate in the minds of the nation's leaders an offensive strategy. But there were also political and bureaucratic reasons for Gamelin's resistance to change. A defensive strategy would have turned France, rather than Belgium, into the battlefield, which would have been an unacceptable option in the light of the traumatic experience of World War I. Had this been discovered, Gamelin's position of commander in chief, in jeopardy especially after March 1940 when Paul Reynaud replaced Gamelin's patron Daladier as prime minister, would have been further undermined. In the army, Gamelin ruled with something less than complete authority. The commander in chief in the French Army was more like a committee chairman than a ruler whose every order was obeyed without question. Most of his subordinate commanders disagreed with his Dyle-Breda Plan, so that any attempt to reverse himself, any show of hesitation or self-doubt, would have eroded his already shaky authority.

The inclination of French commanders to overreach themselves was again apparent at Dien Bien Phu in 1953–1954. After the battle, the French commander in chief in Indochina, General Henri Navarre, blamed French intelligence for his defeat, complaining that his Deuxième Bureau failed to warn him of Vietminh capabilities. However, Deuxième Bureau documents demonstrate beyond a doubt that Navarre was extremely well informed on Vietminh capabilities.[10] As was the case with Joffre and Gamelin, it was not the role of the Deuxième Bureau to talk Navarre out of a particular course of action. The staff simply presented the evidence. It is up to leaders to know the limits of intelligence, as well as the capabilities of their own forces. In other words, net assessment is not a job for intelligence alone. At this point, it is leaders' judgment that comes into play. The irony in Navarre's case is that he rejected his own strategy, the so-called Navarre Plan devised with the Americans in the summer of 1953, which called for the French to adopt a defensive posture based in the Tonkin Delta. He had adopted this plan precisely because the Vietminh, with substantial Chinese aid, had grown in strength in the north to the point that offensive operations against them were no longer considered profitable. Like his predecessors Joffre and Gamelin, Navarre appears to have become unhinged by the increasing power of his adversary. He concluded that a defensive posture was a strategy for defeat in the long term and adopted a strategy anchored in the wishful thinking that a dramatic initiative would somehow confound the plans of his Vietminh adversaries.

Charles de Gaulle must also shoulder a great share of the blame for the distortions in the relationship between intelligence and decision making that exists in France. De Gaulle sought to compensate for French weakness through diplomatic surprise and policy offensives aimed to bolster French prestige and influence. Any intelligence organization that tried to challenge that vision based on more realistic assessments of French capabilities and interests would be reduced to irrelevance and conveniently ignored. Therefore the role of intelligence in de Gaulle's mind was to support his policy of choice, not to provide information that might challenge it. De Gaulle's attitude that intelligence was the servant, not the partner, of policy was apparent in World War II. From June 1940, the task of the Bureau Central du Renseignement et d'Action, the Free French intelligence service organized under André Dewavrin (known as Colonel Passy), was tactical: organize the Resistance into a political force to support de Gaulle and derail American plans to impose a military government on liberated France. The emphasis was on covert operations, not analysis. In the 1950s, de Gaulle utilized segments of the intelligence services, in particular the 11ème choc and its network of reservists, as the nucleus of a Gaullist political party. In the 1960s the general sought to carve out an arena of influence independent of the two power blocs. The SDECE was thrust into the task of fighting the Organisation Armée Secrète (OAS), securing French control over the liberated African colonies, and subsidizing Quebec separatism. A primary consequence was that the politicization of the French services, especially SDECE, a trend apparent since the

1920s, was accentuated. Rather than a relatively neutral service dedicated to informing a fixed vision of French national interests, French intelligence was subsumed into serving the interests of the hegemonic party, that is, the Gaullists. A second tendency accentuated in the first decade of the Fifth Republic (1958–present) was that the traditional tasks of intelligence services—the collection and analysis of information, providing of estimates, and so on—continued to cede primacy of place to a muscular form of counterintelligence and covert action, which still permeate French intelligence culture.

Intelligence-State Relations in France

The politicization of the French services highlights the second problem of French intelligence—a poor history of state-intelligence relations. The pattern of politicization of the French services offers an example of how France differs from the "Anglo-Saxon" paradigm. In Great Britain and the United States, for example, intelligence becomes "politicized" when the services tell the leaders what they want to hear. While this certainly happens in France, the real difference is that the French services have been politicized from within, in that sections of the intelligence service have at various times become part of the political process.

The distrust of French intelligence dates from the end of the nineteenth century, when the French political system was cast into turmoil by the conviction in 1894 of artillery captain Alfred Dreyfus for espionage on charges brought by the French Army's statistical section.[11] The trend of the politicization of French intelligence services accelerated in the interwar years, when they defined themselves as resolutely anticommunist and anti-German. Such a position made loyalty to Vichy the natural response of the intelligence services, to the point that de Gaulle had to create the BCRA from scratch. In the post–World War II years, the French services found it difficult to maintain their professional detachment. The turbulence and fragmentation of power of the Fourth Republic (1944-1958)—caused by a weak executive and a multiparty system, and a political system and culture divided and churned by political scandal—was a challenge to all government agencies. But these relied on a tradition of administrative autonomy in the middle ranks, reinforced by the quasi monopoly of the upper echelons of bureaucratic posts claimed by graduates of the Ecole Nationale d'Administration.

The tradition of a stable civil service developed over two centuries when French political regimes changed often but the continuity of the "state" was guaranteed by the administration. It also remained weak in the secret services, where, with few exceptions, the upper echelons have been reserved in the postwar years for veterans of the Resistance and eventually policemen, generals, and admirals with political connections. Of course, administrative turnover at the top can afflict all intelligence services. The difference in France is the context in which this has taken place, for there are simply fewer checks and balances applied on the secret services by the democratic process in France than in other mature democracies. First, naked careerism, especially apparent in sections of the police and the army, remains untempered in France by an "Anglo-Saxon" sense of reserve. This might mean that ethical or institutional restraints are less likely to be placed on more ambitious, less scrupulous elements in the secret services. An attitude of careerism based on political expediency at the top can communicate itself to the middle ranks. Second, counterintelligence especially fell prisoner to a police culture that combined lower-middle-class recruitment with an administrative attitude that the police could put themselves above the law to save the French people—undisciplined, recalcitrant, volatile—from themselves. Third, a tradition of parliamentary oversight has been weak, allegedly because of large numbers of communist deputies in the legislative chambers. Finally, one must count the covert operations tradition that French intelligence inherited from the Resistance years, one developed and extended in the post-1945 colonial wars.

When this culture of careerism and political expediency, a traditional lack of policy accountability, and covert action meets a no-holds-barred French political culture in which politicians are not above using intelligence to advance their personal agendas, then the boundaries between intelligence and politics become blurred, and the services enter the political arena, either on their own initiative or enticed by politicians. Virtually every serving president of the Fifth Republic was the target of a scandal or "dirty trick" with origins deep in secret service conspiracies: de Gaulle in the Passy affair and later during the Ben Barka kidnapping;[12] François Mitterrand in the *affaire des fuites* (aka Elysée-gate);[13] Georges Pompidou in the Marcovic episode;[14] and Giscard d'Estaing in the scandal of the Bokassa diamonds.[15] Jacques Chirac stayed well away from the Gaullist Service d'Action Civique (SAC), responsible for intelligence and dirty tricks, though he was very close to one of its main organizers, former interior minister Charles Pasqua. And while Chirac has not appeared to use the intelligence services for political gain within France, his continued use of them for economic espionage has riled "allies" like the United States, Great Britain, and Germany and may have contributed to the now infamous papers from Niger that supposedly confirmed the presence of an active nuclear weapons program in Iraq prior to the 2003 invasion.[16]

After 1958, the idea of the services as an autonomous, neutral bureaucracy eroded further, as it endured almost a quarter century of service under conservative governments that valued loyalty above truth or efficiency. In these years, it became difficult to trace the boundary between intelligence and policy, as intelligence was used in a tactical and operational role, rather than a policymaking one.

For French intelligence there have been three consequences of this history of poor civil-intelligence relations in France. First, because French leaders fear that their position will be diminished, even sabotaged, by intelligence functionaries, they place little faith in their services. This increases the tendency to ignore intelligence that runs counter to preconceptions or deflates wishful thinking regarding France's power. Indeed, President Mitterrand, who soon after taking office in 1981 denounced the SDECE as a "costly farce" whose sole purpose was to serve as a vehicle for the intrusion of American influence into French politics, was so distrustful of his intelligence services that he suspected that the Farewell Dossier—evidence produced by French intelligence that the Soviets were carrying out extensive spying in France—was a plant to destabilize his government.[17]

Second, French leaders prefer loyal, inefficient, or parallel services. Back-channel intelligence is a feature of many political systems and certainly existed in the Third Republic (1870–1940). But under the Fifth Republic, it became institutionalized when de Gaulle turned to Jacques Foccart and the SAC, a Gaullist "special action" organization, to supply "intelligence" and especially to keep the liberated African colonies in line.[18] Mitterrand, whose distrust of his intelligence services at times bordered on paranoia, continued this tradition through the so-called Elysée cell under gendarme Christian Prouteau. This caused intelligence professionals, especially in the SDECE (whose name was changed in 1982 to the Direction Générale de la Sécurité Extérieure), to become demoralized because their product was ignored, they lacked influence, and their services risked being dragged, willingly or not, into the squabbles of French politics. The abuse of intelligence to serve political ends was yet again demonstrated in February 1995, when Interior Minister Charles Pasqua leaked reports alleging widespread CIA spying in France. His transparent purpose was to distract attention from a scandal involving illegal telephone taps that he had authorized.[19] The result, however, was to continue the vicious circle of distrustful civil-intelligence relations. Given French political culture, this pattern will be difficult to break.

A third consequence for French intelligence is a convoluted structure, parts of which are inefficient and even unaccountable. French intelligence is fragmented and enclosed within narrow orbits of different services or parts of services. This results in a certain duplication of effort. But worse, there is not a structure that encourages healthy debates among alternatives, and no system of competitive intelligence serves as a check on interpretations or madcap schemes, like that to sink the Greenpeace ship *Rainbow Warrior* in July 1985. Instead, the president listens—or not, as the case may be—to his parallel service. In this way, he can always find the information that supports his preferred course of action. The prime minister, when he is not left out of the loop altogether, as appears to have been the case with Laurent Fabius during the *Rainbow Warrior* episode, listens to another. The defense minister controls foreign intelligence and other, purely military intelligence organizations. The interior minister commands the DST and the Renseignements Généraux, another domestic intelligence service that keeps voluminous files on citizens and carries out polls for the government. Even the prefect of Paris has his own intelligence service, Renseignements Généraux de la Préfecture de Police de Paris (RGPP), which duplicates the functions of the RG in the Paris region.

The rivalries among these services for resources and influence are intense. This encourages further fragmentation, duplication of effort, distrust of rival services, fear of leaks, secretiveness, and compartmentalization. Decisions are made not on the basis of a balanced assessment of intelligence data but on a very limited spectrum of information. The *Rainbow Warrior* episode is a good example of a decision made within a very narrow circle of the DGSE, the defense ministry, and probably the military adviser at the Elysée Palace. Because there is no organization to coordinate the French services, which therefore do not communicate among themselves, there is no mechanism to control harebrained schemes.

Civil-Military Relations in French Intelligence

A third characteristic of French intelligence that departs from the ideal type of an independent civilian agency standing outside of policy is that, in France, foreign intelligence is the preserve of the military. This arrangement has exacerbated poor civil-intelligence relations. Because the army occupies a controversial place in the political history of France, the ambiguous nature of civil-military relations is reflected in civil-intelligence relations. What this also means is that intelligence is one of the players in the process. This contributes to two of the most serious problems that have afflicted French foreign intelligence—poor quality analysis and the difficulties of acceptance by policymakers.

Poor analysis is a criticism of all intelligence services to a greater or lesser degree. The difficulties of persuading leaders to trust intelligence and integrate it into the decision-making process are also common to all countries. However, these problems for France are accentuated by the military character of its foreign intelligence. Military values, which emphasize loyalty and obedience, adapt badly to an intelligence culture, which requires independence of mind, skepticism, and pursuit of "truth." Unless there is an ethos within the military that encourages such thinking, military analysts are less likely to supply information that challenges command perceptions. And there is no such ethos in France. Intelligence is neither a separate branch of service nor a good career path in the French armed forces. Officers, chosen by cooption, appear for short tours. When they return to their original arm of service for the "command time" necessary for promotion, they find that they are given the least attractive assignments. Therefore the most ambitious and dynamic officers see no future in intelligence, which too often abandons the ranks of middle management—the analysts— to officers looking for sinecures in Paris.

Finally, the fact that foreign intelligence is controlled by the armed forces, which are definitely viewed as on the right of the political spectrum, has not always increased its credibility with decision makers, especially those on the left, whose historical memory of civil-military conflict is long: the brutal suppression of the Paris Commune of 1871; the Dreyfus Affair (1894–1906); the tremendous bloodletting of 1914 to 1918, which many blamed on the profligacy with which career soldiers expended the life of the nation to advance their careers; the mutual recriminations between soldiers and left-wing republicans following the fall of France in 1940; the quasi-unanimous military support for the collaborationist Vichy government between 1940 and 1944; and finally, the military coups of 1958 and 1961 during the Algerian War.

In other countries, a situation in which foreign intelligence had been monopolized by an institution with such a contested political record would be ripe for reform. The sad truth for France is that this has been very difficult to do. The Socialist president Mitterrand began to place policemen from the DST in top positions of the DGSE in 1989. But this attempt to "civilianize" foreign intelligence was reversed by the right-wing parliamentary victory of March 1993. Conservative politicians supported French generals who insisted that the DGSE was "their" service. The Right made continued military control of the DGSE a political issue, sent the civilian leadership packing, and restored military control over foreign intelligence, naming Jacques Dewatre, a former military officer acceptable to the French generals, as director in 1993. Since Dewatre's departure in 1999, however, civilians have been in control of the agency, with two career diplomats, Jean-Claude Cousseran (1999–2002) and Pierre Brochand (July 2002 to the present), serving as DGSE director. Reportedly, both have worked to lessen the impact of the military within the intelligence agency. Still, military culture pervades the DGSE, which virtually guarantees that the agency will continue to occupy a marginal place in the French political process.

The "Action Culture" of French Intelligence

A fourth characteristic of French intelligence has been the persistence of a strong "action," or covert operations, culture. This, like other characteristics, is not specific to France. The difference has been, however, that it is more under control in other countries. Intelligence services of several countries emerged from World War II with a strong commitment to covert operations and clandestine warfare. The commitment has persisted longer in the SDECE/DGSE and has had more significant consequences there for three reasons. First is the heritage of the French Resistance, which is especially potent in France. That the French played a significant role in their own liberation through intelligence collection, sabotage, and guerrilla actions against the German occupiers became a "necessary myth" in postwar France. The memory of Resistance became a psychological crutch that helped France limp beyond the humiliation of 1940, the event that announced France's fall from world power status. The Resistance had saved both France's honor and her soul. It was the foundation of Charles de Gaulle's claim to be the legitimate ruler of France in 1944 and served subsequently as the moral foundation for a Gaullist attitude of independence vis-à-vis France's wartime allies. For political reasons, then, it has been very difficult to question the value of the Resistance, especially if some historians might conclude that it had been ineffective, profligate with lives to little purpose, and ultimately had contributed little to France's own liberation. Furthermore, an active Resistance record became the *sine qua non* for a successful political and administrative career in post–World War II France.[20]

The value of "action" and special operations became a dogma that many officers, ex-*maquisards* of the Resistance, carried with them into the colonial conflicts of Indochina and Algeria. In both wars, much of French strategy was determined by the requirements of special operations. "Action" became an operational substitute in the absence of viable policy or coherent strategy. Not surprisingly, these veterans of the Resistance sought to duplicate the Resistance experience by raising native *maquis* "behind enemy lines." This caused no end of problems in both Indochina and Algeria. It is now clear from Deuxième Bureau documents that Dien Bien Phu was initiated to rescue a montagnard maquis run by the Groupes des Commandos Mixtes Aéroportées (GCMA), the army's special operations section, under threat of Vietminh extinction.[21] Also, attempts to disrupt the National Liberation Front–National Liberation Army (FLN-ALN) in Algeria by subsidizing armed groups that were meant to challenge the insurgents in the countryside often proved more trouble than they were worth, either because the groups were infiltrated and "turned" by the FLN or because they degenerated into bandit gangs who did not serve the ends of French strategy, which required French military intervention to suppress them. The kidnapping by the Deuxième Bureau of Ahmed Ben Bella, one of the FLN's *neuf historique* leaders, in 1956 probably did more to undermine France's diplomatic position than any other single act in the war, other than the attack on Suez in that year.[22] In short, "action" in both wars offers examples where the tail wagged the dog, where operations became a substitute for strategy.

While an exaggerated preference for "action" also characterized the CIA in the 1950s and 1960s until curtailed by the Church Committee, its persistence in France is a sign of the lack of maturity of French intelligence culture. This is true because of factors already mentioned: the military domination of SDECE/DGSE; the persistence of thinking in the short term; and the fact that France has traditionally sought to play a role beyond its powers. Here again, as in the case of Joffre and Gamelin, soldiers are more likely to look for panaceas and simplistic solutions, especially to persistent strategic or political problems. In this respect, the reliance on "action" bears a resemblance to 1914, when French officers grasped at the doctrine of the offensive as a way out of what appeared to be an intractable strategic dilemma.

Likewise, the *Rainbow Warrior* episode demonstrates the dangers of seeking a "quick fix," special operations solution to persistent strategic problems that France is powerless to influence by more conventional diplomatic or military means. Like Dien Bien Phu, the decision to blow up the *Rainbow Warrior* in Auckland Harbor, New Zealand, offers a striking example of how intelligence and special operations can court disaster when fed into a nonrational political process.[23] And when this happens, the intelligence services invite derision, which lowers morale and prestige and harms civil-intelligence relations.

A final problem is that "action" translates very much into "special operations" rather than "covert operations." So long as the military retains control of the foreign intelligence service, this is unlikely to change. This is especially the case in France because "action" has strong support on the Right. In the 1950s, the special operations unit of SDECE, the *11ème choc*, became a gathering place for many Gaullist sympathizers with strong links to the Gaullist SAC. The SAC and its action veterans served as a power base for Jacques Foccart, who used intelligence and special operations networks to establish French influence in the former French colonies of sub-Saharan Africa.[24] This has meant that French "covert" operations adopt a very muscular approach, lack subtlety, and call attention to themselves. For instance, in November 1983, the "action" section of the DGSE parked a jeep loaded with explosives outside the Iranian embassy in Beirut in retaliation for the attack on the French barracks there, which killed fifty-eight French paratroopers. In the incident, the detonators failed to work, and the Iranians had no trouble tracing the jeep and the explosives to the French and then launching an embarrassing protest. Mitterrand, already badly disposed toward the DGSE, fumed at the "incompetence" of the "action" service.[25] Still, this episode leaves an outside observer to wonder if the only thing worse than failure for "action" is "success," if the measure of that success is something like the *Rain-*

bow Warrior debacle or the carnage that would have ensued from a car bomb in Beirut.

Primacy of Domestic Security

A final distinguishing characteristic of French intelligence culture is the predominance of domestic intelligence or counterintelligence. This departs from the Anglo-Saxon model, which sees counterintelligence as police work or repression, rather than intelligence per se.[26] This does not make sense in the French case, where the line between internal and external enemies has not always been easy to draw, and where taking a position on a foreign issue can place one in a very delicate position domestically. In this respect, French attitudes toward domestic intelligence are more like those of the old USSR or modern Iran than of a democratic, Western country. But this offers another example of how culture shapes French intelligence priorities. Indeed, because of France's divided political culture and vision of nationhood as a cultural and linguistic communion in constant danger of subversion or overthrow by groups whose national origin, religious beliefs, or political allegiances cause them to be insufficiently integrated into the national community, it is hardly surprising that French leaders have on occasion shown a marked inability to distinguish between the two. In short, any threat to national identity is a threat to national security. Nor must one forget, as Monsieur Pasqua's early 1995 use of wiretaps and leaked DST reports reminds one, that zealous pursuit of political or personal advantage requiring the assistance of domestic intelligence or counterintelligence has been a common feature of French political life.

The precedent of mixing surveillance of foreigners, colonial subjects, national and religious minorities, and external intelligence was set during the first ministry of Georges Clemenceau (1906–1909). So long as surveillance of "foreigners" in France, supplemented by intelligence on them gleaned from abroad, was carried out, then France could be protected from outside influence and could enjoy real political freedom at home.[27] It is hardly surprising that secret services charged with standing watch over French security, especially the DST and the RG, may offend many of the principles they claim to uphold. The tendency might be given full reign when a conspiratorially minded interior minister takes charge. For instance, Raymond Marcellin, de Gaulle's minister of the interior in 1968, saw the outbreak of the troubles in May of that year as the product of an implausible conspiracy of "Germans and Jews."[28]

A political culture that views the world in such a way as to make fellow citizens suspect and transform political adversaries into subversives, a political system that thrives on scandals and dirty tricks, and secret services with a strong "action" culture, invite abuses and, as a result, a further decline in prestige and respect. French history in the twentieth century has served to reinforce that culture, to institutionalize bad habits inherited from the past rather than work against them. "Black chambers," whose job it was to intercept the mail of the political opposition and of foreigners, have a long and venerable history in France stretching back to the ancien régime. In the twentieth century, this expanded into telephone taps, especially in the post-1945 era when prime ministers, the fate of their governments suspended by a frail threat of a few parliamentary votes, took advantage of an extensive network of tap lines left behind by the Gestapo to stay informed of the opinions of friends and enemies alike. The Algerian War, with its turbulent civil-military relations that culminated in the emergence of the subversive OAS, caused this rather ad hoc system to be expanded and formalized into a Groupement Interministériel de Contrôle (GIC). The war ended in 1962; however, Gaullist politicians found it difficult to wean themselves from the system, which in theory required "requests" for taps from the Ministries of the Interior, Defense, and Posts, Telegraphs, and Telephones (PTT) to be approved by the prime minister. To all appearances, requests for taps on opposition politicians, trade union leaders, journalists, left-wing intellectuals, even on other Gaullist politicians, were accorded on a regular basis. For instance, in the 1960s, the telephones of François Mitterrand, Jean-Paul Sartre, Melina Mercouri, François Sagan, and even the singer Barbara were under permanent surveillance by the GIC.

In theory, "political" taps were suspended by President Valéry Giscard D'Estaing in 1974, furious, it was said, when the GIC intercepted his telephone conversations with a celebrated actress. But "administrative" and "juridical" taps, called *interceptions de sécurité*, remain authorized by a 1991 law, so long as they are approved by the prime minister's office. A Commission Nationale de Contrôle des Interceptions de Sécurité, chaired by a senior government official but including opposition politicians, is meant to oversee the activities of the GIC. However, one may question the effectiveness of outside oversight for at least two reasons, one technical-administrative and the other political. First, un-authorized taps, called *écoutes sauvages* by the French, continue. The distrust of Mitterrand for traditional services, a distrust exacerbated by "cohabitation" after 1986, when the Socialist president had to deal with a conservative prime minister, caused the Elysée Palace to set up its own listening service in the 1980s, which bypassed those of the GIC and hence did not require the approval of the prime minister. Although the Elysée services pointed to the rise of terrorism in the mid-1980s to justify its existence, it is now clear that it extended its taps to more than a thousand politicians, journalists, intellectuals, and even the actress Carole Bouquet.[29] *Ecoutes sauvages* are made all the easier by the ex-pansion of cellular telephones that may be intercepted by off-the-shelf commercial devices. If oversight has made it more difficult for func-tionaries of the GIC simply not to record a request, there are private services, often run by retired policemen who make their living tapping phones.[30]

The second problem with controlling these abuses is political. In a political culture where expediency takes precedence over ethics, the ability of parliamentary oversight to prevent abuses is limited because attempts to extend controls over the intelligence services places poli-ticians in an impossible dilemma. This was amply demonstrated in 1995 after it was revealed that Interior Minister Charles Pasqua had convinced prime minister and presidential candidate Edouard Bal-ladur to approve a tap on a judge investigating illegal use of Gaullist Party funds. Pasqua successfully shifted the focus of what was called the *affaire Maréchal-Schuller* from a scandal over internal political spy-ing into a debate about justifying telephone taps to prevent what he claimed was a massive CIA conspiracy to steal French technological and trade secrets. Given French insecurity over the future of the na-tion's economic competitiveness, a national mind-set prepared to be-stow upon foreign, especially American, intelligence services the same mythical influences as they accord their own, and a political culture that sets *raison d'état* above individual liberties,[31] parliamentary over-sight of the intelligence services is a minefield into which few politi-cians with a sense of self-preservation care to venture.

This response is only deepened when internal autonomist groups of Bretons, Basques, Corsicans, or a growing Muslim population threaten the homogeneity, and consequently the security, of the national cul-ture. The potential for "internal subversion" offers the excuse for maintaining some of the least attractive features of French counter-intelligence—secret microphones, telephone taps, and the opening of mail. Interior ministers like Marcellin and Pasqua have felt no need to justify these practices. On the contrary, they stake their professional reputations on their ability to make them more effective.[32] Because the threat of internal subversion is taken seriously by the French, who appear prepared to tolerate an invasive police bureaucracy, the DST has long been considered the most effective of French services and has acquired the greatest share of resources, even under Mitterrand.

CONCLUSION

Although the intelligence process of collection and analysis of information causes problems for all intelligence services, France's unique pattern of decision makers' "acceptance" of analyzed information has developed an intelligence culture that exaggerates the dilemmas and distorts each stage of the procedure—global ambitions that exceed France's power, a history of poor state-intelligence relations, military control of foreign intelligence, a strong "action" or special operations culture, and a focus on counterintelligence. Attempts to reform and upgrade capabilities since the end of the cold war have met only limited success. A Military Intelligence Directorate was created in 1993 to centralize military intelligence. An Interdepartmental Intelligence Committee made up of representatives from several agencies meets on a regular basis to work up a consolidated intelligence briefing for the president of the Republic. Finally, a Domestic Security Council was created in 2002 to improve cooperation between the DGSE and the DST. However, the problems of transparency, cooperation, and inadequate technological capabilities remain. "In France, intelligence has never interested or thrilled the administrative, intellectual, academic and political elites," writes Swiss major general Alain Faupin. "It has traditionally been considered as a necessary evil, to use with caution and if possible in your own interests or for the interests of the organization which is initiating it."[33] Therefore it seems fair to conclude that French intelligence limps into the twenty-first century burdened by the baggage of the twentieth.

NOTES

1. Gustave Bertrand, *Enigma où la plus grand enigma de la guerre, 1939–1945* (Paris: Plon, 1973). F. W. Winterbotham recounted much of the same material in *The Ultra Secret* (London: Weidenfeld and Nicolson, 1974).

2. This is especially the case for the 1930s and World War II. See, for example, Paul Paillole, *Services spéciaux (1935–1945)* (Paris: Laffont, 1975) and *Notre espion chez Hitler* (Paris: Laffont, 1985); Henri Navarre, *Le Service de renseignements 1871–1944* (Paris: Plon, 1978); Jean Bézy, *Le S.R. Air* (Paris, 1979); Michel Garder, *La guerre secrete des services spéciaux française, 1935–1945* (Paris: Plon, 1967); Gen. M. Gauché, *La deuxième bureau aux travail (1935–1940)* (Paris: Amiot-Dumont, 1954).

3. See Lt. Col. Jean Della Santa, "Cassandra, ou le renseignement jamais cru," *Revue militaire Suisse*, no. 3 (March 1972): 117–130. "I believe that I already told you, my goal is to offer once again proof of the efficiency of the French 'service du renseignement' and in this way to demonstrate the incompetence of Allied government" (letter from Paul Paillole to David Kahn, March 26, 1984, in possession of David Kahn).

4. See, for instance, Pierre Marion, *Le pouvoir sans visage* (Paris: Calmann-Lévy, 1990) and *Mission impossible* (Paris: Calmann-Lévy, 1991); P. L. Thyraud de Vosjoli, *Lamia* (Boston: Little, Brown, 1970); Philippe Bernert, *Roger Wybot et la bataille pour la DST* (Paris: La Cite, 1975) and *SDECE Service 7* (Paris: La Cite, 1980).

5. Thierry Wolton, *Le KGB en France* (Paris: Grasset, 1986) and *Le grand recrutement* (Paris: Grasset, 1993); Pascal Krop (with Roger Faligot), *La picine: Les services secret français 1944–1984* (Paris: Seuil Paris, 1985), and *Les secrets de l'espionnage français de 1870 à nos jours* (Paris: JC Lattes, 1993); Roger Faligo (with Remi Kauffer), *Service B* (Paris: Fayard, 1985), and *Au Coeur de l'Etat: Espionnage secret en Afrique* (Paris, 1982); Pierre Péan, *Secret d'état* (Paris: Fayard, 1986), *La menace* (Paris: Fayard, 1987), *L'homme de l'ombre: Eléments d'enquête autour de Jacques Foccart, l'homme le plus mystérieux et le plus puissant de la Ve République* (Paris: Fayard, 1990), and *Le mystérieux Docteur Martin, 1895–1969* (Paris: Fayard, 1993).

6. Michael Handel, "Intelligence and Military Operations," in Handel, ed., *Intelligence and Military Operations* (London: Frank Cass and Co., 1990), and "The Politics of Intelligence," in Handel, ed., *War, Strategy and Intelligence* (London: Frank Cass and Co., 1989); Richard K. Betts, "Analysis, War and Decision: Why Intelligence Failures Are Inevitable," *World Politics* 31 (October 1978): 61–89, and *Surprise Attack: Lessons for Defense Planning* (Washington, DC: 1982); Roberta Wohlstetter, *Pearl Harbor: Warning and Decision* (Stanford, CA: Stanford University Press, 1962); John Ferris, "Intelligence-Deception Complex: An Anatomy," *Intelligence and National Security* 4, no. 4 (October 1989): 719–734.

7. There was an attempt in 1999 by two members of Parliament to create

some sort of parliamentary oversight system, but their proposal never made it into the parliamentary agenda for debate. See Alain Faupin, "Reform of the French Intelligence Services after the End of the Cold War," paper presented at the workshop "Democratic and Parliamentary Oversight of Intelligence Services," Geneva Centre for the Democratic Control of Armed Forces, October 3–5, 2002, 6–7.

8. Paillole, *Services spéciaux*, 185–186, and interview with the author, July 1991.

9. When the final intelligence briefing was given around May 5, 1940, Major Baril, head of the Deuxième Bureau Northeast, would only say that no attack was likely through Switzerland or against the Maginot Line. Gauché, *Deuxième bureau*, 213.

10. Henri Navarre, *Agoni en Indochine, 1953–1954* (Paris: Plon, 1956), and *Le temps des verités* (Paris: Plon, 1979). For intelligence reports, see "Service historique de l'armée de terre" (SHAT), Château de Vincennes, 10H 273, 614, and 1161.

11. Dreyfus was innocent. His conviction rested on false documents provided by the statistical section. When high-ranking officers realized this, they attempted to cover up the mistakes. Emile Zola exposed the affair in a famous open letter to the French president, entitled "J'accuse!"

12. André Dewavrin, alias Colonel Passy, established de Gaulle's intelligence service during the Resistance. He was later accused of pilfering money intended for French intelligence and was jailed for four months before the charges were dropped. Barka, an opposition leader in Morocco in the 1960s, fled to Paris and was subsequently sentenced to death in absentia in Morocco. He was abducted from a Paris café, and his whereabouts have never been accurately ascertained. See Jean Lacouture, *De Gaulle: The Ruler*, 509–513, or the French edition, *De Gaulle: Le souverain, 1959–1970* (Paris: du Seuil, 1986), 628–632. Krop and Faligot, *La picine*, 231–238; Bernert, *SDECE Service 7*, 319–405.

13. Mitterrand set up a cell of security officials in the Elysée Palace to protect secrets such as the existence of his illegitimate daughter and to spy on his political enemies.

14. Stefan Marcovic, who had reputed ties with organized crime and was the bodyguard of one of France's most celebrated movie stars, Alain Delon, was found murdered in 1968. The subsequent inquiry revealed scandalous accounts of drug dealing, blackmail, and compromising photos that touched many parts of the French cinematic and political world, including Pompidou's soon-to-be wife.

15. Jean-Bédel Bokassa seized power of the Central African Republic in 1966 through a military coup. He later became president and eventually named himself emperor in 1976, with France supporting his coronation. Giscard d'Estaing reportedly received diamonds from Bokassa as a reward for his support.

16. The French make no secret of their intent to engage in economic espionage. Retired DGSE director Pierre Marion noted, "This espionage activity is an essential way for France to keep abreast of international commerce and technology. Of course, it was directed against the United States as well as others. You must remember that while we are allies in defense matters, we are also economic

competitors in the world." See John A. Nolan III, "A Case Study in French Espionage: Renaissance Software," http://www.hanford.gov/oci/maindocs/ci_r_docs/frenchesp.pdf. With respect to Niger, French intelligence was engaged in an operation to safeguard Niger's uranium industry, from which France benefited, that led to the forging of documents relating to an apparent clandestine uranium trade with Iraq. See Mark Huband, "French Probe Led to Fake Niger Uranium Papers," *Financial Times*, August 2, 2004.

17. Pierre Favier and Michel Martin-Roland, *La décennie Mitterrand*, vol. 1, *Les ruptures 1981–1984* (Paris: Seuil, 1990), 513.

18. See Péan, *L'homme de l'ombre*. Also see *Rapport de la commission d'enquête sur les activités du Services d'Action Civique*, Assemblée Nationale, session ordinaire de 1981–1982, no. 955 (Paris: 1982), 2 vols.; and Philippe Gaillard, *Foccart Park: Entretiens avec Philippe Gaillard* (Paris: Fayard, 1995).

19. *Le Point*, no. 1171, February 25, 1995, 8–9.

20. Roger Faligot and Rémi Kaufer, *Les Résistants: De la guerre de l'ombre aux allées du pouvoir* (Paris: Fayard, 1969); André Gillois, *Histoire secrète des Français à Londres de 1940 à 1944* (Paris: Hachette, 1973), who quoted de Gaulle's belief that "the Resistance was a bluff that came off," 164. For a more traditional interpretation of the Resistance as savior of France's honor, see M. R. D. Foot, *Resistance* (London: Paladin, 1978), 318–320.

21. For the intelligence and special operations dimensions of Dien Bien Phu, see Douglas Porch, *The French Secret Services: From the Dreyfus Affair to Desert Storm* (New York: Farrar, Straus and Giroux, 1995), chaps. 13 and 14.

22. Ibid., 373–375.

23. Ibid., chap. 19.

24. Péan, *L'homme de l'ombre*.

25. Favier and Martin-Roland, *La décennie Mitterrand*, vol. 2, *Les épreuves* (Paris: Seuil, 1991), 31–37; Pierre Marion, *Le pouvoir sans visage* (Paris: Calmann-Lévy, 1990), 103.

26. The rise of Islamic fundamentalism among Muslim immigrants and the creation of entities like the U.S. Department of Homeland Security, however, may be changing that.

27. His-Hue Liang, *The Rise of Modern Police and the European State System from Metternich to the Second World War* (Cambridge, UK: Cambridge University Press, 1992), 45–46.

28. Raymond Marcellin, *La guerre politique* (Paris: Plon, 1985), 46–51.

29. "Les Villaines manières français," *Le Point*, no. 1171, February 25, 1995, 38–40.

30. Ibid., 39–40; Georges Moréas, *Ecoutes et espionage* (Paris: Edition No. 1, 1990), 27–28, 59; Jean Guisnel and Bernard Violet, *Services secrets: Le pouvoir et les services de renseignements sous François Mitterrand* (Paris: La Découverte, 1988), 274–275.

31. For an excellent summary of the contrasting American and French views

on individual liberty and the role of the state, see Charles G. Cogan, *Oldest Allies, Guarded Friends: The United States and France since 1940* (Westport, CT, and London: Praeger Publishers, 1994), 199–215.

32. Marcellin, *La guerre politique*, 130, 181.

33. Faupin, "Reform of the French Intelligence Services," 2–10.

PART TWO

DEMOCRATIC CONTROL OF INTELLIGENCE IN NEW DEMOCRACIES

SIX

STRUCTURAL CHANGE AND DEMOCRATIC CONTROL OF INTELLIGENCE IN BRAZIL

Marco Cepik

S tructural change has been the main feature of the Brazilian intelligence sector since 1999. In order to evaluate the achievements, failures, and consequences of this structural change, this chapter will explore two separate paths simultaneously.

Regarding the first path, one must start searching for an explanation for the causal nexus between the processes of institutional transformation (i.e., organizational and legal changes) and degrees of democratic control. It is important to know how much the changes observed in a country are congruent with the nature of a political regime. It is similarly important to note how different levels of democratic control over intelligence activities are affected by these same empirically observed structural changes. The second path is also a rough one, because the information that exists regarding the aforementioned structural changes is varied and diverse. The intent in this chapter, then, is to show the processes that exist within the reformed Brazilian intelligence system and to analyze both their limits and their potential.[1] In order to do this, the chapter is organized into four parts. First, in this introduction, two general premises about intelligence are briefly stated, and the working hypothesis that bounds this work is specified. Next, I will discuss the nature of the present Brazilian political regime, as well as some indicators of the current level of the state's capability to conduct intelligence activity. Then changes in the organizational and legal framework of the intelligence system of this country throughout the period 1999–2005 will be presented. I will conclude with a brief and tentative evaluation of the impact of such changes on the level of democratic control and on the effectiveness of Brazilian intelligence services.

The first premise supposes the presence of intelligence services that are legitimate and effective as a necessary condition for a democratic country to guarantee the safety of its citizens and to promote its public interests.[2] In this sense, intelligence services are an essential part—together with the military forces, the police, and the diplomats—of the bureaucratic apparatus of any state with minimal intentions of having autonomy in the international system.

The second premise is related to the inherent tension that exists between the requisites of security and the minimal procedural criteria of democracy, especially in the areas of defense, foreign policy, and provision of public order. Besides the problems that are common to democratic controls existing in other areas of the state's action, in the area of security there are specific tensions and difficulties that may be summed up in two dichotomies: state security versus individual security, and governmental secrecy versus the right to information. Obviously, these two dichotomies are not inherent only to developing countries or to those countries that have been through authoritarian regimes but also manifest themselves in the more established democracies.[3]

I consider, however, that the challenge in bringing intelligence services under democratic control and making them effective (and efficient if it can be known) in the so-called new democracies is particularly fundamental for democracies like Brazil. This is primarily due to the institutional and behavioral inheritance received from the previous dictatorship and the relative frailty of the state in these countries. The problem of democratic control over intelligence services is a part of the more general challenges associated with the solution of civil-military relations and of the building up of the state's capability.[4]

The working hypothesis that informs this chapter is that although the Brazilian political regime is comparatively democratic and consolidated, Brazilian total capability in the area of security is relatively low, which makes it harder to maintain both democratic control and the effectiveness of the new intelligence structures that were implemented after 1999. In the current phase of development in the country, a persistent vulnerability in terms of state capability tends to be detrimental for both the stability and the quality of democracy. Although the democratic legitimacy and the effectiveness of intelligence services are closely related, in the case of Brazil the present challenges related to the institutionalization of these services are more strongly related to effectiveness than to democratic control.[5]

THE BRAZILIAN POLITICAL REGIME:
DEMOCRATIC CONSOLIDATION?

I accept with reservations some minimum and necessary criteria that enable us to characterize a political regime as democratic: First, the leaders both of the executive power and of the legislative power are selected through periodic, competitive elections, which are considered clean by participants and external observers accepted by the candidates. Second, the political rights of voting and being voted for include the whole adult population. Third, basic political and civil rights (speech, organization, and physical integrity) of each citizen are not violated without the political and legal indictment of the governing leadership. And fourth, the elected representatives can govern without the tutelage of nonelected groups of power, be they military, of the business community, foreign governments, or any other groups of interest.[6]

Whether one agrees or not with such criteria, as far as Brazil is concerned there is a consensus in the literature about the democratic nature of the country's political regime.[7] By the same token, in projects that use continual measurements of democracy instead of static classifications, such as the Polity Project of the University of Maryland or Freedom House's index, Brazil is evaluated as being strongly democratic.[8]

Although the duration of the Brazilian democratic regime has not yet gone beyond the threshold of twenty years of stability, as proposed in a study by Arend Lijphart,[9] whether one considers the year of transference of a military president to a civilian one (1985) or the year of the first democratic direct election of the country's president under a democratic constitution (1989), the country is now closer to that threshold, and all prospective international evaluations of a political risk for a period of five years are consistent in stating that, in the case of Brazil, there is no possibility in sight of an interruption of the democratic process.[10]

Finally, the election itself of President Luiz Inácio Lula da Silva, known commonly as Lula, at the end of 2002 and the ascension into power in the federal level of the Workers' Party (PT—Partido dos Trabalhadores) has been pointed to as a sign of maturation and consolidation of the Brazilian democracy.

It is important to notice, however, that the criteria of classification mentioned in the beginning of this section are strictly procedural. This implies a negative and/or weak conception of a democratic consolidation represented by the mere absence of backsliding. In other words, it is the external observation of behaviors of relevant collective subjects (civilian elites, various social groups, foreign governments, the military, etc.) and the empirical verification of the occurrence (or not) of a singular event (a violent interruption of the democratic procedures above defined). As Andreas Schedler and Guillermo O'Donnell correctly argue, consolidation measurement problems tend to become exponential if one adopts a "positive and strong" conception of consolidation, with more-demanding normative expectations of depth of the desirable characteristics of a democratic regime "with adjectives." [11]

Whatever the case may be, the central point here is that the ability to establish control over intelligence services is vastly different, depending on the prior political regime. In this sense, it is fair to say that the structural changes that have taken place since 1999 in the Brazilian intelligence community should be consistent with the evaluation of the Brazilian political regime as a consolidated democracy. In order to assess that, those changes are presented in the next section.

BRAZILIAN INTELLIGENCE SYSTEM: STRUCTURAL CHANGE AND CONTROL

Having established the context in which recent structural changes have been made in the area of intelligence in Brazil, it is necessary now to look at these changes and analyze the problems of democratic control associated with the emergence of these new organizations and procedures. This will be done in four stages. Initially, I will summarize the most important legal changes to the Brazilian intelligence structure. Second, I will discuss organizational changes within the intelligence community that affect its control. Third, the priorities and thematic emphases over the last two governments will be examined. Finally, I will discuss the theme of effectiveness in the current Brazilian system, examining professionalization and resource problems.

Legal Framework for Intelligence in Brazil

The current framework of the intelligence sector in Brazil was established by Law 9.883 of December 7, 1999, through which the Congress created the Brazilian Intelligence Agency (ABIN) and instituted the

Brazilian Intelligence System (SISBIN). Legally, ABIN is considered a central agency of the system and is responsible for regulating the flow of information produced by the institutions linked to it. Enactment of this law not only reflected the weight of a tradition of very generic definitions about the legal mandate of intelligence agencies in Brazil but was also the result of several legislative initiatives presented by the leftist parties and by the government, internal negotiations in the executive, and pressure from civil society throughout the 1990s.[12]

In the first articles of Law 9.883, intelligence activity was defined as that which intends to "obtain, analyze, and disseminate knowledge within and outside the national territory on facts and situations of immediate or potential influence on government actions and decision processes and about the protection and security of society and the State." Equally generic, counterintelligence was defined as "the activity that intends to neutralize adverse intelligence." The specific content of the priorities and thematic emphasis of both activities was left to be defined by a national intelligence policy to be established by the president after hearing suggestions from the external control agency in Congress.

Initially quite slowly, but with a quickening tempo in the last few years, an important legal structure regulating intelligence activities has emerged in Brazil. For a comprehensive view of this legal framework, it would be necessary to analyze the Federal Constitution of 1988, as well as existing legislation that defines crimes against the security of the state and of individuals, regulates instruments combating crime (including telephone tapping), establishes the policies of information security and government secrecy, establishes the procedures for the control of public administration in general, and so on. Obviously, such a legal analysis is far beyond the possibilities of this text.[13]

That said, it is worthwhile to emphasize a number of decrees and administrative guidelines of the executive (e.g., that which in 2002 regulated the functioning of SISBIN), as well as some specific laws (such as the law defining a career path for the analysts of the intelligence system, approved in 2004) that have contributed decisively in shaping the activity in the sphere of federal government. Even considering that different organizations and functions of the Brazilian intelligence system receive more or less attention in terms of explicit regulations, it can be said that today Brazil has fairly developed legislation in the areas of intelligence and information security (see Table 6.1 for a list of the main legal instruments).

TABLE 6.1   BRAZILIAN FEDERAL INTELLIGENCE AND RELATED LAWS

Type of law	Number	Year enacted	Main focus	Comment
Constitution	Art. 5	1988	Freedom of expression and right to information	State security-related exceptions
Constitution	Art. 142	1988	Roles and missions of armed forces	External defense; uphold the Constitution and, by request of the constitutional government, keep internal law and order
Ordinary law	7.170	1983	National security	Passed under military rule; still in place. Congress is examining a bill (6.764/2002) dealing with crimes against the state and democracy
Ordinary law	8.028	1990	Termination of the National Information Service (SNI)	SNI was the powerful intelligence and security service of the Brazilian military regime
Ordinary law	8.159	1991	National archives policy	Main regulation regarding access to government files
Executive decree	4.553	2002	Information security	Security classifications and clearances
Ordinary law	9.034	1995	Use of operational means (i.e., technical surveillance) to prevent and repress crime	Some articles changed by Law 10.217/2001

TABLE 6.1 CONTINUED

Type of law	Number	Year enacted	Main focus	Comment
Ordinary law	9.296	1996	Judicial advance authorization for telephone interceptions	ABIN is not allowed either to ask for such an authorization or to engage in tapping operations
Ordinary law	9.883	1999	Establishes the Brazilian Intelligence Agency (ABIN) and the Brazilian Intelligence System (SISBIN)	Missions are defined in fairly general terms based on a broad definition of intelligence and counterintelligence
Complementary Law	97	1999	Establishes the Defense Ministry (MD) and the EO Defense General Staff (EMD)	MD structure and resources were detailed by Decree 4.735/2003 and Policy Directive MD 1.037/2003
Executive decree	3.695	2000	Establishes the Public Security Intelligence Subsystem (SISP)	SENASP/MJ as coordinator; Decree 3.348/2002 first defined ABIN as SISP central agency, but the Ministry of Justice was able to regain its coordinator role for the SISP
Executive decree	4.376	2002	Specifies SISBIN's organization and membership	Defines members of the SISBIN and its Consulting Council; complemented decree 4.872/2003
Policy directive, Ministry of Defense	295	2002	Establishes the Defense Intelligence System (SINDE)	Strategic Intelligence Department (DIE) of the MD as the central organ

TABLE 6.1 CONTINUED

Type of law	Number	Year enacted	Main focus	Comment
Ordinary law	10.862	2004	ABIN's Special Career Plan	Defines the information analyst career, from entry through training and advancement, until retirement; includes ethos and ethics requirements
National Congress's internal resolution	08	2000	Joint Commission for the Intelligence Activities Control (CCAI)	CCAI was established in 2000; as of December 2006, the Brazilian Congress had not approved the commission's internal rules

Organizational Changes in the Brazilian Intelligence System

With regard to the most important organizational changes that occurred after the establishment of ABIN in 1999, it is important to highlight at least four: subordination of the ABIN to the Institutional Security Cabinet (GSI) of the President of the Republic; the creation of the Joint Commission for the Control of Intelligence Activities (CCAI) and other control committees in Congress; regulation of the participation of the ministries in the sphere of SISBIN; and creation of two intelligence subsystems, the Public Security Intelligence Subsystem (SISP) and the Defense Intelligence Subsystem (SINDE). Figure 6.1 depicts the current Brazilian intelligence system.

In the case of subordinating ABIN to GSI, the government tried to justify this decision, made during the second term of President Fernando Henrique Cardoso (1999–2002), citing the need to guard the president from the daily managerial demands and the potential crises resulting from scandals and tensions inherent to the relation between intelligence and policymaking. In practice, the subordination of ABIN to GSI corresponded to a number of responsibilities that GSI had acquired over time because of the trust the president had in General Alberto Cardoso (no relation). GSI became the main instrument for bringing together the flow of information from various federal agencies and the center for managing crises in internal and external security. Although ABIN is legally defined as *the* central agency of the intelligence system and, in practice, plays the role of *primus inter pares*, its subordination to the GSI increased the control of the decision makers in setting priorities and collecting and analyzing information, while at the same time reducing the ABIN's authority over the other participating agencies.

The second relevant structural development since 1999 was the creation in November 2000 of the Joint Commission for the Control of Intelligence Activities (CCAI) in the Congress.[14] After eleven meet-

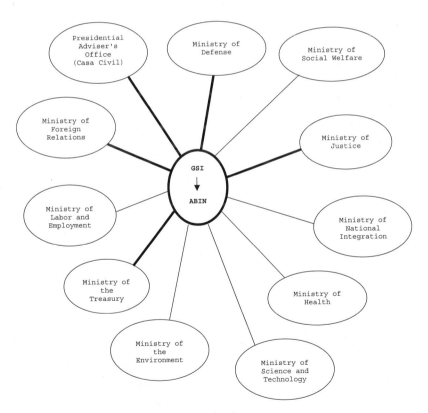

FIGURE 6.1. *Brazilian Intelligence System. The bold rules link the members of the SISBIN Advisory Council.*

ings up through July 2004, the CCAI faced enormous difficulties in carrying out its control functions. These difficulties result in part from the very institutional design of the agency—it is presided over each year in turn by the president of the Commission of Foreign Relations and National Defense of the Senate and the House of Representatives. But problems have also arisen because of a lack of technical resources and personnel. For example, the only employee of the Senate who specialized in intelligence and decisively contributed to the existence of the CCAI also worked to support several other commissions and different tasks of the heads of the Senate. From 2000–2003, parliamentary members of a center-left coalition presided over CCAI and carried out important joint initiatives with agencies of the executive. These included the first-ever seminar on intelligence control (which was actually broadcast to the public) and consultation with civil society in 2003 (another first) about the priorities of the National Intelligence Policy. In spite of this, as of July 2006, the CCAI still had not managed to get its bylaws approved by Congress, and the sporadic meetings and activities were overly occupied with reaction to scandals and accusations in the press, rather than intelligence control priorities.

In addition to CCAI, four other commissions have been established in Congress to support the control of intelligence activities: the defense commissions in both the House of Representatives (CREDEN) and the Senate (CRE); the Commission of Public Security against Organized Crime (CSPCC) of the House of Representatives; and the permanent subcommission of Public Security of the Commission of Constitution, Justice, and Citizenship in the Senate. With regard to budgets, monitoring intelligence is the responsibility both of the Internal Control Office of the President of the Republic and of the Union Accounts Tribunal (TCU).[15]

The publication of Executive Decree 4.376 in 2002 was an important step in outlining the organizational frontiers of SISBIN and represents the third important structural change in the Brazilian oversight regime. The spirit of the 1999 law was to incorporate not only ministries and agencies of indirect federal administration but also state and municipal organizations and even private companies and entities from civil society. By 2004, SISBIN was made up of GSI, ABIN, the Ministry of Defense, the Ministry of Foreign Relations, the Presidential Adviser's Office (Casa Civil—the agency responsible for managing the Amazon Protection System), the Ministry of Justice, the Ministry of National Integration, the Ministry of Science and Technology, Ministry of the Environment, Ministry of Health, Ministry of Social Welfare, as well as the Ministry of Labor. As can be seen in Figure 6.1, at least two ministries participate in SISBIN through three units or more (Justice and Defense), whereas the Ministry of the Treasury participates through both the Office of Tax Revenue and also in the Intelligence Unit of the Central Bank. Together with GSI and ABIN, these two ministries, along with the Ministry of Foreign Relations and the Presidential Adviser's Office (Casa Civil), make up the Advisory Council of SISBIN. Some organizational stability has been obtained in SISBIN in that each ministry has appointed a single person responsible for interaction with SISBIN.

Finally, it is important to highlight the establishment of two important intelligence subsystems in Brazil: the SISP and the SINDE.

PUBLIC SECURITY INTELLIGENCE SUBSYSTEM

The Public Security Intelligence Subsystem (SISP) was established in 2000 through Executive Decree 3.695 and is coordinated by the Public National Security Office (SENASP) of the Ministry of Justice. The main operational components of SISP are the Department of Federal Police (DPF) and the Department of Federal Highway Police (DPRF), in the Ministry of Justice, as well as members of the Ministry of Treasury (SRF, the Federal Revenue Secretariat; the Central Bank; and COAF, the Financial Activities Organizing Commission), the Ministry of National Integration, the Ministry of Defense (SPEAI), the Institutional Security Cabinet of the President of the Republic (ABIN and SENAD, the National Anti-Drug Secretariat), as well as the civil and military police of the twenty-six states and the Federal District.

Although defined as a subsystem of SISBIN, in practice the number of organizations involved in the police intelligence networks tends to transform SISP into a system only partially integrated to SISBIN, in spite of the participation of ABIN and other federal agencies in both advisory committees.

Through an unusual initiative in the first half of 2003, efforts to formulate a national plan of public security intelligence (PNISP) within SISP were under way. This was, unfortunately, interrupted. A policy such as this would have been essential for the country to fight organized crime and urban violence, which present the gravest threats to the security of citizens and to the state itself.

Generally, the SISP is not operating as effectively as it could be- cause not much has come from the potential to integrate the flow of information in the areas of criminal (internal) security intelligence, counterintelligence, and counterterrorism.

THE DEFENSE INTELLIGENCE SYSTEM

The Defense Intelligence System (SINDE) was formally established in June 2002, through an internal administrative decision within the Ministry of Defense (Regulation 295/MD). This subsystem was cre- ated to bring together intelligence components of the navy (CIM), the army (CIE), the air force (SECINT), the defense heads of staff (EMD-2), and the Ministry of Defense. The Strategic Intelligence Department of the Ministry (DIE-SPEAI), which is also responsible for representing SINDE in SISBIN and in the National Congress, is responsible for coordinating the SINDE effort. The intelligence ser- vice of each branch of the armed forces is subordinated both to the Ministry of Defense and to the offices and heads responsible for stra- tegic and operational intelligence, though they each operate in a very decentralized manner.

The idea of "system" derives precisely from the idea of a whole that is maintained by the functional differentiation of its parts. Unfortu- nately, this is not the case with SISBIN, SISP, and SINDE. One reason is that the degree of hierarchical centralization that SISBIN carries out is low. Another is that all three systems tend to focus on either na- tional issues or the operational aspects and bureaucratic imperatives of the organization itself, rather than focusing on areas or functions that they are best organized to support. I will come back to this issue later in the chapter. In the best of all possible worlds, the overall systems of intelligence have the potential of integrating vital informal flows and improving the security of the state and of citizens. In addition, the new comprehensive "systems" have simplified the process of external con- trol, since they create more-focused points of interaction between a number of intelligence organizations, the interested politicians in the Congress, in the executive, and in society itself.

In summary, Figure 6.2 represents the relationship between the three systems, which, in my opinion is closer to the real dynamics of power and distribution of resources than the formally based idea that military and police intelligence are merely subordinated to GSI and ABIN through the SISBIN rules of operation.

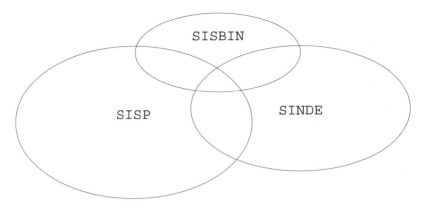

FIGURE 6.2. *The three intelligence systems in Brazil.*

Policies and Priorities in the Last Two Governments

According to the law that created SISBIN, intelligence priorities are established for the system as a whole, through both National Intelligence Policy (PNI) and annual guidelines. The executive branch, with approval from the Joint Commission of Congress, is responsible for establishing the PNI and annual guidelines. The current PNI was sent to Congress in May 2000 and approved by CCAI in November 2001, with some amendments. However, the PNI dealt mainly with procedures, limits, and responsibilities of the newly created SISBIN and provided little clarification about intelligence priorities.

A more precise indicator of intelligence guidelines may be found in public statements by heads of the intelligence sector during the second term of President Cardoso (1999–2002). For example, in the opening ceremony of a seminar held in the National Congress in November 2002, General Alberto Cardoso (then head of the GSI) mentioned several areas in which the intelligence agencies had made significant impacts on government decisions. Among the areas General Cardoso mentioned were the monitoring of separatist movements; the monitoring of answers to demands from social movements; land issues; the protection of the indigenous population; biodiversity and the environment; opportunities and obstacles to national development (mainly in areas of leading technologies and the use of natural resources); squatting (mainly in the Amazon region); the proliferation of weapons of mass destruction (in support to the Brazilian delegations and multilateral agencies); public security in the Brazilian states (in partnership with SISP); the fight against transnational organized crime, drug, and weapons trafficking, and money laundering; the prevention of terrorism and monitoring the movements of members of international terrorist organizations; monitoring and evaluation of external conflicts (and their potential impact on Brazil); and monitoring actions resulting from Plan Colombia and their possible consequences in Brazil. General Cardoso also mentioned the implementation of the National Program for the Protection of Knowledge (PNPC) and the work of the Research Center for Safe Communications (CEPESC/ABIN), both of them very important for the initiatives of information security, cryptography, and counterintelligence in Brazil.[16]

Although there is not yet a similar public discussion of the full range of issues on intelligence work in the Lula government (2003–present), the Foreign Relations and National Defense Chamber of the Government has defined four main themes as priorities in 2003: public security and organized crime (including terrorism and illegal immigration); information security (including protection of sensitive knowledge); threats to national interests and opportunities, mainly in South America; and internal and external threats to the state and to democratic order.

In July 2004, President Lula gave a speech at the inauguration of the new ABIN director, Mauro Marcelo de Lima e Silva, in which he emphasized that the intelligence agency should once and for all put behind it the heritage from the past by strengthening its collective analytical capacity and the relevance of its products, an effort that clearly depends directly on professionalizing ABIN's employees.[17] Undoubtedly, these are some of the challenges faced by the Brazilian intelligence services after the implementation of the current structural changes. A further difficulty is the allocation of the scarce resources to carry out an intelligence mission that has been defined in a very generic and vague way—according to the political crisis of the moment. This can be seen in the wide range of issues and the emphasis on internal security themes (which is rarely questioned). These two themes—resources and professionalization—need further comment.

Ongoing Difficulties: Effectiveness of the ABIN

The wider context of the difficulties of institutionalizing the new intelligence structures in Brazil highlights a lack of willingness of the political elites in the executive and legislative branches in dealing with the problem of effectiveness in the services. In Brazil, effectiveness can be observed in professionalization of intelligence personnel and the state's capacity to develop these personnel. Professionalism can be observed in three categories: professional training and educational standards, a viable career path, and a code of ethics.[18]

PROFESSIONAL TRAINING AND EDUCATIONAL STANDARDS

In Brazil the federal government's intelligence organizations, both in the armed forces and in the civil sphere (ABIN, the Federal Police, the Treasury Ministry, and so on), maintain their own continuing education and refresher course centers for their collectors and analysts. The two best-known centers of this kind are ABIN's Intelligence School, which offers short courses and specific training to a number of other areas in the federal public administration, and the army's Intelligence School, which serves mainly the ground forces.

The curriculum at the ABIN school is primarily divided into two areas: intelligence methodology and a broader set of courses that include foreign language instruction. Overall emphasis is on the methods and techniques that develop specific abilities in the employees and that complement academic knowledge already acquired by these personnel (ABIN analysts are required to have a college degree). The focus of the curricula is on strategic intelligence rather than tactical intelligence, and great emphasis is placed on the employee's ability to analyze and summarize information, to think logically, and to work under pressure. Interestingly, a number of institutions devoted to the formation of professions for the federal administration (among them the Advanced School of Treasury Administration and the National School of Public Administration, to note just two examples) collaborate with the professionalization process at ABIN. In the case of the Escola Superior de Guerra (ESG), there is even an exchange on a regular basis, so some instructors from ABIN's Intelligence School instruct in the Advanced Strategic Intelligence Course at ESG.

ABIN also promotes symposia and gives courses to private and public companies about how to protect sensitive information, as occurs with the Financial Intelligence Course at the Federal University of Rio de Janeiro, as well as in a course given at the Brazilian Bar Association.

A VIABLE CAREER PATH

The existence of a professional career track in intelligence is very important in developing a cadre of officials to provide stability within the intelligence services. In ABIN's present structure, two functional personnel categories have been created: the information analyst, which requires a university degree, and the information assistant, for which a high school diploma is necessary. The Special Career Plan of ABIN (Law 10.862 of 2004) defined the educational and promotion criteria for the intelligence career and also addressed retirement issues. The plan outlined intelligence personnel development in four distinct phases. The first phase is a Profession Familiarization Course, designed to qualify new candidates for specific assignments within ABIN. A second phase includes a three-year period in which the analyst must achieve qualification to become a part of the agency's staff and leads to a first functional advancement. After eight years at ABIN, selected personnel go to a Post-Qualifying Course, a third phase. Seven years after that they attend an advanced course, the fourth phase. The passage of this Career Plan law was a critical step toward greater professionalization of the Brazilian intelligence system.

CODE OF ETHICS

Defining the ethical standards of an intelligence organization is much more complex than doing so in other professions, such as dentistry or medicine. A survey administered to forty-seven permanent ABIN employees (twenty-five managers, twelve senior analysts, and ten intelligence analysts) set out to determine whether ethical standards did, in fact, exist within ABIN. Respondents were asked about the type of professional characteristics needed (in terms of personal qualities, attitudes, capacities, and intellectual abilities), the products of intelligence (nature of the information, kinds of problems), and the status of the profession (profile of tasks, degree of institutionalization, relations between decision makers and analysts).

Although the data collected were widely dispersed, information provided by the managers in particular offers a glimpse of the professional ethos being developed in ABIN. Not surprisingly, values pointed out as desirable by the managers were performance of lawful duties, tasks, and responsibilities. They also noted that the practice of "intelligence" must be carried out with sound judgment, security awareness, and impartiality. These respondents also saw intrinsic value in the search for "truth" as a basic element of analyst behavior, expected discretion when employees dealt with work-related issues, and presupposed that professionals would not make use of the information they have access to as public agents for private purposes. These expressions of behavioral expectations on the part of intelligence professionals of the Brazilian government imply their adoption of a set of beliefs and values that guide attitudes and behaviors, contributing to the necessary confidence in personal and professional actions, even after they retire or leave intelligence service—in short, a code of ethics.

STATE CAPACITY TO DEVELOP INTELLIGENCE

It should also be noted that overall effectiveness of developing intelligence will partly depend on the relative importance that intelligence is given within the state. One way to view this is simply by reviewing the resources allocated to intelligence. As indicated in the introduction to the book, estimating government spending on intelligence is a difficult process and one that is prone to error. Roughly speaking, one may estimate the Brazilian spending on intelligence by adding the budget of ABIN to the sums that appear in the subfunction "intelligence and information" in all the units of the Ministry of Defense and the Ministry of Justice. The estimate derived in this way is $63.6 million.[19] While I recognize that the margin of error in the figure presented here is quite high, it does represent a reasonable estimate of intelligence spending. Relative to overall defense spending of about $11 billion, this figure represents slightly less than 0.6 percent. The fact that so much of the budgets of defense, public security, and intelligence are committed to personnel and debts makes the challenge of professionalization even harder. As Dunning puts it, "in spite of the difficulties in estimating the relationship between input indicators and consequences, in terms of capacity, usually, most of the governments end up receiving the level of services they are capable of paying for."[20] In short, you get what you pay for.

In summary, overall effectiveness in the Brazilian intelligence system is improving because the professionalism of those individuals serving in the system is advancing. Effectiveness is, however, hindered by the state's relatively low interest in developing intelligence vis-à-vis other defense issues.

CONCLUSION

Brazilian structural reforms in intelligence have been mostly successful from the point of view of adapting to the context of a consolidated democratic regime. Even more, they are an important part of democratic consolidation itself. The question one must ask is whether the intelligence services are both under democratic control and effective.

In reviewing the control of Brazil's intelligence apparatus, one can say that democratic institutions are in place. The executive and legislative offices clearly have structures and procedures to define intelligence missions, review intelligence practices, and apportion funds. The establishment of the CCAI is particularly noteworthy. The fact that ethical standards have developed within the intelligence services themselves also speaks well to the degree of control the government has over the intelligence community. This is quite an accomplishment when one considers that the entire intelligence community has been redeveloped over the last fifteen years.

With regard to effectiveness, Brazil has created interesting structures in an attempt to coordinate and control intelligence in the two main integrating instances (the GSI itself and the councils of the three systems). Defining ABIN as the central agency of SISBIN is clearly important, but Brazil has gone a step further by incorporating into the system the most important civil ministries, such as the Presidential Adviser's Office and the Ministries of Justice and Foreign Relations. That the same structure is reproduced in the case of the intelligence system of defense, coordinated by the Strategic Intelligence Department of the Ministry of Defense, also speaks well of the intelligence services potential. Although in the case of SINDE, the degree of autonomy of the intelligence agencies of the three branches of the military may be considered excessive, it is in part neutralized by the very allocation of resources, mostly controlled by the civilian members of SISBIN.[21]

Development of a cadre of intelligence professionals with a viable career path and a professional ethic is clearly on the right path, though increased spending in this arena would be beneficial to effectiveness, as well as to control.

In the final analysis, it is fair to say that the intelligence services in Brazil are under democratic control. Their effectiveness, while on the right path, remains in need of further development.

NOTES

1. This text was developed from two previous essays published in coauthorship with Priscila Antunes: Priscila Antunes and Marco A. C. Cepik, "The New Brazilian Intelligence System: An Institutional Assessment," *International Journal*

of Intelligence and Counterintelligence 16, no. 3 (July–September 2003): 349–373; and Cepik and Antunes, "The Professionalization of Intelligence in Brazil: Knowledge, Career Path, and Values," in Russell Swenson and Susana Lemozy, eds., *Intelligence Professionalism in the Americas* (Washington, DC: JMIC Edition, 2003).

2. "Legitimate" in this context means that the intelligence services are under democratic control of elected officials.

3. *The 9/11 Commission Report: Final Report of the National Commission on Terrorist Attacks* (New York: W. W. Norton and Co., July 2004) highlights these issues; available at http://www.gpoaccess.gov/911/. See especially chaps. 11, 12, and 13.

4. The need for a stronger connection between intelligence studies and the area of civilian-military relations is pointed out by Tom Bruneau and Steve Boraz in the introduction to this book. For an excellent general view of these studies on civilian-military relations in Latin America, see David Pion-Berlin, ed., *Civil-Military Relations in Latin America* (Chapel Hill: University of North Carolina Press, 2001); Harold Trinkunas, "Crafting Civilian Control in Emerging Democracies: Argentina and Venezuela," *Journal of Interamerican Studies and World Affairs* 42, no. 3 (Fall 2000): 77–109; Ruth Stanley, "Modes of Transition versus Electoral Dynamics: Democratic Control of the Military in Argentina and Chile," *Journal of Third World Studies* 18, no. 2 (Fall 2001): 71–91; Samuel Fitch, *The Armed Forces and Democracy in Latin America* (Baltimore: Johns Hopkins University Press, 1998). For a useful comment on the different epistemic communities in the areas of intelligence and international relations, see Michael G. Fry and Miles Hochstein, "Epistemic Communities: Intelligence Studies and International Relations," *Intelligence and National Security* 8, no. 3 (July 1993): 14–28.

5. For Samuel Huntington, the level of institutionalization of a political system can be measured according to the following pairs of variables: adaptability/rigidity, complexity/simplicity, autonomy/subordination, and coherence/separation. If such variables could be unfolded into measurable indicators, it would be possible to evaluate empirically and comparatively the degree of institutionalization of specific organizations and procedures within a political system (such as the intelligence services). See Samuel P. Huntington, *A ordem política nas sociedades em mudança* (São Paulo: Forense/EdUSP, 1975), 24–25. For a more normative perspective, see Robert E. Goodin, ed., *The Theory of Institutional Design* (Cambridge, UK: Cambridge University Press, 1999), 39–43. Goodin offers some useful principles of an institutional design that might work also as parameters for the evaluation of organizations, rules, and procedures: revisability, sturdiness, sensitivity to motivational complexity, publicity, and variability.

6. With minimal differences in wording and emphasis, these are the same criteria proposed by Scott Mainwaring, Daniel Brinks, and Anibal Perez-Linan in "Classifying Political Regimes in Latin America, 1945–1999," *Studies in Comparative International Development* 36, no. 9 (2003): 1031–1067. Their criteria, in turn, derived from the concept of polyarchy proposed by Robert Dahl, *Polyarchy: Par-*

ticipation and Opposition (New Haven, CT: Yale University Press, 1971). These are procedural criteria, but while the first two components are relatively simple to measure in concrete situations, the two others are much more demanding in logical and empirical terms. For a recent discussion of such classification criteria of authoritarian regimes, see Barbara Geddes, *Paradigms and Sand Castles: Theory Building and Research Design in Comparative Politics* (Ann Arbor: University of Michigan Press, 2003).

7. See Adam Przeworski (series ed.), Michael E. Alvarez, Jose Antonio Cheibub, and Fernando Limongi, *Democracy and Development: Political Institutions and Well-Being in the World, 1950–1990* (Cambridge, UK: Cambridge University Press, 2000); and Arend Lijphart, *Patterns of Democracy: Government Forms and Performance in Thirty-six Countries* (New Haven, CT: Yale University Press, 1999).

8. In the last *Country Report* available within Polity Project IV (2003), Brazil was classified as highly democratic (8 points on a 0-to-10 scale), and the last transition to democracy was placed as the year of 1985. Available at http://www.cidcm.umd.edu/inscr/polity/.

9. Lijphart, *Patterns of Democracy.*

10. See Peter Kingstone and Timothy Power, eds., *Democratic Brazil: Actors, Institutions, and Processes* (Pittsburgh: University of Pittsburgh Press, 2000). Also see Political Risk Services 2004, http://www.prsonline.com.

11. See Andreas Schedler, "Measuring Democratic Consolidation," *Studies in Comparative International Development* 36, no. 1 (Spring 2001): 66–92; and Guillermo O'Donnell, "Comparative Politics and Democratic Theory," *Studies in Comparative International Development* 36, no. 1: 7–36.

12. During the military regime (1964–1985) and in the first government after the transition (1985–1989), the National Information Service (SNI) was the central agency of a powerful state security apparatus. The central information agencies of the three armed forces (navy, army, and air force) received new names after 1990, and the SNI was disbanded by President Fernando Collor de Melo in that same year. For a review of this period and the legislative debates in the executive about substitutes for the SNI, see Priscila Antunes, *SNI e ABIN: Uma leitura da atuação dos serviços secretos brasileiros no século XX* (Rio de Janeiro: Editora da Fundação Getulio Vargas, 2001); and Antunes and Cepik, "The New Brazilian Intelligence System."

13. For the complete Portuguese text of the Brazilian legislation, as well as follow-up of various kinds of proposals in the National Congress, see http://www.interlegis.gov.br.

14. The CCAI was initially called the Agency for Control and External Inspection of the National Intelligence Policy (OCFEPNI), established by Law 9.883, December 7, 1999. The Joint Commission was established about one year later.

15. Marco A. C. Cepik, *Espionagem e democracia* (Rio de Janeiro: Fundação Getulio Vargas, 2003).

16. For the full text of General Cardoso's speech, see Brasil Congresso, *Anais*

do Seminário Atividades de Inteligência no Brasil: Contribuições para a soberania e a democracia (Brasília, DF: ABIN e Congresso Nacional, 2002), 179–198.

17. Ricardo Mignone, "New ABIN Director Says the Agency Will Be Transparent," *Brasília Folha Online*, July 13, 2004, http://www.folhaonline.com.br. The full speech of the president is available at http://www.info.planalto.gov.br/download/discursos/pr471.doc.

18. This section was adapted from Cepik and Antunes, "The Professionalization of Intelligence in Brazil."

19. In the case of ABIN, the budget for 2003 was about $40 million, of which 73 percent was committed to personnel expenses, 21 percent to costs of and investments in the agency's activities (or about $8.5 million), and 6 percent for other types of expenses. In the case of the Ministry of Defense, the values authorized for subfunction 183 (information and intelligence) in 2004 amounted to approximately $1 million. As an analytical exercise, if the same proportions were maintained as found in ABIN for the relation between the end activity and expenses with personnel (respectively 21 percent and 73 percent of a hypothetical total), the allocation of resources for activities related to "intelligence and information" in the area of defense would be about $5.1 million in 2004. In the case of the Ministry of Justice, the subfunction "information and intelligence" received expense authorization of about $3.9 million for 2004, which leads to an extrapolation of about $18.5 million for the effort of that ministry. The total here is $63.6 million.

20. James Dunning, *How to Make War: A Comprehensive Guide to Modern Warfare in the 21st Century*, 4th ed. (New York: Quill, 2003), 633.

21. In contrast to Brazil's case, in the United States the Pentagon is reported to control more than 80 percent of the available intelligence resources and capabilities. Of SISBIN's approximately 1,600 workers in 2004, about 400 were analysts.

SEVEN

TAIWAN'S INTELLIGENCE REFORM IN AN AGE OF DEMOCRATIZATION

Steven E. Phillips

Four factors shaped the reform of security and intelligence agencies in the Republic of China (ROC) on Taiwan: democratization; Taiwanization of the state and the Nationalist Party; continuing concerns over the People's Republic of China (PRC); and scandals related to intelligence failures or malfeasance.[1] For most of the cold war, the Nationalist regime was authoritarian but never sought the degree of totalitarian control that its rivals across the strait, the Chinese Communists, did. Beginning in the 1980s, security services on Taiwan followed a pattern seen elsewhere—organizations with no external oversight, and not independent of the dominant political party or the state. Reform created institutions along the model of "bureaus of domestic intelligence" that focus on threats to the state rather than to a ruling political party or individual leader, do not use coercion, and accept "external inspection."[2] Since the late 1980s, the chief rival to the Nationalist Party (Kuomintang) has been the Democratic Progressive Party (DPP).[3] DPP leaders had long hoped to limit the role of the security and intelligence agencies in domestic politics and were able to take advantage of electoral victories to move ahead in this endeavor. Once in control of the executive branch after the 2000 election, however, DPP leaders found that reshaping loyalties while maintaining discipline within intelligence and security agencies was difficult.

Several unique aspects of Taiwan's recent history merit attention. Much of the literature on intelligence services in democratizing states builds on the experiences of postcommunist Eastern Europe. The intelligence efforts of these democratizing regimes now focus on their former ally, Russia, and they must also attack organized crime and terrorism. Taiwan's main external threat, however, has remained constant over the past half century. Chiang Kai-shek, his son Chiang

Ching-kuo, Taiwan-born Nationalist Lee Teng-hui, and DPP leader and current president Chen Shui-bian all shared concern over PRC intentions and military capabilities. These leaders, who range from authoritarian to cautious reformer to comprehensive reformer to democratic activist, also sought to build support among émigré communities and policymakers in the United States and Japan. Other than a few bombings by Taiwanese independence activists in the 1970s, terrorism has not been a major problem in pre- or post-reform Taiwan.

As they reform their intelligence services, many democratizing states debate how to define the national interest. On Taiwan, even the fundamental issue of national identity remains open to question. For decades the PRC and the ROC each advocated a one-China policy, which stated that there is but one China and that Taiwan is part of that China. (Each, of course, claimed to be that one legitimate China.) Beginning in the 1980s, Taiwanization meant that mainland-born Nationalists who came to the island with Chiang were gradually replaced in the military, security, and intelligence services. Taiwanese, Chinese immigrants from the mainland prior to 1945, have less commitment to the ideal of national unification; most of them have never visited the mainland.[4] The heated conflicts over loyalty to a unified China, to the ROC on Taiwan, or to an independent Taiwan that exist in the public sphere have become endemic within all parts of the government.

HISTORICAL CONTEXT: SUCCESSFUL DEMOCRATIZATION

After fifty years of Japanese colonial rule, the Nationalists arrived on the island in 1945 with the promise of restoring the island to China. By 1949, however, the Nationalists faced defeat at the hands Mao Zedong's Communist Party and retreated to the island, which became their final redoubt. As the regime collapsed on the mainland, the central government announced the "Temporary Provisions for the Period of Mobilization for the Suppression of Rebellion." This essentially gave the president dictatorial powers and suspended the constitution. These provisions meant that the president could ignore the legislature if he deemed it necessary and could remain in office indefinitely. In May 1949 the island was placed under martial law. Arrests and executions of those suspected of ties to the Chinese Communists or Taiwanese independence groups increased through 1949 and 1950, marking the start of what became known as the White Terror. By the time the

Korean War began in June 1950, Chiang was president of the ROC, director general of the Nationalist Party, and commander in chief of the armed forces, giving him the top positions in the state, the party, and the military. American support after the Korean War began ensured that the Nationalists would survive, even if Chiang's dream of retaking the mainland proved impossible.

The Nationalists' authoritarian rule and economic success planted the seeds for their downfall. The regime's attempt to co-opt some islanders by allowing them to participate in the state and party enabled Taiwanese to take over the Kuomintang and the Republic of China from the inside—a process known as Taiwanization. The oppression and brutality of the state pushed other islanders to oppose the Nationalist government and to reject the Nationalists' ideology. Despite imprisonment and harassment, in the 1970s non-Kuomintang politicians and intellectuals, called *tangwai* ("outside the party"), grew more vocal. They formed the Democratic Progressive Party (DPP) in 1986, the largest opposition party on the island. Further, economic progress enlarged and emboldened a reformist middle class. The United States also played a role by promoting reform with increasing urgency in the late 1970s and by providing a safe haven for exiled democracy activists.

Within the government, Chiang Ching-kuo, who succeeded his father in 1975, came to realize that the cold war approach of one-party rule and limited political participation for the Taiwanese was no longer viable. Domestic political reform became one way for the regime to build its legitimacy in the face of growing international isolation. Wide-ranging reforms followed, including the relaxation of controls over the press, speech, assembly, and political opposition, and the lifting of martial law. After Chiang Ching-kuo's death in January 1988, native-born Lee Teng-hui assumed the presidency and pushed ahead with Taiwanization and comprehensive reforms that truly democratized the island. Lee repealed the temporary provisions of the constitution. Taiwanization represented a conscious choice—Chiang Ching-kuo and Lee needed to legitimize their rule and cultivate support. It was also inevitable, as those born on the mainland retired. Further, many of their children had married Taiwanese and felt less commitment to the "old" Nationalist goals of retaking the mainland and national unification. Lee's final term as president ended in 2000, and the election that year marked an important transfer of power. After a closely fought race, DPP standard-bearer Chen Shui-bian was victorious. Reforms to intelligence and security services followed on the heels of Taiwan's successful democratic transition.

INTELLIGENCE AND SECURITY ORGANS

Taiwan's security and intelligence establishment grew out of institutions developed on the mainland during the struggle against the Chinese Communists, along with ad hoc bodies created to stabilize the regime after its retreat to the island.[5] At the apex of the pre-reform system stood the Political Action Committee, created by Chiang Kai-shek in 1949. The committee included Chiang, his son, and leaders of the major military, internal security, and intelligence organs on the island. All security and intelligence services answered directly to the president. In fact, until legislation passed in late 1993, the committee and its successors had no legislative mandate, much less oversight. The military, police, and intelligence agencies were above the law, as the survival of Chiang Kai-shek and his party was equated with the fate of China. Intelligence and security efforts concentrated on maintaining internal control, subverting mainland China, and building support in Japan and the United States and among overseas Chinese communities. In light of China's unfinished civil war, the lines between domestic security and foreign intelligence activities were indistinct as the Nationalists focused their resources on what they claimed was part of their own nation—the mainland.

The first steps toward separating domestic and foreign intelligence functions occurred not because of any democratic impulse but as part of the search for administrative efficiency. The Political Action Committee became the National Defense Committee in 1955 and finally the National Security Council (NSC) in 1967. Also in 1955, the National Security Bureau (NSB) was established. The NSB was designed to bring order to the plethora of security and intelligence services operating through the party, state, and military on the island.[6] The NSB oversaw security and intelligence organizations in the military, the Interior Ministry, the Justice Ministry, the National Police Administration, and the Kuomintang. During the 1950s and 1960s the NSB was widely feared as Taiwan's KGB, with a "secret" headquarters on Yangmingshan, north of Taipei.

The NSB also oversaw the Taiwan Garrison Command, which had its own security and intelligence bureaus. Also within the Ministry of

Defense was the Military Police Command, which served as a military police force and a supplement to the civilian police during times of crisis. The National Police Administration (NPA) shared control of police forces on Taiwan with the Ministry of Interior. The police system in Taiwan was, and is, much more centralized than in the United States and includes an international affairs component. The duties of the NPA include monitoring immigration affairs—roughly the equivalent of the Immigration and Naturalization Service in the United States.

As part of the 1955 reforms, the Military Intelligence Bureau (MIB) was established within the Ministry of Defense. The MIB inherited the personnel and mission of the feared Security Bureau, which had been created on the mainland to ferret out dissent. In theory, domestic investigation work was given to the Interior Ministry's Investigation Bureau when the MIB was created. The Investigation Bureau also absorbed the domestic security work performed by the Central Committee Bureau of Investigation and Statistics, a Nationalist Party organization technically separate from the state. The Bureau would later move to the Ministry of Justice (MJIB) and continue as the key counterintelligence organization on Taiwan.

DEMOCRATIZATION AND SCANDALS SPUR CHANGE

The introduction to this book details mechanisms to monitor intelligence agencies, including the separation of domestic and foreign intelligence and the establishment of oversight bodies. Such institutional changes began in Taiwan in the 1980s. Security services now focus on police functions and counterintelligence, and their role in monitoring unions, political parties, universities, and other civic groups has been circumscribed. In many case studies of democratization, the rise of civilian authority over the military is held as a key measurement of success. The military was influential during the martial law era, but the Nationalists on the mainland and on Taiwan did not establish a military regime. Since his rise to power in the mid-1920s, Chiang had been concerned about the power of his generals and was adept at balancing personal, factional, and institutional rivalries in the officer corps. Reform of the military, security, and intelligence organizations on Taiwan would be less a transformation to civilian control than an effort to reduce the power of the Nationalist Party.

Democratization and Taiwanization set the stage for reform, but actual policy changes occurred in reaction to malfeasance or bungling by the intelligence or security agencies. Because of an increasingly free press and electoral competition, information on ROC intelligence failures (or allegations of failures) became widely available. The first major embarrassment was the Jiang Nan Incident of 1984. "Jiang Nan" was a pseudonym for Henry Liu (Liu I'liang), a businessman and writer who authored a critical biography of President Chiang Ching-kuo. In October 1984, he was murdered outside his California home by members of the Bamboo Gang, a criminal organization with ties to the Nationalist Party.[7] Several Nationalist officials, including the head of the MIB, Wang Hsiling, were implicated in the killing and would be sentenced to prison on Taiwan. The court's verdict on retired vice admiral Wang stated only that he had a "personal reason" for wanting to silence Liu.[8] Although the trial was unique in the history of the Nationalist government, many of those involved in the plot gave only brief testimony.[9] Wang claimed that he expected the gangsters only to "rough up" the author. Wang's account seemed to suggest that the criminals were using the intelligence agencies as much as the other way around. These gangsters had come to him through intermediaries, he claimed, because they were worried about their culpability in other crimes and wished to become good citizens—they hoped that assisting the intelligence community would reduce their criminal penalties.[10]

The *Wall Street Journal* accurately put the Henry Liu assassination in the context of a struggle between older, mainland-born Nationalists in the military and intelligence establishment and younger, often Taiwan-born citizens who favored democratic reform.[11] The Jiang Nan Incident was a major watershed that opened the door to criticism of intelligence and security agencies. It also sparked investigations and anger in the United States, thus making America a stronger force in advocating reforms. Jiang Nan became a rallying cry for all critics of the Nationalists. Even if the full extent of the government's involvement in the affair remains murky, the fact that high-ranking officials faced prosecution and prison indicated that the political environment was changing.

The uproar over Jiang Nan forced the government to make its first meaningful reform of an intelligence or security service since 1967. In 1985 the MIB was placed under the direct command of the chief of the general staff, rather than answering to the NSB and the president. The Office of the Deputy Chief of the General Staff for Intelligence was created, and the individual holding this position commanded the bureau. Under the revised system, the MIB was to gather intelligence related to military matters, to avoid political domestic issues, and to eschew covert action.

INSTITUTIONAL REFORM UNDER LEE TENG-HUI

Lee Teng-hui would lead the institutional reform of intelligence and security agencies. He received legislative support from Taiwan-born members of the Nationalist Party and the growing number of DPP legislators. Reform at the top ranks of the ROC military would be a precursor to changes in intelligence and security organizations. Military reform emphasized nationalization—the attempt to disengage the interests of the Nationalist Party from those of the state.[12] More often than not, nationalization meant Taiwanization, the replacement of mainland-born officers with Taiwanese. The last major battle by mainlanders to maintain their influence was led by Hau Pei-tsun in the early 1990s. The Taiwan-born president enticed Chief of the General Staff Hau into retirement by offering him the post of defense minister in 1989. Lee then promoted Hau to premier and finally forced him to retire in 1993. Mainlanders continued to hold the chief of staff post through the 1990s, but they did not challenge Lee's Taiwanization efforts. In 1999, army commander in chief General Tang Yao-ming became the first Taiwanese to hold this post.

In January 1994, legislation was passed to provide a legal mandate for the NSC and the NSB. The reformed NSC includes the president, vice president, premier, minister of defense, minister of foreign affairs, the chiefs of the MJIB and NSB, and others on an ad hoc basis.[13] The 1996 Organic Law of the Presidential Office established the structure of the presidency and agencies that answer directly to it, including the NSC. The NSC and NSB budgets are now monitored by the Legislative Yuan's Intelligence Committee, but most of the budget remains secret from the public.[14] The NSC is not, however, as powerful as the body with the same name in the United States. It has a small staff, meets rarely, and to date has had little direct impact on policies. Although Presidents Lee and Chen did not create "shadow" intelligence or security services, they may have been wary of organizations dominated by mainlanders. In fact, mainlanders in intelligence and security agencies probably tried to undermine Lee. For example, rumors

FIGURE 7.1. *Taiwan's intelligence and security services. Adapted from the National Security Bureau website, http://www.nsb.gov.tw.*

of secret documents that would show President Lee had been a Communist Party member in his youth were common.[15] To date, Chen's interest in working through the NSC appears to have increased with his ability to name the heads of member agencies and bureaus.

The NSB mandate remains the coordination of national intelligence, but it is now expected to separate intelligence from law enforcement, a key theme of reform. NSB integrates and manages the intelligence- and security-related activities of the MIB, the Military Police Headquarters, the NPS, the Coast Guard Command, the MJIB, and other agencies through the interagency Coordinating Meeting for National Security Intelligence (CMNSI) (Figure 7.1). Today the NSB publicly acknowledges approximately 1,500 personnel divided into six departments: mainland operations, overseas operations (basically everything outside of Taiwan or the mainland), internal security intelligence, national strategic intelligence, science and technology intelligence/information security, and cipher/cryptography. The bureau also includes three other units: a computer center, a secretariat, and a general affairs office that provides administrative support and security for NSB facilities. Finally, the NSB now oversees personal security for the president and other top officials.

Covert operations are coordinated through the NSB's Special Operations Center. In 1998 the Legislative Yuan passed a law governing the covert actions managed by the center. Nothing better illustrates the changing situation on Taiwan than this law, which detailed the individuals authorized to approve covert actions and even when force may be used by covert agents.[16] It is, however, unclear whether other agencies continue to engage in covert actions. The latitude for covert operations directed against the PRC appears to be limited by geopolitics as much as institutional reform. Until the 1970s the Nationalists engaged in raids and other activities in order to destabilize the mainland government. Today, in light of Taiwan's international isolation, such an action would spark international criticism and, quite possibly, a military response from Beijing. It is clear, however, that intelligence-gathering efforts on the mainland remain an NSB priority.

Legislation in 1998 reorganized the Ministry of Justice and MJIB. MJIB duties were clearly defined to include investigating treason, sedition, espionage, disclosure of national security information, and other activities related to crime.[17] In this context, the MJIB resembles the United States Federal Bureau of Investigation. One recurring problem is the division of supervision of the MJIB. Its duties involving more-traditional criminal investigation work are overseen by the Ministry of Justice, while national security efforts are led by the NSB.

PRC MISSILE DISCLOSURES AND PROBLEMS OF NATIONAL LOYALTY

Scandals continued to shape public attitudes and state policies. The intelligence services were no longer untouchable but faced accusations of incompetence in the media and before the legislature. For example, in February 2000 the *Washington Post* and sources on Taiwan reported that in 1996 the ROC Defense Ministry inadvertently revealed information that led to the execution of a People's Liberation Army (PLA) general, his wife, and at least one other PLA officer. Nationalist officials had stated that there was little to worry about when the PRC tested missiles in the Taiwan Strait, as they contained dummy warheads—a fact never revealed publicly by the PRC. This remark allegedly sparked a PRC investigation that led to the executions of these alleged spies for Taiwan.[18] This fiasco called into question the ability of the ROC to obtain one day's warning of any missile attack—a key goal and public measurement of the services' effectiveness.[19]

This failure became connected to domestic politics, personal agendas, and issues of national identity on Taiwan. The *China Post* reported in June 2001 that mainland-born Chang Chih-peng, a former employee of the MIB, wished to go to the mainland but was prevented by the Ministry of Justice, for fear of the secrets he might reveal. He claimed that Lee Teng-hui was responsible for revealing information obtained from the two high-ranking PLA officers concerning the dummy warheads. Chang, under his previous cover as a businessman in China, allegedly obtained this information and passed it along to military intelligence. Chang had planned to turn himself in to the PRC in exchange for a reduced sentence for Yao Jiazhen, a manager at a factory Chang used as a front who had been arrested by PRC security forces. Chang also said that he suffered financial setbacks due to Lee's revelations, which led to the confiscation of the factories he had an interest in.[20] Chang's biography, written with his cooperation, reveals his dedication to Taiwan's unification with the mainland and his hatred of Lee Teng-hui, who he deemed as a traitor to China. Chang suggested that the Nationalists and Communists shared as much as they disputed—the DPP and disloyal Nationalists like Lee were the subversives.[21] Chang epitomized a problem in the military, intelligence, and security services—aging mainland-born officials felt that Taiwanization meant abandoning the dream of a united China. He also revealed the ways that private financial interests frequently combined with public service.

In fact, since the late-1990s, supporters of Lee and DPP politicians have become increasingly concerned over the loyalty of mainlanders and their heirs. As one media source noted, "Some of the loudest voices calling for a crackdown [on leaks] come from the democracy activists and Taiwan independence advocates who, in the bad old days, received the often murderous attention of the security authorities." Critics decried the lack of clear procedures for security clearances.[22] President Chen Shui-bian pledged to create new procedures to investigate intelligence officers' contacts with China and dedication to the goal of unification with the mainland—which would now suggest disloyalty to the ROC on Taiwan rather than loyalty to the Nationalists and their ideology. In other words, support of unification with the mainland is no longer a litmus test for government employment but may instead indicate a potential conflict of interest. This represents a tremendous shift in political culture and ideology within the intelligence and security services.

CHEN SHUI-BIAN AND INTELLIGENCE REFORM

When Chen Shui-bian took office in May 2000, the major institutional reforms to security and intelligence agencies had been implemented. The new president would, however, face difficult problems of changing personnel and attitudes within these organizations while maintaining their effectiveness. Chen would not only press for reforms to protect individual rights but also promote new laws to protect national security information. The new ruling party, the DPP, lacks experience in this realm, and some politicians are rightly suspicious because of their personal experiences of arrest and harassment. In light of cross-strait tensions, however, there exists a general acceptance that foreign intelligence gathering and domestic counterintelligence are vital. From Chiang Kai-shek, with his dream of national unification, to Chen Shui-bian, with his hopes of eventual independence, Taiwan's main foreign threat remains the People's Republic.

In a September 2000 press conference, President Chen Shui-bian summed up many of his concerns and goals concerning intelligence and security reform. He noted that he began his career in the opposition and had suffered under the Nationalists' White Terror. Chen called for neutrality in intelligence and crime-fighting operations and in the military and intelligence agencies. Finally, he stated that these organizations should focus on national security, economic and social security, and crime prevention.[23] His discussion of neutrality was understood to mean that promotion of Kuomintang politicians and policies was no longer the goal of security and intelligence organizations. His approach could be summarized as "de-Nationalization," that is, to reduce the interest of this political party.

As the DPP became more accustomed to holding power, its leaders began to worry more about balancing effective intelligence-gathering efforts with democratic reforms. In March 2002, Chen articulated the problems of military, security, and intelligence reform, noting that "the nationalization of military forces and the institutionalization of the intelligence agencies remain goals undertaken by the government after the transfer of political power." In another speech in April, he added, "Only when we forge a democratic supervisory mechanism can we rally the greatest possible support in the legislature and among the general public for the NSB's normal operations."[24] The new president also said, however, that he had concerns about the exposure of some government malfeasance. He claimed that no opposition or contradiction existed between a free press and national security and that no one should use the excuse of national security to limit press freedom. Chen added, however, that "in the delicate balance between national security and press freedom, the protection of one should not compromise — nor be compromised in lieu of — the other."[25] Chen made clear that military, intelligence, and national security organizations were vital in light of events like the PRC missile tests in the Taiwan Strait.[26]

Legislation and regulations concerning the intelligence community refined and clarified laws passed during Lee Teng-hui's tenure. The duties of the deputy chief of staff for intelligence and the MIB were last revised in February 2002. The regulations highlight that the MIB duties are related to military intelligence only and include establishing military intelligence policies, budgets, and education; collecting international intelligence; planning for military needs; and preparing strategic and tactical estimates.[27] The most recent legislation on the duties and organization of the NSB was passed in January 2003. The NSB is to provide guidance, support, and coordination for the MIB, the Military Police Headquarters, the police force, the MJIB, and Coast Guard, and other agencies. The law details for the public the number of top staff and the budget process, even if the actual budget amounts are revealed only to a committee of the national legislature.[28]

Under Chen, Taiwanization reached to the top ranks of the intelligence and security services. His minister of justice, Chen Ding-nan, is Taiwanese. The minister's political career began as an anti-Kuomintang politician in Ilan County in the 1980s. He then became a member of the national legislature. Another important personnel change is the rise of Yeh Sheng-mao. The first Taiwanese to hold the directorship of the MJIB, Yeh replaced Wang Kuang-yu in August 2001. Yeh had a close relationship with the president, as he had been in charge of government ethics in the Taipei city government when Chen served as mayor in the 1990s. Bureaucratic politics and personal rivalries also shaped these personnel shifts. For example, newspapers reported a conflict between Minister of Justice Chen Ding-nan and the MJIB director over MJIB duties.[29] One version of Wang's removal posits that he proved unable to control the MJIB bureaucracy or to promote the creation of a new anticorruption organization.[30]

In 2001, President Chen reshuffled the top NSB and NSC staff. Like many NSB heads, Taiwan-born Lieutenant General Ts'ai Chao-ming moved into this position after commanding the MIB. He began his career at the ROC military academy in 1962 and gradually rose up the ranks into posts involving international affairs and intelligence. He served as deputy director of the NSB and the NSB representative in the United States. He studied at the Command and General Staff College of the U.S. Army and the RAND Graduate School. Chen named him head of the NSB in August 2001. Another sign of change was that Major General Pan Ai-chu was promoted to director of the political warfare department in the MIB in December 2001. She was only the third female general in ROC history (the other two were promoted in the 1950s and 1960s), and the first Taiwanese woman to achieve this rank. The remaining high-ranking mainlander was MIB head Hsueh Shih-ming, who was promoted to his position by Chen from his post as commander of ROC forces on Kinmen Island off the mainland coast.

Nothing better exemplifies the changing political fortunes of Taiwan's former opposition than the rise of Kang Ning-hsiang. Taiwan-born Kang, a prominent democracy activist in the 1970s and 1980s, became the secretary general of the NSC in 2003. He was considered a relatively moderate DPP figure with an early interest in foreign policy that began with his efforts to unite overseas Taiwanese with dissidents who remained on the island.[31] Although Kang's position today has less influence than the American assistant to the president for national security affairs, it has great symbolic importance.

GREEN TERROR?

Intelligence and security organizations became politicized in a new way, as Chen and the DPP stood accused of using them for their own purposes. In 2000 a group of MJIB officials, primarily mainlanders, organized the Investigation Reform Committee (IRC). The committee was supported by the opposition parties, including James Soong's People's First Party (PFP), and the Nationalist Party.[32] In particular, allies of the current mayor of Taipei, a longtime rival of Chen Shui-bian's who was facing an MJIB corruption investigation, decried the "green terror" led by the DPP. "Green" in this case denotes the color of the DPP flag. They called for the separation of intelligence and law enforcement and for rules to keep the MJIB out of politics—reforms the DPP as opposition had advocated for decades.[33] It is important to remember that almost every official under investigation for corruption claims that the MJIB is engaged in a political vendetta. IRC representatives stated that the MJIB received oral instructions from the NSB to monitor political figures on Taiwan. A PFP spokesman stated that ten politicians had been targeted for investigation.[34] They also stated that the MJIB and NSB prepared a secret daily report for the president detailing domestic political developments.

Chen denied the existence of this report but stated that he was kept informed of criminal investigations. The president noted that he supported the reforms proposed by the committee to separate the military and intelligence agencies and to separate intelligence and crime-fighting operations. The issue had become politicized further, and Chen criticized the committee, noting that its supporters were from opposition parties.[35] In response to IRC accusations, MJIB director Wang Kuang-yu announced in October 2000 that this organization was no longer responsible for "political surveillance" work. According to press reports, Chen's new premier, Chang Chun-hsiung, approved the change while admitting, "In the past, the MJIB conducted political surveillance under the supervision of the NSB." The new MJIB "domestic security survey" was to include items such as the PRC's activities on Taiwan, activities of foreign nationals, unlawful activities, information security, and threats to domestic public order. President Chen Shui-bian backed this reform.[36] Wang's replacement, Taiwan-born Yeh Sheng-mao, did little to reduce criticism that MJIB activities were politicized by the DPP and President Chen Shui-bian.

LEE TENG-HUI'S SLUSH FUND AND THE LIMITS OF REFORM

Democratization, Taiwanization, and intelligence reform left some longtime members of the intelligence community embittered against Chen and the DPP. At an increasing pace since the 1990s, mainland-born officials have engaged in contacts with the mainland or even moved there, leading to concerns over the disclosure of sensitive information. It is impossible to know to what extent reforms to the NSB, MIB, and MJIB—or sincere concern that Lee Teng-hui and Chen Shui-bian lacked commitment to the ideal of unification with the mainland—motivate these defections. For example, Major General Pan Hsi-hsien, who worked in the Military Intelligence Bureau, began working for a Taiwanese company and moved to Shenzhen (near Hong Kong) immediately after retiring in May 2000.[37] Since early 2001, even the Control Yuan has complained that many retired intelligence officials were traveling to China, including two former deputy directors of the MIB and the MIB station chief in Hong Kong. The Control Yuan, an independent watchdog branch of the government somewhat analogous to the Congressional Budget Office or the Government Accountability Office in the United States, had been a toothless watchdog when it came to military, intelligence, or security agencies.[38] The Yuan's National Defense and Intelligence Committee also performed an investigation of the travels of retired officials—something unheard-of until recently.[39] The fact that legislators and independent government organizations like the Control Yuan were now probing such matters highlighted the new political atmosphere in Taiwan. The Yuan's criticism caused then secretary general of the NSC Ting Yu-chou to resign in 2002.[40]

The NSB was damaged by a major scandal in March 2002, when Taiwanese publications such as *Next* weekly magazine were prevented from publishing reports on a secret fund managed by Lee Teng-hui.[41] The fund was allegedly created in the early 1990s to boost Taiwan's diplomatic stature and to enhance intelligence-gathering activities in China.[42] The magazine's offices were searched and materials confiscated by the High Court Prosecutor's Office at the request of Ts'ai Chao-ming, then director of the NSB. The betrayal of the secret fund was tied by some observers to "military and intelligence officers who are not native to Taiwan. Those officers who claim their heritage in mainland China have not been shy about proclaiming their doubts about the loyalties of Taiwan's new political leaders to the idea of 'One China.'"[43] The scandal was magnified when Liu Kuan-chun, chief financial officer for the NSB, was accused of embezzlement and of revealing Lee's fund. Liu apparently threatened to disclose the documents and defect if he did not receive a pardon, which did not occur. The materials went through James Soong's People's First Party—primarily made up of mainlanders who despised Lee and Chen. Someone in the party, in turn, provided the documents to *Next* weekly magazine and *China Times*, two publications known for being pro-Nationalist and pro-unification. In fact, *Next* was owned by a Hong Kong businessman closely tied to Beijing.

This incident sparked public debate on the need for further supervision of intelligence agencies. Some Taipei media reported that the MJIB's money-laundering unit had been investigating NSB employee Liu, but the NSB insisted on first assisting the probe, then made it into its own internal investigation.[44] This raised questions about the shared supervision of the MJIB, as the Ministry of Justice seemed uninvolved in these controversies. In 2002 the Control Yuan impeached two NSB officials, both mainland-born, for failing to take action against Liu's embezzlement of government funds, to monitor Liu after his retirement, and to block his flight to China. Public opinion seemed divided between those who criticized Lee's extralegal fund and others who attacked its exposure.

In March 2002, President Chen called for further reform, beginning with a state secrets law and a government information access law. He said that the embezzlement scandal revealed the need for greater legislative oversight and strengthened internal discipline.[45] Revelations over the secret fund seem to have worried Chen as much as the Nationalists, as he and the DPP sought any tool to increase Taiwan's international stature. Taiwan's leaders have hinted that the PRC was behind the disclosures. Ts'ai Chao-ming called publicly for greater wiretapping ability in the wake of the uproar. Without naming any specific threat, he did note, "Our enemy has made every effort to break up our defense."[46] At the same time, many DPP legislators, who might be expected to be most hostile toward the intelligence and security agencies, suggested that the revelations were a plot by the pro-unification PFP or the mainland, thus making them now favor tighter controls on information and personnel.[47] Other legislators proposed laws to require greater transparency in government funding of diplomatic activity.[48]

In August 2002, new regulations went into effect to restrict the ability of government personnel to travel to the mainland. Now employees of the NSB, the Ministry of Defense, the MJIB, related agencies, and retirees must obtain permission from the Interior Ministry's Immigration and Emigration Management Bureau.[49] DPP legislators have in fact called for more-stringent security procedures and for a security clearance system mirroring that implemented in the United States. This debate has become embroiled in partisan politics, as "Pan Blue," the Nationalist Party, and the People's First Party have stalled legislation on loyalty checks, in the name of protecting the rights of government employees. Ex-president Lee Teng-hui's Taiwan Solidarity Union, a new political party formed in 2001, has allied itself with the DPP and has fiercely attacked Pan Blue for endangering national security.[50]

In January 2003, the DPP-controlled cabinet proposed to the Legislative Yuan new legislation to regulate official secrets. This would limit the ability of officials to declare information classified and would require that various categories of documents be declassified in ten to thirty years. The proposed laws, which were a reaction to the publication of information on Lee's secret fund and mainland visits by retired officials, would also provide for clear penalties for revealing classified information. The National Secrets Protection Law was passed quickly.[51] The freedom of information law proposed at the same time, however, languished in the legislature. The failure of this legislation probably stemmed from two factors. First, Chen represented the executive branch and had less interest in making himself vulnerable by revealing information about intelligence gathering and influence peddling. Second, Nationalist Party figures feared that it would require disclosure of political contributions and assets held by political parties.[52]

THE FUTURE OF INTELLIGENCE REFORM

By any measure, democratization has been successful and peaceful on Taiwan. Reform of the intelligence and security agencies is being achieved without bloodshed, and there is little interest in revenge or trying retired officials for past injustices. The major institutions now face outside scrutiny and legal limits on their activities, and there is little chance that Taiwan's reforms will be reversed. Furthermore, competence and effectiveness in the performance of professional duties, or at least the perceptions of effectiveness, has become a key factor in determining the tenure of security or intelligence officials. For example, Ts'ai Chao-ming resigned in 2004, taking the blame for not preventing an assassination attempt on Chen and his vice president on the eve of the March elections. He was replaced by General Hsueh Shih-ming, a mainlander who headed the MIB since 2001. The fact that Chen selected Hsueh for this post was a hopeful sign that the heated conflict between native-born and mainland-born might fade.

There exist, however, several unresolved issues. Will the DPP remain committed to reform? Now that Chen Shui-bian holds power and has placed Taiwanese in the top ranks of the intelligence community, will the DPP build upon its heritage as "outsiders" and continue to promote change? The evidence suggests that even if the DPP falters, the "new" opposition parties and the press will serve as watchdogs. However, Taiwan's divided government, where the opposition Nationalist Party and People's First Party remain in control of the legislature, has meant that partisanship pervades all aspects of intelligence and security reform. The island has been mired in political paralysis, particularly after Chen's razor-thin margin of victory in the March 2004 election.[53] While political leaders have not resorted to violence, conflicts are heated. The Nationalists and allied parties have already attempted to impeach President Chen Shui-bian once during his first term, and there is a danger that the DPP will find itself stymied by opposition for its own sake (commonly called *wei fan er fan* in Chinese) throughout the second term. This may lead to greater cynicism toward intelligence and security efforts, as every error in judgment becomes a major public scandal and each criminal investigation is labeled a political vendetta. The most significant change in the last two years was the January 2005 National Intelligence Work Law, which mandates that employees of the NSB, the MIB, the MJIB, and the National Police Administration avoid political activity and that these agencies answer to the legislature and provide written reports on their efforts each year. The NSB, MJIB, and MIB might find themselves buried in a blizzard of accusations and investigations. This has not occurred to date, as public sympathy has tended to shift when citizens feel that partisanship is excessive.

Further institutional reforms have been discussed but have yet to be implemented. For example, it remains to be seen whether the Control Yuan has the necessary expertise and access to information to monitor intelligence and security activities, as opposed to simply reacting to scandals. Nationalist and DPP enthusiasm for a freedom-of-information law has waned. The ROC has yet to establish an organization like the U.S. President's Foreign Intelligence Advisory Board (PFIAB) or other control and oversight organizations discussed in Chapter 1. Finally, the management of national security and intelligence functions is still rather ad hoc, as the NSC has yet to fulfill its mandate.

Increasing economic integration with the mainland has raised several security concerns on Taiwan. During the pre-reform era, it was the most conservative Nationalists who warned against economic ties to the mainland. Today it is the DPP, which is responsible for national security and has a long-term interest in preventing unification. Some legislators established the Alliance Against Selling Out Taiwan to draw attention to security threats arising from mainland ties. First, investment made the island more dependent on the mainland. Second, it raised the specter of intellectual property rights violations, industrial espionage, and influence peddling. Third, economic ties have created a cadre of businessmen who act as lobbyists for Beijing. In March 2003, NSB head Tsai Chao-ming announced the formation of a task force to prevent the loss of high-technology information. This came in the wake of claims that at least one Taiwan semiconductor company with a factory on the mainland may have disclosed sensitive data. Press reports detailed the brain drain from Taiwan to the PRC. Many researchers with the Chung-Shan Institute of Science and Technology (a part of the Ministry of Defense roughly equivalent to the Defense Advanced Research Projects Agency, or DARPA) were retiring to work in the private sector and then moving to the mainland. In 2003 at least one institute employee was arrested for supplying information to the PRC.[54] Like all national security issues, this incident has become politicized, as the chairman of the Nationalist Party denied that two of his relatives were involved in the institute espionage case.[55] Scandals even reached the top levels of the intelligence community. An NSC staff member, the personal secretary to Secretary-General Kang Ning-hsiang, resigned in August 2003 when press reports alleged that she had extensive mainland investments connected to the PRC's Ministry of Railways.[56]

The chief problem of reform thus far has been the embarrassing disclosures by supporters of the "old" Nationalist Party. Will tensions within intelligence and security agencies decrease as mainlanders and even their children pass from the scene, or will the transition spark further defections to the mainland and disclosures of ROC efforts? These conflicts will be worsened if the current president makes significant moves toward independence. Will intelligence and security efforts be hampered by the fact that many important documents and much institutional knowledge remain with the Nationalist Party rather than with the ROC state? Simply put, will the reformed institutions be effective at monitoring the mainland and limiting the activities of PRC personnel on Taiwan? The key test will be the ROC's ability to predict and evaluate the next cross-strait crisis.

From the start of the Korean War until the United States switched recognition to the People's Republic of China in 1979, military, diplomatic, economic, and intelligence cooperation between Taipei and Washington was strong. The abrogation of the mutual security treaty and the unofficial nature of diplomatic ties after 1979 downgraded, but did not entirely end, this relationship. Taiwan was and is an important conduit for information about political and military developments in the People's Republic of China. The ROC has many advantages that make it a vital resource for understanding the mainland—geographic proximity, growing cross-strait contacts, a common language and culture, and advanced technology. If the potential difficulties that have accompanied reform can be surmounted, Taiwan will remain significant to China watchers. The Taiwanese and the DPP, like the mainlanders and the Nationalists before them, have a vested interest in seeking to increase political, military, and intelligence ties to the United States.[57] Due to the one-China policy, such cooperation must be discreet in order to avoid antagonizing Beijing.

TAIWAN AS A MODEL FOR REFORM?

Duplicating Taiwan's democratization experience, which served as the base for intelligence reform, would be difficult. Democratization took place over the course of two decades and built upon three decades of extraordinary economic growth, a relatively equitable distribution of income, a cadre of young people who had studied in the United States, and persistent American pressure for liberalization. The scars of authoritarian rule are not as deep as might exist in other democratizing regimes. The Nationalists were never as brutal as the Chinese Communists, and few Taiwanese ever called for radical social or economic change. Ethnic, racial, religious, or class-based violence has been almost nonexistent. Finally, the ROC's unique international isolation forced Nationalist leaders to seek to build legitimacy at home to compensate for the lack of recognition abroad—a problem no other state has to confront. The ROC has been relentless in its efforts to publicize its successful reforms, in part as a rebuke to Beijing's continued one-party rule of the mainland. In light of international sensitivities over the PRC's one-China policy, however, few democratizing regimes will be eager to publicize that they might benefit from Taiwan's experiences.

The institutional aspects of intelligence reform, however, do provide a model for other democratizing states. The laws and regulations, the organization of the NSC and NSB, and the roles of the legislature, the Control Yuan, and the press can be imitated elsewhere. Taiwan also offers two important lessons. First is the need to focus on the sequence of political change: constitutional reform, guaranteed rights, free elections, viable opposition parties, and a political culture that generally eschewed violence all preceded reform to intelligence and security agencies. Second is the perception of a common external threat. Despite conflicts over Taiwanization and Taiwan's national identity, most Nationalists and DPP leaders see the PRC as Taiwan's most likely adversary. This shared concern may give both parties an incentive to limit the damage to intelligence or security agencies stemming from reform or political competition.

NOTES

1. The Republic of China is also known as Nationalist China. This state was guided by the Kuomintang (the Nationalist Party). The Kuomintang was formed around the ideology of Sun Yat-sen called Three Principles of the People — nationalism, democracy, and people's livelihood — and was dominated by Chiang Kai-shek after Sun's death in 1925.

2. On the use of these concepts, and evidence on Eastern Europe, see Kieran Williams and Dennis Deletant, *Security Intelligence Services in New Democracies: The Czech Republic, Slovakia, and Romania* (London: Palgrave, 2001), 3–4.

3. For personal names and places, this paper uses the romanization system presently utilized by the ROC, and the pinyin system promoted by the PRC for Communist leaders. For other terms and organization names, which are rarely romanized, I have used the Wade-Giles system. Note that romanization may change, as the ROC on Taiwan is currently adopting a system called *tongyong pinyin*, a modified version of the mainland's romanization.

4. Most Taiwanese came from provinces along the southeast coast of the mainland during the Qing dynasty (1644–1912), prior to the Japanese occupation in 1895. "Mainlanders" are Chinese who came to the island after 1945, the majority arriving between late 1948 and mid-1950 as the Nationalist government faced defeat at the hands of the Chinese Communists.

5. "Security" denotes efforts to prevent subversion, espionage, and civil unrest, usually within national borders; "intelligence" suggests attempts to gather information (both secret and open-source) abroad. Until recently, on Taiwan the boundary between security and intelligence was blurred.

6. Kao Minghui, *Chingchih tang'an* [Political Intelligence Archives] (Taipei: Shangyu chouk'an, 1995), 137–138.

7. The Bamboo Gang *(Chulin lienmeng)* was formed in 1956 by young refugees from the mainland. This became the largest criminal gang on the island. Chen Qili, leader of the Bamboo Gang, may have even met with or had ties to Chiang Wei-kuo, Chiang Ching-kuo's brother.

8. Liu was accused of supplying information to Nationalist and Communist intelligence agencies and was possibly planning a trip to the PRC when he was killed.

9. Maria Shao, "Liu Case Tests Taiwan's Claims to Democracy," *Wall Street Journal*, April 29, 1985, 1.

10. Wang Shihch'un, *Chung yu kuo Chingchih shouchang Wang Hsiling te ch'iluo* [A Matter of Honor: The Rise and Fall of Wang Hsiling] (Taipei: Tianhsia yuanchian, 1999). Chapters 13 and 14 contain the complex story of how the Military Intelligence Bureau and the Bamboo Gang became involved in the author's death. In fact, Wang's book is by far the single best account of ROC intelligence and influence peddling operations in the United States, for he was stationed in Washington in the 1970s and 1980s.

11. Maria Shao, "Liu Case Tests Taiwan's Claims to Democracy," 1.

12. On nationalization, see "Kuofang chungyao shihcheng" [Major Policies to Implement for National Defense], chap. 6 in the July 2002 National Defense Report of the ROC, http://www.mnd.gov.tw/report/defence/chinese/IND.HTM.

13. For more information on the national defense organizations of the ROC, see David Shambaugh, "Taiwan's Security: Maintaining Deterrence amid Political Accountability," *China Quarterly* 148 (December 1996): 1284–1318. For the best overview of the ROC national security organs, see Michael Swaine, "Taiwan's National Security, Defense Policy, and Weapons Procurement Processes," MR-1128-OSD, RAND National Security Research Division, 1999.

14. See *Kuochia anch'üanhui tsuchihfa* [Organic Law of the NSC], December 30, 1993.

15. On anti-Lee conspiracies, see Yu Chengwen's oral history, prepared by Huang Chihming et al., *Paise k'ongpu mimi tang'an* [Secret Archives of the White Terror] (Taipeihsian: Tuchia wenhua, 1995), 241–253; and Su Enmin, *Chiench'a tiao fahsien: Guo'anchü fan Li shihli* [Prosecutor's Investigation Reveals NSB Anti-Lee Teng-hui Efforts], *Tzuli wanpao*, March 26, 2002, 2.

16. *Kuochia anch'üanchü t'echung ch'inwu shihshih panfa* [Laws on the Special Operations of the NSB], December 21, 1998.

17. As of 1998, the Ministry of Justice's mandate included: prevention of civil strife; prevention of foreign aggression; prevention of disclosure of national secrets; drug prevention; prevention of organized crime and criminal gangs; prevention of corruption and bribery related to elections; prevention of major economic crimes and money laundering; national security investigations; and investigations involving high-level organizations for national security and the national interest.

18. Note that this is the version put forth on the mainland and Taiwan. It is unknown if the PRC security agencies learned of People's Liberation Army contacts with Taiwan through other means.

19. John Pomfret, "Taiwanese Mistake Led to Three Spies' Executions," *Washington Post*, February 20, 2000, A1.

20. "Ex-Spy Barred from Leaving Taiwan," *China Post*, June 29, 2001, 1.

21. Chang's story is told in Wang Paoyuan, *Ch'ingpao tsochan chishih* [A Record of Fighting an Intelligence War] (Taipei, 2001).

22. Laurence Eyton, "A Stern Test of Loyalty: The Government Imposes New Security Checks," *Asiaweek*, October 9, 1998; accessed at http://www.asiaweek.com/asiaweek/98/1009/nat6.html.

23. A Chinese-language transcript from President Chen Shui-bian's September 16, 2003, press conference is available at http://www.president.gov.tw/1_president/subject-06a.html.

24. Lin Chieh-yu, "Chen Issues Call for Overhaul of Security Agencies," *Taipei Times*, March 26, 2002, 1; Sofia Wu, "Intelligence Work Needs Democratic Oversight: President," Central News Agency (Taiwan), April 10, 2002.

25. Deborah Kuo, "President Chen Reiterates Stance on Safeguarding Freedom of Press," Central News Agency (Taiwan), March 26, 2002.

26. See the Chinese-language transcript from Chen Shui-bian's press conference of September 16, 2003, at http://www.president.gov.tw/1_president/subject-06a.html.

27. *Kuofangpu ts'anmo penpu panshih hsitse* [Rules and Regulations for the Ministry of Defense Chief of Staff Duties, part 6, February 27, 2002.

28. *Kuochia anch'üanchü tsuchih fa* [Organic Law of the NSB], revised January 22, 2003.

29. Jou Ying-cheng, "Group Urges MJIB Reform," *Taipei Times*, September 10, 2000, 3.

30. Jou Ying-cheng, "MJIB's New Chief Takes Command," *Taipei Times*, August 22, 2001, 4.

31. Lin Mei-chun, " 'Old Kang' a Political War-Horse," *Taipei Times*, February 10, 2003, 3.

32. The People's First Party was an offshoot of the Nationalist Party. Most members of this party are mainlanders who feel that the Nationalist Party has abandoned its commitment to China's unification.

33. "Editorial: Intelligence Roles Need Clarifying," *Taipei Times*, September 13, 2000, 8.

34. Lin I-hsien, "Tiaokaihui ch'engli: chengchih t'anfang tzoju lishih?" [Investigation Reform Committee Established: Political Surveillance Passing into History?], Taiwan *Sinorama* (Chinese edition), October 2000, 76.

35. The Chinese-language transcript from President Chen Shui-bian's September 16, 2003, press conference is available at http://www.president.gov.tw/1_president/subject-06a.html.

36. Sofia Wu, "MJIB Formally Ceases Controversial 'Political Surveillance' Work," Taipei, Central News Agency wire, October 25, 2000; accessed through LexisNexis.

37. Julian Baum, "Security Lapse: A Top Intelligence Official Takes a Retirement Job in China," *Far Eastern Economic Review* 163, no. 28 (July 13, 2000): 22.

38. The ROC has five branches of government: executive, legislative, judicial, control, and examination. The Examination Yuan was created to manage the hiring and placement of government bureaucrats, but it has little power.

39. Sofia Wu, "Watchdog Body Concerned about Intelligence Network Safety," Taipei, Central News Agency wire, January 7, 2003; accessed through LexisNexis.

40. Ting had served as head of the NSB from 1999 to 2001. The best overview of politics in the intelligence agencies in the late 1990s and early 2000s is found in Ting Yu-chou's memoirs, *Ting Yu-chou hui-yi-lu* [Memoirs of Ting Yu-chou] (Taipei: T'ian-hsia yuan-chien, 2004).

41. Liu Kuan-chun, chief cashier of the bureau from 1997 to 2000, allegedly revealed that NSB director Ying Tsung-wen, with the approval of President Lee, in 1994 established a $3.5 billion fund. It may have been used to delay South Africa's shifting of diplomatic relations from the ROC to PRC. John Pomfret of the *Washington Post* reported that the fund totaled US$100 million. Funds went to South Africa, Nicaragua, Panama, Japan, and the United States. John Pomfret, "Secret Taiwan Fund Sought Friends, Influence, Abroad," *Washington Post*, April 5, 2002, A1.

42. Wu Tung-yeh, "No Saints to Be Found in NSB's Scandals," *Taipei Times*, March 25, 2002, 8.

43. John Tkacik, "Secrets, Scholars, and Spies," *China Brief (Jamestown Foundation)* 2, no. 10 (May 9, 2002). http://www.jamestown.org/publications_details .php?volume_id=18&&issue_id=650.

44. "Intelligence Bureaus Ripe for Reform," *Taipei Times* (online edition), September 29, 2000, http://www.taiwanheadlines.gov.tw/20000929/2000092902 .html.

45. "Chen Issues Call for Overhaul of Security Agencies," *Taipei Times*, March 26, 2002, 1. Tso Ching-wen, "Chen tsungt'ung: Kuo'an yu hsinwen tzuyu weipi tuili" [President Chen: National Security and Media Freedom Are Not in Opposition], *Tzuli wanpao*, March 26, 2002, 3.

46. "Intelligence Official Calls for Legalized Bugging in NSB," *China Post*, March 14, 2002; accessed through LexisNexis.

47. "Lawmakers Clash over Leaked NSB Files," *China Post*, March 22, 2002; accessed through LexisNexis.

48. "Lawmakers Target Secret Government Funding," *China Post*, May 5, 2002; accessed through LexisNexis. Lai Jenchung, "Kuochia chimi paohufa" [National secrets protection law], *Tzuli wanpao*, March 22, 2002, 19.

49. Taiwan tichu jenmin chinju talu tichu hsuk'e panfa [Methods for Obtaining Permission for Those in the Taiwan Area to Travel to the Mainland Area], revised August 28, 2002. "Ministry Tightens Rules on Overseas Trips by Security Officials," Taipei, Central News Agency wire, October 2, 2002.

50. "TSU Says KMT-PFP Stonewalling Poses Significant Danger to National Security," Central News Agency dispatch, *Taipei Times*, August 13, 2003, 3.

51. *Kuochia chimi paohufa* [National Secrets Protection Law], February 6, 2003.

52. Dennis Engbarth, "State Secrets Act Approved," *Taiwan News*, January 15, 2003. See also Huang Weichu, "Shechi kuo'an ch'ingpao kuantao hsu yungchiu paomi" [The Pipeline for National Security Intelligence Must Always Be Kept Secret], *Tzuli wanpao*, January 15, 2003, 1.

53. Chen was behind in most polls on the eve of the March 20 election. A botched assassination attempt that wounded Chen and his running mate, Annette Lu, probably swung votes to the DPP. Chen won by about 30,000 votes out of more than 13 million cast. Leaders of the Pan Blue opposition hinted that the assassination attempt was a DPP trick and claimed that a state of emergency declared after the shooting prevented many soldiers from voting. In the month after the election, Pan Green (the DPP and allied parties) and Pan Blue leaders fought over the scope of the recount.

54. Fiona Lu, "Watch for Spies, CSIST Told," *Taipei Times*, August 7, 2003, 3.

55. "KMT Denies Info Leads Involving Lien's Family," *China Post*, August 8, 2003; accessed through LexisNexis.

56. Roger Liu, "NSC Denies That Secrets Were Sold," *Taipei Times*, August 10, 2003, 4. The official who resigned was an expert on China's economy. An NSC spokesman claimed that her husband had made the investments in China and that he had been held by the PRC government in Shanghai over a business dispute.

57. Taiwan-U.S. intelligence relations are often adversarial, as the ROC attempts to monitor dissidents among immigrants and to influence politicians in Washington, while the United States seeks to discover ROC intentions and, in one incident, prevent Taiwan from developing nuclear weapons. David Albright and Corey Gay, "Taiwan: Nuclear Nightmare Averted," *Bulletin of Atomic Scientists* 54, no. 1 (January 1998): 54–61.

EIGHT

ESTABLISHING DEMOCRATIC CONTROL OF INTELLIGENCE IN ARGENTINA

Priscila Carlos Brandão Antunes

The involvement of the legislative branch in setting up and controlling intelligence activities is a crucial aspect of establishing democratic control and effectiveness. This supervision must be in accord with two basic parameters: the control of the intelligence operations (which, in order to be effective, need to be secret); and budgetary control, because intelligence is an activity that is highly specialized and, at least in some areas of tradecraft, involves significant technological requirements.

Based on these premises, this chapter discusses the overall importance of the legislative and judicial branches in asserting control over intelligence activities (with the greatest emphasis on the legislative); briefly discusses intelligence reform in the context of civil-military relations reform; describes in detail the path Argentina followed in order to reform intelligence; and analyzes the position of Argentine congressmen in this process, particularly in enacting the National Intelligence Law, finally approved on December 21, 2001, after nearly twenty years of debate.[1]

In so doing, this chapter explicitly highlights two points emphasized by Tom Bruneau and Steve Boraz in the introduction: reform is both difficult to achieve and often the last major hurdle in democratic consolidation efforts.

LEGISLATIVE AND JUDICIAL CONTROL OF INTELLIGENCE

The institutional consolidation of a democratic system demands the control of intelligence activities. Initially, the discussion about the control of intelligence activities typically raises a high degree of resistance by the intelligence community, since it may result in the exposure of methods, activities, and people, which in turn could pose a significant threat to the effectiveness of the intelligence agencies. Therefore it is worth remembering that any discussion of the control of intelligence should include the way in which this control will be implemented, and by whom. As pointed out in the Introduction to this book, there are various levels of control over intelligence and security activities, including the executive; the legislature, which determines the legal mandates that outline the functions and missions of the intelligence community; congressional committees; the judiciary; the inspectors general internal to the agencies; the media; and other mechanisms that can be created by the executive and the legislative branches to control intelligence.[2] In this section I examine the two branches within the government—legislative and judicial—that balance executive authority and provide some means of control of an intelligence community.

Legislative Control

Among the control mechanisms noted above, the legislative branch is undoubtedly the most important. This is true because legislatures provide a review of intelligence that is not a part of the intelligence apparatus, yet still resides in the government. This is not the case with the executive branch, which can and does provide oversight in some instances, because the intelligence community is organized *within* the executive. In general, legislatures exert control over intelligence through specific commissions, made up of representatives from both the House of Representatives and the Senate. These commissions may be made up only of congressmen or only of senators, or they may be mixed. The institutional design of these commissions varies from country to country and depends on congressional interest in legislating national security. As the main instrument of control of the intelligence system in countries where there is in fact control, legislative control has received the attention of many scholars who have sought to define its general characteristics.

The Argentine expert, Marcelo Saín, argues that congressional control should include inspection of all the operations and tasks carried out by the intelligence services, the set of sources and methods used to obtain data and information, and the identity of the agents carrying out these activities, in order to justify their classification. Control should also refer to existing files, the information produced, and the set of secret norms that regulate their missions, as well as all the expenses involved. In order to carry out adequate inspection of intelligence activities, controlling authorities should have the necessary legal mandates, including access to classified information; power to carry out inspections and investigations in all public or private offices; and, with judicial warrant, a mandate to require any document or other source considered important. The effectiveness of this control in discovering functional irregularities and deficiencies of intelligence activities and consequent formulation of measures for their improvement will also depend on an institution with permanent and routine control.[3]

For Saín, these control commissions should have a central role in drawing up the budget for intelligence, which must correspond to the guidelines formulated by the government in relation to proper functioning of the intelligence services. He argues that to attribute a more active role to legislative participation in drawing up guidelines for the area of intelligence, which in presidential democracies is an exclusive prerogative of the executive, should result in greater degrees of effectiveness and democratic legitimacy of intelligence activities.[4]

The main bases of supervision by a congress are as follows: legislative authority itself and the annual approval of the budget; the authority to approve international treaties and to demand reports and information from the executive; the power to confirm individuals nominated by the president to certain key positions within the intelligence community; and authority to call hearings and witnesses and begin investigations of issues that are considered relevant.[5]

Some countries also authorize the legislative branch to have prior knowledge of covert actions just after they are approved by the executive branch, as in the United States. In these cases, this powerful control instrument may pose a high risk for the congress itself: the capacity to establish critiques about its actions increases its responsibility for the expected results of intelligence operations. In the case of scandals and possible political embarrassments resulting from these actions previously approved by the commissions, the capacity of the congress to criticize the action of the agencies is extremely reduced.

As its main challenges, legislative control must face limits imposed by government secrecy and the problems related to security; the risk of co-optation of the members of the congress by the intelligence community; becoming too involved in intelligence activities so as to reduce their effectiveness; and the overall quality of the work of the legislative branch itself.[6]

This last challenge is extremely important insofar as the actual exercise of oversight by a congress depends on the quality and intensity of the matters identified by its members in their supervisory work. The main barrier to this type of control is the willingness that members have for studying intelligence and energetically controlling it. This discussion is disheartening when we find that democratically elected civilians, even in long-established democracies such as the United States, may not be interested in controlling the intelligence apparatus because they lack the incentives and instruments to do so.[7]

With the exception of crises, most politicians are not interested in themes related to the routine control of intelligence activities. The legislators that choose to dedicate themselves to this subject normally have an interest in using these positions as a springboard to more senior national security positions, have links with interest groups relevant in their electoral base, or, to a lesser degree, have ideological concerns or preferences relating to security as a public good.[8] Therefore, reforms in the intelligence sector tend to occur as a result of intelligence scandals or failures, which force politicians to adopt unusual and activist postures.

This low level of normal legislative participation does not negate the importance of congressional supervision. It is precisely because congressional committees that specialize in defense, intelligence, and/or international relations have a mandate to approve legislation, decide on budgets, and have access to the documents and information produced by intelligence services that their control is so necessary.

Unfortunately, the lack of interest by the legislative branch is true both in the established democracies and in democracies in the process of becoming consolidated. However, older democracies have an advantage over newer democracies in that the degree of legislative involvement in the overall system at the outset of attempting to establish control over intelligence is much greater than in those previously authoritarian countries in which, in many cases, spaces have not yet been opened up for a discussion about intelligence at all.

Judicial Control

Judicial control of intelligence is typically most directly related to those areas affecting the privacy of the population. In several democracies, legislation gives the judiciary the responsibility for issuing warrants so that agents linked to the intelligence system can secretly access the private life of citizens or residents. Its task is to assure that these actions are carried out exclusively for the purposes for which they were authorized and that, preferably, they should intrude minimally in the private sphere. In previously authoritarian regimes, the judiciary may also be legally equipped to verify the cases in which those carrying out intelligence operations are accused of criminal activities. For instance, judges may be empowered to determine if, in committing illegal activity, members of the intelligence community acted in their own interest or were following orders from the intelligence agencies.

Although the judicial branch may be called on to solve disputes between citizens and the behavior of the services of intelligence, it rarely does so, as pointed out by Elizabeth Parker and Bryan Pate in chapter 2. They also point out both the legal and political difficulties for the judicial branch to work as an independent reviewer of government decisions in areas of interest in institutional security, such as access to classified information and expertise in intelligence matters.[9]

ESTABLISHING A DEMOCRATIC INTELLIGENCE SYSTEM IN ARGENTINA: AN OVERVIEW

The political debate and struggle to reform the Argentine intelligence system followed the experience of other democratic countries in defining greater degrees of coordination, transparency, and effectiveness in the activities carried out within the military, the police, and the intelligence sector. In addition in Argentina, the intelligence services, together with the police forces and the military, were responsible for a great number of deaths, kidnappings, and torture, mainly, but not only, during the military dictatorship. Trying to establish some limits on the operation of the intelligence services through laws, regulations, and control over their operations and protecting civilians from these types of atrocities were the main objectives of the legislators who presented proposals for reforming the intelligence system during the first civilian government that replaced the military regime in 1983. The development of the National Intelligence Law has its foundation in two early phases of reform following Argentina's democratic transition: establishing control of the armed forces and developing an Internal Security Law.

Civil-Military Relations Reform

The first stage in reforming intelligence in Argentina actually began with the process of bringing the military under control following the transition to civilian government in 1983. The first measures taken at the beginning of the Raúl Alfonsín presidency (1983–1989) were to remove the possibility that military personnel could occupy positions in government structures outside the armed forces; to prohibit the command of civil intelligence services by the military; and to truly strengthen the role of the National Intelligence Center (CNI)[10] as the agency responsible to coordinate intelligence. Although the CNI was set up to fill this role, it did not possess the instruments to do so.

Civil-military reform continued with the passage of the National Defense Law (23,554) of 1988. The debate on "the military issue" at that time centered on the theme of human rights violations, the roles and missions of the Armed forces, and the effort to legally subordinate the military to civilian power. The most controversial points in this debate were related to the definition of internal security in the concept of national defense and the consequent involvement of the armed forces and military intelligence in internal intelligence operations.

The passage of the National Defense Law in 1988 brought significant legal-institutional advances in civil-military relations and provides the context through which to view intelligence reform. National defense was established as an institutional projection of the state, with the exclusive function of guaranteeing *external* security. The armed forces were relieved of the responsibility to protect *national security*, an old euphemism for *internal political control*, carried out by the armed forces since at least the 1960s. This law gave a period of one year for the National Defense Council, which was established by this law, to draw up and send regulations on the National Intelligence System and state secrets to the executive. The law directly affected the performance of the intelligence system when it prohibited the intelligence services of the armed forces to work in the fields of internal politics. According to article 15, "the body of highest level of intelligence will provide the information and intelligence necessary for the national strategy of defense" and "the questions about internal politics of the country may not in any event be the work of military intelligence bodies." As a way of clearing up any doubt about the conceptual definition, the new law defined national defense as "the integration and coordination of the action of all the forces of the nation to solve those conflicts which require the use of the Armed Forces, in a confrontation with *external* aggression" (emphasis added). As well as distinguishing national defense and internal security, this law also envisioned the future elaboration of a separate law to regulate the issues of internal security.

A significant accomplishment of the approval of the National Defense Law was that it initiated a new way of working in the Argentine Congress with regard to the laws on security and defense. The drafting and discussion of the themes presented in the law were by a team of special advisers and representatives of the most significant political parties in order to attenuate parliamentary debates as the bills were being voted in the respective houses.

The Internal Security Law of 1992

The next phase of institutionalizing the process of intelligence control occurred during the debates on the creation of the Internal Security Law (24.059/92), which strengthened the conceptual distinction between what should be considered defense and what should be considered security. Internal security, which implies the use of human and material elements of all the police and security forces of the nation, was defined as "the *de facto* situation based on the right in which are protected the freedom, life and belongings of inhabitants, their rights and guarantees, and the full operation of the institutions of the republican and federal representative system established in the national constitution."[11] The responsibility for internal security was passed to the Ministry of the Interior, which would be responsible for the political control of the Federal Police, the provincial police forces, and the security forces of the state, giving the Ministry of the Interior the responsibility for coordinating intelligence within these agencies.

In order to do this, the National Directorate of Internal Intelligence (DNII) was created with the mission of assisting the interior minister, who could "require of the national or provincial civil intelligence organizations and those of the security and police forces all the information and intelligence necessary."[12] The law also approved the creation of a Bicameral Commission for the Supervision of Intelligence Agencies and Activities (hereafter referred to as the Bicameral Commission on Intelligence) in Congress to supervise and control these departments. This marked the first time that the Argentine Congress was given the power to establish control mechanisms over intelligence activities.

THE CONGRESSIONAL PATH TO AN
INTELLIGENCE LAW IN ARGENTINA

To better understand the contents of the Intelligence Law and how it eventually passed, it is worthwhile to review the fundamental concerns that marked the fifteen-year-long intelligence debate in Argentina. This discussion went through several phases between 1986 and 2001. It began with a focus on human rights, moved to a review of legislative control mechanisms, then to budgetary control, and finally to examining the overall effectiveness of intelligence activities. It should be noted that until the National Intelligence Law was finally approved in December 2001, the primary law in effect was a remnant from the previous military regimes and remained classified.[13]

Debate Leading Up to the Internal Security Law of 1992

The debate in the National Congress about legislative control of intelligence began in 1986, when Congressman José Luis Manzano (Justicialist Party—PJ) presented a bill entitled "Preservation of Individual Rights in the Law of Intelligence Agency." The draft was divided into three sections. The first discussed individuals' access to their intelligence files and gave them the right to request that errors or false data in their files be corrected. If they were denied this, they could appeal to the courts. The second proposed the creation of a new intelligence school, which would include courses about the preservation of democratic norms. The last section sought to establish the Legislative Committee for Oversight, made up of ten senators, to control the intelligence services. The objective of this section was to assure the Congress the capacity to "intervene and investigate the existing intelligence organizations and those to be created." This section was eventually codified in title 7 of the Internal Security Law of 1992, when the aforementioned initial regulation on the control of Argentine intelligence services was enacted. Another highlight of the Manzano bill was that when proposing regulations on the control of intelligence activities, it sought to apply them over a broad range of intelligence activities that might be established, including those by the private sector. The control in the Manzano bill would apply to the CNI and the military intelligence agencies, as well as any other public or private organization working with intelligence activities.[14]

The second attempt to regulate intelligence activities was the bill named Organic Regime of Information and Intelligence of the National State, presented by a group of Radical Party (Unión Cívica Radical, or UCR) legislators on June 28, 1990, and headed up by Congressman Victorio Bisciotti. This bill proposed legislative oversight of intelligence and the decentralization of the intelligence system by subordinating the areas of defense, foreign, and domestic intelligence to their respective ministries. The intent was to limit the number of agencies with their own collection capability while at the same time to stop various departments from carrying out counterintelligence operations. With regard to control itself, the bill proposed a complex scheme of legislative and judicial oversight of the intelligence community.[15]

In 1991, Senator Eduardo Vaca (PJ), who was president of the National Defense Committee at the time, proposed the National Intelligence System, which also envisioned the creation of a legislative control commission made up of six senators, representing at least the first two minority parties. The supervision and control would be carried out with the presence of the president of the commission and his deputy in the councils of the National Intelligence System, which would also implement budget control. The argument at that time was that the intelligence agencies would collaborate only if the Congress actually controlled their money. In addition, the proposal forbade intelligence organizations to carry out police functions or to reveal information about any Argentine citizen or organization (except in the cases where it was of public interest, and even then only with court order). The Vaca plan also sought to give the CNI the exclusive right to intercept communications.[16]

While all these proposals failed to pass, they were important because they became the foundation for intelligence bills considered by the Argentine Congress in the years ahead.

The Internal Security Law of 1992

Passage of the Internal Security Law of 1992 (24.059/92) was the result of a high-level consensus achieved over a bill proposed by Congressman Miguel Angel Toma (PJ) in 1989 and by Congressman Victorio Bisciotti (UCR) in 1990.[17]

Interestingly, these bills initially did not include control mechanisms on internal security.[18] It was not until debates were held in the Congress in June 1991 that Congressman Manzano (PJ) proposed that legislative control mechanisms, through a mixed congressional commission (the Bicameral Commission on Intelligence), be instituted over intelligence and security departments. His proposal also defined the congressional commission's composition, mission, and attributions, all of which were incorporated into the Internal Security Law.

The establishment of this commission was the first attempt by the Congress to legally include control mechanisms in the security activities in Argentina. The commission was to be made up of twelve members, six from the Senate and six from the House. It was to be permanent and to have its own bylaws. Among its attributes were the authority to demand necessary information from public agencies (though it did not have the ability to obtain classified information), to subpoena (through the judiciary), to prevent people under investigation from leaving the country, and to propose measures to the executive that were necessary to correct faults that might be found in internal intelligence agencies. It was also to be responsible for the annual production of both a public report, for the Senate and House, and a secret report for the Congress and the executive branch, in which it assesses the results obtained in its inquiries. In the case of divided opinions, as many reports as necessary would be produced.[19]

Once established in this manner, the Bicameral Commission on Intelligence was responsible for controlling the activities of intelligence and security. However, these functions presupposed that control already existed over different intelligence community activities and organizations, and this assumption received some of the greatest criticism following enactment of this law. The broad scope of activities that the commission would have to control would, in and of itself, limit its real capacity and effectiveness. In order to be effective, control mechanisms need a set of instruments that allow oversight of the *structures* and *functional dynamics* of intelligence activities. From the point of view of democratic civilian control and effectiveness, the Argentine committee had only been given the scope to inspect the structures of the intelligence community.

Another significant limitation was that even after the creation of the Law of Internal Security, the norms and legislation that regulated the organization and functioning of intelligence agencies still remained secret. The commission was not given the authority to access the classified information it desired; thus it could only attempt to affect control as a result of information that might become public through a scandal or leak. The functioning of the commission was compromised from its inception because it had not been given the necessary power.

Scandals and Fiascos Affecting Argentine Intelligence Reform

Two important events occurred in 1993 and 1994 that galvanized perceptions in Congress of the need to control and reform intelligence. First, in 1993, evidence became public of intelligence service surveillance of citizens in order to update existing intelligence files and became known as the "ideological-surveillance scandal." The second event, in 1994, was the bombing of the Asociación Mutual Israelita Argentina (AMIA), a Jewish community center in Buenos Aires.

ILLEGAL SURVEILLANCE

Regarding the ideological-surveillance scandal of 1993, the impact on public opinion was so strong that it generated comments from all corners of Argentina on how to manage internal intelligence. Although the Internal Security Law had established the Bicameral Commission on Intelligence, it had not yet been institutionalized and still was without the authority it needed to do its job. Following public disclosure of the surveillance, several bills were proposed to regulate the Bicameral Commission. The public outcry literally *forced* Congress to discuss legislative control of intelligence.

The first bill presented was that of the opposition congressman, Victorio Bisciotti, who had previously fought for the regulation of intelligence activities. He proposed the "Law of Information and Control of Intelligence and Information." This draft called for the creation of intelligence committees in the House and the Senate, with proportional representation and rotation; demanded debate about intelligence, by proposing regular weekly meetings; provided incredible detail on what the internal procedures of the Bicameral Commission on Intelligence should be; and proposed strict control and circulation requirements for secret information. It further regulated judicial control of communications intercepts, by creating a Judicial Observation Office, which would be responsible for the technical operations of interceptions approved by the judiciary, as well as establishing penalties for those who violated citizens' privacy. The regulation highlighted the need for a large intellectual investment that would make it possible to measure, quantitatively and qualitatively, the actions of intelligence departments.[20]

In 1993, Senator Vaca sent another draft, the "National Intelligence Law," to be considered in Congress. Among the changes from his previous draft was that the commission would be able to intervene in the budgetary process of the State Intelligence Secretariat (SIDE),[21] to call for and receive classified information, and to review the annual secret report produced by the SIDE. It further proposed that the responsibility for interception of communications would be transferred from the CNI to the SIDE, which would be the only department with a mandate to do so. This draft, in fact, did not have many structural changes when compared with the existing centralized system, and it was arguably a step backward in relation to the proposals already presented in the bill by Congressman Bisciotti.[22]

THE BOMBING OF THE AMIA

On July 18, 1994, a car bomb exploded in front of the Jewish social center AMIA, killing eighty-six people and rekindling the debate about intelligence in Argentina. This was the second attack against Jewish targets in three years: on March 17, 1992, another car bomb had blown up the Israeli embassy, leaving thirty dead and more than a hundred injured. This time, however, there was a new aspect that entered into the debate about the control of intelligence: its effectiveness. The question was why the SIDE had not been able to gather information in advance of this attack, especially after the explosion at the Israeli embassy in 1992. The attacks, especially the second, had shown the government's low capacity for anticipating and preventing terrorism. This served to reinforce the debate on the legislative obligation to regulate the intelligence services. The main discussion was about the link that should be established between intelligence and terrorism and about how to justify and distribute the secret expenses. Politicians and civil society blamed the SIDE and the "hands-off" presidential doctrine for failing to prevent this new attack, because this policy clearly demonstrated how poorly Argentine intelligence behaved when left to regulate itself.[23]

Once again, an intelligence fiasco drove legislative debate about intelligence and brought about Senate approval of the Vaca proposal in August 1994. This bill passed, however, only after the incorporation of some issues driven by Radical Party pressure. First, the intelligence commission was to be bicameral. Second, the members of the commission were to be a part of a newly created department, called the Permanent Council, designed to assist the secretary of intelligence in drafting the National Strategic Intelligence Plan (PIN). Third, the bill demanded the dissemination of intelligence to the commission. Fourth, it widened the power of the commission in budgetary control, including part of a bill presented in 1993 by Congressman Raúl Baglini that had proposed regulations on secret expenses.[24]

Also of note, other proposals were made by UCR and the newly formed Front for a Fair Country (FREPASO). Two UCR bills were presented by Jesus Rodriguez and Antonio Berhongaray, respectively. Both bills focused on secret expenses and the decentralization of the intelligence services.[25] The draft "Law of State Information and Intelligence" was spearheaded by FREPASO congressman Carlos Álvarez and proposed an increase in the powers of the Bicameral Commission on Intelligence, which, besides controlling the activities of the intelligence community, would control its budgets and formulate proposals to improve the National Intelligence System.[26] Under the Álvarez bill, the executive would have the responsibility to design and formulate the "National Strategic Intelligence Program" and send it to the commission for review. Álvarez's proposal also sought to guarantee that covert actions should be carried out only with the express and written approval of the president of the republic and immediately communicated to the Bicameral Commission on Intelligence. The text forbade intelligence departments to have any functions of policing or repression and of obtaining information or producing intelligence about any Argentine inhabitant, which had also been proposed in the UCR drafts.

While the Vaca bill became the first proposal on intelligence ever passed in Argentina, an inability to reconcile differences between Justicialist Party preferences, which primarily updated the existing system, and those of the Radical Party, which advocated a decentralized system and more-structured controls, doomed the bill in the House. Thus the Senate-approved bill eventually died in the lower house, and intelligence reform in Argentina unfortunately was put on hold yet again.

AMIA Revisited and a New Round of Proposals

In what many criticized as very late in coming, the Argentine Congress formed the Special Bicameral Commission for Monitoring the Investigation on the Attacks on the Israeli Embassy and the AMIA Building in 1996. With the establishment of this commission, the need for intelligence oversight was reiterated. The AMIA investigatory commission made progress in discussions about intelligence and its capacity for providing warning for and analysis of international terrorism. When the commission concluded its work in April 1997, it proposed "a rapid updating both in the objectives and priorities in the qualification of the intelligence system, as well as the norms and doctrines that guide it." In addition, it called the Argentine intelligence system "inefficient in the work of producing and disseminating general intelligence, especially with regard to the 'new threats' against the State." To address these issues, the commission proposed a systematic control of secret budgets, assigned the judiciary the exclusive responsibility for approving communications intercepts, and reinforced the coordinating role of the CNI.[27]

While this commission carried out its investigation, congressmen were updating legislation for intelligence control. FREPASO Party congressman Jesus Rodriguez, who had support of UCR officials as well, put forward a recommendation that reinforced the discussion on the control of secret budgets, and UCR congressmen Antonio Berhongaray and Edgardo Barberis sent drafts to the floor in 1998 that incorporated the major issues about control the UCR had been championing since 1990—namely, a decentralized system with significant legislative and judicial control mechanisms. Again, Congress was unable to reconcile differences and passed no new intelligence law, though debate had advanced somewhat and the issue continued to be of interest in Congress.

TOWARD A NEW INTELLIGENCE LAW

The next phase in creating an Argentine intelligence law began in early 2000 with discussions on how best to proceed. Building on lessons learned from the drafting of the National Defense Law in 1988, Congress delegated the drafting of a new intelligence law to a new commission consisting of a team of advisers who were responsible for presenting various proposals for regulating intelligence. Many commission members were academics responsible for providing analysis of legislation on defense and security.

In order to prepare the draft, the advisers considered a litany of proposals, which were still in the pipeline in both chambers of the Congress. These bills, as noted throughout the previous section, covered broad issues that would help establish both democratic control and enhance the effectiveness of the Argentine intelligence system. The commission was both deliberate and meticulous about its work, meeting weekly and also establishing a *mesa chica* (small table), a smaller group of advisers as well as some representatives from the SIDE. It was in the *mesa chica* where decisions were actually made and the draft text was drawn up (though the commission was heavily criticized for incorporating SIDE members and was accused of giving in to SIDE organizational interests).

In theory, the intelligence commission considered seven bills, the most important being the following: one from the SIDE, presented by Secretary Carlos Becerra; one from Senator Beatriz Raijer (PJ), who was president of the Bicameral Commission; and separate proposals from Senator Nestor Rostan (UCR), Senator Carlos Corach (PJ), Senator Ricardo Branda (PJ), Congressman Dario Alessandro (FREPASO), and Congressman Ricardo Quintela (PJ).[28]

Aside from the large number and diversity of the proposals, the intelligence commission faced several other challenges in drafting a new intelligence law. Foremost of these issues was the difficulty in defining the typical functions of intelligence activities in which the borderline between internal and external intelligence is unclear.

In order to guide the discussions, the drafting commission established some terms of reference upon which all members generally agreed:

1. That there must be a legal reference framing the performance and professionalism of intelligence personnel

2. That effectiveness in intelligence operations could not override democratic precepts

3. That a set of standards be created to punish those who violated civil rights

4. That specific *legislative* mechanisms be created to guarantee the permanent work of overseeing intelligence activities

5. That the legal reference should be the result of a true consensus, so that the law would become effective

6. That the bill should reach a balance in the distribution of the roles attributed to each organization of the intelligence community with respect to its functions and attributions[29]

Although each of the members of the commission drafting the intelligence law accepted these basic ideas, the means to achieve these goals in their respective proposals varied a great deal.

It should also be noted that debate over the intelligence bill followed the so-called labor reform crisis, which began when then Vice President Carlos Álvarez resigned in October 2000. Álvarez, who had helped ensure the election of President Fernando de la Rúa in 1999 through their *Alianza* (alliance) ticket formed between the Radical Party and FREPASO, submitted his resignation in protest to de la Rúa's failure to fire close presidential advisers, including Intelligence Secretary Fernando de Santibañes, who were implicated in a bribery scandal. Money was paid to senators, using SIDE accounts, to gain passage of a labor reform bill supported by de la Rúa. With no coalition in place to support him, de la Rúa was forced to resign about one year later, in the midst of probably the worst economic crisis in Argentine history.[30]

Reconciling Issues of the National Intelligence Law

From the framework established above, the commission set to work on reconciling differences in each of the intelligence reform proposals, and four issues came to the fore as the most important. The first, the protection of human rights, was not controversial, and in fact each of the bills had some reference to preserving the liberties of Argentine citizens. The remaining three issues — communications intercepts (primarily wiretapping), the makeup and professionalization of personnel in the intelligence community, and the specific mechanisms the legislature would have in exercising control — were more contentious.[31]

PROTECTING CIVIL AND HUMAN RIGHTS

The debate regarding the protection of human rights sought to define which rights should be preserved and what the ideal form to guarantee these liberties should be. The bills presented were almost unanimous in prohibiting the intelligence community from gathering information about people based on their sex, race, faith, association, and so on; carrying out repression; and interfering in the political process or manipulating public opinion. All these premises were incorporated into the bill drawn up by the intelligence commission and approved in the final law, which also included the term "inhabitants," in place of

Argentine citizens, as a way of extending this protection to all those who lived on Argentine soil.[32]

While all agreed that intercepting communications (primarily wire-tapping) needed to be legally defined, consensus was not achieved in determining the department that would be responsible for conducting these operations. There was great divergence among those who would have liked to take this responsibility away from the SIDE and transfer it to the judiciary and those who wanted to maintain this function in the SIDE.

On the one hand, the SIDE had a history—and, some would argue, a culture—of illegally wiretapping phones to spy on citizens, blackmail individuals and corporations, and interfere in politics. On the other hand, the judiciary had no experience in these types of operations, and others argued that corruption in the Argentine judiciary system would make it impossible to guarantee the secrecy of operations or the appropriate decision making on when to approve wiretapping.

In the final bill, the SIDE was given the responsibility for phone taps, but strict limits were imposed, using the judiciary as an appropriate balance against potential misconduct. In order to receive approval for a phone tap, the SIDE had several requirements. First, it had to prove that there was a viable need to intercept communications. Second, it had to request to do so in writing and had to include telephone numbers and addresses of persons to be surveilled, along with information about any other means to obtain the information desired. Third, the request had to come from the secretary of intelligence or his delegate to a federal judge in order to obtain a warrant. Finally, these actions would be carried out under the control of the Judicial Observations Board within the SIDE. The law further stipulated that if the interceptions did not result in a court case, they had to be destroyed.[33]

The next step in the discussion on control was related to the personnel who would make up the staff of the new civilian intelligence agency and their qualifications. All bills set the condition that no one could be hired who had a record of violating human rights. Congressman Alessandro's bill included a proposal to block employment of anyone who was currently being prosecuted for human rights violations. The bills proposed by the SIDE and Congressman Alessandro included restrictions on military personnel entering into civilian intelligence agencies, requiring them to leave active service if they wanted to work in the new intelligence agency. The bill of Senator Corach sought to limit the total number of personnel in the agency to two hundred and called for an open and competitive employment process, though it gave priority to those coming from other intelligence services. Senator Rostan's bill proposed prohibiting journalists, clerics, and former intelligence officers who were then working in the private sector from joining the intelligence agency, unless they had been out of these positions for more than two years. Eventually, the bill prohibited applicants in a category termed "offender," by establishing that they would be so considered if they had a record in the Human Rights Office.[34]

Relating to professional issues, the law established a qualification system for intelligence personnel based on a system of higher education within the School of National Intelligence (ENI). The school was encouraged to establish agreements with selected private and state universities and with the judiciary and the Prosecutor's Office to improve its education core. An advisory council, made up of members of all departments in the National Intelligence System, was created to develop the curriculum at the intelligence school, which is the primary means for training qualified personnel to be appointed into the intelligence agency. The law also states that personnel should have ethical and respectable behavior and a capacity for critical thinking.

LEGISLATIVE CONTROL MECHANISMS

One of the most important discussions the intelligence commission held was about the way legislative control was to be implemented. Prior to the bill, the only consensus was on the need to establish strict control, but the desired form was not clear. The SIDE bill and that of Senators Raijer and Quintela proposed control over internal security and intelligence, but there was no agreement on which structures would be created to implement this control. Eventually a compromise was reached, and the Bicameral Commission on Intelligence was given broad authority over intelligence activities (discussed in the next section).

According to the coordinator of the group of advisers in the *mesa chica*, Jaime Garreta, the maximum tension in the discussion occurred when the Congress proposed establishing strict control on the secret expenses used by the agency. The intelligence community considered this form of control to be excessive congressional interference in executive branch issues. This rationale was used to defend the interests of the intelligence agencies, which for years used these resources as they pleased, without any form of accountability to the National Treasury. Until the approval of the National Intelligence Law, the intelligence community had to declare only the total expenses for intelligence. Not surprisingly, this complete lack of control was criticized as an endless source of corruption and seemed more important because of the contemporary context in which the bill was being debated—the labor reform scandal and the SIDE's use of funds for bribery. In spite of all the resistance, the commission managed to impose control on the budget, a criterion considered indispensable to assure the democratic control of intelligence.

The National Intelligence Law

Through its diligence, the *mesa chica*, which continued to work to resolve conflicts that existed within the main political parties, was able to achieve consensus, and a draft bill was sent to President de la Rúa in May 2001. The president sent the bill to a vote in August that year, after delivering a presidential message drawn up by the SIDE, in which he presented his main comments on the draft law. The National Congress rapidly processed the bill, few alterations were made, and the law was promulgated on December 3, 2001. The bill reorganized the intelligence community and established democratic controls in the Congress, through the Bicameral Commission on Intelligence.

INTELLIGENCE COMMUNITY ORGANIZATION

The National Intelligence Law reorganized the Argentine intelligence community into civilian, military, and security/police agencies. The key national agencies were as follows:

1. The Secretariat of State Intelligence (SIDE) was named the principal agency responsible for collecting and producing foreign and domestic intelligence and counterintelligence. It was designated as the lead agency in the National Intelligence System and was given the mission of directing and controlling the system. A civilian, appointed by the president, was to head the agency, as had been the case in Argentina since 1983.

2. The National Directorate for Criminal Intelligence was designated as a coordination body responsible for the intelligence effort related to domestic security, under the jurisdiction of the Minister of the Interior.

3. The National Directorate for Strategic Military Intelligence was responsible for the production of military intelligence, under the jurisdiction of the Ministry of Defense.

In addition, the army, navy, and air force intelligence units and the joint intelligence organization within the Joint Staff became part of the National Intelligence System. Police and security intelligence services in National Gendarmerie, the Argentine Coast Guard, the Argentine Federal Police, and the Federal Penitentiary Service were also included in the National Intelligence System.[35]

DEMOCRATIC CONTROL

Regarding democratic civilian control, the Bicameral Commission on Intelligence was given permanent and exclusive control over intelligence activities. Including the authority already mentioned regarding control of the intelligence budget, the Bicameral Commission was empowered to

1. Verify the legitimacy and effectiveness of the agencies belonging to the National Intelligence System

2. Review the National Intelligence Plan (PIN) submitted by the executive and provide recommendations to improve it

3. Provide an annual secret report on intelligence activities to the entire Congress that must include suggestions for enhancing the effectiveness of the intelligence system

4. Issue opinions about any bills linked to intelligence activities

5. Receive and investigate accusations of people and companies filing complaints against the intelligence services

6. Analyze the curriculum of the National Intelligence School (ENI)

7. Request information, including classified information, from the Justice Ministry and its offices around the country, to determine

if the interceptions of communications corresponded to those authorized by court orders

8. Gather data from the intelligence agencies regarding their internal, doctrinal, and functional norms.

For its part, the Bicameral Commission was forbidden to reveal information that might damage the intelligence agencies or affect the internal security or defense of the country, and it was subject to legal penalties for any disclosures of such information (similar penalties were to be applied to members of the intelligence community for disclosing classified information).

CONCLUSION

The implementation of a control system over the Argentine intelligence community resulted from congressional initiative, though the process was iterative and took more than fifteen years. The difficulty in finally passing legislation was due in large part to the overall political conflict between members of the Radical and Justicialist parties and their opposing ideas regarding intelligence reform. Moreover, intelligence reform may not have occurred if intelligence fiascoes had not been exposed. The Argentine case serves to highlight the exceptional difficulties many countries face in enacting intelligence reform.

Argentina eventually settled on a system with strong legislative controls over the budget, significant investigatory capabilities, and the authority to underwrite executive proposals in the National Intelligence Plan. The oversight system also brought about some judicial controls to balance congressional authority and to provide legal review of the intelligence community's use of communications intercepts.

The evidence available so far shows that the oversight regime in Argentina has not yet been fully institutionalized, and political debate on the control of intelligence continues. Issues remain regarding the relationship between Congress, intelligence agencies, and the executive branch. The main challenges for Argentina now are to ensure that intelligence remains an issue of interest in Congress, to develop further mechanisms to support intelligence control, and to ensure that priorities, resources, and capacities are congruent. This final challenge requires special attention by the Argentine Congress, since it is now just as responsible for intelligence inefficiencies and excesses as for intelligence successes. Regardless of these challenges, passage of the National Intelligence Law of 2001 was clearly a significant accomplishment and established the basis for future institutionalized control of intelligence in Argentina.

NOTES

1. In October 2002, in Buenos Aires, I interviewed those officials most responsible for formulating regulations for the new Argentine intelligence system and examined all relevant documents, many unpublished. Those interviewees included Mariano Bartolomé, international relations expert specializing in intelligence; José Manuel Ugarte, political scientist and legislative adviser; Eduardo Estévez, legislative adviser, on the re-creation of the intelligence service in the Argentine armed forces since 1983; Luiz Alberto Somoza, professor of the intelligence course for the Argentine armed forces; Marcelo Saín, political scientist and legislative adviser, on legislative proposals for the re-creation of the Argentine intelligence services; German Montenegro, lieutenant, Argentine Air Force, and political adviser; Pablo Martinez, parliamentary adviser; Jaime Garreta, parliamentary adviser who led the work on the final version of the bill on Argentine intelligence (Garreta is also president of the nongovernmental organization SER en el 2000 (Seguridad Estrategica Regional en el 2000) and, between 2004 and 2006, vice minister of defense); Colonel Eduardo Gonzalez Villamonte, director of the School of Intelligence of the Argentine armed forces; Ricardo Colombo, director of the Argentine Internal Security System in 2002; Mario Baizán, parliamentary adviser, who also defended the creation of the Argentine Intelligence Service at the National Defense Commission; Luiz Tibilleti, parliamentary adviser who joined the committee for the final discussion of the bill, and director of SER en el 2000 (Tibilleti became secretary for security, Ministry of Interior in mid-2005); Miguel Pesce, former secretary of the treasury, responsible for discussing secret budgets for national defense; and others who requested their identities not be revealed.

2. For a list of these means, see also, for example, Marco A. C. Cepik, *Espionagem e Democracia* (Rio de Janeiro: Fundação Getulio Vargas, 2003).

3. Marcelo Saín, "Democracia e inteligencia de Estado en la Argentina," unpublished manuscript, May 1999.

4. Ibid.

5. Cepik, *Espionagem e Democracia*, 178–185.

6. Ibid.

7. See, for example, Amy B. Zegart, *Flawed by Design: The Evolution of the CIA, JCS, and NSC* (Stanford, CA: Stanford University Press, 1999); and Thomas C.

Bruneau, "Controlling Intelligence in New Democracies," *International Journal of Intelligence and Counterintelligence* 14, no. 3 (Fall 2001): 323–341.

8. Cepik, *Espionagem e Democracia*, 214.

9. Also see ibid., 201.

10. The National Intelligence Center (CNI) was a coordination and analytical body with some operational activities; created in 1972 it was based on a secret presidential decree. Although its name implied a central role in intelligence, it hasn't had a prominent role, and since 1983 several efforts were made to reinforce its role as head of the community. See Eduardo E. Estévez, "Argentina's Intelligence after Ten Years of Democracy: The Challenge of Reform and Congressional Oversight," Buenos Aires, December 1993, http://www.fas.org/irp/world/argentina/estevez.htm.

11. See title 1, art. 3, of Internal Security Law (24.059/92).

12. Ibid.

13. Jaime Garreta interview with Thomas Bruneau, May 18, 2001, in Buenos Aires.

14. Estévez, "Argentina's Intelligence," sec. 6, par. 2.

15. Expediente 983-D-90. ("Expediente" here means a proposed bill, which when submitted by the executive or member of Congress, receives a number; its number makes it accessible.)

16. Expediente 729-791.

17. Expedientes 738-D-1989 and 983-D-1990. The information about the bill of Congressman Miguel Angel Toma is from Saín, "Democracia e inteligencia."

18. The Commission of National Defense and Constitutional Issues of the Congress also proposed reform bills, drawn up in 1990, based on the joint bill drawn up by these same congressmen that did not specify control mechanisms. See Saín, "Democracia e inteligencia."

19. See sec. 7 and art. 37 of the Internal Security Law (24.059/92).

20. See arts. 2, 5, 25, 27, 28, 31, and 34 of Expediente 4865-D-92.

21. The SIDE is the lead intelligence agency in Argentina.

22. Expediente 58-S-94, in parliamentary process no. 90.

23. There is an ongoing investigation as to whether SIDE had information about the presence of Iranian Shiite fundamentalists in the country and whether it was blocked from acting by various interests who were defended by then President Carlos Menem. Allegations exist that Menem did not allow a thorough investigation of the source of the attacks and did not allow the political, diplomatic, and judicial prosecution of Iranian representatives who were at the Iranian embassy, after Iranian ambassador Hadi Soleimanpour promised a ceasefire in Argentine territory. See Jorge Boimvaser, *Los sospechosos de siempre: Historia del espionaje en la Argentina* (Buenos Aires: Editora Planeta, 2000), 28.

24. Expediente 4031-D-93.

25. Expedientes 4131/4132-D-94 and 4121-D-94, proposed by Jesus Rodriguez and Antonio Berhongaray, respectively. Congressman Rodriguez's draft reiter-

ated the discussion about secret expenses presented in 1993 by Congressman Raúl Baglini.

26. Expediente 4085-D-94.

27. Eduardo E. Estévez, "Estructuras de control de los sistemas, organismos, y actividades de inteligencia en los estados democráticos" paper presented at Seminario Internacional: La Inteligencia en las Organizaciones del Siglo XXI, Instituto de Ciencia Política, Universidad de Chile, November 3–4, 2000.

28. Draft Laws 1670/00, 1771/00, 2558/00, and 2577/00.

29. Jaime Garreta, "El diseño de un nuevo marco jurídico regulatorio para la actividad de inteligencia del estado en la Argentina," *Security and Defense Studies Review* 2, no. 2 (Winter 2002/2003): 268–282, http://www.ndu.edu/chds/Journal/ PDF/2002-3/Garreta-Jaime.pdf. Translation mine; emphasis added.

30. A rich set of information on the crisis of this political alliance is available in Martín Granovsky, *El divorcio* (Buenos Aires: El Ateneo, 2001).

31. This information was drawn from a table created to analyze the drafts presented and the various versions of the proposal drawn up by the commission.

32. National Intelligence Law (25.520/2001), art. 4.

33. Ibid., title 6.

34. Ibid., art. 23.

35. See National Intelligence Law; and Eduardo E. Estévez, "Executive and Legislative Oversight of the Intelligence System in Argentina: A New Century Challenge," paper presented at the workshop "Making Intelligence Accountable," September 19–20, 2003, Oslo, Norway, http://www.dcaf.ch/legal_wg/ev_oslo_030 919_estevez.pdf.

NINE

ROMANIA'S TRANSITION TO DEMOCRACY AND THE ROLE OF THE PRESS IN INTELLIGENCE REFORM

Cristiana Matei

Since the end of the Communist regime, Romania has tried to consolidate its democracy by gaining acceptance from elites and civil society, reforming and restructuring the economy, and bringing the armed forces and intelligence agencies under democratic, civilian control. Years after the end of the cold war, the postcommunist intelligence community, once *persona non grata* has, surprisingly, become one of the more trusted state institutions in Romania. Two factors can be credited with this transition of the intelligence services. First, and most interesting, is that civil society, primarily through an aggressive media, helped force the government's hand and bring about democratic reforms. Second was the imperative throughout Romanian political, economic, and civil society to institute reforms that the European Union and NATO would accept in order for Romania to accede to these pillars of the international democratic system.

To paraphrase Adam Przeworski, after 1989, joining the European and Euro-Atlantic "club" has more or less become the "only game in town" for the Romanian postcommunist governments.[1] But EU and NATO accession required, *inter alia*, complete reform and genuine civilian and democratic oversight of the military and intelligence apparatus. Having new security services, which people could trust rather than fear, was what Romanians wanted too. And while formal oversight mechanisms exist, informal control, mainly through the media, has been the primary oversight mechanism to ensure that both the popular demand for democratic norms and the Western requirements for accession have been fulfilled. The media have exposed scandals and government bungling to domestic and international audiences, thus forcing the hand of the decision makers to institute reforms. This chapter will discuss Romania's path toward democratic control of its intelligence services, while highlighting the role that external forces have played in achieving said oversight.

THE CEAUSESCU REGIME

From 1947 to 1989, Romania was an authoritarian communist regime, characterized by one-party rule in the form of the Romanian Communist Party (PCR) and a cult of personality around dictator Nicolae Ceausescu and his wife, Elena.[2] The population was forced to participate in continuous meetings and to attend demonstrations, congresses, and conferences that no one actually believed in or supported. The Ceausescus had unlimited power over all the facets of the country. As in other authoritarian regimes, the country's intelligence apparatus, the Department of State Security (DSS), was the core for the regime's maintenance of political power.[3] The DSS, better known as Securitate, was the political police force of Ceausescu and his regime, and he used it ruthlessly to impose his rule and coerce society.

Organized in the late 1940s to defend the new regime, Securitate (derisively called Secu[4]) was a specially trained force entrusted to watch over the internal security of the Ceausescu regime and suppress any unrest, opposition, or dissident group that criticized or defied it. It collaborated with guerilla movements as well as terrorist and organized crime groups, especially in its attempts to commit terrorist acts and assassinate selected émigrés.[5] Members of Securitate enjoyed special treatment from the communist leaders in order to ensure their loyalty.[6] The PCR selected many Securitate officers ("Securisti" in Romanian slang) and bodyguards from among children living in Romanian orphanages. Their loyalty was very easy to earn, and they were inculcated with the belief that Elena Ceausescu, Nicolae Ceausescu, and the PCR were the only family they had.[7] A huge number of citizens, who either voluntarily offered their services to Securitate for personal reasons or were forced by Securitate officers through various coercive measures, collaborated with Securitate. The Securitate was, on a per capita basis, the largest secret police force in Eastern Europe.[8] Like so many other Eastern Bloc intelligence organizations, Securitate frequently operated against both imaginary and real "enemies" of the regime without regard to any objective framework for analysis and assessment. These "enemies" were intimidated and beaten, had their property broken into or confiscated, and were imprisoned and murdered. The Securitate officers themselves were in turn under observation by their superiors. Most problematic was that many Securitate officers were illiterate and single-minded.[9] Securitate paranoia and incompetence were so great that, in one notorious case, some Securitate officers tried to "interrogate" a talking parrot to find out who taught him to say "Nicu Prostu" (Stupid Nicu), a reference to Ceausescu's son. They eventually decided to kill the bird because it refused to answer their questions.[10]

According to researchers, Securitate kept files on approximately one million people, and up to 25 percent of the population acted as collaborators.[11] Securitate succeeded in instilling in the population a "fear of their own shadow" and the belief that the visible presence of officers was only an infinitesimal element of an omnipresent network of officers, agents, informers, and collaborators who were watching them. It was indeed a state of mind as much as the instrument of state oppression.

Other than the control exercised by Ceausescu and his wife, there was no oversight of the military, police, and intelligence agencies. To prevent the development of an opposition power base, the regime frequently rotated government officials who were not relatives of the Ceausescu family from one job to another. The regime forbade any autonomous social organizations that did not come under the state's sphere of control. Although unions and associations existed, formed mainly by PCR members, they were not allowed to express views that differed from those of the Party and the regime. Religion was taboo too; not only had Ceausescu forbidden free expression of religious belief, but he also had a great many churches demolished. Oddly, there were priests who were PCR members and Securitate agents.

There was no real civil society, let alone a liberalizing faction within the regime.[12] Nor was there a free press: newspapers, magazines, radio, and television were under the control of the dictator or the PCR and were severely censored. Newspapers and television programs were mainly dedicated to the Romanian Communist regime, its leadership, and their "great accomplishments." Starting in the late 1970s, there was only one television channel, and it broadcast a maximum of six hours a day.[13]

Ceausescu's callous economic and political policies had cost him the support of many government executives, including the most loyal Communist Party cadres. With the collapse of the Berlin Wall, social and political discontent against Ceausescu and communism led to a mass revolt in December 1989, which culminated in the execution of the Ceausescus after a brief trial and set Romania on a path toward democracy.

The Securitate forces, the symbol of the Communist "inquisition," were subsequently placed under the control of the military. DSS files and reports were also taken by the armed forces. Important Securitate leaders were arrested, sent to trial, and convicted. "Deactivating" Securitate was critical, not only for deterring elements still loyal to the regime but also for the success of regime change. Romania could have easily ended up in civil war between pro-communist and pro-democratic factions had the Securitate not been dismantled and its leaders arrested.

Because of the absence of any liberalizing faction, Romania's transition to democracy was not a protracted negotiation between Ceausescu's old guard and pro-democratic elements; it happened with violence and the deaths of students, intellectuals, and common people.[14] The construction of civil society, political institutions, constitutionalism, and rule of law were nonexistent and had to be created from scratch. This transition has undergone four distinct phases:[15] 1990-1991—the wake-up period, characterized by uncertainty and insecurity; 1991-1996—first steps toward building new institutions, establishing legal bases, opening processes;[16] 1997-2000—reform and adjustment, NATO summits in Madrid and Washington; and 2001-present—continuation of reform and anticorruption actions, NATO membership, and the latest developments regarding EU accession in 2007.

INTELLIGENCE IN THE POST-TRANSITION PERIOD

Romania's new government took the form of a republic, organized under the principle of the separation and balance of powers—legislative, executive, and judicial. Political pluralism was a condition and a guarantee of the Constitution. The Constitution and the National Security Law of 1991 established oversight of all governmental activities related to national security, including intelligence and security organizations.

Building new intelligence agencies and bringing them under a legal authority and democratic oversight was problematic in a country

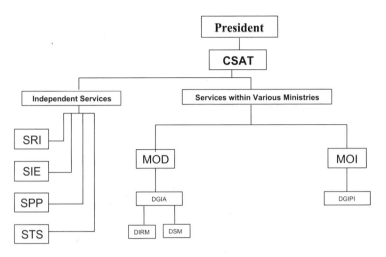

FIGURE 9.1. *Intelligence community in Romania.*

where the populace's rage at the prior intelligence apparatus was immense. As previously mentioned, during the revolution the former Securitate was placed under the armed forces; for a certain period of time, the government did not want to deal with it. However, due to a number of events that threatened the state's national security (for example, ethnic unrest in two of the counties with large Hungarian minorities), the newly formed transitional government considered the creation of an intelligence system to be important. Establishing one service was out of the question; a return to a concentration of power was not what the Romanian people wanted after the overthrow of the Communist regime. The government decided to divide the former intelligence sector into several agencies.[17] Currently, there are at least six intelligence agencies (Figure 9.1). Their legal basis is founded in the Constitution and the Law of National Security 51/1991.[18] The new intelligence services can be divided into two categories: independent agencies and those that are part of a specific ministry. The independent intelligence services include the Romanian Intelligence Service (SRI), the Foreign Intelligence Service (SIE), the Guard and Protection Service (SPP), and the Special Telecommunication Service (STS). Those working in specific ministries include the General Directorate for Intelligence and Internal Protection (DGIPI) and the Directorate for General Information of the Army (DGIA).

Independent Intelligence Services

The Romanian Intelligence Service (SRI) is responsible for collecting information pertaining to Romania's national security.[19] It gathers and analyzes intelligence on both domestic and foreign threats and has an antiterrorism protection and intervention role, which it shares with the Foreign Intelligence Service (SIE) and the Guard and Protection Service (SPP). It also carries out technical collection. The SRI was established under Decree 181 of March 26, 1990, and placed under a statutory basis under Law 14/1992, Organization and Functioning of the Romanian Intelligence Service.[20]

The Foreign Intelligence Service (SIE) is responsible for foreign intelligence activities with respect to Romania's national security and safeguarding of its national interests.[21] The SIE was set up in January 1990 and is regulated by Law 1/1998, entitled Organization and Functioning of the Foreign Intelligence Service, and by the Romanian Government Emergency Ordinance on the modification and completion of the respective law.

The SPP is an independent military-administrative authority set up on May 7, 1990, under Decree 204 of the Provisional Council of National Unity, to ensure the protection of the president, Romanian party leaders, and foreign diplomats.

Created in 1996, under Government Resolution 229 of May 27, 1993, the Special Telecommunication Service (STS) is charged with ensuring military and government communications security and providing national signals intelligence. In addition, the STS is believed to have agents operating undercover.

Ministerial Intelligence Services

The Directorate for General Information of the Army (DGIA) in the Ministry of Defense (MoD) was created by the Emergency Ordinance 14 of January 26, 2001, and is charged with intelligence collection and analysis on domestic and external military and nonmilitary threats to national security. It is responsible for ensuring the protection of security information and cryptographic activities, as well as the geographical intelligence needed by the military.[22] The Directorate for Intelligence and Military Representation (DIRM), which monitors the service's foreign activities, and the Directorate for Military

Security (DSM), the former Counterespionage Department, are now subordinated to DGIA.[23]

The counterintelligence department of the Ministry of the Interior (MoI), originally known as UM 0215, was set up on February 1, 1990, with President Ion Iliescu's approval and included Securitate officers previously placed on reserve. After several failed attempts, UM 0215 was finally placed within a legal framework in June 1990.[24] Due to constant criticism by both the media and Western governments and nongovernmental organizations (NGOs) on the presence of ex-Securiști in the unit and its dubious modus operandi, UM 0215 was restructured and underwent a significant personnel reduction in 1998. A special commission under the direction of the first deputy minister of the interior was assigned to do background checks on the remaining personnel, in order to decide where to assign them. In 1999 the unit was renamed UM 0962, the General Directorate for Intelligence and Internal Protection (DGIPI), and now consists of two bodies responsible for countering corruption and for crime prevention.

ESTABLISHING DEMOCRATIC CONTROLS

The creation of multiple agencies at the outset of the transition had the unintended consequence of diluting intelligence oversight, as government agencies were unable to deal with the new bureaucratic challenges posed by multiple intelligence services. The impact was that oversight was virtually nonexistent, although the National Defense Supreme Council, discussed below, was providing some coordination of the services' activity. A summary of current oversight mechanisms is presented in Figure 9.2.

Executive Oversight

The National Defense Supreme Council (CSAT) was created by Law 39 of December 13, 1990, to ensure the unified coordination of all activities pertaining to defense and state security.[25] The CSAT consists of the president (chair); the prime minister (vice chair); the ministers for industry, defense, interior, and foreign affairs; the president's national security adviser; the SRI and SIE directors; and the chief of the general staff. It is responsible for coordinating SRI, SIE, and SPP

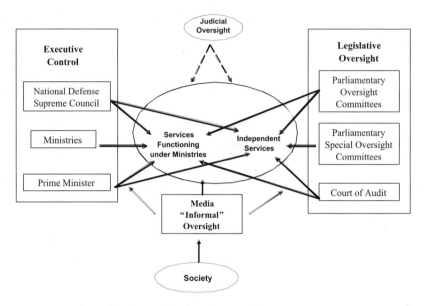

FIGURE 9.2. *Control and oversight of intelligence in Romania.*

activities, and council members are empowered to decide on collection policies as well as to regulate the information flow throughout the intelligence community. CSAT has taken a keen interest in intelligence and national security matters. For example, CSAT is required to meet at least quarterly, but members actually meet monthly to do analyses, make reports, endorse intelligence drafts and handle other security-related issues. This represents a positive measure of executive control.[26]

Executive oversight improved further in 2001 after the CSAT's approval of an interministerial cooperation protocol for managing crises, which empowered the prime minister to exercise control over the intelligence services in crisis situations.[27] This procedure improved both democratic control and effectiveness of Romanian intelligence, in that it gave the prime minister coordinating authority over all of the intelligence services (the prime minister would normally have jurisdiction over only those services that are organized under the ministries). It also forced the intelligence community to act jointly. Essentially, the prime minister may now, in coordination with the president, summon the directors of the intelligence agencies.

Legislative Oversight

Legislative oversight was initially instituted following the services' involvement in party politics.[28] Oversight of the intelligence agencies is carried out through the committees for defense, public order, and national security in both chambers of the Parliament. Special parliamentary committees were set up to oversee the activity of the independent intelligence services, and they consist of nine members: seven deputies from the lower chamber and two from the Senate. Each of the parties in Parliament is represented on these committees.[29] Both committees overseeing the SRI and the SIE are empowered to verify constitutional and legal compliance of the services' activities; investigate allegations of illegal intelligence collection; hold hearings on the presidential nominees for director positions; and assess the directors' annual reports, submitting their reviews to the full Parliament. The committees are also able to request SRI and SIE data, and the services are required to respond to the requests within a reasonable period of time, unless it jeopardizes ongoing operations, the identities of agents, or sources and methods.[30] The committees are authorized to investigate the directors of the agencies and their staff members and have the right to conduct unannounced visits to the services, at which the services are required to grant the committees full access to personnel, data, and facilities.[31] Such visits have been very important. Committees have uncovered corruption, links to organized crime, and violations of civil rights and liberties. The committees have also followed up, discussing the necessity to improve the legal framework to prevent these illegal activities.

Despite the above, the effectiveness of the parliamentary oversight has been hampered by a series of factors. First, the state has focused on issues it has reasonably deemed more important: elections, building new institutions, and supporting economic reforms.[32] A second factor was the deficient parliamentary experience in intelligence matters, though this has been ameliorated of late, especially after the creation of the Higher National Security College (discussed below). A third shortcoming is that the members of parliamentary committees have been selected more on political affiliation and less on professional merit; thus the activity of parliamentary oversight is sometimes affected by political interests. Cross-party consensus on national security policy also discourages the creation of a strong opposition minority or serious parliamentary debates on security issues. A fourth problem is that legislative oversight has suffered from poor cooperation and coordination among parliamentary committees. Despite procedural norms that allow legislative members' access to information, the SRI typically responds to queries with an aloof attitude and is not well trusted by the intelligence services, which represents a fifth problem. Finally, though the intelligence services normally comply with legislative requests for data, they often submit reports with irrelevant or redundant information.[33] Parliamentary oversight of the ministry services is carried out in compliance with the constitution's provisions, with the ministerial heads accountable before Parliament.

One particular component of this oversight is the control over the budget. The Court of Audit, the accounting body, is the authority that annually assesses whether public funds were legally spent, though information regarding the budget is scarce, primarily because of classification issues but also because intelligence agencies are sometimes permitted to use nonbudgetary funds and resources that cannot be easily monitored.

Judicial Oversight

Judicial oversight was established by the Romanian Constitution and the 1991 National Security Law. However, legislation does not provide for a system of judicial supervision. For example, statistics revealed that 14,267 warrants were requested from 1989–2002 by the intelligence agencies for wiretapping, and the general prosecutor did not deny a single one. Of the warrants issued, only about 2 percent led to an indictment[34] while the services claimed the remaining 98 percent were "used for prevention."[35] Concerns remain that this surveillance is being conducted for political purposes or in order to monitor citizens. Judicial oversight is further undermined by a high degree of corruption existing at all levels of public and political life, the judicial system included.[36] Judicial oversight in Romania exists on paper, but in reality it is nonexistent.

Oversight by Civil Society and the Media

The media in Romania have played a huge role in overseeing the intelligence community and forcing reform, and much of the rest of this chapter is devoted to detailing this phenomenon. Suffice it to say here that the press and civil society have held the government and the intelligence services to very high standards regarding democratic control, transparency, and requirements for integration with NATO and the EU.

Following the cold war, there was a need to adjust intelligence to meet the new spectrum of threats and challenges to national and international security, as well as to align the intelligence community to democratic values. Reform of intelligence processes, organizations, personnel, doctrine, and strategy has all taken place, and the driving force for much of this reform is the media's constant criticism and a parallel concern for meeting NATO/EU membership requirements. Reforming intelligence in Romania was neither an easy nor a short process. It took years, and myriad obstacles, many of them within the services, had to be overcome in order to complete an overhaul of intelligence services. The main obstacle was the legacy of the past: the Securitate and its personnel were reluctant to give up their positions, and many succeeded in staying on by concealing their Securitate background.[37] This problem, coupled with the inability or unwillingness of the new government to deal with intelligence, helped perpetuate the old institution's methods and mentality within the postcommunist institutions.

Consequently, there was insufficient trust in the state institutions, and a fear that any successor of the Securitate would be the reincarnation of it. While both Romanians and the West wanted to ensure that the Securitate was a closed chapter, there were attempts to rehabilitate the DSS and its personnel at the beginning of the transition.[38] The continuity of former Securitate officers in the Romanian intelligence network was a drawback for Romania's full membership to NATO for a number of reasons. One was that the former Securisti were viewed as a potential danger to safeguarding allies' classified information after Romania's accession to NATO.[39] The public's initial concern has been ameliorated as the number of former Securitate personnel has been gradually reduced, to a current level between 12 and 14 percent of the positions in the SRI and SIE, and no positions in the DGIA. The remainder of this personnel is scheduled to retire in 2006. It is, however, uncertain what the percentage is in the services operating under ministries other than the Ministry of Defense.

Removing the Securitate personnel created other problems for Romanian intelligence, specifically a lack of expertise, poor personnel recruitment, and substandard education. In the attempt to deal with the lack in personnel with a background in intelligence, the services kept some of the ex-DSS officers as specialists. Unfortunately this had a negative impact on the new generation of intelligence officers, as the ex-Securisti continued to apply Securitate methods.

Staffing and training have also been a major problem, due partially to people's reluctance to join the secret services still associated in people's minds with the former Securitate. To fill the staffing gap, a campaign was started in early 1990 to recruit representatives from the civil society, especially new university graduates who would be more open to reform, following Euro-Atlantic standards and procedures. Although special attention has been given to training and specialization of the newly recruited personnel, building primarily on Western standards, recruiting and training have been less than perfect.[40] These standards have helped in redefining SRI missions. In addition, the SRI created the National Intelligence Academy, which offers courses specific to NATO intelligence officers and uses foreign faculty, predominantly from NATO countries.[41] The SRI leadership identified the lack of intelligence expertise and its legitimate functions among civil society as constituting one of the most significant challenges to the effective performance of the SRI. To address the issue, the SRI created the Higher National Security College (HNSC) in 2002. The HNSC provides instruction on security and intelligence issues to public authorities and parliamentarians, other intelligence structures, civic organizations (particularly those with preoccupations in the defense and security sectors), journalists, and independent analysts.[42]

An additional shortcoming is that intelligence education and training have focused more on the tradecraft of intelligence and less on the operational aspects.[43] Romania's participation in international endeavors to fight terrorism and organized crime has proven useful for strengthening the services' professionalism.[44] The demilitarization of the SRI and SIE would also help improve professionalism.

Although downsizing and removing Securitate personnel from the intelligence services have occurred, ex-Securisti still have a residual influence in the intelligence sector, both in culture and through current business contacts. Former Securitate personnel often represent sources of corruption and illegal businesses such as smuggling of cigarettes, alcohol, oil, and guns; targeted bankruptcy; and fiscal frauds.[45]

Special attention should also be given to the private security firms, whose activity is not overseen by the legislature although they are part of the security sector. As their budget exceeds that of the state-owned intelligence institutions, they can afford ultramodern equipment and experienced personnel; the danger comes from hiring staff without ethical considerations, who are willing to break the law for money.[46]

THE ROLE OF CIVIL SOCIETY AND THE MEDIA
IN ROMANIA'S INTELLIGENCE REFORM

Civil society in Romania was essentially born immediately after the revolution, in Bucharest's University Square, where a small group of students protested against a new government that opted for "communism with a human face" as opposed to democracy. Representatives of newly created NGOs and private associations, labor union members, intellectuals, artists, and the media joined the protesters. From this dramatic beginning, over time numerous associations and NGOs have been founded and function throughout the country to monitor the activity of government institutions, including the intelligence apparatus.

The media have led the way in monitoring the government and intelligence agencies after the fall of communism. The freedom of the press that arose following the 1989 revolution set off important institutional changes in the media: privately and publicly owned television and radio stations appeared and began broadcasting twenty-four hours a day (including programs in minority languages), while numerous local and nationwide newspapers and magazines sprang up. The key institutional change though, was that journalists, who during communism were trained and monitored by the PCR, were able to take on a new role: exercising their profession based on their personal judgment and analysis.

This change did not occur right away, however. In the immediate aftermath of the communist collapse, the press was aggressive and indiscriminate, opting for sensationalism rather than serving the public interest.[47] The media's role as "watchdog" was therefore not entirely constructive. Of late, the situation has changed for the better. Legislation protecting both media and individuals has been passed, and there are now laws regulating journalist ethics, free access to information, audiovisuals, slander, and libel. Departments teaching media, communications, journalism, and public relations have been created within almost all universities to ensure professional and academic training, and the use of foreign expertise has opened doors for Romanian journalists. The press has increasingly become more professional, ethical, and spirited.

Although the press was very active during President Iliescu's first term, 1992–1996, and then during Emil Constantinescu's term (1996–2000), its increased professionalism became most conspicuous during the second term of President Iliescu (2000–2004), when it turned out to be an even better opposition and oversight mechanism. The campaign that the media conducted against Iliescu and his party, as well as corruption, abuses, and past involvement with Securitate, heavily influenced the 2004 elections that culminated with the victory of the opposition's reform-oriented leader, Traian Basescu. In response, the government, primarily Iliescu's Social Democratic Party, had tried to censor the media.[48]

Regarding the press's role in overseeing intelligence, the media have continuously watched the government and intelligence services, pointing out every mistake to the national and international audiences and thereby ensuring that the intelligence apparatus does not regress into the former oppressive service under communism and that the NATO and EU requirements are fulfilled. While media coverage has shown the intelligence services in a poor light, the intelligence community has attempted to manipulate or discourage the media from doing so, thus far without success.[49]

Numerous media disclosures on the intelligence agencies have occurred, and it is worth mentioning those that have pressured the government to start investigations, sped up reform, and forced passage of new legislation or amended existing legislation.

Criticism of Intelligence Structure

First, the Romanian media, along with Western governments and NGOs, have constantly criticized the existence of so many intelligence agencies and asked the officials to reduce their number; pointing out the legal framework that would allow such reductions.[50] In 2004, Parliament started to debate whether to decrease the number of services in order to avoid duplication and facilitate oversight. By 2006, the number of Romanian intelligence agencies had decreased from nine (as there were in the mid-1990s) to six. In addition, a National Intelligence Community (CNI) was created in November 2005 to gather all agencies under the same umbrella and foster interagency cooperation.

Second, the media frequently accused the intelligence services—in particular the SRI, the SPP, and the former UM 0215—of meddling in politics and reviving Securitate-type methods and mentality.[51] The press also covered cases of corruption and organized crime within the intelligence services. In response, parliamentary committees started internal SRI and SIE investigations and inquiries that resulted in removal of personnel.[52] Officials claimed they would continue the reform in the legal sector to better prevent and counteract violations of civil rights and liberties, emphasizing changes in surveillance and wiretapping. A positive step was the revocation of the Emergency Ordinance 29/2001, which had broadened the power of DGIPI to collection, wiretapping, surveillance, search, and seizure without a warrant from the general prosecutor.[53]

Third, one of the most criticized issues regarding intelligence services was the presence of former Securisti in key positions within the government and intelligence agencies and the slow process of removing them from those services. In 2002 a newspaper printed a list of Securitate officers sitting in key positions within the intelligence services. It claimed these ex-Securisti represented a roadblock to intelligence reform.[54] Later, a number of newspapers translated and republished a *Wall Street Journal* article warning that NATO may be unwilling to share classified information with former Securisti.[55] NATO press officers declined to comment on whether the presence of former Securitate agents in intelligence services was among the issues under consideration by the alliance in assessing Bucharest's bid to join NATO, but they stressed that respect for all democratic values— including freedom of the press, respect for the rights of minorities, and fighting corruption—were key issues. However, the U.S. Congress passed a provision that the president report to Congress by January 1, 2004, on the progress made by the seven new NATO members on intelligence reform, to ensure that they were interoperable with NATO in protecting intelligence sources.[56] In response, Romania adopted measures to screen all intelligence officials who may share NATO secrets.[57] In 2002–2003, NATO Office of Security (NOS) inspectors visited Romanian intelligence services and the new body created to deal with NATO classified information, to ensure that Romania was on the right track regarding NATO membership. In 2003 DGIA declared that there were no former Securitate officers among its personnel, and the rest of the services claimed they were downsizing their ex-Securitate officers.

Fourth, the media backed the initiative to gain access to former Securitate files, which became law in 1998 (and was upheld in a 1999 judicial ruling), allowing Romanian and foreign citizens who had Romanian citizenship after 1945 access to their own files. The so-called Ticu Law (named after a former political prisoner, Ticu Dumitrescu, who was the driving force behind its passage) led to the creation of the National Council for the Study of the Securitate Archives (CNSAS), which took into its custody more than 65,000 files.[58] In compliance with the law, the CNSAS is responsible for checking the Securitate archives for proof of which current candidates for political office have been past Securitate collaborators. The law was considered a success; access to the once-unattainable Securitate files marked a move away from the bitter past, exposed former Securisti who were running for office, and opened a new chapter in Romanian transparency.[59]

The impact of this new culture of an open society has not been lost on the intelligence services. Both the SRI and the SIE have made significant efforts to make information publicly available, especially after 9/11. Press conferences are organized on a regular basis to brief the media representatives and the populace on the current level of threat or ongoing missions. The end result is that the SRI has initiated a "security culture strategy" by establishing a partnership with the civil society. Through this partnership, the secret services make available expertise and analyses for the population. Although certain sectors of civil society criticize this as a way for the services to get the information they desire while transmitting only what they want to, others have lauded it for its transparency and willingness to work with the public.

Analysis of the Media's Role in Oversight

The relationship between the media and the intelligence agencies in Romania is both tense and symbiotic.[60] It is tense because there is conflict in the way the news is conveyed and interpreted and the way the government wants to be perceived: the media want to ensure that intelligence is accountable and transparent to society, by letting the citizens know what is going on within the intelligence system, whereas the intelligence agencies want to operate in secret. The relationship is symbiotic because each party has something the other wants and needs: the media need a "story," which the secret services usually have, and the intelligence community needs to look good in the public's eye, something that can generally happen only if the media report it that way. Overall, the media's unofficial supervision of intelligence agencies has sometimes proven to be more efficient than the formal oversight.

CONCLUSION

Intelligence reform in Romania has not been easy. Critics argue that the cultural legacy from the prior regime remains in place, that the same clandestine activities that infringed upon human rights continue, and that there is no genuine civilian, democratic control. Others argue that reform has occurred, that the new services have rid themselves of their communist past and are under civilian control. The reality regarding democratic control of the Romanian intelligence services is somewhere in between the aforementioned points.

The existing problems in the intelligence services—corruption and presence of ex-Securitate officers, for example—are being mitigated by continuing downsizing, improving recruiting procedures, and decreasing the number of redundant agencies. Oversight is currently hampered by the limiting legal framework, the knowledge base of overseers, judicial corruption, and a lack of trust between the controlling agencies and the intelligence services being controlled, but improvements can be made by revamping the legal framework of oversight and increasing civilian understanding of intelligence—trust is sure to follow. The current president, Traian Basescu, has already asserted his intentions to improve control of intelligence. His appointment of the independent and respected Monica Macovei to the position of minister of justice provides some optimism in counteracting corruption within the judicial system itself. Basescu has also noted the need for increasing the professionalism of the security services and has promised to make changes within the agencies, based not on political grounds but rather on professionalism.

As Romania continues to consolidate its democracy, interaction between the intelligence services, their oversight bodies, and civil society should intensify to decrease the gap between secrecy and transparency and to make the security sector more accountable to the larger public. The path the security services followed after the end of the communist era has had ups and downs, but nearly two decades after the Romanian Revolution the intelligence agencies are generally compatible with those within the European and Euro-Atlantic sphere and work hand in hand with them in fighting the difficult challenges of the current security environment. Romania's accession into NATO in May 2004 and into the European Union in January 2007 have shown that Romania's reforms have succeeded in developing transparency and that the nation is a trusted partner in democratic security. This is a significant accomplishment.

NOTES

1. Adam Przeworski, *Democracy and the Market* (New York: Cambridge University Press, 1991). Przeworski gives particular attention to the importance of "location, location, location" for the Eastern European new democracies.

2. Barbara Geddes would describe the Romanian case as "personalist." See Geddes, *Paradigms and Sand Castles: Theory Building and Research Design in Comparative Politics* (Ann Arbor: University of Michigan Press, 2003), 50–87.

3. Functioning within the DSS was the Department of External Information (DIE), which was Romania's principal organization focusing on foreign intelligence and counterintelligence, including technological espionage, disinformation to promote Romania's national interests and foreign policies, and monitoring of the activities of exiled dissidents criticizing Ceausescu's regime. For more information, see http://www.sie.ro/En/index_e.html and http://www.ceausescu.org/ceausescu_texts/revolution/die.

4. A play on words mocking the illiteracy and stupidity of the Securitate officers: *sec* in Romanian means "empty."

5. Several terrorist acts on Radio Free Europe (RFE) in Germany, and the deaths of three consecutive directors of the RFE, which have been attributed to DIE and were later acknowledged by President Iliescu to have been committed by the Securitate. See http://www.globalsecurity.org/intell/world/romania/securitate.htm and http://www.rferl.org/about/speeches/301101.asp.

6. Securitate personnel earned higher salaries, as compared with other military/police employees, had better living standards and also enjoyed the possibility to travel abroad.

7. Orphans were also known as "Ceausescu's kids."

8. See http://www.free-definition.com/Securitate.html.

9. Marius Oprea, *Mostenitorii securitatii* (Bucharest: Humanitas 2004), 25.

10. See http://www.free-definition.com/Securitate.html.

11. Bianca Guruita, "The Shadow of Securitate: Leaked Files and Political Machinations Mark Romania's Struggle to Open Its Secret Police Archives," *Transitions Online*, September 15, 1998, http://www.tol.cz.

12. Chris D. Ivanes, "Romania: A Kidnapped Revolution and the History of a Pseudo-Transition," http://www.arts.monash.edu.au/eras/edition_2/ivanes.htm.

13. There were three hours a day during the week (mainly worshiping the president and communism), and up to six hours a day on the weekend that included some entertainment and old American movies. Occasionally, Romanians were also able to watch live soccer games.

14. I use Diamond and Plattner's definition of democracy: free and fair elections; freedom of belief, expression, organization, protest, and other civil liberties, including the following: protection from political terror and unjustified imprisonment; a rule of law under which all citizens are treated equally and due process is secure; the political independence and neutrality of the judiciary and of other institutions of "horizontal accountability" that check the abuse of power; an open, pluralistic civil society, including free mass media; and civilian control over the military. Larry Diamond and Marc F. Plattner, eds., *The Global Divergences of Democracies* (Baltimore: Johns Hopkins University Press, 2001), ix–xi.

15. See Liviu Muresan, "Security Sector Reform—A Chance for the Euro-Atlantic Integration of Romania," paper prepared for the workshop "Security Sector Reform in Central and Eastern Europe: Criteria for Success and Failure," Geneva Centre for the Democratic Control of Armed Forces (DCAF), November 22–23, 2001, 2–3; http://www.dcaf.ch/cfs/ev_geneva01_papers_muresan2.pdf. Note that Muresan's analysis stops at 2001.

16. In April 1991 the first meeting between civilian and military representatives took place to draft a national security strategy. The meeting established the security services, and the U.S. Congress assisted the Parliament in oversight issues.

17. There were at least nine agencies in the early 1990s.

18. Károly F. Szabó, "Parliamentary Overview of Intelligence Services in Romania," paper presented at the workshop "Democratic and Parliamentary Oversight of Intelligence Services," Geneva Centre for Democratic Control of Armed Forces, October 3–5, 2002; http://www.dcaf.ch/legal_wg/ev_geneva_10.02_Szabo.pdf.

19. See http://www.sri.ro.

20. Kieran Williams and Dennis Deletant, *Security Intelligence Services in New Democracies: The Czech Republic, Slovakia, and Romania* (London: Palgrave, 2001), 220.

21. See http://www.sie.ro.

22. See http://www.mapn.ro.

23. Doru Dragomir, "Hurricane in the Army's Secret Services," *Ziua*, April 9, 2003.

24. Williams and Deletant, *Security Intelligence Services*, 226–227.

25. The text of the law is available at http://diasan.vsat.ro/pls/legis/legis_pck
.htp_act_text?idt=7873.

26. Larry L. Watts, "Control and Oversight of Security Intelligence in Romania," Geneva Centre for the Democratic Control of Armed Forces, Working
Paper Series, no. 111 (2002), 9; http://www.dcaf.ch/publications/Working_Papers/
111.pdf.

27. Radu Tudor, "Romanian Government to Revamp Intelligence Services
Structures," *Ziua*, November 16, 2001, 3.

28. SRI's first director played a tremendous role in replacing the first prime
minister; for more information, see Tom Gallagher, *Furtul unei natiuni: Romania
de la comunism incoace* (Bucharest: Humanitas, 2004), 136.

29. Joint Standing Committee of the Chamber of Deputies and Senate for
Control and Supervision of the SRI (June 23, 1993); Special Parliamentary Commission for Overseeing the Foreign Intelligence Service (Rule 44/1998.). Also see
http://www.sri.ro.

30. Watts, "Control and Oversight," 12.

31. Ibid., 30. Also see Williams and Deletant, *Security Intelligence Services*, 245–
246.

32. Ibid.

33. For more information, see Razvan Ionescu and Liviu Muresan, "Monitoring Exercise of Instruments and Mechanisms for Parliamentary Oversight of
the Security Sector in Romania," pilot project of the EURISC foundation, the
Commission for Defense, Public Order, and National Security of the House of
Deputies, Parliament of Romania, and with the support of the Geneva Centre for
the Democratic Control of Armed Forces (DCAF) (Bucharest, Romania, 2004),
30–40.

34. "Ministerul Public acuzat ca a incalcat viata private a cetatenilor" [Pub-
lic Ministry Accused of Violation of Citizens' Private Lives], *Ziua*, December 17,
2003.

35. Christian Levant, "SRI asculta tot mai mult. Degeaba?" [SRI Is Wiretapping More and More. In Vain?], *Evenimentul Zilei*, December 16, 2003.

36. According to Transparency International, Romania occupies the 89th
position out of 146 countries ranked on level of corruption. Corruption is widespread in the customs authorities, the judiciary, the police, the state property fund,
Parliament, and the ministries.

37. For example, the first SRI director was in office for seven years before his
Securitate background was revealed.

38. V. G. Baleanu, "The Enemy Within: The Romanian Intelligence Service
in Transition," Conflict Studies Research Centre, Royal Military Academy Sand-
hurst, Camberley, UK, January 2005, available at http://www.fas.org/irp/world/
romania/g43.html.

39. Eugen Tomiuc, "Romania: Authorities to Screen Officers Likely to Work

with NATO Secrets," Radio Free Europe/Radio Liberty, May 16, 2002, http://
www.rferl.org/features/2002/05/16052002082653.asp.

40. In the summer of 2004, for example, two off-duty SPP officers stopped a
member of the Audiovisual Council of the Secretary of State and beat him in front
of his family. The ensuing investigation revealed that one of them had a criminal
record. *Ziua*, August 9–13, 2004; and *Romania Libera*, December 17, 2004.

41. SRI sources.

42. Watts, "Control and Oversight." It should be noted that CCMR conducts
annual seminars in Bucharest on intelligence issues and reform that are sponsored
by the SRI, but with participation of all the intelligence agencies, oversight bodies,
and sectors of civil society, including the media.

43. SIE sources.

44. Romania identified and expelled al Qaeda cells and Iraqi embassy officials
engaged in espionage; it also participates in the Iraq and Afghanistan wars with
intelligence units.

45. See "Sittings of the Chamber of Deputies of November 5, 2002," http://
www.cdep.ro/pls/steno/steno.stenograma?ids=5348&idm=1,15&idl=1; and Marius Oprea, *Mostenitorii Securitatii* (Bucharest: Humanitas, 2004): 214.

46. For example, a television reporter pretended to be a business owner and
contacted a private detective company to negotiate surveillance of certain persons (listening to their phones) and theft of the databases of supposed business
competitors. The detective company said they could do these things. Although
violation of citizens' rights is severely sanctioned by the Constitution and laws
(the company could lose its operating license, and the detectives could get up to
twelve years in prison), they do such things anyway, despite the consequences.
"Detective Companies Offer Illegal Intelligence for Money," *Pro TV Bucharest*,
October 27, 2004.

47. For instance, news media reported alleged links between Radu Timofte
and the KGB before the 2000 elections when he was proposed for SRI director,
demanding his withdrawal from consideration for this position. But it turned out
that Timofte had not been involved with the KGB; in fact, his career in the military was terminated by the Securitate in the 1980s because his sister emigrated to
the United States. See Watts, "Control and Oversight," 18. SRI later published
the names of several SRI officers who had faked information to discredit Timofte.
See Anca Hriban, "Ofiterii implicati in fabricarea dosarului Timofte-KGB, dati
pe mana CSAT" [Officers Involved in Faking the Timofte-KGB File Turned in
to CSAT], *Ziua*, May 8, 2001, and http://old.revistapresei.ro/RO/articol.cfm?
Sectiune=7zile&ID=8101.

48. See Soria Blatmann and Jean-François Julliard, "Roumanie: Entre vieux
réflexes et avancées démocratiques, la presse roumaine à la croisée des chemins,"
http://www.rsf.org/IMG/pdf/Rapport_Roumanie.pdf.

49. For example, the first SRI director tried to close a newspaper that the gov-

ernment considered a "problem," in order to curb the newspaper's investigative coverage; see Tom Gallagher, *Furtul unei natiuni: Romania de la Communism Incoace* (Bucharest: Humanitas, 2004), 136. Also, former defense minister Ioan Mircea Pascu tried to get a journalist to "moderate" his coverage, with the threat that the "minister of defense knows all he [the journalist] is doing, where he is going, what and with whom he is talking," implying that the journalist was under surveillance by the intelligence directorate within the Ministry of Defense. For more information, see Christian Levant, "Ioan Mircea Pascu, un nou atac la adresa presei" [Ioan Mirecea Pascu, a New Attack on the Media], *Evenimentul Zilei*, October 11, 2004; and Radu F. Alexandru, "Radu F. Alexandru ii cere lui Iliescu sa ia masuri in cazul Ivanciuc," *Ziua*, October 12, 2004.

50. See Doru Dragomir and Bogdana Paun, "SPP a fost transformat in serviciu secret" [SPP Transformed into a Secret Service], *Ziua*, December 4, 2002.

51. See V. G. Baleanu, "A Clear and Present Danger to Democracy: The New Romanian Security Services Are Still Watching," n.d., http://www.fas.org/irp/world/romania/csrc12045.htm.

52. Watts, "Control and Oversight," 17.

53. Ibid., 28.

54. "Armageddon of Securitate People," *Ziua*, March 28, 2002, i–iv.

55. Eugen Tomiuc, "Romania: Journalists Condemn Defense Ministry Intimidation, Officials Deny Threats," Radio Free Europe/Radio Liberty, May 14, 2002, http://www.rferl.org/features/2002/05/14052002081156.asp.

56. "NATO's Intelligence Concerns," *Jane's Intelligence Digest*, September 5, 2003, http://www.janes.com.

57. Tomiuc, "Romania: Authorities to Screen Officers."

58. Although the law also provides that the SRI must hand over the entire Securitate archive to the CNSAS, not all files have been transferred to date.

59. It should be noted that having access to the files has sometimes uncovered painful information. Romanians found out just how involved present-day officials had been in the former Communist Party; discovered the depths to which some in society had sunk in order to gain extra income by collaborating with the Securitate; and learned that their relatives or best friends had betrayed them to the Securitate.

60. The idea of tense and symbiotic is borrowed from Pat M. Holt, *Secret Intelligence and Public Policy: A Dilemma of Democracy* (Washington, DC: Congressional Quarterly Press, 1995), 169–172.

TEN

TRANSFORMING INTELLIGENCE
IN SOUTH AFRICA

Kenneth R. Dombroski

By most objective standards, intelligence sector reform in South Africa seems to be a model for success. Not only have the intelligence services been transformed from militarized and highly repressive instruments of internal control into what appear to be more transparent and democratically accountable civilian-led agencies designed to inform policy, but they have done so in a systematic manner that conforms to policy prescriptions and theories of experts in the field of democratic transformation. From a theoretical standpoint, South Africa's transformation process is a political scientist's dream come true: models were adapted to policy prescriptions, which in turn were codified into law and operationalized into new structures and procedures. One can study where the South African intelligence sector stood during the apartheid era, how the transformation process was designed and implemented, and what were the tangible results of these reforms on the intelligence sector. What remains to be seen is if the transformation process has realized the high standards set by the reformers, and how these reforms have impacted the effectiveness of the South African intelligence services. After more than a decade into the transformation process, the long-term effects of these reforms remain uncertain, but several trends have become evident. This chapter assesses the intelligence sector transformation in South Africa and offers lessons learned that might be instructive to other democratizing states. The questions to be considered include the following:

- Why did F. W. de Klerk's administration make it a priority for intelligence to be more accountable to the executive branch of government?

- Why did the Government of National Unity under Nelson Mandela embrace intelligence reforms as one of their first priorities?

- How does the reality of the South African intelligence community compare with the idealized picture of that community?

- Can the South African experience be generalized to offer guidance to other democratizing countries attempting to gain control of independent intelligence services?

A MODEL FOR COMPARATIVE ANALYSIS

In the case of South Africa, the structure and evolution of the nation's security intelligence institutions during the period of apartheid rule were key factors in preserving the white-minority regime's power. Understanding the theory behind the structural change from apartheid to democracy is as important as the chronology of its evolution. Peter Gill's definition and classification of security intelligence organizations provides an excellent basis for developing a model for comparative analysis. Gill defines security intelligence as the "state's gathering of information about and attempts to counter perceived threats to its security deriving from espionage, sabotage, foreign-influenced activities, political violence and subversion."[1] Gill elaborates on the earlier work of W. W. Keller by creating a typology for security intelligence services in modern states, from which it is possible to classify and compare the services of different states.[2] According to Gill, security intelligence services can be classified by the degree of power they possess, measured in the degree of autonomy from external political control and oversight they enjoy, and in the degree of their penetration of society. The classification of the services can then be used to draw some conclusions about the nature of the state. Gill groups security intelligence services found in various types of political regimes, whether authoritarian or democratic, into three general categories, or ideal types:

- Bureau of domestic intelligence: The desired type of security intelligence service for a modern liberal democracy, this organization has limited and specific powers derived from a legal charter or statute. Its primary function is to gather information relating to the criminal prosecution of security offenses, and it does not conduct aggressive countering operations against citizens. The British MI5 is a good example of this type of security intelligence service.

- Political police: This type of organization tends to be found either in authoritarian regimes or in decaying democracies. These operatives have greater autonomy from democratic policymaking and are more insulated from legislative and judicial scrutiny than a bureau of domestic intelligence. This type of security intelligence service responds almost exclusively to the political elites or party in power. Typically, political police focus on internal political opposition groups, often gathering intelligence unrelated to specific criminal offenses, and conducting aggressive countering operations against domestic political opposition to the existing regime. The security intelligence services in many authoritarian regimes in the communist bloc, as well as right-wing regimes in Latin America and Southeast Asia during the cold war era, would fall into this category.

- Independent security state: This is a security intelligence service characterized by a lack of external controls and oversight, even from the authoritarian regime it is supposedly protecting. It differs from the political police because it determines its own goals, which may not coincide with those of the political elite. Enjoying a high degree of autonomy from the routine political process, this type of security intelligence service keeps its funding and policies hidden from the governmental policymaking process, and its targets and countering activities are authorized by the service itself. Examples of independent security states include the South African intelligence apparatus during periods of the de Klerk regime, and the Securitate in President Nicolae Ceausescu's Romania.

Among these three general types of security intelligence services, the independent security state's penetration of society is the most extensive, and it wields virtually unchecked power over the regime and population. Not only does it collect intelligence, but it also sets its own agenda. The political police, by comparison, wield less power and are more responsive to the regime in power. The domestic intelligence bureau is the ideal type of security intelligence service for a democracy. It does not conduct countering operations against its citizens, and it may not even have arrest authority, but its monitoring nevertheless remains a form of power and thus is potentially susceptible to political misuse.

Gill's typology gives nine possible classifications for security intelligence services; however, only three types are specified. While useful,

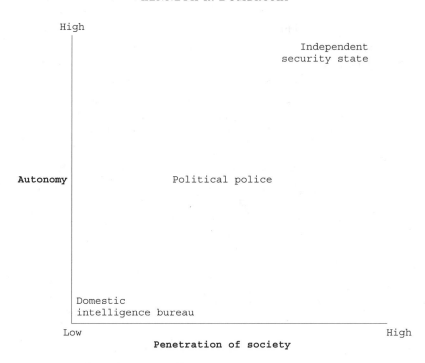

High

Independent
security state

Autonomy   Political police

Domestic
intelligence bureau

Low   High

Penetration of society

FIGURE 10.1. *Types of security intelligence services.*

Gill's typology table suffers from its limited ability to compare and contrast relative changes in security intelligence agencies over time. Moreover, it labels only one-third of the possible combinations of agencies based on their autonomy from and penetration of society. A more accurate graphical depiction is shown in Figure 10.1. While maintaining the three general categories developed by Keller and Gill, this graph can be used to rank and compare security intelligence agencies by accounting for change in the independent variables of autonomy and penetration of society. In the case of South Africa, over the last fifty-five years its security intelligence organization could be plotted in all three of the categories.

THE SOUTH AFRICAN INTELLIGENCE
APPARATUS UNDER APARTHEID

To comprehend the significance and extent of the reforms undertaken in the South African intelligence sector, it is important to understand the nature of the intelligence services prior to the transformation process. This section explores the transformation of the South African intelligence apparatus during that nation's transition from apartheid to a post-apartheid regime. Because of its peculiar heritage and the dramatic transformation that it has undergone, the South African transition to democracy presents a vivid picture of intelligence abuses and a determined dedication to bringing intelligence under democratic control.

While apartheid was practiced from the beginning of white rule in South Africa, the apartheid era is generally agreed to have been institutionalized beginning in 1948, when D. F. Malan formed a National Party (NP) government led by Afrikaner nationalists that immediately began to introduce apartheid legislation. Malan's successor, Hans Strijdom, instituted changes to the South African Constitution to further consolidate white-only rule by disenfranchising nonwhite voters. In 1961 the apartheid government under Hendrik Verwoerd broke from Great Britain, turned South Africa into a republic, and left the Commonwealth. Under Prime Minister John Vorster the National Party regime reached its peak of power. Vorster's successor, P. W. Botha, attempted a process of reform, but he failed because the black majority was excluded from a new constitutional arrangement that culminated in a unique tricameral parliament and an executive presidency. By 1989, the apartheid regime was in serious trouble. The USSR was collapsing, thus depriving the regime of one of its chief excuses for its repressive policies. Civil unrest, coupled with controversial military ventures in Angola and Namibia and the growing impact of international isolation and economic sanctions, led to a revolt in the top ranks of the National Party. Botha's cabinet forced him to resign, and F. W. de Klerk was elected president by the Parliament with the mandate to reform the apartheid regime and achieve a negotiated settlement with the opposition forces of the African National Congress.[3]

The intelligence apparatus in South Africa originated from within the police and military organizations, with many of the security intelligence agencies[4] descended from the Special Branch of the South African Police. From the beginning of the apartheid era, their primary objective was to gather intelligence relating to internal security threats posed by liberation movements, principally the African National Congress (ANC), that the apartheid regime considered to be under the control of external communist powers. This perception was enhanced by the cold war international climate and by the influence of the Afrikaner doctrine of Christian Nationalism, internalized by both the ruling elites and the security officers who served them. Throughout the apartheid era, national security focused primarily on combating the ANC and other communist-supported groups, whether inside the country or in neighboring states. As internal and external resistance to the apartheid regime increased and the threat of Soviet expansion in Africa grew, the South African intelligence agencies continued to expand in size and power. Officers from the South African Police Security Branch (SB) were attached to the national civilian intelligence organizations, the Republican Intelligence and its successors, the Bureau for State Security (BOSS), the Department of National Security, and the later National Intelligence Service (NIS). These internal security intelligence services and the military's Department of Military Intelligence were responsible for collecting, analyzing, and disseminating intelligence, as well as conducting counterintelligence operations. Over time, intelligence activities expanded to include elements from the Department of Information, Foreign Affairs, the Railways Police Security Branch, and the Prisons Service.[5] The SB collected intelligence on subversive elements and conducted operations both within South Africa and in neighboring frontline states. Toward the end of the apartheid era, the de Klerk administration dismantled the SB and created the Criminal Investigation Service to handle its political intelligence functions.[6]

Military officers seconded to internal security intelligence duties dominated this security intelligence apparatus. These "securocrats," as they became known, flourished under the Botha administration (1975–1989), and the internal security intelligence structures they operated became the primary institutions used by the NP government to maintain white minority rule. The State Security Council (SSC), established in 1972, coordinated strategic intelligence policy. The SSC was chaired by the prime minister (state president after 1984) and consisted of the ministers of Defense, Foreign Affairs, Justice, and Police (later Law and Order), the senior representatives of the South African Defense Force (SADF), Security Intelligence (later NIS), and the South African Police, as well as other ministers as needed. SADF influence over the SSC was evident with the appointment of generals with clandestine operations experience to the key post of SSC secretary general. National intelligence policy developed by the SSC was implemented through a vast intelligence network known as the National Security Management System (NSMS). Influenced by a series of senior SADF generals, the SSC used the NSMS, teamed with a corresponding National Welfare Management System (NWMS), to implement an aggressive counterrevolutionary "Total Strategy" to address security and welfare needs by the "Winning the Hearts and Minds" (WHAM) approach to defeat the ANC. The NSMS structure was extensive and penetrated deeply into society through 14 joint management committees (JMCs) headed by SADF regional commanders, down through 60 submanagement centers, further down through 350 mini-joint management centers, to hundreds of local management centers in neighborhoods, townships, and villages.[7]

During the Botha administration, the NIS became less influential, having been relegated to the roles of strategic analysis and foreign liaison service. Shaun McCarthy credits the demise of the civilian-led NIS to personal animosity, strategic policy differences, and bureaucratic competition in the Vorster administration between P. W. Botha, then serving as defense minister, and Hendrik van den Bergh, director general of BOSS. SADF and its Directorate of Military Intelligence (DMI) in the 1970s advocated a counterrevolutionary strategy based on a geopolitical view of the strategic role of South Africa as a "bulwark against communist aggression" allied with the West and engaged in a "war by proxy" against the frontline states supported by the Soviet Union. Van den Bergh was opposed to this military strategy, particularly the SADF operations in Angola. When Botha became president in 1975, the military gained in prominence, and the DMI became the dominant intelligence agency, assuming responsibility for clandestine and covert operations from BOSS. Counterintelligence fell under the Police Security Branch. The DMI and its directorates of counterintelligence, military intelligence, and communications operations, along with its special forces were extensively involved in covert operations targeting the liberation movements both within South Africa and in neighboring countries. Right-wing "securocrats" from the DMI were the praetorian guards of the apartheid regime under Botha.

In modern democracies such as the United States and Great Britain, national intelligence organizations exist for one primary purpose: to inform and support policymakers. National intelligence organizations provide threat assessments to support the development of plans and identify emerging issues that impact on long-term assessments and the strategic environment. Counterintelligence is a purely secondary mission in these intelligence organizations, whether military or civilian. Domestic security intelligence is primarily a "high policing" function, and in most modern democracies it is a function assigned to a civilian agency such as the Federal Bureau of Investigation in the United States or the Security Service (MI5) in the United Kingdom.

This was not the case in South Africa, where, like in most authoritarian regimes, the boundaries and functions of military intelligence and police organizations overlapped or became indistinguishable from each other. The militarized South African security intelligence services of the NSMS functioned more as "political police" than domestic intelligence bureaus subject to a democratic process and responsive to ministerial control and legislative and judicial oversight. During the Botha administration they acquired greater autonomy from policymakers and became insulated from most legislative or judicial scrutiny. As the SADF and its DMI became more influential, they tended to be responsive to, and derived their powers and responsibilities from, the executive authority of the president and the SSC rather than legal mandates. They gathered political intelligence on a considerable number of people, usually related to subversion rather than specific criminal offenses. These security intelligence organizations were the apparatus the apartheid regime used to conduct aggressive countering operations against political opposition and to maintain white minority rule. By the time de Klerk came to power in 1989, these military-dominated intelligence services resembled what Keller and Gill have called the "independent security state." This extreme form of security intelligence organization is characterized by a lack of external controls on intelligence activities. It is different from the political police because the security intelligence organization determines its own agenda, and its goals may not coincide with those of the ruling elite. Its funding and policies remain hidden from the rest of the policy-making process, and the organization itself selects the targets for its information-gathering and countering activities.[8] All of these characteristics were present in the South African intelligence apparatus in the last decade of the apartheid regime.

F. W. de Klerk was determined to bring this military-dominated independent security state under control in order to advance his political agenda of democratization. Consequently, the NSMS was diminished in power, subordinated to the NIS, and, along with the SSC, placed under a civilian deputy minister of information services, Roelf Meyer. To diminish the military's preeminent role in the intelligence sector that had been established under the Botha administration, de Klerk made the civilian-led NIS the dominant South African intelligence organization. McCarthy argues that during the last years of the apartheid era under de Klerk, the NIS "remained the most enlightened and least controversial" of the South African intelligence agencies. Its active role in the covert operations campaign against the ANC had been minimized by the securocrats in the SSC during the Botha administration, and the NIS was the intelligence agency most in favor of seeking a political, rather than military, solution. The NIS also was involved in facilitating the early negotiations between the de Klerk administration and ANC leaders.[9] Henderson maintains that de Klerk, first as a minister and member of the SSC under Botha, then later as president, both helped shape intelligence requirements and shared in responsibility for the covert operations targeting the ANC and other organizations opposed to the apartheid regime. Once he became president, de Klerk attempted to make the security intelligence apparatus more accountable to him, but by then it had become an independent security state. Attempts by de Klerk to reign in some of the excesses of the DMI operators as part of his campaign to reach a political solution with the ANC were often thwarted by rogue elements within the DMI and SADF. Purges of senior SADF officers of questionable loyalty to the administration and the presence of "Third Force" elements conducting unsanctioned covert operations deeply divided the military. Resistance from senior and midgrade officers in the police and military to change their oppressive tactics complicated de Klerk's attempts to effect political change.[10] This is not to say that de Klerk was not above using the security intelligence apparatus he inherited. Quite the contrary, as Henderson argues, "de Klerk and his key cabinet advisors found clandestine operations an essential instrument for their reform strategy, while their control over those who managed the operations was weak."[11]

During the final years of the apartheid regime leading up to the Transitional Executive Council, de Klerk struggled to reform the security intelligence apparatus, only to find that secret units supported by hidden funds defied government control and oversight. Despite his efforts to gain control over the security intelligence apparatus, de Klerk continued to be plagued by revelations through the media and courts of the persistence of violent "Third Force" operations being conducted by a network of former and current members of the security intelligence apparatus without government sanction. During the latter stages of Botha's administration and throughout de Klerk's, the South African media played a significant role in exposing dubious activities of the security intelligence apparatus. Though at times under-mining de Klerk's negotiating position by their revelations, the media, in the absence of any effective legislative oversight mechanism, pro-vided the only real, albeit sensationalized, oversight of intelligence in South Africa.[12]

INTELLIGENCE SECTOR TRANSFORMATION UNDER THE GOVERNMENT OF NATIONAL UNITY

With the election of Nelson Mandela as president of the Government of National Unity (GNU) in April 1994, South Africa entered a period of momentous political transition that included the integration, reori-entation, and reorganization of the intelligence and security sectors. Although the GNU included ministers from the National Party (in-cluding de Klerk as second vice president) and the Inkatha Freedom Party, all the security portfolios (Defense, Safety and Security, Intel-ligence, Justice, and Foreign Affairs) were held by ANC members.[13] This would have a profound effect on the future shape and course of the new South African intelligence community. The integration of the intelligence and security sectors would be the most daunting task of the democratic consolidation.[14]

Discussions between the NIS and the ANC's Department of Intel-ligence and Security (ANC-DIS) during 1993 led to proposals dur-ing the Transitional Executive Council (TEC) period for legislation to transform the intelligence apparatus once the new GNU came to power. Recognizing that merely integrating the intelligence and secu-rity services would not solve the underlying problems of the persis-tence of an independent security state, the TEC's Sub-Council on Intelligence developed principles and guidelines to map the transfor-mation course for subsequent legal mandates and a new organizational structure. The origins of these guidelines for the new intelligence community were an earlier set of guidelines published in an ANC re-port in 1992. These guidelines reflected the desire to adhere to demo-cratic principles and transparency and specified that the new intel-ligence community would be organized and governed by new legal mandates, subject to a code of conduct, accountable to the legislature, and subject to legislative oversight.[15]

In developing a new intelligence "dispensation," the Sub-Council on Intelligence and GNU legislators and policymakers were influenced by the British, Canadian, and Australian models of intelligence communities. The South Africans closely studied the Canadian Security Intelligence Service Act and the Australian Security Intelligence Organisation Act and adapted several of the organizational structure, executive control, and parliamentary oversight features of both in their new intelligence sector legislation. The Canadians were particularly concerned with issues of public accountability, while limiting the scope of the oversight process to avoid politicization of the intelligence community. The U.S. and British models apparently were viewed less favorably due to perceived problems in legislative oversight.[16] Considering the lack of effective legislative oversight mechanisms during the apartheid regime, the rise of a militarized independent security state, and the reliance on leaks and media stories for exposing intelligence problems, it was only prudent that the GNU lay the groundwork for intelligence control and oversight as one of their first priorities in reforming the intelligence community.

After taking office in May 1994, the GNU followed through on the TEC's efforts toward comprehensive intelligence reform with an October 1994 White Paper on Intelligence that outlined the "philosophy, mission and role of intelligence in a democratic South Africa," with a "focus primarily on the mandates of the proposed new civilian services (domestic and foreign)."[17] Reforms for the military intelligence organizations were addressed in the May 1996 White Paper on National Defense.[18] In late 1994, the GNU passed legislation authorizing and regulating intelligence activities that became the principal legal mandates for the new South African intelligence organizations:

- The Intelligence Services Act created the civilian National Intelligence Agency and the South African Secret Service to replace the existing apartheid-era services.

- The National Strategic Intelligence Act defined the functions of the national intelligence agencies and created a National Intelligence Coordinating Committee to replace the NIS.

- The Committee of Members of Parliament and Inspectors-General of Intelligence Act created intelligence oversight mechanisms.

In addition, the 1995 South African Police Services Act and the 1996 National Crime Prevention Strategy addressed aspects of security intelligence pertaining to the police.[19]

The interim constitution developed during the transition period did not deal with the restructuring of the intelligence community, as it had for the police and military. Consequently, the White Paper on Intelligence became a crucial document for outlining the overarching philosophy, organizational structure, legal mandates, control and oversight mechanisms, code of conduct, and future policies for the new South African intelligence community. According to the White Paper, the new South African intelligence services would be governed by principles such as political neutrality; legislative sanction, accountability, and parliamentary control; a balance between secrecy and transparency; and the separation of intelligence from policymaking. In addition, members of the intelligence services would be required to follow an ethical code of conduct that called for the following: adherence to an ethical code of conduct by members of the intelligence services that called for the following: allegiance to the constitution and other democratic institutions; subordination to the rule of law; compliance with democratic values; submission to an oath of secrecy; adherence to the principle of political neutrality; commitment to integrity, objectivity, and unbiased evaluation of information; and promotion of mutual trust between policymakers and intelligence professionals.[20] The White Paper also contained language that severely limited the use of covert operations both internally and externally, stating: "Measures designed to deliberately interfere with the normal political processes in other countries and with the internal workings of parties and organisations engaged in lawful activity within South Africa, must be expressly forbidden."[21]

The constitution adopted in 1996 stipulated the governing principles of the intelligence services as compliance with the rule of law (including international law), civilian executive control vested in the president, legislative regulation and oversight, transparency and accountability, political neutrality, and the duty of intelligence service members to disobey illegal orders.[22]

The GNU set about consolidating the intelligence community by integrating the intelligence and security apparatus inherited from the former apartheid regime with its counterparts the black homeland security and intelligence services[23] and the ANC-DIS. Before 1990, the ANC's intelligence apparatus included directorates for counterintelligence and strategic intelligence analysis, as well as the military intelligence service of the Umkhonto we Sizwe ("Spear of the Nation," or MK), the ANC's military arm.[24] Besides being bitter enemies, these organizations had very different ideologies, core competencies, operating procedures, and experiences. The existing South African intelligence services were tainted by their role as the guardians of the apartheid regime. The ANC services, trained by the Soviets and their allies, were rooted in unconventional warfare and were unaccustomed to performing the various tasks and functions needed of sophisticated national intelligence agencies in a liberal democracy. The homeland security and intelligence services were problematic. A mixed bag of former lower-ranking SB and SADF members known for corruption, they were seen by the ANC as extensions of the apartheid regime security and intelligence apparatus.

THE NEW SOUTH AFRICAN INTELLIGENCE COMMUNITY

The South African intelligence community structure that developed during the GNU period resembled the British, Canadian, and Australian models, with modifications to accommodate the differences in the South African government structure (Figure 10.2). The following section describes the functioning of the new South African intelligence system as developed under the GNU up through the consolidation of power of the ANC and reelection of Thabo Mbeki for a second term as president in 2004.

As outlined in the 1996 constitution and subsequent legislation, executive control of the intelligence community is vested in the president and passes down to the cabinet through the Cabinet Committee for Security and Intelligence Affairs, to the Ministry for Intelligence Services. The two new civilian intelligence agencies, the National Intelligence Agency (NIA) and the South African Secret Service (SASS), are under the Ministry for Intelligence Services. The NIA is charged with domestic intelligence and counterintelligence missions (similar to the British MI5), while the SASS conducts foreign intelligence activities (similar to MI6). The president appoints the directors of both the NIA and the SASS. Military intelligence under the South African National Defence Force (SANDF) is separate and distinct from the civilian agencies. Within the South African Police Service (SAPS), the Crime Intelligence Division conducts criminal intelligence. Coordination among these agencies is handled by the National Intelligence Coordinating Committee (NICOC), which consists of the intelligence coordinator and staff, the director generals (DGs) of NIA and SASS, the chief of Defense Intelligence of the SANDF,

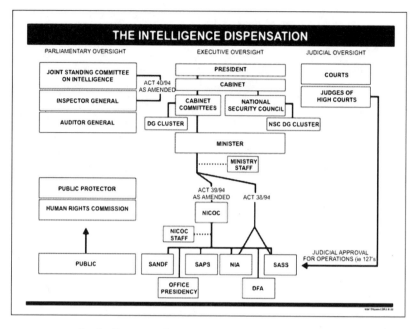

FIGURE 10.2. *South African intelligence community. From the South Africa National Intelligence Agency website, http://www.nia.org.za.*

and the head of the Crime Intelligence Division of the SAPS, and other members of departments, such as the Department of Foreign Affairs (DFA).[25]

Legislative oversight is conducted by the Joint Standing Committee on Intelligence. The committee is empowered to conduct investigations of intelligence community activities, make recommendations on intelligence-related legislation, and control the accounts and financial statements of the intelligence services. An inspector general for intelligence, appointed by a two-thirds majority vote in the legislature, has considerable access to intelligence information in order to conduct investigations and report to the Joint Standing Committee. The auditor general and Standing Committee on Public Accounts monitor the intelligence budgets, and the public protector and the Human Rights Commission provide additional protections from abuse of state power.[26] Judicial oversight is exercised primarily as a check on executive control over the legality of intelligence operations and through the resolution of legal actions brought against the government.[27]

National Security Council

A National Security Council (NSC) was established in June 2000 and consists of the president, deputy president, and ministers from the Safety and Security, Defense, Intelligence, Foreign Affairs, Home Affairs, and Finance and Justice ministries. Other ministries may participate as needed. The primary function of the NSC is to develop national security policy and coordinate that policy between the cabinet committees. This nonstatutory cabinet committee was not a feature of the GNU, and it seems to have been designed to move national security policy making out of the realm of the larger cabinet. In addition to the NSC, subordinate joint operational and intelligence structures (Joints) linking the NIA, SASS, SANDF, SAPS, and other government agencies were created in 1999 to deal with internal security issues.[28]

Ministry for Intelligence Services

The Ministry for Intelligence Services was created in 1996 as the primary office for intelligence policy formulation. Charged to provide guidance and direction for the transformation process, the ministry is the executive office for civilian intelligence and performs the community management function. Under the National Strategic Intelligence Amendment Act of 1998, the minister for intelligence is responsible for ensuring effective cooperation between the civilian intelligence services (NIA and SASS), SANDF, and the SAPS, in consultation with their ministers. The NICOC staff, under the direction of the intelligence coordinator, handles day-to-day intelligence coordination between the national intelligence organizations. The NICOC also produces and disseminates national strategic intelligence products to the president, the cabinet, the Cabinet Committee for Security and Intelligence Affairs, and other clients within the national government departments, provincial governments, and parliamentary committees. The NICOC has established Provincial Intelligence Coordination Committees (PICOCs) in the nine provinces and created several functional committees to facilitate coordination below the national level.[29] The creation of PICOCs resembles the JMC structure in the old apartheid-era National Security Management System. However, unlike the NSMS, the current system is not dominated by the military.

A Presidential Support Unit (PSU) was created within the NIA in October 2001. Originally, it was designed to provide logistical backing to the presidency and provide support services such as ensuring secure communications and countering electronic surveillance measures when the president travels, but it has evolved into a three-hundred-member unit with the official mandate to advise the presidency on strategies for conflict prevention, management, and resolution. The PSU is not supposed to have an intelligence collection function.[30] However, its functions remain somewhat murky, and there are indications that it has become Mbeki's personal intelligence service.

Intelligence priorities for the ministry include combating subversion, sabotage, terrorism, corruption, crime, and arms smuggling; conducting counterespionage; addressing domestic protective security problems, regional security issues, stability issues in Africa, international economic and technological threats directed at South Africa; preventing involvement of private security companies in African conflicts; and ensuring safety for local elections.[31]

Ronald Kasrils was appointed the minister for intelligence services in April 2004 during the cabinet reshuffle following Mbeki's reelection to a second term of office. Kasrils was a senior ANC military intelligence official trained in the former Soviet Union. He replaced Lindiwe Nonceba Sisulu, who served as intelligence minister from 2001 to 2004. Sisulu had succeeded Joe Nhlanhla, who suffered a stroke in July 2000. Prior to becoming minister, she was deputy minister of home affairs from 1996 to 2001, a member of Parliament since 1994, chairperson of the Parliamentary Joint Standing Committee on Intelligence, and personal assistant to Jacob Zuma (deputy president in Mbeki's first term). Reported to be close to Mbeki, Sisulu joined the MK in exile and received military and intelligence training in the late 1970s. She later served in key positions in ANC-DIS and was a member of the Sub-Council on Intelligence in the Transitional Executive Council.[32] Nhlanhla's tenure as minister was marked by several scandals, and the intelligence ministry suffered from lack of public confidence, charges of corruption, and a perception that it was being misused by the ANC to control internal dissent. Sisulu was described as a "smooth operator," and she received good marks for her administration of the Intelligence Ministry. While there, she set in motion several reforms, including mending fences within the intelligence agency by improving the integration process of former NIS and ANC intelligence officers, with several recent senior appointments going to white officers. She also pushed for greater compartmentalization within the NIA to prevent leaks, and for the creation of a new national intelligence academy.[33] In the cabinet reshuffle, Sisulu was appointed minister of housing.

National Intelligence Agency

The NIA, created by amalgamating the former NIS with ANC-DIS and the homeland intelligence services, has the domestic intelligence mandate. The National Strategic Intelligence Act of 1994 defined the legal mandate of the NIA: to gather, correlate, evaluate, and analyze domestic intelligence, in order to identify any threat or potential threat to the security of South Africa and to supply intelligence regarding such threats to the NICOC; to fulfill the national counterintelligence responsibilities; to provide, where necessary, intelligence regarding such threats to the South African Police Service (SAPS) for the purpose of investigating alleged offenses; and to gather and evaluate intelligence at the request of other interested departments of the government.[34]

The NIA's domestic intelligence function includes threat indications and warnings, crisis monitoring, analysis, and identifying "opportunities for the government"; the national counterintelligence function, including offensive counterespionage, to "impede or neutralize the effectiveness of foreign or hostile intelligence services, to protect classified intelligence, to counter subversion, terrorism, and sabotage aimed at the Republic of South Africa"; and a departmental intelligence responsibility to liaison with and provide assistance to other government departments requiring intelligence. The NIA also has responsibility for conducting security investigations, vetting of intelligence personnel and others for access to classified information, providing internal protective security and information technology security for the ministry, developing security standards policy, and assisting other departments in the government's anticorruption campaign.[35] The NIA does not have law enforcement powers, but it does support SAPS with intelligence as needed and authorized. In 2000 the NIA underwent a further reorganization, aimed at decentralizing intelligence activities into the provinces to focus on domestic security threats.[36] This was probably related to the creation of the PICOCs.

Manala Elias Manzini was appointed acting director general of the NIA in October 2005, and later confirmed as director, following the suspension of Billy Lesedi Masetlha by Intelligence Minister Kasrils. Masetlha's suspension was reportedly tied to an ongoing struggle within the ruling ANC and was apparently the result of the NIA's investigation of Saki Macozoma, a former ANC parliamentarian and potential successor to Mbeki. Masetlha had succeeded Vusi Mavimbela as the director general of the NIA in early 2005. Both Mavimbela and Masetlha previously served as political advisers to Thabo Mbeki. All three of the NIA directors were trained in either the Soviet Union or East Germany. Mavimbela and Masetlha served in the ANC-DIS. Manzini was part of the ANC team that negotiated the intelligence reforms during the transition period. Although the NIA's primary job is to collect domestic intelligence and conduct counterintelligence, it does monitor patterns involving organized crime and passes that information on to the police.[37]

South African Secret Service

The SASS is the foreign intelligence agency, and its mission is to gather, evaluate, and analyze foreign intelligence, excluding foreign military intelligence, and to conduct counterintelligence measures within the service. The National Strategic Intelligence Amendment Act of 1998 allows the SASS to conduct counterintelligence operations outside the country. Reportedly, the SASS received the "cream of the crop" of personnel from the old NIS and ANC intelligence organizations when it split off from the NIA.[38] Hilton Anthony "Tim" Dennis was appointed the director general of the SASS in December 1999. He took over the SASS from Billy Masetlha. From 1994 to 1999, Dennis served as deputy general manager and later general manager of counterespionage in the NIA. His background was in counterintelligence in the ANC, and he received military training in Angola and attended various courses in counterintelligence in East Germany.[39] After Nhlanhla's stroke and the public discovery that an NIA counterespionage division surveillance camera had been collecting information against the German embassy in Pretoria, Dennis was promoted by Mbeki to head the SASS. The SASS intelligence products reportedly are not held in high regard, which may account for the formation of the PSU. With Dennis as its director general, counterespionage is likely to be a priority function for the service.

South African Police Service

The SAPS reports to the Ministry of Safety and Security and is the primary domestic security service. It is a national force, with 149,000 personnel (including 33,000 civilians) spread across the nine provinces. During the transition period, it faced a significant problem with personnel competency, since an estimated one-fourth of the police officers were functionally illiterate. Insufficient and low-quality personnel, corruption in the service, low morale, and a high level of murder of police officers remained problems within the force for years.[40] Crime in South Africa continues to be a serious national security problem, and the SAPS is on the front line of the government's National Crime Combating Strategy (NCCS) campaign to stabilize crime rates, particularly in designated "hot spots." The Directorate of Special Operations, better known as "the Scorpions," is the SAPS leading crime-fighting unit, reportedly modeled after the FBI. The Crime Intelligence Division is responsible for the management, collection, and analysis of crime intelligence and counterintelligence, providing technical support to crime prevention and investigation. Crime Intelligence is the fastest-growing program in the Safety and Security budget. The Crime Intelligence Division was involved in various cross-border operations such as Operation Rachel in Mozambique, which focused on the destruction of arms caches. It also generates intelligence reports in support of the SAPS, including crime prevention and crime investigation intelligence.[41] To support the NCCS, the division is shifting its emphasis from reactive to proactive intelligence and to investigate suspected criminal activities before a crime has been committed. The Crime Intelligence Division does conduct covert actions.[42] While not militarized or integrated into the security intelligence network to the degree seen during the apartheid era, the SAPS does have representatives in the Joint Standing Committee and PICOCs, and its minister sits on the NSC. The commissioner of the Crime Intelligence Division represents the SAPS on the NICOC.

Charles Nqakula was appointed minister of safety and security in May 2002. Close to President Mbeki, he had served as deputy minister of home affairs, and before that as a parliamentary counselor to the president. He was the former secretary general of the South African Communist Party. Nqakula has a background as a journalist. He underwent military training in Angola and joined MK, and he later trained in the Soviet Union and East Germany. Nqakula infiltrated back into South Africa as one of the commanders of Operation Vula, as part of the ANC plan to build underground military capabilities, and served as commander in the Western Cape from 1988 to 1991.[43] Described as a "low-key police minister," Nqakula owed his position to his close relation to Mbeki, rather than to "any obvious aptitude for dealing with crime or managing the bureaucratic behemoth of the South African Police Service."[44]

Defense Intelligence

Demilitarization of the intelligence apparatus was a key goal of the intelligence sector transformation process. By dismantling the "securocrat" structure, creating a civilian-led Defense Department, and limiting the scope of military intelligence to the functions specified in the 1994 National Strategic Intelligence Act, the GNU and its successor administrations achieved that goal. The act limits Defense Intelligence (formerly the Military Intelligence Division) to collecting, correlating, evaluating, and using foreign and domestic military intelligence and to conducting counterintelligence within the SANDF. It is excluded from collecting nonmilitary intelligence and from conducting covert collection except under very specific circumstances limited by law, and only when authorized by the chairperson of the NICOC with the concurrence of the NICOC and the cabinet. The DI is forbidden from participating in any non-intelligence-related operations, and the SANDF does not have the powers of arrest, detention, or search and seizure under the new constitution. However, DI is involved in supporting the top two high-priority Defense Department missions: border control and cooperation with SAPS for internal security. Neither the SAPS nor the SANDF is comfortable with the military being involved in what are essentially police functions, but until the SAPS can demonstrate a capability to assume these missions, the SANDF will remain a major player in internal security.[45] Oversight of the DI is shared between the mechanisms designed for the intelligence community and an inspector general for defense intelligence.

Lieutenant General Mojo Motau, the former head of MK military intelligence, became the defense intelligence chief following the sacking of General Georg Meiring and several other top SANDF officers in 1998.[46] The DI was severely criticized at the time, both within and outside the government, for its allegations in what came to be known as the Meiring Report, which claimed that there was a left-wing coup plot led by Winnie Madikizela-Mandela and others to overthrow the GNU of Nelson Mandela. The report, which Meiring gave directly to the president, had not been coordinated with the other intelligence agencies, and Meiring bypassed the intelligence coordination system set up to avoid such problems.[47] The DI came under renewed criticism for its poor intelligence estimates of the Royal Lesotho Defense Force analysis during the Lesotho incursion shortly after Motau took over.[48]

CONCLUSION: FUTURE PROSPECTS AND LESSONS LEARNED

Since the election of Thabo Mbeki in 1999 to succeed Nelson Mandela as president, there have been some subtle but significant changes to the intelligence community, not all of which bode well for the high standards set for it by the Constitution and the intelligence acts. Mbeki's placement of old comrades from the ANC's former intelligence network into virtually every key security-sector position has worried some observers. Moreover, the extent of effective oversight of the intelligence community has become a concern. An inspector general of intelligence, Fazel Randera, resigned in January 2002 after only six months on the job, supposedly for personal reasons, but reports indicated that the real reason he left had to do with the nature of the job. Because the job placed whoever held it in an untenable position of having to confront an intelligence community with close ties to the presidency, as well as having unclear roles and reporting lines, it had remained vacant for most of the first decade after the GNU came to power.[49] Former Home Affairs Minister Mangosuthu Buthelezi, leader of the Inkatha Freedom Party and coalition partner with the ANC-led government until the second Mbeki administration, questioned the independence of the oversight mechanisms, calling the top ANC leaders "untouchable."[50]

Amendments to the intelligence acts were enacted in 2002, and while several of the provisions were designed to clarify some of the ambiguities of the earlier legislation, critics saw the changes as a move by the government to make the intelligence services less transparent and accountable to parliamentary and judicial oversight.[51] While such comparisons probably would not be welcomed by the Mbeki administration, the NSC and the new Presidential Intelligence Support Unit were beginning to look and function more like the old apartheid regime's Cabinet Committee for State Security and its subordinate SSC. If this trend continues and the security intelligence sector begins to backslide into a political police mode of operation, owing its allegiance to the ANC rather than the constitution, South Africa's democratization process would be put in jeopardy.[52]

Lessons learned from the South African case show that reform of the intelligence sector is a key element of the democratization process. Intelligence reform should begin earlier rather than later in the overall progression of democratization. The South Africans developed a road map of where they wanted to take these reforms through a white paper that outlined why reform was necessary, what the intelligence community structure would look like, where the intelligence functions were to be distributed, to whom it would be accountable, and how the intelligence agencies and their personnel were expected to act. From this outline, South African legislators crafted legal mandates to govern the operation of the intelligence community, placing emphasis on the need to balance security with transparency, establishing legislative oversight, building in civilian control, and separating intelligence from policymaking. Operationalizing these mandates has proven to be more difficult than anticipated. Integrating, amalgamating, and transforming a variety of intelligence agencies that were once mortal enemies into a cohesive and efficient community is a long-term undertaking. Professionalization of the intelligence community is the key to success, and that aspect has been a struggle for the South Africans. It took several years to purge the old guard securocrats, and it is likely to take quite a bit longer to replace the communist-trained ANC group now in control. After a two-year hiatus, the intelligence community late in 2002 established the South African National Academy of Intelligence (SANAI) to provide training to members of the NIA, SASS, NICOC, and Presidential Support Unit, as well as the SANDF-DI and SAPS.[53] The graduates of the SANAI are the future of the South African intelligence community, but it will be years before they rise to the top echelons.

A practical problem for most emerging democracies involves the organizational dynamics of transforming a bureaucracy. One of the most persistent arguments against reforming intelligence agencies is that the transformation process will leave the nation vulnerable to both internal and external threats. In most organizations, a radical transformation process will inherently involve a period of declining organizational task efficiency. This certainly happened in the South African case. The goals during the transformation process were to limit the decline in organizational task efficiency while minimizing the time it would take for the organization to recover. As a former South African senator described it, a dilemma occurs when the organizational level of efficiency reaches a lower plateau and seems to stagnate rather than improve toward the level of the old organization. A common reaction to this problem is to attempt to reorganize in order to improve efficiency (or as one longtime intelligence officer opined, to increase managerial control over the organization). The result is another decline in organizational task efficiency as the agency adapts to the changes. The problem can become systemic if the agency's leadership does not recognize this trend and allow the organization sufficient time to adapt and gradually improve efficiency.

The South African intelligence community has undergone at least three major reorganizations since 1989: first under de Klerk, then during the GNU period, and again in 2000 under Mbeki. In addition, most of the agencies have endured numerous internal reorganizations and amalgamations during the same period. Unless the government gives these agencies time to adjust and develop standing operating procedures, they are unlikely to reach their optimal level of efficiency for a very long time.

South Africa made a remarkable transformation of its security intelligence sector from what had clearly become an independent security state during the later stages of the apartheid regime to a bureau of domestic intelligence in the GNU. However, with the consolidation of the ANC's hold on power, the Mbeki administration has shown a tendency to inch the security intelligence services more toward a political police mode of operation. Rather than being dominated by the military securocrats, the new intelligence community is dominated by ANC members, most of whom were trained in the Soviet Union, East Germany, or Cuba and served together in the ANC's intelligence services during the struggle against the apartheid regime. The placement of so many key security sector positions in the hands of communist-trained former intelligence operatives is a remarkable exception to the general trend in new democracies. How South Africa consolidates its democracy is being closely watched by other emerging democracies, and its success or failure will have an impact on the region and the continent.

NOTES

1. Peter Gill, *Policing Politics: Security Intelligence and the Liberal Democratic State* (London: Frank Cass, 1994), 6.

2. The classification of security intelligence service types is based on Gill, *Policing Politics*, 60–61, 79–83, and his interpretation of William W. Keller, *The Liberals and J. Edgar Hoover: Rise and Fall of a Domestic Intelligence State* (Princeton, NJ: Princeton University Press, 1989), 13–16.

3. See "Internal Affairs, South Africa," *Jane's Sentinel Security Assessment: Southern Africa*, March 18, 2003, http://www.janes.com. For in-depth studies of national security strategies in the South African apartheid era, see Annette Seegers, *The Military in the Making of Modern South Africa* (London: Tauris Academic Books, 1996); James M. Roherty, *State Security in South Africa: Civil-Military Relations under P. W. Botha* (London: M. E. Sharpe, 1992); Chris Alden, *Apartheid's Last Stand: The Rise and Fall of the South African Security State* (London: Macmillan, 1996); and Jacklyn Cock and Laurie Nathan, eds., *Society at War: The Militarization of South Africa* (New York: St. Martin's, 1989).

4. British and Commonwealth scholars prefer the term of art "security intelligence" to describe intelligence activities aimed at countering internal threats. Counterintelligence is usually associated with foreign intelligence threats. Security intelligence is primarily domestic intelligence, and unlike criminal intelligence, which is associated with police work, it usually concerns activities to counter political crimes. See Gill, *Policing Politics*, 6–7.

5. Shaun McCarthy, "The Relationship between the Academic and Intelligence Communities in a Post-Apartheid South Africa," *South African Defence Review*, no. 13 (1993), available at http://www.iss.co.za. See also Kevin A. O'Brien, "Counter-Intelligence for Counter-Revolutionary Warfare: The South African Police Security Branch, 1979–1990," *Intelligence and National Security* 16, no. 3 (Autumn 2001): 27–59.

6. Shaun McCarthy, "Challenges for the South African Intelligence Community," in William Gutteridge, ed., *South Africa's Defense and Security into the 21st Century* (Brookfield, VT: Dartmouth, 1996), 68–69.

7. Robert D'A. Henderson, "South African Intelligence under de Klerk," *International Journal of Intelligence and Counterintelligence* 8, no. 1 (Spring 1995): 53–56.

8. See Gill, *Policing Politics*, for the typology of security intelligence organizations based on W. W. Keller, *The Liberals and J. Edgar Hoover: Rise and Fall of a Domestic Intelligence State* (Princeton, NJ: Princeton University Press, 1989), 13–16, 60–61. Gill categorizes the three types of security intelligence services with respect to levels of autonomy from and penetration of society.

9. McCarthy, "Challenges," 66–67.

10. McCarthy, "Challenges," 64–72.

11. Henderson, "South African Intelligence," 79.

12. Ibid., 52, 67–68, 73, 78–80.

13. Kevin O'Brien, "South Africa's Evolving Intelligence and Security Structures," *International Journal of Intelligence and Counterintelligence* 9, no. 2 (Summer 1996): 192.

14. On the security sector transformation, see James Winkates, "The Transformation of the South African National Defence Force: A Good Beginning," *Armed Forces and Society* 26, no. 3 (Spring 2000): 451–472; Kent Hughes Butts and Steven Metz, *Armies and Democracy in the New Africa: Lessons from Nigeria and South Africa*, Strategic Studies Institute Monograph, U.S. Army War College, January 9, 1996; Jakkie Cilliers, "The Security Agencies and the South African Constitution," Institute for Security Studies Occasional Paper no. 3, March 1996; and Jabu Kuzwayo, "Developing Mechanisms for Civilian Oversight over the Armed Forces," *African Security Review* 7, no. 5 (1998), available at http://www.iss.co.za.

15. McCarthy, "Challenges," 73–74. See also his article, "South Africa's Intelligence Reformation," *International Journal of Intelligence and Counterintelligence* (Spring 1996): 63–71. For an ANC perspective, see Joe Nhlanhla, "The Transformation of Military Intelligence and Special Forces: Towards an Accountable and Transparent Military Culture," *South African Defence Review*, no. 12 (1993), available at http://www.iss.co.za.

16. See O'Brien, "South Africa's Evolving Intelligence," 205–206, 227–228. Shaun McCarthy claims that the GNU policymakers were influenced by the writings of Barry Buzan on national security policy and the principles recommended by the Canadian Security Intelligence Review Committee on legislative accountability and oversight of intelligence activities. McCarthy, "South Africa's Intelligence Reformation," 65, 71. For a list of Barry Buzan's works, see http://www.lse.ac.uk/people/b.g.buzan@lse.ac.uk/publications.htm. His most influential work on the South African national security reformers, according to McCarthy, is *People, States, and Fear: The National Security Problem in International Relations* (Chapel Hill: University of North Carolina Press, 1983); and his revised second edition with the new subtitle *An Agenda for International Security Studies in the Post–Cold War Era* (Boulder, CO: Lynne Rienner, 1991). For the Canadian experience with oversight issues, see Reg Whitaker, "The Politics of Security Intelligence Policy-Making in Canada: 1984–91," *Intelligence and National Security* 7, no. 2 (1992).

17. South African White Paper on Intelligence, 1994, sec. 1, "Objective," available at http://www.intelligence.gov.za/Legislation.asp.

18. White Paper on National Defense for the Republic of South Africa, chap. 3, "Civil-Military Relations," May 1996, available at http://www.polity.org.za/html/govdocs/white_papers/defencewp.html#3c.

19. These documents are available at http://www.polity.org.za.

20. South African White Paper on Intelligence, 1995.

21. Ibid.

22. Constitution of the Republic of South Africa, as adopted on May 8, 1996, and amended on October 11, 1996, by the Constitutional Assembly, arts. 198, 199, 209, and 210, available at http://www.polity.org.za. For a discussion of the new Constitution and its impact on the intelligence community, see Cilliers, "The Security Agencies."

23. Transkei, Bophuthatswana, and Venda had civilian and military intelligence services, but the Ciskei Intelligence Service had been disbanded in August 1991. O'Brien, "South Africa's Evolving Intelligence," 224.

24. Ibid., 221. For background on the MK, see Tsepe Motumi, "Umkhonto we Sizwe—Structure, Training, and Force Levels (1984 to 1994)," *African Defence Review*, no. 18 (1994), available at http://www.iss.co.za.

25. "Security and Foreign Affairs, South Africa," *Jane's Sentinel Security Assessment: Southern Africa*, March 18, 2003, http://www.janes.com.

26. For the most current information on the South African intelligence community organizational structure, see the NIA homepage, http://www.nia.org.za. For more-detailed discussions on the roles and missions of the various agencies, see O'Brien, "South Africa's Evolving Intelligence"; Cilliers, "The Security Agencies"; and the Federation of American Scientists Intelligence Resource Program website, http://www.fas.org/irp/world/rsa.

27. For example, courts ruled against the SAPS policy of denying a group of ten white police officers promotions to captain because the positions were reserved for other racial and minority groups. A labor court ordered the SAPS to promote them. "SAPS Lose Appeal in White Officers' Case," *Independent Online*, March 7, 2003, http://www.iol.co.za.

28. For a brief discussion of the new NSC structure, see "Security and Foreign Affairs, South Africa." The assessment of key players is based on informal discussions with U.S. intelligence analysts.

29. NIA website, http://www.nia.org.za.

30. Marianne Merten, "Spy Unit for Mbeki," *Mail and Guardian* (Johannesburg), February 22, 2002, available at http://allafrica.com/stories/200202210470.html. In the 2003 budget, there was a mention of Defense Intelligence providing early warning reports to a "Presidential National Early Warning Centre." See *National Medium Term Expenditure Estimates—Justice and Protection Services (February 2003)*, Vote 22: Defence, Programme 6: Defense Intelligence, 501–502, available at http://www.polity.org.za/pdf/Expest_Justice.pdf. See also Robert D'A. Henderson, "South Africa," in *Brassey's International Intelligence Yearbook*, 2003 ed. (Washington, DC: Brassey's, 2003), 172.

31. Ministry for Intelligence Services priorities are as reported in "Security and Foreign Affairs, South Africa."

32. See her biography at South African Government Online, http://www.gov.za.

33. "The 2002 Report Card," *Mail and Guardian Online*, December 20, 2002, http://www.mg.co.za.

34. *National Intelligence Agency, Annual Report, April 2001–March 2002*, 1st ed., 9, http://www.nia.org.za.

35. Ibid.

36. Ibid.

37. Pule Molebeledi, "An Intelligent Approach to Spying," *Business Day* (Johannesburg), November 7, 2002, available at http://allafrica.com/stories/2002110 80144.html.

38. "The People behind the Cabinet: Who Does What in the Ministries," *Mail and Guardian* (Johannesburg), November 12, 1999, available at http://allafrica .com/stories/199911120209.html.

39. Statement on Appointment of Directors-General, issued by Office of the Presidency, December 4, 1999, available at http://www.polity.org.za/govdocs/pr/ 1999/pr1204.html.

40. "Security and Foreign Affairs, South Africa."

41. See *National Medium Term Expenditure Estimates—Justice and Protection Services (February 2003)*, Vote 25: Safety and Security, Programme 5: Crime Intelligence, 576–577, available at http://www.polity.org.za/pdf/Expest_Justice.pdf.

42. Delien Burger, *South Africa Yearbook 2002/03*, Government Communication and Information System, http://www.gcis.gov.za/docs/publications/year book.htm.

43. See his biography at South African Government Online, http://www .gov.za. For a detailed discussion on Operation Vula, see Robert D'A. Henderson, "Operation Vula against Apartheid," *International Journal of Intelligence and Counterintelligence* 10, no. 4 (Winter 1997–1998): 418–455.

44. "The 2002 Report Card."

45. Winkates, "Transformation," 461–462.

46. Ray Hartley, "11 Days That Led to War," *Sunday Times*, September 27, 1998, http://www.suntimes.co.za/1998/09/27/news/news23.htm.

47. See Rocky Williams, "Before We Forget: Writing the History of Umkhonto We Sizwe between 1961–2000," *Journal of Peace, Conflict, and Military Studies* 1, no. 1 (March 2000), http://www.uz.ac.zw/units/cds/journals/volume1/ number1/article2.html.

48. Winkates, "Transformation," 458–459.

49. "The 2002 Report Card."

50. Ranjeni Munusamy, " 'Untouchable' SA Leaders Bend the Law, Says Buthelezi," *Sunday Times*, November 11, 2001, http://www.suntimes.co.za/2001/11/ 11/news/news02.asp.

51. See Kevin O'Brien, "Controlling the Hydra: An Historical Analysis of South African Intelligence Accountability," in Hans Born, Loch K. Johnson, and Ian Leigh, eds., *Who's Watching the Spies? Establishing Intelligence Service Accountability* (Dulles, VA: Potomac Books, 2005), 199–222, http://www.dcaf.ch/legal_wg/ ev_oslo_030919_obrien.pdf. See pages 41–47 for a discussion of the amending acts passed by the South African Parliament between 1998 and 2003.

52. For an interesting article regarding South African attitudes toward the ANC government, see Rory Carroll, "Nostalgia Grows for Apartheid System," *The Guardian*, December 12, 2002, http://www.guardian.co.uk/international/story/0,3604,858369,00.html: The following is an excerpt: "In a rebuke to the African National Congress government, more than 60% of all South Africans polled said the country was better run during white minority rule. One in five black people interviewed gave the regime which jailed Nelson Mandela and denied them the vote, a positive rating—a result which analysts attributed to crime and unemployment. In 1995, fewer than one in ten gave apartheid a positive rating. A growing number of white people voiced confidence in the future of the state, as did blacks who have prospered since democratic elections replaced apartheid in 1994. Perceptions that the new elite is corrupt have also diminished. The study was conducted by Afrobarometer in September and October on behalf of the Institute for Democracy in South Africa, Ghana's Centre for Democratic Development and Michigan State University."

53. Thabo Mokgola, "Intelligence No Longer Associated with Dirty Tricks: Zuma," *BuaNews* (Pretoria), February 28, 2003, available at http://allafrica.com/stories/200302280534.html.

ELEVEN

TERRORISM'S THREAT TO NEW DEMOCRACIES

The Case of Russia

Mikhail Tsypkin

In this chapter, I address the relationship between democratic civilian control over intelligence and security agencies in the Russian Federation.[1] Since the mid-1990s, Russia has had to deal with increasingly frequent acts of terror committed by (or sometimes only attributed to) the Chechen separatists. I examine the relationship between the government's response to terrorism and the reform of the intelligence agencies.

Russia is perhaps the most difficult case of all postcommunist states when it comes to democratic civilian control over intelligence and security agencies. The Soviet Union could be characterized as the archetypal counterintelligence state. This term, coined by John Dziak, refers to a political system where the security service "permeates all societal institutions" and is "the principal guardian of the Party," where "the two together constitute a permanent counterintelligence enterprise to which all other major political, social and economic questions are subordinated."[2] Russia has inherited from its communist past a uniquely powerful system of intelligence and security agencies. In this chapter, I first briefly address the institutional culture inherited by the Russian agencies from their Soviet predecessors. Second, I discuss the current status of democratic civilian control over these agencies. Third, I explain the factors behind the current state of affairs; in the process, I answer the question of the impact of counterterrorism on democratic civilian control of intelligence agencies.

The origins of the Russian intelligence services suggest that their transition to real democratic civilian control is not likely to be easy. The postcommunist Russian state inherited the old cadre of the Committee of State Security (KGB), split during the last month of the existence of the USSR into several agencies. By the end of 1992, the former First Chief Directorate of the KGB, responsible for foreign intelligence, became the External Intelligence Service (SVR) of the Russian Federation (RF); the Second and Third Chief Directorates (responsible for counterintelligence and military counterintelligence, respectively), the Fourth Directorate (transportation security), the Directorate for Protection of the Constitution (formerly the infamous Fifth Chief Directorate that dealt with dissidents, by 1991 responsible for counterterrorism, ethnic problems, etc.), the Sixth Directorate (economic crime and corruption), and the Seventh Directorate (surveillance and wiretapping) became the Ministry of Security, which subsequently became the Federal Security Service, or FSB. The Eighth Chief Directorate (communications and signals intelligence, or SIGINT) became the Federal Agency for Government Communications and Information. The Ninth Directorate (physical security of high officials) became the Main Guard Directorate. The Border Guards became the Committee for the Protection of Russian Borders.[3] The Fifteenth Directorate (maintenance and protection of secure underground facilities for the leadership) became the Main Directorate for Special Projects, attached to the office of the president of RF.[4] The intelligence arm of the military, the Main Intelligence Directorate of the General Staff (GRU), has not undergone any visible change; so little is known about the GRU that I largely exclude it from this discussion. This probably incomplete list gives us a good idea of the huge scale of the KGB activities under the Soviet regime.

THE SOVIET LEGACY

The legacy of the Soviet intelligence and security services is of great importance because of the continuity between the Soviet and Russian agencies. The Soviet intelligence agencies were directly responsible for one of the worst campaigns of mass terror in the twentieth century. The competence of the "organs," as the intelligence and security services were known in the vernacular, embraced until Stalin's death in 1953 practically all spheres of human activity. Not only did the intelligence services gather information about real and purported enemies of the regime, but they also were involved in the development of new weapons, especially nuclear ones; controlled a substantial part of the economy where prison labor was employed; closely monitored and manipulated cultural developments; punished industrial managers, engineers, and scientists for failures; enforced secrecy; and so on.

The issue of civilian control over the intelligence services in the Soviet times should be viewed in the light of the fact that the worst brutalities committed by the secret police—Cheka and it successors (the NKVD, MVD, and MGB)—were a manifestation of the will of the political elite. The Soviet intelligence services acquired their wide-ranging extralegal character as a result of a conscious political decision of a radical minority group, which had seized power and resolved to maintain it against all odds and without legitimate political authority. Like any bureaucracy, the Soviet intelligence services attempted to pursue their corporate self-interest even under Stalin, but there is little doubt as to who really called the shots. This civilian (if one may call it so) control did not happen by itself: Stalin was a vigilant dictator, aware of the tendency of any bureaucracy to pursue its self-interest rather than the desires of the supreme leader; the intelligence services, because of their knowledge of the darkest secrets of the dictator, and because of their access to his person, required particular vigilance from Stalin, who purged them thoroughly on several occasions, as well as split the Commissariat of Internal Affairs (NKVD) of the era of the Great Terror into two agencies, the MVD (Ministry of Internal Affairs) and MGB (Ministry of State Security).

During Stalin's rule the personnel of the intelligence services developed into a closed, relatively large and highly privileged group, separated from the rest of the population by a gulf of fear. While the officers in the intelligence services received benefits more modest than often imagined in the West, it was the fear of the nearly unlimited power that the security services had over the Soviet citizens, from a collective farmer up to generals and government ministers, that allowed the officers of the security services to obtain many tangible and intangible benefits for themselves and their families. They maintained a huge network of coerced or bribed informers that penetrated every corner of the Soviet society and added to the image of power and omniscience of the "organs."

The events following Stalin's death demonstrated that civilian control, even dictatorial civilian control, over the intelligence agencies could not be taken for granted. Lavrenti Beria assembled all security agencies into one super-ministry (MVD) and apparently planned to use it as an instrument in his bid for supreme power. When the Communist Party oligarchs decided, with the greatest trepidation, to remove Beria, they discovered that they had no ready tools of coercion at their disposal: Beria controlled their bodyguards, investigators, arrest squads, prisons, and so forth. As a result, the Party bosses had to choose a very distasteful (from their point of view) option of bringing the military into politics in order to arrest, incarcerate, try, sentence, and execute the much-feared Beria and several of his henchmen.[5] In the aftermath of the Beria affair, the Communist Party took several steps to strengthen its control over the intelligence services. The MVD super-ministry was split into two in 1954: the MVD remained in charge of the less feared and less prestigious uniformed police, internal security troops, and prison and labor camps system, while the intelligence, counterintelligence, border guard troops, and associated secret services were put under the Committee of State Security (KGB), its status as a committee rather than a ministry indicating demotion. (The relationship between ministry and committee is approximately the same as between department and agency in the U.S. government.) The KGB officials at the regional level from then on had to keep local Party authorities informed about their activities, and they were prohibited from spying on high-ranking officials. The indiscriminate terror and mass use of torture were ended immediately after Stalin's death, while Beria was still in charge. At the helm of the KGB the old-school "professionals" were replaced by a succession of former Communist Party officials who brought with them a number of Party functionaries, a policy that was supposed to strengthen the Party's control over the services.

As much as Khrushchev may have disliked the KGB, it was an essential element of the Soviet order, and it continued to act during Khrushchev's reign against any manifestation of discontent, however mild, within the regime. The old cadre responsible for the horrors of Stalin's era were left, for the most part, in charge of the KGB, despite the presence of a number of high-level recruits from the Party. Criticism of the security agencies' actions under Stalin, unleashed from time to time by Khrushchev, did little to weaken the corporative spirit of the KGB officers who considered themselves unfairly singled out for criticism by Party officials who had had the ultimate responsibility for the terror. The KGB took part in the plot that ousted Khrushchev in 1964; despite the prohibition on spying against high-ranking officials, the KGB tapped the telephones of Khrushchev and his family members for months before the coup.

Between 1964 and 1985, the KGB, like the other elements of the Stalinist state and ideology, experienced partial restoration: the Party oligarchs, who overthrew Khrushchev, believed that the Soviet system could not be maintained without fear, and fear was the KGB's vocation. Brezhnev decided to guarantee the Communist Party's control over the KGB by appointing Yuri Andropov, one of the secretaries of the Central Committee, as the KGB chairman. At the time (1967), this appointment was viewed as a demotion: no Party official had ever returned from the intelligence and security agencies to aspire for political leadership. Andropov's appointment came at a propitious moment for the "organs": the Soviet and Warsaw Pact troops were used to prevent a disintegration of the communist system in Czechoslovakia in 1968. The same year saw student demonstrations in Poland; in 1970, deadly force was used to quell worker protests in that country. The Soviet system was entering a crisis; the reaction of the Kremlin was increasingly to rely on the KGB to suppress any manifestation of protest in the USSR.

The KGB, during the last two decades of the Soviet system, appeared to be able to pursue its self-interests to a greater degree than under either Stalin or Khrushchev. This was due to the general weakness of the political leadership of the Soviet Union; that group of old men was dedicated only to preservation of the status quo, which allowed several powerful bureaucracies (military, defense industry, KGB) to pursue their corporate agendas within the limits set by the well-established preferences of the political leadership. The KGB under Andropov provided the political leadership with analyses designed to exaggerate the external and internal threats to the Soviet Union. This suited the self-interests of the KGB and did not go against the instincts of the political elite. Under Andropov, a massive media campaign was launched to enhance the KGB's image: hundreds of movies and books about the "brave *chekisty*" were released; Russia's president Vladimir Putin credits such books and films for giving him the dream of joining the KGB.[6] KGB personnel (their number was estimated to be about 500,000) enjoyed various and considerable formal and informal privileges.

The KGB's foreign intelligence activities were of little importance to the Soviet citizens in comparison with the enormous impact that the KGB domestic operations had on everyday life in the USSR. A negative reference from the KGB could ruin a person's chances for college admission, job placement, the coveted privilege of traveling abroad, and promotion at work. The KGB reported to the highest Communist Party authorities on the attitudes of various sectors of the public and played an important role in all matters of self-expression. Even thirty years after the end of Stalin's terror, Soviet citizens would refer to the KGB in a manner of primitive tribesmen, who used taboos and euphemisms to denote something utterly frightening and beyond their control: instead of just saying "the KGB," a finger would be pointed at the ceiling in a silent warning.

The KGB was at the center of events leading to the end of the Soviet communist system and the disintegration of the Soviet Union. After Mikhail Gorbachev ordered the KGB to stop its repression of dissent in 1986–1987, there was nothing else to stop various political movements from forming and competing with the Communist Party for power. Once Gorbachev felt threatened by these movements, he began to encourage the KGB to provide him information on his political opponents; he must have also at least permitted the KGB to prepare for an introduction of martial law or emergency rule. A number of Gorbachev's reform-minded associates complained later that the KGB, in pursuing its own self-interests, tried to frighten Gorbachev with imaginary plots by the pro-reform politicians. These associates warned Gorbachev, but his usual response was that he knew how to deal with the KGB. Apparently, he didn't: using Gorbachev's acquiescence in preparations for an imposition of martial law, the KGB organized the August 1991 anti-reform coup that temporarily removed Gorbachev from power.[7] The coup crumbled apparently after the KGB commando unit refused to storm the center of resistance to the coup, the building of the parliament of the Russian Federation, and arrest or kill Boris Yeltsin and his supporters. Finally, the symbolic act of the end of communism was the removal, to the cheering of a large crowd, of the statue of the secret police founder, Felix Dzerzhinsky, from the square in front of the KGB building. This was a backhanded compliment to the KGB, recognition of its centrality to the survival of the communist regime—no monument to Lenin was removed or destroyed in Moscow at the time.

THE ISSUES FOR ANALYSIS

Which agencies are we going to consider? The editors' guidance to authors suggests that there are "four primary functions of intelligence:

collection, analysis, counterintelligence, and covert action." The following agencies in Russia clearly are engaged in such activities: the Federal Security Service[8] (Federal'naya sluzhba bezopanosti—FSB), which is engaged in a broad range of counterintelligence activities; the External Intelligence Service (Sluzhba vneshnei razvedki—SVR), engaged in gathering and analyzing political and economic intelligence about foreign countries; and the military's Main Intelligence Directorate (Glavnoe razvedyvatel'noe upravlenie—GRU), whose main mission is gathering intelligence about military capabilities of other nations. As far as their current activities go, the greatest amount (and it is not very great) of reliable information is available about the FSB, much less about the SVR, and even less about the GRU. There is one more agency that is likely to engage at least in some counterintelligence activities: the Federal Protection Service (Federal'naya sluzhba okhrany—FSO), which provides security for Russia's top officials. Very little is known about the current FSO; still, reading the official documents on its missions suggests that it engages in some domestic collection.[9] All agencies are militarized: their personnel have military ranks and are considered to be members of the armed services.

The questions that one might potentially address in order to evaluate the state of civilian democratic control over the agencies are these: the legal framework for intelligence work; the hierarchy of accountability; the existence of an intelligence community and the identity of its main customers; the relationships between counterintelligence and intelligence, and between covert operations and analysis; and, naturally, executive and legislative oversight.[10] It is impossible within this one chapter to answer all these questions; I attempt to address the issues of agencies' oversight by the executive, legislative, and judicial branches of the Russian government, as well as the relationship of the agencies with the mass media.

THE ROLE OF THE EXECUTIVE BRANCH

The Russian Federation inherited the Soviet-era constitution, which granted great powers to the parliament (Supreme Soviet), obviously because the drafters of that document never imagined that anyone would ever have to take it seriously. Russia's first president, Boris Yeltsin, found himself in a gridlock with the parliament when the legislative branch rather naturally attempted to use its constitutional prerogatives, combined with popular discontent with the desperate economic situation in 1992–1993, to weaken Yeltsin and possibly remove him from power. The result was Yeltsin's crushing of the rebellious parliament by force, and the approval of a new constitution in December 1993 by a nationwide referendum (widely believed to have been rigged). Drafted in response to Yeltsin's political needs and personal preferences, this document gave the president of the Russian Federation far greater powers than the legislative and judiciary branches, especially in the area of security.

The executive branch of the Russian state, as it emerged after the adoption of the 1993 constitution, is peculiarly bifurcated. The president is the top official of the executive branch, while at the same time he is above it. The constitution, written to satisfy both President Yeltsin's ego and his desire to be put out of reach of the parliament, assigns to the president the role of the "guarantor of the Constitution of the Russian Federation, of the human and civil rights and freedoms." The president provides for coordinated functioning and cooperation of the bodies of state power.[11] Under Putin, this interpretation of the unique presidential role has been taken to new and extraordinary lengths. The website of the president of the Russian Federation says that the system of government requires checks and balances—and then promptly excludes the president from such:

> Each of the bodies (institutions) of state power only partially provides for the functioning of the constitution. Only the President has the mission to protect the foundations of the state as a whole, the sovereignty and integrity of the state. . . . While being legally distant from all branches of government, the President at the same time is "closer" to the executive than to any other branches of government.[12]

This extraordinary president leaves day-to-day operational control of such fields as the economy, education, health care, and social security to the government (Pravitel'stvo) of the Russian Federation, whose prime minister is appointed by the president and confirmed by the State Duma. (The Duma has no right to confirm appointments of the ministers.) Given the disastrous state of all these fields, it is in the interest of the president to entrust them to an expendable prime minister, who could serve as a useful scapegoat. The president, however, has not been left idle: he is directly in charge of the "presidential block," a collection of twenty-one ministries and other agencies dealing with external and internal aspects of the security of the Russian state (and its president), including the FSB, SVR, FSO, and, with the GRU, as part of the Ministry of Defense.[13] This situation is not the invention of Putin. The presidential block was first established by Boris Yeltsin, while Putin, thanks to his vastly superior work habits and natural interest (given his background as a KGB officer) in the agencies, has taken his predecessor's arrangements further.

It appears that the intelligence agencies communicate the results of their work directly to the president, the partial exception being the head of GRU, who normally reports to the minister of defense and the chief of the General Staff but can also, according to the former GRU commander General Fedor Ladygin, report directly to the president, as long as he files the same reports to the minister of defense and the chief of the General Staff.[14] There is no indication that Russia has anything like the American system of national intelligence estimates, drawing together the collective judgment of all the intelligence agencies. A former GRU commander states that his agency reports directly to the president and usually has no information about the content of reports on the same subject by the foreign intelligence.[15] The president himself "coordinates" the work of different agencies.[16] Russia's agencies are not organized into an intelligence community, as they are in the United States; there are no formal horizontal links between these agencies. Some coordination of intelligence and security activities may be carried out at the level of the Security Council, which acts as the president's chancellery.[17] There is no equivalent to the post of the director of central intelligence, let alone the new position of director of national intelligence.

MISSIONS OF THE AGENCIES

Missions of the agencies are defined in a number of laws and presidential directives. External intelligence is conducted by the SVR, GRU, and, to a certain degree, FSB. The SVR is tasked with collecting intelligence in the areas of politics, economy, military strategy, and science and technology. The GRU is supposed to collect information on the military power of other nations: military art and weapons, as well as defense industry.[18] The FSB can also engage in external intelligence activities; the published laws and directives contain no specific information as to the character of such intelligence operations, but they do contain a provision that such intelligence operations should be coordinated with the agency or agencies established specifically to conduct external intelligence.[19] The FSB is tasked with conducting counter-terrorism operations throughout the Commonwealth of Independent States (CIS) in cooperation with security services of these states; the deputy director of the FSB serves as the director of the CIS Counter-terrorism Center.[20] The director of the SVR insists that Russia follows the agreement with other CIS members, reached in Almaty in 1992, not to conduct intelligence operations against one another.[21] This may be true as far as the SVR is concerned—it is much more natural for the FSB, which has likely kept at least some of its vast network of informers throughout the former Soviet republics, to engage in intelligence collection there.

The ability of Russia's external intelligence to run high-value foreign spies has been demonstrated quite dramatically in the recent cases of penetration of the CIA and FBI. In contrast, little is known about the quality of the intelligence analysis by the GRU and SVR. The GRU provides no unclassified products. The SVR has made four of its reports publicly available; they uniformly deal with innocuous subjects, such as proliferation of WMD (1993), extension of the Non-Proliferation Treaty (1995), the ratification of the Chemical Weapons Convention (1996), and antipersonnel mines.[22] The subjects are uncontroversial, the position of the Russian government on all these issues well established at the time of the publication; the reports demonstrate good knowledge of Western open sources. In the mid-1990s, at least a couple of purported SVR reports were leaked to the press. This appears to have been done on orders of the SVR leadership, since the reports were obviously meant to convey Russia's concerns about NATO enlargement and Western activities in the former Soviet republics.[23] Both reports focus on advocacy of Russian positions and on negative consequences of Western actions for the prospects for Russia's democratic consolidation. This is hardly the stuff for analytical reports of an external intelligence service; one is justified in suspecting that these two documents were a case of post-Soviet "active measures."

According to credible Russian sources, the SVR failed to predict the outcome of the elections in Yugoslavia in 2000, which cost Slobodan Milosevic his job. Both of these agencies failed to predict the course of the phase of "major military operations" in Iraq. In the case of Iraq, the GRU supposedly predicted a rather prolonged conventional conflict. At the same time, statements and actions of the Russian government, as well as leaks to the press, suggest that the Russian intelligence correctly estimated the threat from the Taliban movement in Afghanistan. Putin's statement in the fall of 2002 that the center of gravity in the war against terror is Saudi Arabia and Pakistan, and not Iraq, also suggest sensible intelligence analysis, although spiced up with the Russian economic interest in keeping Saddam Hussein's regime afloat.[24] It is difficult to judge whether external intelligence agencies report to the political leadership as objectively as they can, or provide intelligence-to-please, or twist intelligence reports to serve their institutional interests, or all of the above. On one recent occasion, what appears to be an organized GRU leak blamed the entourage of Minister of Defense Sergei Ivanov for allegedly ignoring GRU warnings about the dangers stemming from the NATO enlargement.[25] Is it an expression of a genuine discontent of the GRU analysts? This is quite possible, since the anti-Western bias is very strong in the agencies. Such a leak, however, could also be another salvo in the conflict between the minister of defense and the Chief of General Staff Anatoly Kvashnin.

Counterintelligence is primarily the function of the FSB. The law is quite vague: it allows the FSB to conduct counterintelligence not only against foreign intelligence services, terrorists, and those attempting a violent change of the Russian political system but also against "other types of activity" directed against the security of the Russian Federation.[26] The Third Directorate of FSB, as in the Soviet days, is in charge of counterintelligence in the military; apparently, the military still cannot be trusted to ensure its loyalty on its own.[27] The two external intelligence services, SVR and GRU, are allowed to engage in counterintelligence among their own ranks.[28]

The FSB apparently also has been charged with a mission most unconventional for a security agency in a democratic society—running the computerized system for processing and reporting election results. The State Automated System "Vybory" (Elections) was established by Boris Yeltsin in 1995, apparently in preparation for the Duma and presidential elections to be held in December 1995 and June 1996 respectively. Although on paper the Vybory system is subordinated to the Central Electoral Commission, it is common knowledge that Vybory was initially run by the Federal Agency of Government Communications and Information (FAPSI), an agency responsible for signals intelligence and secure communications; when the Duma decided to discuss the functioning of the system during the 1999 elections, it invited the director of FAPSI to testify.[29] Subsequent discussions of the system again involved the FAPSI experts.[30] The FAPSI was disbanded in March 2003, and its assets were distributed among the SVR, GRU, FSB, and FSO. It is assumed that now the FSB operates the system via an information technology center under the Central Electoral Commission. A lengthy law provides specifics for the operations of the Vybory, but fears that it can be and has been abused by the authorities persist.[31]

PARLIAMENTARY OVERSIGHT

Parliamentary oversight of the services in Russia can be fairly described as nonexistent. The two-chamber parliament—the Federal Assembly—has been progressively weakened in general since 1993, both under Yeltsin and especially under Putin. The upper chamber, the Federation Council, consists of representatives of regional bureaucracies that have become completely dependent on Putin. It has a Committee on Defense and Security, whose activity is very vaguely documented. The documentation that is available suggests that the committee deals primarily with the issues of salaries and benefits for the personnel of the military, uniformed police, and intelligence and security services.[32] When members of the Federation Council address issues of terrorism and intelligence services, the dominant themes are condemnation of terrorism in general and specifically in Chechnya; exhortations of the West to drop the subject of human rights violations in Chechnya and to extradite Chechen activists, who find refuge in the West, to Russia; and the need to strengthen the intelligence services. On those rare occasions when members of the Federation Council address specifics of intelligence operations, they seem to be less than interested in the issues of democratic civilian control. For instance, the representative of the Ingushetia in the Federation Council, Issa Kostoev (a former well-known police investigator), who is a member of the Federation Council's Committee on Law and Judiciary, warned about uncontrolled activities of Islamic religious organizations and proposed that the Soviet-era department for oversight of religious organizations be restored in the FSB and that special expert councils evaluate whether pronouncements by clergy in mass media contribute to the rise of Islamic extremism.[33]

The activities of the Committee on Security of the lower chamber (State Duma) of parliament are much better documented. The membership of that committee is quite interesting. Out of the twenty-nine members of the Duma Committee on Security, eight are former KGB/FSB officers, another eight are former MVD officers, four are former military officers, one is a Soviet-era prosecutor, and only eight do not have such previous affiliations.[34] Vladimir Vasil'ev, its chairman until recently, was the first deputy minister of internal affairs and an MVD general. The practice of selecting "experts" to the membership of parliamentary committees whose duties include oversight of the military and intelligence and security agencies goes back to the last days of the Soviet Union and to the first experiment with parliamentary democracy—the Supreme Soviet elected in 1989. That the Supreme Soviet had a Committee on Defense and State Security, whose members were also primarily selected on the basis of their "competence," implied that Ivan Public obviously could not be trusted to exercise oversight over his own security; "experts" were required for this task. The result was that out of forty-three members, nineteen were employed by the defense industry, six were military officers, and three were KGB officers. The rest were Communist Party officials and reformist intellectuals.[35] Thus the trend toward "competence" in parliamentary oversight of national security has become more pronounced over the last fifteen years, helped, no doubt, by the fact that liberal political forces now have only minuscule representation in the Duma. Some informed observers argue that the majority of the laws produced by the Security Committee are in reality ghostwritten by the staff of the Security Council of the Russian Federation, an advisory body working directly for the president of Russia.[36]

The Duma's activities in the area of intelligence primarily focus on writing, adopting, and amending new legislation. Indeed, the Russian Federation has laws on fighting terrorism,[37] on the FSB,[38] on criminal investigation,[39] on state secrets,[40] on national security,[41] and on external intelligence.[42] The problem is that both chambers of parliament have been left by the 1993 Constitution with no right to conduct investigations of any kind, let alone investigations of the agencies. The Federation Council and the State Duma are given a very vague right to conduct "hearings" on subjects of interest.[43] They approve the budget of the agencies, which is published openly (subdivided into twelve categories).[44] The Accounting Chamber—a quasi-independent body modeled on the General Accountability Office, whose chairman is appointed by the parliament (which today is completely subservient to the president)—can audit expenditures in any program, including those in the agencies, but not their operations.

The Law on the FSB (adopted in 1995 and amended in 1999) speaks in very general terms about the rights of members of parliament to obtain information about the FSB and SVR "in accordance to law."[45] The Law on External Intelligence prohibits members of parliament from receiving information about Russia's foreign intelligence from any sources but the appropriate parliamentary committees, whose members and staffers all have to receive appropriate security clearances, a process in which the FSB plays a decisive role. A special group in the Accounting Chamber can request information from the SVR on its execution of the budget, but apparently on nothing else.[46] While the parliament is to keep away from the agencies, the FSB is not allowed to recruit members of parliament as secret informers.[47] The constitutional ban on parliamentary investigations is, however, enforced selectively: the State Duma had special commissions investigating the causes of the financial crash of 1998 and the operations of the Port of Novorossiisk.[48] These investigations, however, were conducted by the much more combative Duma of the Yeltsin era.

A review of the agenda of the meetings of the Security Committee of the State Duma from January to July 2004 suggests that no reports on operational activities of the agencies were heard. The committee writes new legislation; it does not oversee operations in any meaningful sense. The scope of responsibilities of the Security Committee is so overwhelmingly broad that it probably couldn't focus more on oversight even if it chose to: the Security Committee deals with the legislative issues related to fourteen agencies, and it lists thirty-nine functional areas as subject to its jurisdiction, even including traffic safety and firefighting.[49]

Some attempts have been made to allow the State Duma to conduct investigations. The draft law, approved by the Duma on July 10, 2003, in the first reading, is very modest; its main goal, according to Nikolai Gonchar, one of its drafters, is to at least punish the executive branch when it refuses the deputies' requests for information or when its officials refuse to show up for the Duma hearings.[50] It is interesting that several of the bill's sponsors are members of the Security Committee and former KGB and MVD officers. The government, however, immediately gave a negative evaluation of the bill as "unconstitutional," which was enough for the Duma to withdraw it.[51] The upper chamber of the parliament, the Federation Council, also registered its opposition to the bill and to the idea of parliamentary investigations itself.[52] As of the writing of this chapter, the bill is being "improved" by the Duma.[53] In the meantime, members of the Duma, including those serving on the Security Committee, find out from the mass media about such events as President Putin's July 11, 2004, decree reorganizing the FSB.[54]

The case of the attack by the Chechen terrorists in October 2002, when they seized more than 800 people in a Moscow theater who were watching the popular musical *Nord Ost*, demonstrated the rather timid reactions of the Russian parliamentarians to the issues of security agencies and terrorism. After a two-day siege, FSB commandos stormed the theater and killed all the terrorists. The commandos used an unknown gas to knock out the terrorists before shooting them; the gas, however, affected the hostages. As a result of a poorly organized evacuation and inadequate medical aid, 129 hostages died. It was the current chairman of the Duma Security Committee (then first deputy minister of internal affairs) Vladimir Vasil'ev, in charge of press relations for the emergency staff of the security forces, who first advocated a ban on direct broadcast from the area of the siege, then tried to deny that the assault was premeditated by saying that it had been an alleged escape attempt by several hostages that had forced the hand of the authorities, and then denied that any hostages died because of the use of the mysterious gas by the security forces.[55]

The Federal Assembly's response to the bloody outcome of the assault was to draft a law to muzzle the media's reporting of terrorist attacks, since some television reports during the siege allegedly endangered the rescue operation. The draft law was so sweeping that Putin vetoed the bill. He also met with representatives of the mass media and expressed his dissatisfaction with their coverage of the so-called *Nord Ost* affair.[56] A call for hearings came from the faction of liberal reformers, the Union of Right Forces (SPS), but was rejected by the Duma's pro-Putin majority. SPS conducted its own investigation. The investigative commission of SPS met for three days in October and November 2002 and interviewed eleven witnesses, mostly physicians. Only four witnesses allowed their names to be published, while others preferred anonymity. The conclusion of the commission was that the high death rate among hostages resulted from extremely poor coordination between the security forces that executed the assault and the medical and other rescue services.[57] Although Putin eventually briefly met with the commission's chairman, Boris Nemtsov, the president reportedly dismissed the investigation as nothing new.[58]

Acts of terror, however, do not necessarily result in reduction of civilian control. Indeed, when citizens believe that the government is not protecting them from terrorism, the Russian government finds it necessary, as a concession to the public opinion, to allow parliamentary investigations. In the spring and summer of 2004, Russia experienced an escalation of terrorist attacks. On April 6, 2004, the president of Ingushetia, General Murat Zyazikov barely survived an assassination attempt.[59] The Kremlin-sponsored president of Chechnya, Akhmad Kadyrov, was assassinated on May 9, when Russians celebrate victory in the Second World War. On June 22, the anniversary of the German attack against the Soviet Union in 1941, Chechen insurgents seized for several hours the city of Nazran', the capital of neighboring Ingushetia, and killed ninety people, mostly law enforcement officials and officers of special services, after which the insurgents escaped without losses; in the aftermath of this attack, Putin ordered a reshuffle of the security forces in the North Caucasus.[60] Apparently the reshuffle didn't help, because on August 24, suicide bombers simultaneously blew up two passenger aircraft, killing ninety people onboard. And on August 31, a suicide bomber struck at the entrance to an underground station in Moscow, killing fifty and injuring more than fifty others.

Finally, on September 1, 2004, a group of terrorists (mostly Chechens) seized a school and more than a thousand hostages, mostly children, in the town of Beslan, North Ossetia. A chaotic storming of the school left hundreds of children dead and both the public and the political elite frightened. Unlike the *Nord Ost* affair, however, the string of terrorist acts culminating with the Beslan tragedy resulted in a revival of interest in the oversight of the agencies on the part of the Russian parliament. The Federation Council and the Duma formed a joint commission to investigate the Beslan massacre. It appears that the Putin administration authorized (or even suggested) this step in order to deflect the public outrage over the government's failure to stop terrorism. The mission of the parliamentary commission (as it became known in the Russian media) has included determination of the exact circumstances of the terrorist attack as well as the culpability of government officials. Although there is still no law on parliamentary investigations, the Federation Council approved the statute of the commission, which empowers it to obtain information from private individuals, as well as government officials and bodies, and to invite officials, as well as private individuals, to answer questions at the commission's hearings. Members of the commission are not allowed to release information about its work.[61]

Until the Beslan tragedy, as we have seen, the government had been pursuing the strategy of keeping the agencies practically free of parliamentary control. Why this reversal of course? The five months before Beslan saw a series of highly damaging acts of terrorism in Russia. With the slaughter of children in Beslan, Putin (whose confidence appeared badly shaken) apparently felt that he had to appoint a parliamentary commission to investigate such a major failure of security, perhaps following the American example in the aftermath of the 9/11 attacks.

The commission published a number of press releases and eleven information bulletins, which provided brief information on the commission activities, primarily names of officials who testified at the commission hearings, the main issues the commission has been investigating, and so on.[62] Initially the commission, according to several interviews of its chairman, Aleksandr Torshin, was highly critical not only of the security services but of the Russian government as a whole: "Complete irresponsibility is flourishing in Russia today. Nobody wants to take charge of any risky situation. Nobody wants to take decisive action; everybody tries to protect themselves with the opinions of their superiors, to place a phone call to the Kremlin, to get through to the president."[63] Torshin accused the "special services" (which really means the FSB) of contempt for the public, which demanded action and instead heard the usual refrain: "Leave the special services alone to do their job." As a result, relatives of the hostages and simply local bystanders "attempted to save the children."

With the passage of time, the government has recovered from the initial shock and seems to be in no hurry to have the report released or to encourage further parliamentary inquiries. Although Torshin promised to release the report by the end of 2005, this has not been done as of the time of this writing (July 2006). Instead, Torshin delivered a brief interim report orally in December 2005. According to his remarks, the commission interviewed many officials, including the head of FSB, but did not interview President Putin. The tone of Torshin's remarks was much less accusatory toward the government in Moscow and the security services. The preliminary conclusions aim most of the criticism at local government and police officials, not at the FSB.[64]

In December 2005 the Duma adopted a law regarding parliamentary inquiries that was drafted by Putin's staff. The language of the law is both vague and restrictive. Parliamentary inquiries are to be limited to cases of "especially flagrant or mass violations of human rights" and of natural or technological disasters, wording that could be construed to bar nearly any inquiry. The bill also bans parliament from inquiring about the activities of the federal president or about actions that are already subject to criminal investigation. The first restriction could shield the entire executive branch from investigation, while the second could allow the judiciary (which readily responds to executive branch pressure) to stop a parliamentary investigation simply by going through the motions of opening a criminal probe. Moreover, the law would require a majority vote of both houses to set up a commission of inquiry and to accept its report as an official document. Given the degree to which the executive branch dominates the upper house through presidential appointments, these provisions give the president an effective veto over the entire inquiry process.[65]

JUDICIAL OVERSIGHT

The laws on the external intelligence and on the FSB assign the oversight of the agencies to the state prosecutor's office. The institution of state prosecutors is part and parcel of the executive branch. The prosecutor general of the Russian Federation is appointed by the federation's president, with the consent of the majority of the Federation Council, a body that is completely in Mr. Putin's pocket. The prosecutor general appoints lower-ranking prosecutors.[66] The concept of prosecutorial oversight as practiced in Russia means that the prosecutor's office monitors government agencies' observance of laws; if prosecutors believe that the law has been violated, they either pass the case on to a court or inform an appropriate government body. One of the goals of prosecutorial oversight is protecting the rights of individuals against abuse by government agencies.[67] The office of the prosecutor general has a department to oversee the legality of operations of the security agencies. (It is not clear from the title of this department if it is involved at all in overseeing foreign intelligence.) There is also a special department in the North Caucasus whose mission is described as "investigation of crimes in the field of federal security and inter-ethnic relations."[68]

The problem with approaching the issues of prosecutorial oversight by simply analyzing the relevant laws is that in today's Russia there is a growing gulf between the laws on the book and the practices of the legal system. One of Russia's most prominent defense attorneys, Yury Schmidt, who took part in several cases involving the FSB, says: "Paradoxically, laws are becoming more liberal. . . . But the more liberal the laws, the more often they are violated, and the court actions become increasingly hard-line compared to the law. . . . The more liberal the law, the more frequently it is violated, because the mentality of the judges has failed to adapt to the new conditions."[69]

The institution of prosecutorial oversight has been inherited by the Russian legal system from the Soviet Union, where it acquired a steady reputation as a sick joke. Amid the horrors of Stalin's torture chambers and extermination camps, prosecutors would appear, from time to time, to inquire of prisoners, in front of their torturers and jailers, if they had any complaints. Soviet prosecutors were nothing more than enforcers of the will of the government, completely unconcerned about legality. Their complicity in the KGB's illegal actions against dissidents in the 1960s–1980s has been abundantly documented. The post-1991 Russian prosecutors, the majority of whom are the product of the Soviet prosecutorial system, have unfortunately inherited the mind-set of the Soviet prosecutors.[70] The system is highly politicized: Putin has successfully used the office of prosecutor general as an instrument for terrorizing Russian tycoons through selective and dubious application of law.

The U.S. Department of State report on human rights in Russia says: "The FSB operated with only limited oversight by the Procuracy and the courts."[71] There is little doubt that the prosecutorial oversight of the agencies is at this point nothing but a sham, as demonstrated by several recent court cases of individuals accused by the FSB of espionage and divulging state secrets. The highest-profile case has been that of Igor Sutyagin, a scholar at the prestigious Institute for the Study of the USA and Canada, who was accused of selling Russian military secrets to foreign intelligence agents, although he had never had access to any classified information. The FSB viewed his analysis of open-source Russian literature as espionage only because Sutyagin drew conclusions that allegedly concerned secret matters. The prosecution based its case on classified Decree 55 of the Ministry of Defense, which "determines categories of data that can be considered secret."[72] Neither Sutyagin nor his lawyers were allowed to read the secret decree. After four years in pretrial detention, Sutyagin was found guilty by a jury (the judge replaced the first jury with a second one without explanation), which asked whether he worked for a foreign entity (something he never denied); FSB experts told the jury such work was a cover for foreign intelligence. No one, however, asked the crucial question of whether his work contained any secret information. Sutyagin was sentenced to fifteen years in prison and is regarded by most human rights organizations as a political prisoner.[73] The logic behind such actions of the Russian legal system has nothing to do with legality. One of my Russian colleagues heard the following from an FSB officer, in reference to the Sutyagin case: if you copy a train schedule at a railroad station and then sell it to a foreigner, your place is in jail.

The FSB has played an important role in the war in Chechnya, where massive human rights violations by the Russian forces (as well as by the insurgents) have been well documented.[74] No actions by prosecutors regarding such allegations have been reported. Moreover, a local prosecutor, investigating numerous cases of disappearances in the Republic of Ingushetia (Chechnya's neighbor), recently disappeared himself immediately after returning from Moscow, where he went to complain about the complicity of the local FSB in the disappearances.[75] Ingushetia's president Murat Zyazikov is an FSB general (probably in active reserve); his election was widely presumed to have been engineered by the Kremlin in order to have its man in Ingushetia helping Moscow fight the insurgency in Chechnya. While legal restrictions on the activities of the FSB have been increasingly ignored, the law on the FSB makes it clear that the prosecutorial oversight should be limited: the identities of FSB informers and any information regarding "the organization, tactics, methods, and means of work of the FSB" do not come under prosecutorial oversight.[76] The Law on External Intelligence contains similar language.[77]

THE ROLE OF MASS MEDIA

The intelligence and security agencies have become very adept at neutralizing and exploiting the mass media in Russia. SVR and GRU dealings with the mass media are relatively rare and are usually limited to releases of historical information. The FSB, on the other hand, has had a very involved relationship with the mass media. Even during Yeltsin's era, characterized by the president's serious commitment to the freedom of the press, the FSB sought ways to influence the media. It began to "attach" its officers to media outlets with the ostensible mission of providing objective information on the FSB activities to the journalists. Very soon, these "attachés" began to plant stories in exchange for favors for journalists: a military flight to Chechnya, or a foreign passport for someone who had had, before becoming a journalist, access to military secrets. The Law on State Secrets, passed in 1993 and amended in 1997, has become an effective instrument in preventing journalists from investigative reporting on the agencies, as well as on other matters of national security. One journalist, a military officer and military newspaper reporter named Grigory Pas'ko, received a prison sentence for "espionage" in connection with his professional activities. Many others have reported harassment by the FSB, receiving "invitations" for "chats" at the Lefortovo Prison, where the FSB investigators rather suggestively have their offices. The issue invariably is an alleged violation of the Law on State Secrets; the Sutyagin case has demonstrated how flexibly it can be interpreted by the FSB, prosecutors, and judges.

The FSB has been very successful in planting a continuous stream of stories in the Russian media, as documented by the Russian *Index on Censorship*.[78] These "active measures" have several goals. One is to improve the reputation of the FSB and SVR by whitewashing their past. Here the favorite subject is the figure of Yuri Andropov, former KGB chairman (1967–1982) and general secretary (1982–1984). Retired KGB officers are filling the media with their memoirs, praising Andropov and justifying the role of this truly sinister political figure in the wide-scale repression within the Soviet Union from the 1960s through the 1980s. While the KGB/FSB archives are now hermetically sealed to the public (with the exception of files of those killed and imprisoned under Stalin), the FSB allows access to favored journalists and historians, enabling them to spread the Andropov myth in the mass media, especially via the increasingly popular Internet.[79]

Another goal of the FSB is to present an uncritical view of its operations today. A very good example of this was an avalanche of "exclusive" interviews by the veterans and active officers of the FSB in the aftermath of the *Nord Ost* assault against the Chechen terrorists; a chorus of expert voices sought to convince the public that despite the loss of 129 lives, the FSB was beyond reproach in that episode. Presenting the war in Chechnya as simply a fight against terrorism is another important goal of the FSB media campaign: terrorist acts by (or attributed to) the Chechen insurgents are played up, while the suffering of the Chechen civilians at the hands of the Russian military and security forces is played down.

The majority of Russians get their news from television; since the government tightly controls the major channels seen throughout the country, critical information about the agencies cannot be broadcast. The print and Internet media are relatively free, but their reach is limited; newspapers are too expensive for many impoverished Russians, and Internet access is limited to 8 to 10 million people, only 20,000 of them having broadband access.[80] Still, many newspapers are available online now, together with other sources of information, as can be seen from the notes to this chapter, which was largely researched on the basis of online sources. Although newspapers and the Internet can raise criticisms of the intelligence agencies, they can rarely do investigative journalism on this subject, because of the lack of access to relevant documents and the severe punishment meted out to officers who may want to provide information to reporters.

Objective press coverage has not been provided in cases of great public significance, such as the trials of alleged terrorists who blew up two apartment buildings in Moscow and one in Volgodonsk in September 1999, killing more than three hundred people. These horrific explosions were immediately attributed by the Russian government to "the Chechen terrorists" and were a key factor in public support for the second war in Chechnya in 1999 and for Russia's commander in chief in the war against terror, Prime Minister and soon-to-be president Vladimir Putin. Only two minor figures in the plot were tried behind closed doors and found guilty. Very little information has been released to the press, which was, for its part, not inclined to ask any questions. And questions should have been asked: neither defendant was a Chechen or from Chechnya, both were from the Karachai-Cherkessian Republic, and the act of terror was allegedly ordered and paid for by a shadowy Arab fighter named Khattab, based in Chechnya and killed in fighting later during the war.[81] Khattab was an Islamic fundamentalist, and his connections and interests could lead far away from Chechnya. One may suspect that since it is in the interest of the Putin government to equate terrorism with the Chechen insurgency, the foreign link of Khattab remained unexplored—or at least not publicly discussed.

SUMMARY AND CONCLUSIONS

It is apparent that democratic civilian control over the intelligence agencies does not exist in Russia. No single cause can completely explain this state of affairs. The main factor is the Russian postcommunist political system, in which the executive branch dominates the legislature and judiciary, and the hypertrophied institution of the presidency dominates all three branches of government. Under such an institutional arrangement, the intelligence agencies are likely to be an instrument of the president's personal power. This predominance of presidential powers and the executive branch is due to the early failure to establish a system of checks and balances, and it precedes the emergence of the terrorist threat. Some argue that the current system, lacking checks and balances, is in response to terrorism; however, Russia suffered the first serious terrorist attacks in 1995, yet the reduction of parliamentary influence began in 1993. That year, long before there was any serious concern about terrorism, Boris Yeltsin stripped the parliament of its oversight powers.

Thus terrorism, from which Russia has suffered since 1995 and particularly since 2002, is only partially responsible for this state of affairs. The restrictive Law on State Secrets was adopted in 1993 and amended in 1997.[82] The law on the FSB was adopted in mid-1995 and therefore must have been in preparation long before the first major terrorist act by the Chechen insurgents, which took place on June 14, 1995, in the town of Budennovsk. The Law on External Intelligence was adopted in December 1995. How much was terrorism on the mind of Russian leaders at that time? It appears that even as late as 1997, terrorism was not a source of very great concern to the Russian leaders: the first National Security Concept of the Russian Federation, adopted in December 1997, mentions "international terrorism" only briefly.

While it is the relative weakness of the legislative and judicial branches of government that is primarily responsible for the lack of democratic civilian control, the situation in Russia has been affected by unfavorable security factors. The same 1997 National Security Concept that barely mentioned terrorism stressed the threat of ethnic separatism to the integrity of the Russian Federation, obviously in reference to the Chechen insurgency, which by the end of 1996 led to Chechnya's virtual independence from Moscow.[83]

Indeed, Russia's war against terror is a war against the Chechen separatists, who use terror as an asymmetric weapon against the infinitely more powerful Russia. In societies at war, the executive branch of government is often stronger than the legislative and judiciary, and democratic civilian control over the agencies is often weakened. The tighter control over the mass media's reporting on security matters may be partially related to this war: one of the key lessons of the war in Chechnya in 1994–1996 was, from the Kremlin's standpoint, that the Russian leaders lost the war in their country's media because journalists could report relatively freely from Chechnya. But the media's increasing inability to report on matters of security is only a part of the general reintroduction of censorship under Putin, who knows quite well that he was created as a political figure by the mass media, especially television, and is determined not to be undone by the same instrument.

Still, the events of 2004 suggest that terrorism by itself does not always have to weaken civilian control in Russia. In fact, sometimes it may have an opposite effect. As described earlier, the series of horrific terrorist acts in 2004 resulted in the creation of the parliamentary commission investigating, among other things, the work of the intelligence agencies. Recent opinion surveys suggest that the Russian public is unwilling to sacrifice basic liberties and democratic institutions for the sake of fighting terrorism.[84]

A cultural factor is also responsible for the weakness of democratic civilian control over the agencies. This factor combines the predisposition of the public to have a positive view of these agencies and their personnel, with an active corporate promotion campaign by KGB veterans and active-duty KGB alumni, who have a vested interest in weak public supervision of their activities. Even in the early 1990s, after years of media attacks against the KGB and revelations of horrible crimes committed by that agency in the recent past, many people viewed the KGB officers as highly intelligent and professional.[85] In March 2002, only 33.7 percent of the public trusted the upper chamber of the parliament, the Federation Council, while 52.5 percent trusted the FSB.[86] In October 2002, the State Duma enjoyed the trust of only 25.2 percent of the public, while the FSB, according to the same survey, was trusted by 40.9 percent.[87] There has never been a wide-ranging public support for lustration of the officers of the former KGB, or something like the Truth and Reconciliation Commission in South Africa. There is no better demonstration of this public attitude than the overwhelming success of Vladimir Putin, a former Soviet KGB officer who proudly speaks about his past affiliation. One of Putin's first acts as prime minister was to dedicate a memorial plaque on the FSB headquarters to honor Andropov. This was not only a gesture toward the KGB/FSB/SVR officers—it was also recognition of Andropov's popularity among a large part of the public.

One of the most important political phenomena of the last several years has been an influx of intelligence officers, or *siloviki*,[88] all of them veterans of the old KGB, into other areas of the executive branch. The process had begun before Putin's ascent to power; in fact, he is the most visible beneficiary of the personnel policy pursued by Yeltsin's regime in its last two years. By early 1999, the post of Russia's prime minister was occupied by Yevgeniy Primakov, who had served as the director of SVR from 1991 to 1996 and has been rumored to have a long-standing relationship with the KGB foreign intelligence. Former KGB officer Nikolai Bordyuzha was the head of the Presidential Administration, a position equal to that of chief of staff to U.S. presidents. Former KGB officers also served as the chief of staff for the cabinet of ministers, as the deputy secretary of the Security Council, as the chief executive of the government-owned arms export company, as the chief military prosecutor, as the chief of personnel of the Presidential Administration (a very important job), as the first deputy chief of the president's press service, and as deputy director of the official ITAR-TASS news agency.[89]

Since Putin's election as president in the year 2000, the induction of a large number of the *siloviki* into senior levels of the civilian bureaucracy has accelerated. According to a recent study, the *siloviki* were 34.9 percent of newly appointed deputy ministers. The largest share of these officers—45.2 percent—came from the FSB and SVR. In most cases, these officers were not recruited by the respective ministries but appointed by the president. Such officers stay in "active reserve," keeping their rank and salary in their intelligence or military agency; they carry out their missions in their current civilian bureaucracy, get their second salary there—and report on their activities to their "alma mater."[90] As a Russian scholar notes, these "trusted agents of the president are supposed to become 'the eye of the tsar' in the economy and thus strengthen the Kremlin's control function."[91] Today the minister of defense and chief of personnel of the armed forces have come from the KGB/SVR and KGB/FSB, respectively. The former director of SVR, a professional intelligence officer and SVR general, is now the first deputy minister of foreign affairs. Out of three deputy secretaries of the Security Council, two are KGB/SVR and KGB/FSB veterans.

This massive infusion has resulted in increased hostility in the high echelons of government to the ideas of checks and balances and of transparency in government operations. The intelligence agencies' veterans and active-duty officers are motivated by both their institutional culture and their self-interest. Ol'ga Kryshtanovskaya, the head of the Center for the Study of Elites at the Institute of Sociology of the Russian Academy of Sciences, provides a plausible explanation of the views of the *siloviki:* "This whole social group was summoned to reestablish order. Order, as *they* understand it. Their understanding is simple and harsh: order means a strong state, and a strong state means one not separated into branches, a state where all power is concentrated."[92]

The mind-set of the KGB/FSB/SVR officers is by itself resistant to oversight, especially because they tend to suffer, in the words of General Yuri Kobaladze, from an excessively good self-image: we are the salt of the earth, and only we know what the state is, what its interests are, and how to defend them. Because we are the special services, we are above reproach, we are not corrupt, we are exceptional.[93]

The natural predisposition of the *siloviki* to weaken or eliminate altogether the system of checks and balances, and thus make democratic civilian oversight of the agencies impossible, neatly dovetails with their desire to maximize their corporate interests. During the roaring 1990s, enormous economic gains were made by various close-knit groups (mafias) operating in secrecy and bypassing the weakened state. The vast social and economic changes of 1991–1999 largely did not benefit these officers. Unlike the bureaucrats involved in managing the economy, these officers could not benefit from the privatization. They were even worse off than many military officers who benefited from selling off military property. According to a former SVR general, some of the FSB/SVR officers who had watched how the state was robbed felt slighted: "How come they sliced the cake without us? Now we will move into the government and also grab our slice."[94]

Under Putin, these people have been given a chance to catch up. The KGB/FSB/SVR officers are positioned to do so, because of their strong corporate spirit[95] and ability to operate in secrecy, conditions required for success in the murky world of the Russian government and economy. Another condition for the redistribution of property in favor of the intelligence agencies' elite is weak oversight by the parliament, judiciary, and media. The need to fight terrorism provides a good excuse for avoiding oversight.

This convenient myth of the superiority of intelligence and security officers will continue to be propagated as long as the Russian public is reluctant to look squarely at its nation's history, and the role played in that history by its intelligence services responsible only to the supreme leader. This moment apparently has not arrived yet. This ambiguous public attitude to the past and present of the political police is well exemplified by the fact that in Moscow there is a street named after the human rights activist Andrei Sakharov, as well as a street named after his tormentor in chief, Yuri Andropov. The dilemma of state power and the society's right to demand accountability from the state continues to be unresolved in postcommunist Russia.

NOTES

All translations from Russian in the text are mine.

1. The term "intelligence" most often refers to the agencies and missions of foreign intelligence, while "security" refers to domestic security and counterintelligence. In Russia, these missions have historically overlapped in the organizations conducting these missions, to the extent that it is sometimes difficult to discern a difference between the two. Inasmuch as this is the case, I attempt to make a distinction where I can within this text. When I cannot, or when I am referring to the whole enterprise of intelligence and security organizations, I use the term intelligence alone.

2. John J. Dziak, *Chekisty: A History of the KGB* (Lexington, MA: D. C. Heath, 1988), 1, 2.

3. Amy Knight, *Spies without Cloaks* (Princeton, NJ: Princeton University Press, 1996), 35.

4. *Glavnoe upravlenie spetsial'nykh program president (GUSP)*, http://www.agentura.ru/dossier/russia/gusp/.

5. Amy Knight, *Beria: Stalin's First Lieutenant* (Princeton, NJ: Princeton University Press, 1993), 196.

6. Natalya Gevorkyan, Natalya Timakova, and Andrei Kolesnikov, *Ot pervogo litsa: Razgovory s Vladimirom Putinym* (Moscow: Vagrius, 2000), 24.

7. See the book by two prosecutors who investigated the attempted coup: V. Stepankov and Ye. Lisov, *Kremlevskiy zagovor: Versiya sledstviya* (Perm': Ural-Press, 1993).

8. The successor to the Ministry of Security.

9. The FSO is supposed, among other things, to gather and process informa-

tion on socioeconomic and political problems, as well as on public opinion. *Prezident Rossiyskoy Federatsii. Ukaz ot 14 iyulya 2003 no. 774. Voprosy Sluzhby spetsial'noi svyazi i informatsii pri Federal'noi sluzhbe okhrany Rossiyskoy Federatsii,* http://www .agentura.ru/dossier/russia/fso/docs/polojeniespecvyaz.

10. Mark Kramer's study of oversight of Russian intelligence and security agencies also suggests other pertinent questions: the relationship between the needs of security and civil liberties, and between external and internal intelligence; the role of the judicial branch of government, as well as the executive and legislative branches, in oversight; partisan political activity by the intelligence and security agencies' personnel; and the proper balance between secrecy and transparency in the oversight process. Mark Kramer, *Oversight of Russia's Intelligence and Security Agencies: The Need for and Prospects of Democratic Control,* PONARS Policy Memo 281, Center for Strategic and International Studies, Washington, DC, October 2002.

11. Konstitutsiya Rossiyskoy Federatsii, art. 80, par. 2, http://www.kremlin .ru/articles/ConstChapter4.shtml.

12. *Sistema vlasti v Rossiyskoy Federatsii,* http://kremlin.ru/articles/instituto1 .shtml.

13. *Prezidentskiy blok,* http://kremlin.ru/print/instituto3.shtml.

14. Igor Korotchenko, "Lyuboe gosudarstvo yavlyaetsya predmetom interesa GRU," *Nezavisimoe voennoe obozrenie,* July 30, 1999.

15. Ibid.

16. "U nas rabotayut umnye, podgotovlennye lyudi," *Izvestiya,* July 15, 2003, http://www.izvestia.ru/politic/article36143.

17. "My uzhe ne boimsya ogorchit' nachal'stvo," *Vek,* December 15, 2000.

18. Federal'nyy zakon, "O vneshnei razvedke," chap. 2, art. 11, http://svr.gov .ru/svr_today/doco2.htm.

19. Federal'nyy zakon, "Ob organakh Federal'noy sluzhby bezopasnosti Rossiyskoy Federatsii," chap. 1, art. 11, http://www.fsb.ru/under/fsb.html#01.

20. Andrei Soldatov, *Litsenziya dlia FSB,* http://www.agentura.ru/dossier/ russia/people/soldatov/colonka/sng.

21. "S kem poidem v razvedku?" *Rossiyskaya gazeta,* December 20, 2002.

22. "Materialy i kommentarii SVR," http://svr.gov.ru/material/material.htm.

23. "Perspektivy rasshireniya NATO i interesy Rossii," *Krasnaya zvezda,* November 30, 1993; "Rossiya—SNG: Nuzhdayetsya li v korrektirovke pozitsiya Zapada?" *Rossiya i sovremennyy mir,* no. 2 (1995): 79–100.

24. "Press-konferentsiya Prezidenta V. V. Putina i Prezidenta Dzh. Busha posle rossiysko-amerkinaskikh peregovorov," November 22, 2002, http://kremlin .ru/appears/2002/11/22/2356_type63380_29579.shtml.

25. Igor' Yur'ev, "Razvedka preduprezhdaet: Minoborony ne reagiruet," *Nezavisimoe voennoe obozrenie,* January 31, 2003, http://nvo.ng.ru/notes/2003-01-31/1_razvedka.html.

26. Federal'nyy zakon, "Ob organakh Federal'noy sluzhby bezopasnosti Rossiyskoy Federatsii," chap. 2, art. 9.

27. *Polozhenie ob upravleniyak (otdelakh) Federal'noi sluzhby bezopasnosti Rossiyskoy Federatsii v Vooruzhennykh Silakh Rossiyskoy Federatsii, drugikh voiskakh, voinskikh formirovanyakh i organakh (organakh bezopasonosti v voiskakh)*, http://www.fsb .ru/under/pologeni.html.

28. Federal'nyy zakon, "Ob operativno-rozysknoi deyatel'nosti," chap. 3, art. 13, http://www.hro.org/docs/rlex/laword.htm.

29. "Gosduma obsudit algoritmy vzloma sistemy GAS," Vybory, http://lenta .ru/internet/1999/12/02/duma-hack/.

30. "Veshnyakov ne ikslyuchaet, chto v budushchem mozhno budet golosovat' cherez internet," http://www.federalpost.ru/russia/print_1526.html.

31. Federal'nyy zakon, "O Gosudarstvennoi avtomatizirovannoi sisteme Rossiyskoy Federatsii," Vybory, http://www.gov-vyatka.ru; "Kakimi budut vybory d Dumu?" http://www.iamik.ru/?op=full&what=content&ident=8868; "Tsentrizbirkom ne kontroliruyet GAS," Vybory, http://www.c-r-t.ru/fluger/24.07 .2003/04.shtml; "I u vas v kvartire GAS," http://dossie.ru/article.php?id=276; "Re: Podtasovki v. GAS," http://daily.webforum.ru.

32. From the committee's website at http://www.council.gov.ru/committee/ item1630091.html.

33. Ibid.

34. Compiled from the website of the State Duma of the Russian Federation Committee on Security, http://www.duma.gov.ru/csecure/deputat/cher.htm.

35. Mikhail Tsypkin, "The Committee for Defense and State Security of the USSR Supreme Soviet," *Report on the USSR* 2, no. 19 (1990): 8–11.

36. Andrei Soldatov, "Bezopasnyy komitet," http://www.agentura.ru/dossier/ russia/people/soldatov/colonka/komitee.

37. *Federal'nyy zakon Rossiyskoy Federatsii o bor'be s terrorizmom*, http://www.fsb .ru/under/terror.html.

38. Federal'nyy zakon, "Ob Organakh Federal'noy sluzhby bezopasnosti v Rossiyskoy Federatsii."

39. Federal'nyy zakon, "Ob operativno-rozysknoi deyatel'nosti."

40. "Zakon o gosudarstevnnoi taine," http://www.fsb.ru/under/secret.html.

41. *Zakon RF on 5 marta 1992 g. N 2446-I "O bezopasnosti,"* http://svr.gov.ru/svr _today/doc04.htm.

42. Federal'nyy zakon, "O vneshnei razvedke."

43. Konstitutsiya Rossiyskoy Federatsii, art. 101.

44. Prilozhenie 32 k federal'nomu zakonu, "O federal'nom byudzhete na 2004 god."

45. Federal'nyy zakon, "Ob organakh Federal'noy sluzhby bezopasnosti Rossiyskoy Federatsii," art. 23.

46. Federal'nyy zakon, "O vneshnei razvedke," art. 24.

47. Federal'nyy zakon, "Ob organakh Federal'noy sluzhby bezopasnosti Rossiyskoy Federatsii," art. 19.

48. "Sledstvie povedut deputaty," *Literaturnaya gazeta*, no. 44 (2003), http://www.lgz.ru/archives/html_arch/lg442003/Polosy/art2_1.htm.

49. "Vremennoe polozhenie o Komitete Gosduarstvennoi Dumy Federal'nogo Sobraniya Rossiyskoy Federatsii po bezopasnosti," http://www.duma.gov.ru/csecure/komitet/01-2.html.

50. "Sledstvie povedut deputaty." Also see Proekt federal'nogo zakona, "O parlamentskikh rassledovaniyakh Federal'nogo Sobraniya Rossiyskoy Federatsii," no. 214764-3.

51. "Ofitsial'nyy otzyv na proekt federal'nogo zakona #214764-3," http://www.government.gov.ru/data/structdoc.html?he_id=101&do_id=1309.

52. Komitet po kosntitutsionnomu zakonodatel'stvu, "Protiv proekta zakona o parlamentskikh rassledovaniyakh federa'nogo Sobraniya RF," http://www.council.gov.ru/inf_ps/chronicle/2002/09/item453.html.

53. RIA Novosti, July 12, 2004, communicated to the author by Aleksandr Golts.

54. Yekaterina Dobrynina and Tamara Shkel', "Obshchestvo i siloviki," http://www.duma.gov.ru/csecure/public/047.html.

55. Soldatov, "Bezopasnyy komitet."

56. Vladimir Putin, *Vstupitel'noe slovo na vstreche s predstabitelyami SMI i zhurnalistskikh organizatsiy*, November 25, 2002, http://president.kremlin.ru/appears/2002/11/25/2300_type63374type63376type63378_29584.shtml.

57. "Sobytiya v Nord Oste: Chto eto bylo? Spasenie zalozhnikov ili unichtozhenie terroristov?" http://www.demoscope.ru/weekly/2002/093/print.php.

58. Sergei Parkhomenko and Aleksandr Ryklin, "Popravki k teraktu," *Yezhenedel'nyy zhurnal*, November 27, 2002, http://ej.ru/046/life/02vlast/index.html.

59. *Kamikadze vzorval avtomobil's prezidentom Ingushetii*, http://www.newsru.com/russia/06apr2004/murat.html.

60. Aleksei Grishin, "V otvete za 22 iyunya," *Vremya novostei*, July 20, 2004.

61. "Parlamentskaya komissiya po rassledovaniyu prichin i obstoyatel'stv soversheniya terroristicheskogo akta v g. Beslane respubliki Severnaya Ossetiya—Alaniya 1–3 sentyabrya 2004 goda," http://www.council.gov.ru/inf_ps/chronicle/2004/09/item2303.html.

62. These are available at http://www.council.gov.ru/inf_ps/chronicle/2004/09/item2312.html.

63. Aleksandra Samarina, "Aleksandr Torshin: 'Beslan byl neizbezhen,'" *Nezavisimaya gazeta*, December 24, 2004, http://www.ng.ru/ideas/2004-12-24/1_troshin.html.

64. "Dyestviya terroristov ne ustupayut zvesrstvam natsistov," *Sovet Federatsii*, December 29, 2005, http://www.council.gov.ru/inf_ps/chronicle/2005/12/item4033.html.

65. "Federal'nyy zakon Rossiyskoy Federatsii of 27 dekabrya 2005 g. N 196-FZ

O parlamentskom rassledovanii Federal'nogo sobraniya Rossiyskoy Federatsii," *Rossiyskaya gazeta*, December 29, 2005, http://www.rg.ru/printable/2005/12/29/rassledovanie-dok.html.

66. *General'naya prokuratura Rossiyskoy Federatsii*, http://genproc.gov.ru/ru/about/basis/.

67. Federal'nyy zakon, "O prokurature Rossiyskoy Federatsii," chap. 3, http://genproc.gov.ru/ru/about/basis/index.shtml?show_item=7.

68. *General'naya prokuratura Rossiyskoy Federatsii*, http://genproc.gov.ru/ru/gen_prokurarura/.

69. "Sudebnaya reforma: uspekhi i neudachi," http://www.polit.ru/lectures/2004/06/04/sudreforma.html.

70. Mark Kramer, "Out of Communism: Reforming the Russian Legal System," *Current History* (October 2003): 331.

71. *Russia: Country Reports on Human Rights Practices—2003*, Bureau of Democracy, Human Rights, and Labor, U.S. Department of State, February 25, 2004, http://www.state.gov/g/drl/rls/hrrpt/2003/27861.htm.

72. "All Charges Are Based on a Secret Decree," http://case52.org/news/index.shtm. The Russian Supreme Court in its decision of September 12, 2001, admitted that some of the provisions of this decree contradict the law, but the decree has not been invalidated or changed to accommodate the Court's opinion.

73. See "Joint Statement on the Case of Igor Sutiagin," by Amnesty International, Human Rights Watch, the International Helsinki Federation for Human Rights, the Moscow Helsinki Group, and the Public Committee for the Protection of Scientists, June 2004, http://www.hrw.org/backgrounder/eca/russia/2004/igor_statement.htm.

74. *Amnesty International Report 2004: Russia Federation*, http://web.amnesty.org/report2004/rus-summary-eng; "The Situation in Chechnya and Ingushetia Deteriorates: New Evidence of Enforced Disappearances, Rape, Torture, and Extrajudicial Executions," joint statement by Amnesty International, Human Rights Watch, the Medical Foundation for the Care of Victims of Torture, and Memorial, http://hrw.org/english/docs/2004/04/07/russia8408.htm.

75. Peter Baker, "Young Men Vanishing in Russian Region: Prosecutor Probing Role of Secret Police Is Among the Missing," *Washington Post*, June 6, 2004.

76. Federal'nyy zakon, "Ob organakh Federal'noy sluzhby bezopasnosti Rossiyskoy Federatsii," art. 24.

77. Federal'nyy zakon, "O vneshnei razvedke," art. 25.

78. Vladimir Voronov, "Lubyanskiy pul," *Indeks: Dosye na tsenzuru*, no. 20 (2004), http://www.index.org.ru/journal/20/voronov20.html.

79. See, for instance, Andrei Sidorenko, "Zhizn', otdannaya Otechestvu," *Spetsnaz Rossii*, nos. 6 and 7 (2004). A list of media publications favorable to the Cheka/NKVD/KGB can be found at the FSB website, http://www.fsb.ru/history/autors3.html. FSB director Nikolai Patrushev has recently contributed two newspaper and magazine articles to the Andropov cult: Nikolai Patrushev, "Chelovek

bol'shogo kalibra," *Politika*, no. 67 (2004), http://www.fsb.ru/smi/liders/patrush8
.html; and Patrushev, "Taina Andropova," *Rossiyskaya gazeta*, June 15, 2004, http:
//www.fsb.ru/smi/liders/patrush9.html. For new "documentary" evidence whitewashing Andropov, see Boris Prozorov, "Yuri Andropov: Bez grifa 'Sekretno,'"
Fel'dpochta, March 8, 2004, http://www.feldpost.ru/N20/prozorov.shtml.

80. "Markets by Country: Russia," *New Media Review*, http://www.etcnew
media.com/review/default.asp?SectionID=11&CountryID=83.

81. "Kaznit' vas nado!" *Izvestiya*, January 12, 2004, http://izvestia.ru/conflict/
article42932.

82. "Zakon o gosudarstvennoi taine," http://www.fsb.ru/under/secret.html.

83. "Kontseptsiya natsional'noy bezopasnosti Rossiyskoy Federatsii," *Krasnaya zvezda*, December 27, 1997.

84. Vladimir Petukhov, "Ugroza terrora i perspektivy demokratii v Rossii,"
Izvestiya, October 5, 2004.

85. Stephen White and Ol'ga Kryshtanovskaya, "Public Attitudes to the KGB:
A Research Note," *Europe-Asia Studies* 45, no. 1 (1993): 174.

86. Survey by ROMIR, http://www.romir.ru/socpolit/socio/2002/04_2002/
russia-life-march.htm.

87. Survey by ROMIR, http://www.romir.ru/socpolit/socio/2002/11_2002/
russia-life-october.htm.

88. The Russians use the word *siloviki*—those representing the agencies that
use force—to describe personnel working for intelligence services and the military. Application of the term by no means implies successful integration of the
military and intelligence agencies. The military has never had an easy relationship
with the domestic security service that spies on it. In recent years, the fights between FSB and the SIGINT agency FAPSI (before the latter was swallowed by
FSB) often spilled out into the press. See, for example, "Russia: FSB, Information
Agency Chiefs Deny 'Confrontation,'" *Moscow ITAR-TASS*, in English, April 7,
1997, FBIS-SOV-97-097.

89. A. G., "Nedra," *Itogi*, February 16, 1999.

90. Ol'ga Kryshtanovskaya, "Rezhim Putina: liberal'naya militokratiya?" *Pro
et Contra* 7, no. 4 (Fall 2002): 167.

91. Ibid., 168.

92. "Siloviki u vlasti," *Radio Ekho Moskvy*, January 16, 2005, http://www.echo
.msk.ru/guests/7699/.

93. Tamara Zamyatina, "Yuri Kobaladze, 'Ropot budet,'" *Vremya novostei*, November 21, 2001. For a discussion of this mind-set among the pre-1917 and post-
1971 Russian and Soviet secret policemen, see Laurent Murawiec and Clifford C.
Gaddy, "The Higher Police," *National Interest* (Spring 2002): 29-36.

94. Zamyatina, "Yuri Kobaladze, 'Ropot budet.'"

95. Ibid.

TWELVE

ETHICAL AND MORAL ISSUES IN INTELLIGENCE REFORM

The Philippines

Douglas J. Macdonald

This nation is at a crossroad: quite simply, it must reform or perish.
—FILIPINO PRESIDENT GLORIA MACAPAGAL-ARROYO

Reform of security services in emerging democracies is one of the most important tasks facing these governments in the process of democratization.[1] This chapter will examine the tortuous road to intelligence and military reform since the overthrow of the Marcos dictatorship in the Philippines in 1986. The Marcos period (1965–1986) was marked by an unprecedented politicization and corruption of the civilian and military security forces of the Philippines, the primary producers of intelligence. This legacy has been and will remain one of the greatest barriers to meaningful reform of democratic institutions and intelligence services. Two fundamental approaches to reform are contrasted: the "top-down," widespread, wholesale reforms aimed at the complete transformation of the security forces simultaneously attempted by the Corazon Aquino government (1986–1992), and the incremental "bottom-up" reforms attempted by its successor, the government of President Fidel Ramos (1992–1998). In addition, the Ramos administration proceeded with a series of creative diplomatic and socioeconomic initiatives that were crucial to its relative success. As additional important elements in this success, Ramos served in a period of relative prosperity in the region of Southeast Asia and, as a former military man, was not the object of suspicion from that quarter, as was President Aquino. Although both the top-down and bottom-up approaches have their strengths and weaknesses, and implementation of intelligence reform as one aspect of broader democratic reforms has been imperfect, the incremental approach utilized by Ramos is the superior strategy in pressing for intelligence reform in the Philippines.

SOME INHERENT CULTURAL OBSTACLES TO REFORM

The Philippines, an archipelago of some 7,107 mountainous islands spread over 500,000 square miles, has long been a dissonant nation with strong centrifugal political and social dynamics, especially those between Manila and the rest of country. There is a strong sense of localism, and the various provinces have a tradition of notable local families who dominate the economics, politics, and social activities in their areas.[2] Since World War II, and especially after independence in 1946, many of the notable families have kept private armies to prevent anyone from challenging the socioeconomic status quo and to protect their power prerogatives. They have always been a source of challenge to the power of the state—under the Spanish, under the Americans, and since independence. Indeed, a recent book about Filipino political culture referred to it without too much overstatement as "an anarchy of families."[3] This localism has fortified a strongly personality-driven, patron-client form of political culture and institutional behavior where loyalty to the family, faction, or friend often takes precedence over loyalty to the state or to abstract principles such as merit or legality.[4] For example, in the 1970s, the U.S. government estimated that about four hundred families essentially controlled the economy and politics of the country.[5] Data today are hard to pinpoint; however, the situation is relatively unchanged.

According to this view, the family—which is most often used in the sense of clan, as Filipinos have unusually broad inclusion standards for familial ties—is a hindrance to the creation of a strong national identity. Thus for geographical, cultural, and historical reasons a political culture evolved with institutions not unlike those of many other Third World countries with economically and politically powerful elite families: a "strong society and weak state."[6] This has led to a history of localist rebellions at the popular and elite levels of society against the rule from Manila, from a variety of rationales.[7] With this historical legacy, it may not be surprising that Filipino society is so prone to violence, even by Third World standards. Yet the power and influence of the notable families are not limited to their provincial strongholds. The families have long dominated the government in Manila, and they have at times been shameless in using public institutions for private gain for themselves, their families, and their allies.

This hierarchical, oligarchic system, with its shifting alliances and violence-prone politics, creates a very weak political party system, with personality-driven political dynasties dominating the Congress and other political institutions, including the uniformed intelligence services.[8] Changing allegiances bears no stigma, since individually providing particular services to constituents is the most important activity for staying in office. According to one study of electoral incentives, Filipino politicians face "some of the most particularistic incentives in any democracy."[9] Despite repeated attempts at decentralization of the old hierarchical system and anticorruption measures under the Aquino, Ramos, and current Arroyo administrations, legislators have successfully reversed or circumvented those reforms in order to maintain their positions as brokers for public goods and "pork barrel" for their constituents.[10]

In summary, the Philippines has a political culture and political system that reward localism, cronyism, corruption, and short-term political goals at the expense of the long-term, or even medium-term, planning necessary for successful policies. The combined culture and political system is inherently unstable at both the elite and mass levels because it arrays incentives in such a way as to entrench corrupt interests along regional, personalistic, and factional lines that resist any real change. A deference to authority figures, the continued importance of patron-client relationships, and the primacy of kinship continue to be obstacles to the development of democracy.[11] This general approach to public life has debilitating effects on attempts to reform the military and civilian intelligence agencies, as loyalties often remain attached to leaders or peers in factions rather than to the nation or appeals to abstract principles.

The Security "Problematique"

Like most developing countries, economic and international organizational issues dominate Filipino foreign policy. Historically, the country's national security had been guaranteed by the "special relationship" with the United States. With the sole exception of the Japanese in the 1940s, external threats to Filipino security on a state-to-state level have largely been nonexistent. The "special relationship" ended in the early 1990s with the withdrawal of U.S. naval and air forces. The primary security threat to the Philippines, and therefore the main focus of its military and intelligence efforts, has been and remains indigenous insurgencies and terrorist infiltration and subversion, not an invasion from without.

There are currently four main sources of sustained armed threats to the government and society: the Moro Islamic Liberation Front (MILF), a Muslim separatist group; the New People's Army (NPA), a Maoist-inspired communist group; the Abu Sayyaf Group, an al Qaeda–backed jihadist Muslim separatist group; and a variety of smaller violent gangs, often partially made up of former soldiers or police officers, generally called kidnap-for-profit gangs (KFPs).[12] The first three groups are ideologically motivated, arguably articulating justifiable grievances in Filipino society, albeit in a violent, terrorist fashion, and have in the past or are currently receiving aid from external sources; the KFPs are not. Yet some KFPs, such as the Pentagon Gang (reportedly made up of former MILF fighters), make tactical alliances with the ideological groups, adding to the menace. As former president Fidel Ramos puts it, however, the Muslim separatists and the NPA are primarily "rebels, not criminals."[13]

This "rebels and criminals" dichotomy is an important distinction for current and future policies. If the rebel groups represent justifiable grievances, then a holistic approach that attends to those grievances must be part of the counterinsurgency effort, as in the programs of President Ramon Magsaysay in the 1950s and those advocated by Ramos and his colleagues today.[14] If one sees the rebels not as ideologically motivated and representing real social problems but as primarily driven by greed or maniacal fanaticism, then one might take a much harsher "law and order" line in dealing with them, seeing them as primarily a military and police problem. The latter is a position currently identified with former national police chief Senator Panfilo "Ping" Lacson.[15] Such arguments should be familiar to American security analysts, given that they dominated the discussion of strategies for counterinsurgency in Vietnam.[16] Indonesia and other Association of Southeast Asian Nations (ASEAN) members complain that the United States views terrorism as primarily a military problem, without taking into account the socioeconomic conditions that breed terrorists.[17] The basic causes of the respective insurgencies or criminal activity such as kidnapping can be usefully simplified into three categories: identity (the Islamist insurgency in the south), ideology (the communist insurgency in the north), and greed (the KFPs.)

By the end of the Marcos dictatorship, an unnamed "senior U.S. official" told an Asian journalist: "The Philippine army has become a Southeast Asian army in the mode of Thailand or Indonesia. It feels it knows better than the civilians how to run the country."[18] It was into this chaotic atmosphere that President Corazon Aquino, the widow of the murdered chief political rival of Marcos, entered as a relative political neophyte in her "People Power" revolution of 1986 as Marcos fled the country. An ambitious program of reform was spelled out in the 1987 Constitution, including sweeping reforms of the military and police intelligence agencies, but actual implementation would prove to be a difficult thing to accomplish.

The Marcos Legacy

It is impossible to discuss the Philippines without spending some time on Ferdinand Marcos. First elected president in 1965, he was reelected in 1969 with the voter fraud and violence that have characterized many Filipino elections. Like most Filipino presidential candidates, he ran as a reformer who would change the system, but by his second term he had created an atmosphere of corruption and general sleaziness that achieved a new low in modern governmental history. In 1972, forbidden by the constitution to run again in 1973, he declared martial law and officially instituted a dictatorship. He was overthrown in 1986, after massive and obvious fraud in an electoral contest with Corazon Cojuangco-Aquino, the widow of Marcos's primary political rival, Benigno "Ninoy" Aquino, who was murdered upon his return to the Philippines in 1983 on what was widely believed to be Marcos's orders. Marcos fled the Philippines in 1986 and settled in Hawaii, where he died in 1989. Mrs. Aquino was named president.

Governmental reforms since 1986, across administrations, have been largely aimed at undoing the politicization, corruption, and institutionalization of the one-party state that Marcos created under martial law. These reform attempts have often been aimed at the military, police, and intelligence services. Since Marcos was driven from power in 1986 by the relatively peaceful People Power Revolution, in what the Filipinos refer to as EDSA I,[19] the country has experienced consistent bouts of political instability.[20] Much of this political instability has been tied to the attempts to reform the security services, including the intelligence agencies that achieved unprecedented power within the government under Marcos.

The main legacy of the Marcos period was the corruption that permeated much of Filipino society, and nowhere more prominently than in the Armed Forces of the Philippines (AFP), the National Bureau of Investigation, and the Philippine Constabulary, or PC (the national police force at the time), which were generally the most important producers of intelligence for the Philippine government. (For a listing of current major intelligence agencies in the Philippines, see Table 12.1.) The AFP was placed under General Fabian Ver, Marcos's cousin, longtime crony, and the man most considered responsible for the murder of Ninoy Aquino. Relatives and provincial cronies were placed at all levels of government. General Ver and therefore the AFP were at the personal disposal of Marcos and were used as often to attack his political enemies as to attend to the internal or external security of the nation. The AFP's senior officers, including those from the intelligence agencies, were allowed to operate private businesses, extort money from various sources, and generally run roughshod over any political forces that stood in their way. The AFP had become thoroughly politicized and corrupted, and perhaps not surprisingly, the communist and Muslim insurgencies grew exponentially. This was a major catalyst in the creation of radicalized reform groups among younger officers that remain a threat to Filipino governmental stability. Near the end of the dictatorship, the military and intelligence organizations were badly polarized along generational lines, as they remain today.[21]

This problem was compounded by Marcos's decision to centralize the intelligence agencies under the tight control of General Ver. By the end of the regime, Ver had virtually total control over the police, military, and intelligence functions in the government.[22] Marcos had been suspicious of the intelligence agencies in particular from the beginning, and it was there that he concentrated much of his attention following the onset of martial law. When he became convinced, for example, that General Marcos Soliman—the head of the premier existing intelligence agency, the National Intelligence Coordinating Agency (NICA)—had informed Marcos's rival Ninoy Aquino of the plans for martial law, he dismissed Soliman and shortly thereafter dissolved the NICA altogether in order to create a super-agency he could control, the National Intelligence and Security Authority (NISA), with far more sweeping powers and General Ver in charge. General Soliman shortly thereafter was reported in the controlled press to have died of a heart attack, but his family and others believed that Marcos had him shot.[23] The NICA would not be restored until after the dictator's overthrow.

To deal with the growing security problems and to win the favor of the military, Marcos increased the AFP budget by a factor of five

TABLE 12.1   GOVERNMENTAL ORGANIZATIONS UNDER THE
COORDINATION OF THE NATIONAL INTELLIGENCE COORDINATING
AGENCY AS OF FEBRUARY, 2006

Aviation Security Group, PNP
Banko Sentral ng Pilipinas
Bureau of Customs
Bureau of Fisheries and Aquatic Resources
Bureau of Immigration
Bureau of Internal Revenue
Central Management Information Office
Criminal Investigation and Detection Group, PNP
Dangerous Drugs Board
Department of Labor and Employment
Department of Tourism
Directorate for Investigation and Detective Management, PNP
Environment Management Bureau, DENR
Firearms and Explosives Division, CSG-PNP
Gate 2, Presidential Security Group
Intelligence, AFP (J2)
Intelligence, Philippine Navy
Intelligence Group, PNP
Intelligence Service, AFP (ISAFP)
Land Transportation Office
Maritime Group, PNP
Narcotics Group, PNP
National Bureau of Investigation
National Capital Region Police Office, PNP
National Drug Law Enforcement and Prevention Coordinating Center
National Maritime Aerial Reconnaissance and Surveillance Center
Office of the Intelligence Service, DFA
Philippine Center on Transnational Crime
Philippine Coast Guard
Philippines Overseas Employment Agency
Securities and Exchange Commission
Traffic Management Group, PNP
Videogram Regulatory Board

Abbreviations: AFP, Armed Forces of the Philippines; CSG, Civil Security Group; DENR, Department of Environment and Natural Resources; DFA, Department of Foreign Affairs; ISAFP, Intelligence Service of the Armed Forces of the Philippines; PNP, Philippine National Police.
Source: Government of the Republic of the Philippines, http://www.gov.ph. (Accessed October 20, 2006)

and doubled its strength to 113,000 troops. Because of the enlargement of the insurgencies, U.S. military aid doubled to $45 million, as Marcos drove some hard bargains over the continued presence of the U.S. naval and air force bases. Alfred McCoy describes the results of this politicization and corruption:

> The armed forces were no longer the servant of the state under martial law, but the bastion of a particular regime. Backed by his generals, Marcos wiped out warlord [i.e., private] armies, closed Congress, and confiscated corporations. The president involved the military in every aspect of authoritarian rule—censorship, repression, and governance. Officers became corporate managers, civil servants, local officials, and judges.[24]

Although many good people remained at their posts, it is hard to conceive of a more unprofessional military establishment. An estimated 3,257 people were killed during martial law (not including the insurgencies), with 35,000 tortured and 70,000 incarcerated. As many times happens with widespread repression, insurgents were created in addition to being captured or killed. By 1985, and especially following the Aquino assassination, Marcos looked as if he could no longer hold on. Strong opposition was widespread, and such unlikely allies as the communist New People's Army and the Catholic Church agreed that Marcos had to go.

This process of politicization of the military during martial law also gradually produced junior officer groups like the Reform the Armed Forces Movement (RAM) that were highly politicized but largely left out of the huge profits of the corruption. As Marcos stacked the AFP and the PC with cronies from his home province, this favoritism gradually led others in the military establishment to become restive. As General Ver took over control of the major military organizations through his control of senior officers via promotion and bribes, Marcos's longtime political crony Juan Ponce Enrile, who was nominally in charge as minister of defense, became increasingly disgruntled. Another Marcos cousin, General Fidel Ramos, who was passed over for high army command and made chief of the PC, joined Enrile in his dissatisfaction. Enrile and Ramos would lead a military revolt against Marcos that was crucial to his fall from power in 1986.

Angry younger officers also flocked to support Enrile, and the growing rift with Marcos was one of the main reasons the AFP turned against the dictator. The rebels ran the ideological gamut: some junior officers were simply idealistic reformers disgusted with the way the AFP was being misused; others were notorious torturers afraid of being held to account. In the period after martial law was declared, young officers like Colonel Gregorio "Gringo" Honasan (now a member of the Philippine Senate), Lieutenant Colonel Eduardo "Red" Kapunan, and Lieutenant Colonel Oscar "Tito" Legaspi formed RAM under the surreptitious patronage of Enrile, an important factor in the overthrow of Marcos and in later coup attempts against President Aquino.[25]

There is less written about the PC or other police agencies during martial law, but they followed a similar evolution of corruption and politicization and acted as a kind of junior partner to the AFP. General Fidel Ramos headed the PC in the latter years. Though Ramos was believed to be personally honest, the PC in martial law played a role similar to that of the army: gathering intelligence on Marcos's political enemies, arresting political dissidents, protecting the interests of Marcos cronies, and generally acting outside the parameters of what is considered acceptable police practice. Repeated charges were made that the police agencies were directly involved in criminal enterprises at all levels of organization. Thus politicization and corruption also permeated the Philippine Constabulary and other local and national police groups. It should also be noted that it was General Ramos, as chief of staff under Aquino, who was most responsible for reforming the police and military institutions after the fall of Marcos.

THE AQUINO REFORMS (1986–1992)

The government of Corazon Aquino was a decidedly reformist government when it first came into office, and also perhaps the most unstable in Filipino history. The intelligence agencies of the Armed Forces of the Philippines were believed most responsible for her husband's murder. Yet Aquino had another legitimacy problem with the military from the very beginning, as the soldiers believed that they, not the civilians, deserved the credit for the overthrow of Marcos. It had been, they believed, the RAM rebels, Defense Minister Enrile, and PC chief Ramos who had removed Marcos from power. Aquino and her political movement, on the other hand, believed it was they who were the liberators of the country, and they were bound that they would reform the Filipino political system to its very foundations and punish the purveyors of repression. Their goals very much included reforms of the military and the police, as these agencies were seen by the reformers as the instruments of repression that had kept Marcos in power, not the instruments of liberation that had swept him from power. These sharp differences in perceptions meant that the civilians and soldiers in the government were at loggerheads throughout the period. As one leader of RAM said of the activities of the Commission on Human Rights set up by Aquino: "What do they want us to do? Flog ourselves?"[26] It appeared to the soldiers and police that while communist and Muslim rebels were being given amnesty, the AFP and PC were under assault. A RAM study bitterly noted that the numerous coup attempts were the result of soldiers being singled out to take the blame for the entire Marcos period.[27]

From the beginning of her government, Aquino concentrated on removing pro-Marcos forces in the AFP and PC that she blamed for the repression under Marcos, by firing them and reorganizing the intelligence agencies wholesale. She simultaneously called for a broadbased "national reconciliation," a controversial and contradictory policy that was bitterly resisted by the military. Thus it was largely a "top-down" reform aimed at the generals at the top of the hierarchy. Yet it was the junior officers who were most opposed to her government. The human rights goals and the governmental institutions to implement them were an integral part of the new constitution promulgated under her direction, which came into being in 1987 and pledged that civilian authority would be "at all times supreme over the military."[28] But many in the military, viewing themselves as the heroes of the overthrow of Marcos, saw the constitution as aimed at retribution, not reconciliation. This perception was enhanced by Aquino's actions, which seemed to them to blame the military almost exclusively for most of the violence in Filipino society. She retired a number of senior generals, signed cease-fires with the NPA and Moro separatists, surrounded herself with leftist critics of the military, released numerous "political" prisoners,[29] and used the newly established Commission on Human Rights to investigate the AFP and the Philippine National Police (PNP), only later adding the NPA. Within this context, military and intelligence reform was going to be resisted, if not fought, at every step.

Samuel Huntington has written that this "blitzkrieg" approach to reform is inherently flawed. By attempting widespread reforms simultaneously, a regime tends to coalesce the opposition to the changes. Using Kemal Atatürk as his paradigmatic reformer, Huntington suggests that an incremental Fabian reformist approach, one that isolates each sector that is to be reformed and avoids such widespread resistance, is the preferable strategy. The Aquino experience in the Philippines appears to bear out this insight.[30] By attempting deep-seated and broadly based reforms in the intelligence services simultaneously, Aquino caused a coalescence of opposition in the PNP, in the AFP, and among elite factions not in her coalition, including some in Congress. Rightly or wrongly, the uniformed security forces believed that they had participated in the People Power Revolution, and, indeed, without the support of Secretary of Defense Juan Enrile and PNP chief Fidel Ramos, the revolution very well might have failed. The uniformed services did not object to purging General Ver and the Marcos cronies; RAM and a more radical spin-off, the Young Officers Union (YOU), after all, had been formed in reaction to the widespread corruption in the AFP under Marcos. But when Aquino included the entire security establishment and rank and file as the object of her reforms, she virtually guaranteed their resistance.

The Aquino government had more military coup attempts against it than any other "third wave" democratizing regime in the world, a total of nine.[31] In comparing Aquino's dilemma with a similar situation in Argentina (another troubled democratizing country in this period), Alfred McCoy writes:

> In this transition [to democracy], the Philippine military, like its Argentine counterpart, seemed wracked by lingering tensions from a long immersion in torture and terror. . . . The Filipino officer corps refused to accept punishment for its crimes in service to dictatorship. By either joining coups or failing to move against them, the military signaled its demands for full amnesty, increased appropriations, and aggressive counterinsurgency. With such support, the RAM rebels were able to launch coup after coup against Aquino.[32]

The repeated attempts to overthrow the government had a devastating effect on the cause of reform and eventually rendered it politically impossible. Over time, President Aquino moved farther and farther from the reforms that she had called for early in her time in power, and she made alliances with moderate and conservative groups in order to stay in power. The more she was saved from coups pushed by younger officers by the upper levels of the professional military, the more beholden she was to them and the harder it was for her to demand unwanted change.[33] In late 1986, she was forced to fire Minister of Defense Juan Ponce Enrile because of his support for an attempted coup, replacing him with General Rafael Ileto.[34] A negative pattern of civil-military relations evolved. Throughout her presidency, Aquino remained extremely unpopular with large sections of the military and police, and it was only the support of political moderates and conservatives, as well as military professionals such as Fidel Ramos and Ramon Montaño, that kept her in power. Thus the ambitious Aquino reforms changed the structures of the intelligence agencies, but in practice there was far less success.

One of the most important reforms that President Aquino made was a direct result of her political problems with the AFP. The most serious coup attempt occurred in early December 1989, when three thousand RAM soldiers and four hundred members of the elite Scout Rangers revolted and took over the Makati section of Metro Manila. Bloody fighting ensued, with the loyalty of the rest of the AFP in doubt until the very end of the crisis. Malacañang Palace was dive-bombed by dissident officers of the Philippine Air Force. At least seventy-nine people were killed, and more than six hundred injured. But Ramos and leading generals remained loyal to the president; they penetrated the rebels' ranks and therefore had good intelligence of their plans.[35] On December 7, the Rangers and RAM members were persuaded to return to their barracks but were allowed to keep their weapons, an ominous sign for the future, given their behavior over the previous three years.[36] Another important development in the crisis was the use of U.S. "persuasion flights," overflights of Malacañang Palace to demonstrate American support for the Aquino government and keep the rebels in the Philippine Air Force on the ground. This action turned many Filipinos against the American military presence and in part led to the ending of the "special relationship" in 1991.[37]

In the aftermath of the December 1989 coup attempt and another that followed in early 1990, the Aquino government moved against the leaders of RAM and expelled them from the AFP. Over time, some were arrested and most were cashiered out of the service. RAM's leader, Gregorio "Gringo" Honasan, however, remained at large berating the administration in press and radio interviews. The inability to capture Honasan only added to the growing perception of Aquino's ineptitude, despite her continuing personal popularity at that time.

A possibly more important consequence of the 1989 coup, however, was that pro-government members of Congress moved in early 1990 to separate the PC and the Integrated National Police (INP)—the premier national police forces existing under Marcos—from the AFP, specifically to use the former two as a counterweight to the latter. Legislation was introduced to abolish the PC (which had been created by the Americans in 1901) and the INP and incorporate them into an enlarged Philippine National Police (PNP), as had been mandated in the 1987 Constitution. For the first time since their creation in the American colonial period, the police and military agencies were to be separate in their training, mission, and orientation. Police cadets would no longer attend the Philippine Military Academy, where the close associations that led to RAM and YOU had been formed.[38] The separation of powers between the military and the police was an important reform of the Aquino period, however imperfectly it has been implemented.

Aquino's policy of generosity and amnesty toward the NPA, the MILF, and the Abu Sayyaf Group ended in failure and enraged elements of the military. The 1987 Constitution had set up the Autonomous Region of Muslim Mindanao (ARMM), and provincial leaders from the MNLF were given control over some elements of local government. In return for this autonomy, they publicly declared that they no longer supported independence; the MILF broke off from the MNLF partly over this issue.[39] This only seemed to whet the appetites of the more radical groups, and the endemic and flamboyant political instability in Manila emboldened enemies of the government while insurgent violence grew. Negotiations with the NPA were broken off in 1987. Aquino increasingly turned to the use of vigilante groups in the villages to fight the communist and Muslim insurgencies, increasing the complaints of human rights violations domestically and from international organizations.[40] It was during the early 1990s that al Qaeda began moving into the Philippines, lending support through Islamic "charities" and nongovernmental organizations (NGOs) to Abu Sayyaf and the MILF, and after establishing Islamic religious schools with the aid of Middle Eastern countries, al Qaeda started using them as political training centers for Islamist radicalism.[41] Some cashiered soldiers and policemen ended up joining the ideological rebels or forming KFP gangs.[42]

As noted above, Aquino increasingly relied on military support as the ranks of the rural insurgencies swelled, and the promising start on reforms—institutional reform, as well as economic measures such as land reform aimed at ending the instability and redistributing the booty taken by Marcos's "crony capitalism"—moved farther and farther to the bottom of the government's agenda. One friendly critic believed that her intentions had been thwarted because she had simply been "shocked into submission" by all the attempted coups.[43] Her own commission to explain why so many coups had been attempted, headed by the respected Supreme Court justice Hilario Davide, while hardly exonerating the military rebels, concluded:

> Despite the installation of the formal structures and the advances in the democratic processes, the EDSA Revolt that installed Corazon C. Aquino as President did not result in the far-reaching revolution many people had hoped for. Most of these expectations were embodied in the [1987] Constitution but have largely remained unfulfilled.[44]

The Davide Commission did recommend some important reforms, including civilian control over the Department of National Defense, the National Security Council, and the newly created NICA, positions that traditionally went to military or ex-military officers. And although the civilianization of the top of the state security apparatus—as advocated, for example, by the Davide Commission—did not occur, civilianization of the middle and upper reaches of the security apparatuses did take place. This was a modest but effective reform that began in the Aquino period.[45]

THE RAMOS REFORMS (1992–1998)

In contrast to the blitzkrieg approach of the Aquino administration, the Ramos administration took a Fabian approach of gradual reforms *in seriatim*. Fidel Ramos won the presidency with 24 percent of the vote in a field of seven candidates. In many ways, however, he was the right person at the right time to further the cause of military and intelligence reform.

First, under the Aquino administration the Filipino economy began to recover from the negative growth of the final Marcos years and joined the economic boom that Southeast Asia enjoyed until 1997. That recovery, of course, had been severely hampered by the political instability and violence of the immediate post-Marcos period. Ramos would further the progress made under Aquino with a number of business-friendly reforms that hastened and strengthened the economic revival. This liberalization policy worked in the short run: by 1994, the Filipino economy was growing at 5 percent a year.[46] In 1998 the Philippine economy was freed from International Monetary Fund supervision for the first time in thirty-five years.

Second, as a military man and former PC commander and chief of staff of the AFP, Ramos knew intimately the relevant forces and the people who ran them, and this knowledge allowed him to plan reform strategies in effective ways. He had a degree of credibility and rapport with these armed forces that Aquino simply never could attain. Although at odds with Gringo Honasan and RAM, he was far more acceptable to them.

Third, unlike many other military or police figures in the Philippines, Ramos was trusted (or at least not distrusted) by the civilian democratic reformers in ways other soldiers were not. It had been Ramos, after all, who had been the key protector of the Aquino presidency and democratic government in the entire national security bureaucracy. The combination of credibility with the business sector, the security forces, and a number of the democratic Left gave him political capital as a reconciler that few could match. Moreover, after the flamboyant Marcos period and the unstable Aquino era, many Filipinos were apparently satisfied with a president whose nickname was Steady Eddie. There were no coup attempts, or even serious rumors of coup attempts, during the Ramos presidency.[47]

Ramos and his supporters in the military had been pushing through reforms from the bottom up since the overthrow of Marcos in 1986, in particular in reaction to the coup attempts of the late 1980s. These reforms were accelerated upon his taking office. Within a month of taking office, he had issued an administrative order revitalizing the National Security Council (NSC) and intelligence agencies, ordering them to reorient their activities "towards attaining broader national goals" rather than the narrow politics of the past. Ramos named his old friend José Almonte, a longtime intelligence operator and a former mentor to RAM, as his national security adviser and gave him control of the NSC and the NICA, the foremost intelligence agency in the executive branch that had been created in the Aquino period.[48] Almonte was a strong believer in civic action and a holistic approach to insurgencies, and his thinking on the subject mirrored Ramos's own.

Realizing the depth of the problem, Ramos, in his words, went "back to basics" and began with the retraining and reorganization of the services to isolate the personalistic networks in police and military intelligence created by President Marcos and General Ver in the martial law period. This was a slow process, but by 1991 the new national police force had been separated from the military in training and structure for the first time in a century with the creation of the reformed Philippines National Police (PNP). This was followed by a wholesale firing of the entire top leadership of the PNP and the prosecution of police officials for rape and robbery in highly publicized cases. It was announced that as many as five thousand police officers of all ranks would be cashiered. Reporters called it the "biggest police shake-up in the nation's history."[49]

In the military realm, intelligence agents were placed at the village level, replacing their concentration in large encampments and aiding in collection tasks immensely. Emphasis was placed on strengthening the "tactical intelligence capabilities" of the intelligence agencies, concentrating on collecting information about targets' families, personal details, and so on. A new system of evaluating this intelligence, borrowed from the United States, allowed for improved analysis of raw data from the villages and neighborhoods. With the growing regional threat of Islamist terrorism, the Philippines took the initiative among its ASEAN neighbors and others in creating the beginning of new international intelligence-sharing relationships in Southeast Asia. Institutionally, Ramos demonstrated the importance of intelligence to security by creating a secretary of intelligence at the cabinet level.[50]

Ramos also changed the strategy for dealing with military and other rebels. He first turned to the RAM and YOU rebels and offered them a general amnesty. Given his legitimacy with the soldiers, and a general fatigue of constantly being on the run, most of the military rebels signed peace agreements with the government in 1994–1995. In negotiations with the MNLF, the government scored another impressive success, with help from Pakistan, Libya, and the Organization of the Islamic Conference (OIC). In September 1996 the MNLF agreed to forgo the promise of a separate Islamic state in exchange for a greater degree of autonomy and an invitation to join the government. Thus two of the most serious threats to political stability and economic progress had been lessened by creative and successful diplomacy. The cease-fire signed at that time remains in force today. As Ramos was to put it later, the first modernization of the AFP and PNP was not in weaponry or tactics but in their collective mind-sets.[51]

To be sure, problems continued with the NPA, the MILF, the Abu Sayyaf Group, and the growing number of KFPs, and the improvements were relative ones. Negotiations with those groups did not progress as smoothly, and in fact the MILF and the Abu Sayyaf Group became more violent in resistance to the increased moderation demonstrated by the MNLF. In April 1995 the Abu Sayyaf attacked the town of Ipil, killing at least thirty-three people, robbing banks, and burning dozens of buildings.[52] Not coincidentally, it was also in the early 1990s that al Qaeda, Libya, Iraq, and other Middle Eastern nations began to take a greater interest in Southeast Asia in terms of funding radical Islamists.[53] Islamist political groups were strengthened in Thailand, Indonesia, Malaysia, and the Philippines. The porous borders of the island nations, in particular, taxed the capabilities of intelligence agencies and military forces. The removal of the U.S. Navy from the region had the unintended consequence of opening up the ASEAN countries to increased infiltration, smuggling, and piracy.[54] Despite the growing crises, opposition political activists in Thailand, Indonesia, and the Philippines were especially wary of giving power back to security institutions, in light of their recent experiences with dictatorship.[55] It would not be until the shocks of the 9/11 bombing of the World Trade Center (the 1993 bombing of which had been partly planned in a terrorist cell in the Philippines) and the Bali bombing of October 2002 that the ASEAN countries and Australia would improve regional coordination of intelligence information.[56]

Moreover, a lack of resources following the onset of the regional recession in 1997 and the persistence of corrupt practices, especially in the PNP, continued to discourage reformers in the Philippines.[57] In one notable embarrassment in 1997, when government agents raided a suspected drug lord's home near Manila, twenty PNP police officers were found moonlighting as bodyguards and drug dealers. In another incident, forty NPA rebels walked into a PNP headquarters building thirty-five kilometers east of Manila and kidnapped the police chief, to the intense embarrassment of the government. Despite all the retraining and replacement of corrupt officers, policemen in Metro Manila continued to earn about the same as an unskilled factory worker—making the temptation of corruption too great. Senator Orlando Mercado, chairman of the Senate Committee on Defense and National

Security, publicly announced in 1997: "The PNP has become a monster. It requires major surgery."[58]

In summary, the Ramos administration was far more successful in putting through reforms than the Aquino administration or administrations that followed. Many of the structural changes proposed in the Aquino period were finally implemented in the Ramos period. Yet even with a concerted effort by major sections of the government and a reformist leader at the helm, the reforms were only imperfectly implemented. Ramos and his backers exacerbated the distrust of government when they tried to amend the Constitution to allow him a second term. Both Corazon Aquino and the Catholic Church successfully opposed the move. When Ramos left office, despite the real improvements, both the military and the PNP were still corrupt, inept, and a drag on democratic consolidation. The worsening of the regional economy made it appear even less likely that the resources for modernization and reform of the security services were likely to be found.[59]

THE ESTRADA DEBACLE (1998–2001)

One of the main reasons for the attempt to grant Fidel Ramos a second term by some was the Manila-based elite's horror at the thought that his popular vice president, Joseph "Erap" Estrada, might become president.[60] Estrada, who at the time of writing is on trial for "plundering," was a hard-drinking, openly womanizing movie actor who played in modern Robin Hood–style films. His appeal was unabashedly populist, and his screen image of a no-nonsense, Dirty Harry–style hero apparently impressed the public. He was elected president in 1998 with 40 percent of the votes in a field of eleven candidates and nearly double the votes that Ramos received, in what one observer calls "one of the freest, fairest, and least violent elections in Philippine history."[61]

Estrada ran on a platform promising to narrow the gap between rich and poor—his campaign slogan was "Erap is for the poor"—but acted quite differently once in office. He tried to implement unpopular constitutional changes; consistently took the side of management in disputes with labor; browbeat and harassed the critical media, including through the use of the Bureau of Internal Revenue; dismissed outstanding legal cases against the Marcos family, who were attempting to regain some of their plunder; and rehabilitated and restored the assets of Eduardo "Danding" Cojuangco, Corazon Cojuangco-Aquino's estranged cousin and one of Marcos's most corrupt cronies. Fairly or not, the Estrada administration was increasingly judged to be a restoration of the corrupt and antidemocratic practices of the past. Not surprisingly, Estrada's actions invited the combined political opposition of the Aquino movement, the Catholic Church, former president Ramos, and, increasingly, the public. By the end of his first full year in office, Estrada's popularity had plummeted, especially in Manila.[62]

In the security realm, the Estrada administration eased off on some of the reforms in the AFP and PNP, although change did continue. Persistent coup rumors began in late 1999 and early 2000, peaking in April, meaning that the government had to keep the military and the police satisfied, which always has slowed reform. Corruption worsened and retraining slowed. Charges that AFP troops were selling weapons to the MILF and Abu Sayyaf rebels increased.[63] Estrada took an increasingly tough line on the insurgencies, unleashing the military in the south in March 2000, a move that was popular with the high command. Those actions, and the failure to implement the 1996 Peace Accord signed by the Ramos government and the MNLF, led to increased violence in Mindanao and record numbers of kidnappings and bombings. The MILF and the government returned to their fight while participating in negotiations that continue to this day. The NPA went on the attack, especially targeting government personnel and economic targets in the countryside in the Maoist style. The Abu Sayyaf Group became even more outrageous in its behavior, beheading two kidnapped teachers on April 19 "as a birthday gift to President Estrada."[64] In April 2000 an allied group in Indonesia, who would also perpetrate the October 12, 2002, tourist bombing in Bali, car-bombed the house of the Philippine ambassador in Jakarta.[65] Although Estrada's popularity actually increased because of his tough line on insurgency, the relative political and economic stability of the Ramos years was disappearing quickly.[66]

Amid long-standing rumors of personal corruption, an estranged crony of Estrada's, Ilocos Sur governor Luis "Chavit" Singson, accused the president of extorting 200 million pesos in proceeds from an illegal gambling racket called *juetang*.[67] Dozens of similar charges of official and unofficial corruption followed.[68] Evidence showed that the PNP, as had long been charged, was deeply involved in the racket.[69]

The political opposition and the press moved to avenge their treatment by Estrada in the past. As opposition in the Congress drew up articles of impeachment, the vice president, Gloria Macapagal-

Arroyo, resigned from the cabinet (but not from the vice presidency) and joined the calls for Estrada's resignation.[70] During his second Senate trial, Estrada was driven from office by the EDSA II, the second People Power Revolution. The six principal players in the removal of the president were business circles, the Catholic Church, the media, the political opposition (especially former presidents Aquino and Ramos and their backers), the military, and the chief justice of the Supreme Court. The first four brought people into the streets, the military tipped the political balance within the government, and the Supreme Court oversaw the trials to remove him.[71] In January 2001, Estrada resigned from the presidency and was replaced by Macapagal-Arroyo. Once again, Filipino democracy appeared to be doomed, only to prove its resilience. Yet such resilience came at a high cost, as political instability and rural violence increased significantly after the relative respite of the Ramos period.[72]

CONCLUSIONS

By any standard of professionalism, the Filipino security forces have played too central a role in the prevention of or the promotion of the consolidation of democracy in the Philippines. Even in the EDSA I and EDSA II People Power rebellions, the military was the national institution of last resort. Democratically elected governments should not have to be supported by the security forces of their nation, or as President Macapagal-Arroyo put it after coup rumors again swept through Manila in 2002: "Clandestine designs creep into the armed services and the law enforcement agencies. There is a sense of constant [political] fragility that cannot be easily overcome."[73] The Philippines has had a tortured, albeit real, period of democratic consolidation. Yet the legacy of dictatorship and its attendant politicization of the security apparatuses of government continue to act as a constraint on further democratization of society. Filipino society appears to coalesce in opposition to authoritarian government, but it has not yet coalesced in creating a civil society that supports further democratic consolidation. Filipino culture, which has yet to produce a consistent, widely accepted ethos of support for nationally based democracy beyond the rhetorical level, acts as an additional constraint within this historical context. Despite attempts made under Aquino and Ramos, legislative and executive control over the intelligence services remains weak, and those elements of the AFP have often been in the forefront of the threats of coups that can undermine the legitimacy of democratic government. Some promising initial efforts have been made; for example, the separation of the training of the AFP and the PNP. But reform of the security forces has to go forward if the intelligence agencies of the nation are to be professionalized; and in this, there have been steps forward and backward.

The Philippines case strongly suggests that the pace of reform is as important as its scope. Prioritized, incremental change appears to be more acceptable to more people than a sweeping, blitzkrieg approach. For example, there has not been a noticeably widespread hostile reaction to the separation of the AFP and the PNP, although pockets of resistance have appeared, and this is an important first step in breaking the stranglehold that the security forces had on Filipino society under Marcos. Although rhetorically most Filipinos appear to want widespread, dramatic change, the forces of opposition must also be taken into consideration. Reform measures that are seen as threatening the security forces as "institutions" are the most likely to lead to political violence and retrenchment. Whether the Macapagal-Arroyo government can maintain this delicate balancing act remains to be seen.

Severe problems remain: that perennial complaint of intelligence services, a difficulty in coordinating inter-institutional intelligence-sharing;[74] continued reports that AFP groups in the south are making deals with the insurgents and terrorists and even selling them weapons, as well as reports of uniformed service members "coddling" insurgents and criminals for bribes (it is no coincidence that crackdowns on such activities correlate strongly at times with rumors of coups);[75] attempts by opposition politicians to weaken the loyalty of security forces to the existing government; continued factionalism and personalism; and a general demoralization in the AFP over the lack of progress in armed forces modernization because of financial problems, poor pay, and an on-again, off-again counterinsurgency strategy.

Although problems remain in the AFP, the PNP and local police forces appear to remain the primary problem and obstacle to reform. Generous civil service benefits and protections make it difficult to fire anyone outright without an overwhelming reason.[76] Police officials who are suspected of corruption or ineptitude are usually sent to remote posts in the countryside. But those very areas are the centers of the insurgencies, meaning that the only real government representatives that many rural dwellers come into contact with are often not the best the nation has to offer.

As is usually the case in the Philippines, however, not all is bleak. There have been real and valuable reforms in terms of civilianization of major institutions such as the NICA and the entire security structure and its concentration in the executive branch. Military mutineers such as those in RAM and YOU seem not to be the dynamic movements they have been in the past, although they lurk in the background and coup attempts and mutinies continue to occur. As President Macapagal-Arroyo, who won reelection in 2004, noted in a speech dedicated to intelligence matters in 2002, the security forces now have a presence down to the individual village level.[77] Additionally, international intelligence cooperation with ASEAN, European, Middle Eastern, and American intelligence institutions has "never been better," according to one Filipino intelligence official.[78] These are all positive signs of security service reform and will add to further democratic consolidation.

Yet the continued collective cognitive dissonance—the gap between beliefs and performance—remains the wellspring of Filipino politics. The demoralization such levels of corruption can cause is the major reason for the endemic violence in the country, not least the political violence, when that demoralization turns into frustration and anger. Politicians who try to bridge this gap are the best hope for further reform. President Arroyo has been accused by her detractors of bowing too often to the desires of the entrenched military, and her calls for reform have not been followed by effective implementation. Until the nation develops a truly professional military establishment and a national ethos that moves beyond patron-client politics and the resulting corruption at all levels of society, the pace of reforms in the intelligence and security forces promises to be slow and incomplete—and for that, all the more necessary.

NOTES

I would like to thank Zachary Abuza, former ambassador to the Philippines Stephen Bosworth, Tom Bruneau, Concepcion "Ching" Clamor, Ken Dombroski, Major General Ramon E. Montaño (retired), former president Fidel V. Ramos, and Jim Wirtz for the gracious help and encouragement they offered. My former student Erin Wickham offered valuable research assistance. Any mistakes of judgment or fact, of course, are mine alone. The source of the epigraph is a quotation in *Manila Times Online*, January 10, 2003, http://www.manilatimes.net.

1. See Thomas C. Bruneau, "Controlling Intelligence in New Democracies," *International Journal of Intelligence and CounterIntelligence* 13 (2001): 323-341.

2. For balanced general overviews of Filipino society, economics, and politics, see David Joel Steinberg, *The Philippines: A Singular and a Plural Place*, 4th ed. (Boulder, CO: Westview Press, 2000); and David Wurfel, *Filipino Politics: Development and Decay* (Ithaca, NY: Cornell University Press, 1988).

3. See Alfred W. McCoy, ed., *An Anarchy of Families: State and Family in the Philippines* (Madison: University of Wisconsin Press; Manila: Ateneo de Manila University Press, 1993). McCoy credits anthropologist Robert Fox for coining the term in the 1950s (8). See also John T. Sidel, "Philippine Politics in Town, District, and Province: Bossism in Cavite and Cebu," *Journal of Asian Studies* 56, no. 4 (November 1997), 947-966. Following the overthrow of Marcos in 1986, fighting among provincial clans again became quite violent. See John McBeth, "Family Clans Fight for Supremacy: Provincial Power Play," *Far Eastern Economic Review Online* (hereafter, *FEERO*) 145, no. 37 (September 14, 1989), http://www.feer.com.

4. In a provocative article comparing this patron-client model of bureaucratic behavior in the region, Springer and Gable argue that this cultural assumption is exaggerated and that organizational values can supersede personalistic ones in bureaucratic settings. J. Fred Springer and Richard W. Gable, "The Impact of Informal Relations on Organizational Rewards: Comparing Bureaucracies in Southeast Asia," *Comparative Politics* 12, no. 2 (January 1980): 191-210. I am arguing not that relatively objective organizational or national values cannot predominate in Filipino institutions, but that they often do not and that this is an impediment to reform.

5. U.S. government study cited in Robert H. Reid and Eileen Guerrero, *Corazon Aquino and the Brushfire Revolution* (Baton Rouge: Louisiana State University Press, 1995), 10. Both Benigno Aquino and his widow, Corazon (née Cojuangco), were members of elite families from Luzon.

6. See Joel S. Migdal, *Strong Societies and Weak States: State-Society Relations and State Capabilities in the Third World* (Princeton, NJ: Princeton University Press, 1988). Alfred McCoy particularly points to the similarities with Latin American polities; see McCoy, " 'An Anarchy of Families,' " in *An Anarchy of Families*, 8-9. In contrast, Patricio N. Abinales argues that it was state formation that shaped local power rather than local power that shaped state formation. I think it is sensible to view it as an interactive process between the two. See Abinales, *Making Mindanao: Cotabato and Davao in the Formation of the Philippine Nation State* (Manila: Ateneo de Manila University Press, 2000).

7. For an overview of the various rebellions in the colonial periods, see

David R. Sturtevant, *Popular Uprisings in the Philippines, 1840–1940* (Ithaca, NY: Cornell University Press, 1976).

8. For example, the current president of the Philippines, Gloria Macapagal-Arroyo, is the daughter of Diosdado P. Macapagal, the fifth president of the Philippines Republic, serving from 1961 to 1965 before being defeated by Ferdinand Marcos. Marcos's widow, Imelda, ran for president in 1998; his son, Ferdinand Junior, is the governor of Ilocos Norte Province, where the Marcos family dominates the political scene; his daughter Imee is a member of the Philippine Congress. The Philippine Senate has as a member Ramón Magsaysay Jr., whose father was president and was killed in a plane crash in 1957. Such relationships in politics are not considered unusual in the Philippines.

9. Kent Eaton, citing a study by Carey and Shugart, in "Political Obstacles to Decentralization: Evidence from Argentina and the Philippines," *Development and Change* 32 (2001): 114.

10. Ibid., 101–127. On patron/party switching as a characteristic of Filipino politics, see also Paul D. Hutchcroft, "Oligarchs and Cronies in the Philippine State: The Politics of Patrimonial Plunder," *World Politics* 43, no. 3 (April 1991): 414–450. "Pork barrel" money is officially allocated to each member of the Philippine Senate.

11. See Rica M. Ligeralde, "Democracy in the Philippines: A Political Cultural Approach," *Asian Profile* 25, no. 2 (April 1997): 123–134.

12. There is another nonjihadist Muslim group, the Moro National Liberation Front (MNLF), that has made peace with the government and is represented in the government at the local, provincial, and national levels and is not considered a security problem.

13. Interview with former president Fidel Ramos, Manila, March 4, 2003. At least one military intelligence officer I interviewed did not share that view; off-the-record interviews with military intelligence officers of the Intelligence Service of the Armed Forces of the Philippines (ISAFP), Manila, March 2 and 5, 2003.

14. Interview with Ramos; interview with former Philippine National Police (PNP) chief Major General Ramon E. Montaño, Armed Forces of the Philippines (AFP; retired), Manila, March 4, 2003. Ramos demonstrated an early interest in a holistic approach to insurgency in writing the foreword for a book by a dissident officer who had actually fought with the communist forces for six years before returning to the PNP in the Aquino amnesty of 1986. See the foreword by then minister of defense Fidel Ramos to Victor N. Corpus, *Silent War* (Quezon City, Philippines: VNC Enterprises, 1989).

15. Interview with Montaño.

16. For example, see the infighting between "reformists" (holistic approach) and "bolsterers" (military/police approach) in Vietnam during the Kennedy administration in Douglas J. Macdonald, *Adventures in Chaos: American Intervention for Reform in the Third World* (Cambridge, MA: Harvard University Press, 1992), chaps. 8 and 9. Similar disputes over reformist versus hard-line policies took place

during the Chinese Civil War (1946–1949) and the Huk Rebellion in the Philippines (1949–1953); see ibid., chaps. 4–7.

17. See Barry Wain, "September 11, One Year On: Unfriendly Fire," *FEERO* (September 12, 2002).

18. Quoted in Nayan Chanda, "A Split Opinion: U.S. Officials Are Divided on Philippine Military Problems," *FEERO* 137, no. 39 (September 24, 1987).

19. "EDSA" refers to the highway named Epifanio de los Santos Avenue, which intersects Manila and was the site of confrontations between pro- and anti-Marcos forces in February 1986. EDSA I ousted Marcos; EDSA II ousted President Joseph Estrada in 2000. A so-called EDSA III consists of the followers of Estrada who periodically try to put him back in power, but so far it has garnered little public support.

20. For a very good overview of Filipino electoral politics, see Julio Teehankee, "Electoral Politics in the Philippines," *Dialogue + Cooperation* 1/2002, 149–202, http://www.fesspore.org/pdf/Electoral%20Politics/PHILIPPINESFINAL.PDF.

21. See Alfred W. McCoy, *Closer Than Brothers: Manhood at the Philippines Military Academy* (New Haven, CT: Yale University Press, 1999), for an interesting study of the socialization processes that prevailed in the Marcos period. He compares a contemporary (1971) class with an earlier (1940) class at the Philippine Military Academy to show how, "[i]n real political terms, there is an obvious and important difference between a class unity that prevents coups and one that promotes them" (344).

22. Interview with Ramos; off-the-record interviews with ISAFP military intelligence officers.

23. David Wurfel, "Martial Law in the Philippines: The Methods of Regime Survival," *Pacific Affairs* 50, no. 1 (Spring 1977): 24.

24. McCoy, *Closer Than Brothers*, 192–193. For a highly critical journalistic account of the U.S. role in this period, see Raymond Bonner, *Waltzing with a Dictator: The Marcoses and the Making of American Policy* (New York: Times Books, 1987).

25. For RAM's role in the anti-Marcos coup, see McCoy, *Closer Than Brothers*, 234–237; and Wurfel, "Martial Law in the Philippines," especially 24–27. By the time of the coup, RAM had a membership of nearly nine hundred in the junior officer corps. All fifteen of its leaders were from the Philippine Military Academy's class of 1971. McCoy, *Closer Than Brothers*, 193.

26. McCoy, *Closer Than Brothers*, 261.

27. Ibid., 261.

28. The text of the 1987 Constitution of the Philippines can be found at http://www.gov.ph/aboutphil/constitution.asp.

29. Including NPA founder José Sison, who soon moved to the Netherlands, where he lives today.

30. Samuel P. Huntington, *Political Order in Changing Societies* (New Haven, CT: Yale University Press, 1968). I have argued that Ramon Magsaysay success-

fully used a similar strategy as secretary of defense and later president during the Huk Rebellion in the 1950s. Macdonald, *Adventures in Chaos*, chaps. 6–7.

31. Greece experienced seven coup attempts after democratization, Argentina five, and Spain three. There is disagreement over the number of coup attempts that occurred during the Aquino period, ranging from seven to nine, depending on how you define "coup attempt." Mark R. Thompson, "Off the Endangered List: Philippine Democratization in Comparative Perspective," *Comparative Politics* 28, no. 2 (January 1996): 179, 198 n. 1. For "third wave" democratization in general, and the discussion from which this comparison is cited, see Samuel P. Huntington, *The Third Wave: Democratization in the Late Twentieth Century* (Norman: University of Oklahoma Press, 1991).

32. McCoy, *Closer Than Brothers*, 260. McCoy is extremely harsh on Aquino, as he is on all Filipino elites.

33. Rodney Tasker, "A Delicate Balance: Ramos and His Generals Seek Bigger Say in Government," *FEERO* 134, no. 50 (December 11, 1986). Eventually a reaction in the Philippine Congress set in against this development, which slowed but did not end it. See Jose Galang, "Military Setback: Congress Rejects Code to Give Ramos More Power," *FEERO* 142, no. 49 (December 8, 1988). See also McCoy, *Closer Than Brothers*, 282–283.

34. Reid and Guerrero, *Corazon Aquino and the Brushfire Revolution*, 63–74. For the buildup to the crisis, see Rodney Tasker, " 'Johnny Be Good': Defence Minister Enrile's Consolidation of Power Causes Concern," *FEERO* 133, no. 32 (August 7, 1986).

35. Interview with Ramos; Reid and Guerrero, *Corazon Aquino and the Brushfire Revolution*, 70; McCoy, *Closer Than Brothers*, 284–285.

36. Interview with Ramos; off-the-record interviews with ISAFP military intelligence officers; John McBeth, "Threat of Another Coup Hangs over Aquino: Time for Toughness," *FEERO* 146, no. 51 (December 21, 1989); McCoy, *Closer Than Brothers*, 284–293.

37. Interview with Ramos. Chairman of the U.S. Joint Chiefs of Staff General Colin Powell called Ramos, who was then minister of defense, to offer troops and other military support. Ramos counseled Powell that these were not necessary and that the persuasion flights would be sufficient. See also Colin L. Powell and Joseph E. Persico (contributor), *My American Journey: An Autobiography* (New York: Random House, 1995), 440–444. As for the influence of the persuasion flights on the U.S. bases agreement, Juan Enrile, after he had been forced to resign as defense minister because of his suspected support for an earlier coup and had been elected to the Senate, thundered at a political rally in 1991: "The U.S. Phantom jets that darkened our skies at the height of the December, 1989, coup attempt are but the most uninhibited demonstration of how poorly the United States regards our sovereignty and independence" (quoted in Reid and Guerrero, *Corazon Aquino and the Brushfire Revolution*, 211).

38. John McBeth, "Partners in Proposed Unified Police Force at Odds: Shot-

gun Marriage," *FEERO* 145, no. 30 (July 27, 1989), and "Police Bolstered as Potential Anti-Coup Force: Pig in the Middle," *FEERO* 147, no. 4 (January 25, 1990).

39. James Clad, "Autonomy and Acrimony: Government and Muslim Separatists Sign Accord," *FEERO* 135, no. 3 (January 15, 1987). ARMM included the provinces of Lanao del Sur (population: 571,000); Maguindanao (population: 662,000); Tawi-Tawi (population: 250,000); the Sulu Islands, including Jolo (population: 540,000); and Basilan (population: 295,000).

40. See Justus M. van der Kroef, "The Philippines: Day of the Vigilantes," *Asian Survey* 28, no. 6 (June 1988): 630–649.

41. Ahmed Rashid, "Schools for Soldiers: Islamic Schools Mix Religion and Politics," *FEERO* 158, no. 10 (March 9, 1995): 25; Mark Turner, "Terrorism and Secession in the Southern Philippines: The Rise of the Abu Sayaff," *Contemporary Southeast Asia* (Singapore) 17, no. 1 (June 1995): 10–13; Marites D. Vitug and Glenda M. Gloria, *Under the Crescent Moon: Rebellion in Mindanao* (Manila: Institute for Popular Democracy, 2000), 118; Al Madarz Jalim, "NGOs Tied to al-Qaida: ISAFP Paper Also Cites Islam Schools," *Manila Times Online*, March 27, 2002.

42. John McBeth, "Military Dissidents Linked to Crime Upsurge: Rebels and Robbers," *FEERO* 151, no. 12 (March 21, 1991).

43. Quoted in Reid and Guerrero, *Corazon Aquino and the Brushfire Revolution*, 152.

44. Quoted in ibid., 191. For an analysis of the Davide Commission, see John McBeth, "Government Panel Looks at Hands behind the Coups: A Common Thread," *FEERO* 150, no. 42 (October 18, 1990).

45. Communication from Concepcion "Ching" Clamor, assistant director of research for the NICA, April 1, 2003.

46. On the combination of businessmen, politicians, and military men in the top decision-making positions in the Ramos government, see Rigoberto Tiglao, "The New Hands on the Helm," *FEERO* 155, no. 35 (September 3, 1992).

47. Interview with Ramos; Steinberg, *The Philippines*, 191–208.

48. John McBeth, "Jose Almonte: Filipino Security Chief Is a Master of Intrigue: Career Soldier Who Understands Social Issues Is the Architect of Ramos' Philippine 2000 Development Game Plan," *FEERO* 156, no. 14 (April 8, 1993).

49. John McBeth, "Clean Sweep: Senior Officers Fired in Effort to Reform Police," *FEERO* 156, no. 19 (May 13, 1993).

50. Interview with Ramos; interview with Montaño; off-the-record interviews with ISAFP military intelligence officers. The United States offered increased aid to the Filipinos for the reform of their intelligence institutions beginning in 1987. See Nayan Chanda, "Here Come the Spies: Reagan Authorizes the CIA to Give More Help to Manila," *FEERO* 136, no. 15 (April 9, 1987).

51. See "Bearer of the Torch," interview with President Fidel Ramos, *FEERO* 159, no. 9 (February 29, 1996); Segundo E. Romero, "The Philippines in 1997: Weathering Political and Economic Turmoil," *Asian Survey* 38, no. 2 (February

1998): 198–199; and Francisco S. Tatad, *A Nation on Fire: The Unmaking of Joseph Ejercito Estrada and the Remaking of Democracy in the Philippines* (Manila: Icon Press, 2002), 102.

52. V. G. Kulkarni, "Mid-Term Blues: Halfway through His Six Year Term, a Series of Crises Has Left President Ramos's Coalition Struggling Ahead of Key Legislative Elections in May," *FEERO* 158, no. 17 (April 27, 1995).

53. For an excellent overview of this problem in the Philippines, see Christos Iacovou, "From MNLF to Abu Sayyaf: The Radicalization of Islam in the Philippines," Institute for Defense Analysis, Greece, July 11, 2000, available at http://www.ict.org.il/articles/articledet.cfm?articleid=116. See also John Mc-Lean, "Manila Expels Iraqi Diplomat," *BBC News Online*, February 12, 2003, http://news.bbc.co.uk/2/hi/asia-pacific/2752765.stm; Joshua Kurlantzick, "Fear Moves East: Terror Targets the Pacific Rim," *Washington Quarterly* 24, no. 1 (Winter 2001): 19–29.

54. See Peter Chalk, "Low Intensity Conflict in Southeast Asia: Piracy, Drug Trafficking, and Political Terrorism," *Conflict Studies*, nos. 305–306 (January–February 1998): 1–36.

55. For evidence that the fear is not unwarranted in Indonesia, see Slobodan Lekic, "Indonesian Military Implicated in Terrorism," *Nando Times*, August 12, 2002, available at http://www.intellnet.org/news/2002/08/12/10862-1.html.

56. Mark Baker and Lindsay Murdoch, "Heat on Jakarta to Crush bin Laden Followers," *smh.com.au (Sydney Morning Herald)*, January 26, 2002, http://smh.com.au; Agence France Presse, Singapore, "Deputy PM Seeks Closer Intelligence Links with Philippines," December 9, 2002, available at http://www.singapore-window.org/sw02/021209a2.htm.

57. Although the Philippines did not suffer as much as some other countries in the region, from the onset of the regional financial crisis in July 1997 to October 1998 the Philippine peso lost 40 percent of its value, and the Philippine stock index 10 percent of its value. Gabriella R. Montinola, "The Philippines in 1998: Opportunity Amid Crisis," *Asian Survey* 39, no. 1 (January–February 1999): 64.

58. See Peter Morgan and Antonio Lopez, "Cleaning Up the Good Guys: Can Manila Rein in Corrupt and Inept Cops?" *Asiaweek*, November 14, 1997, http://www.asiaweek.com/asiaweek/97/1114/nat7.html.

59. For an overview, see Romero, "The Philippines in 1997," 196–202. More generally, see Renato Cruz De Castro, "Adjusting to the Post–U.S. Bases Era: The Ordeal of the Philippine Military's Modernization Program," *Armed Forces and Society* 26, no. 1 (Fall 1999): 119–138.

60. Romero, "The Philippines in 1997," 196. In the Filipino presidential system, the vice president does not have to be of the same party as the president.

61. Montinola, "The Philippines in 1998," 65. See also Nicholas Nugent, "Estrada: Movie Hero or Villain?" *BBC News Online*, December 10, 2000, http://news.bbc.co.uk/2/hi/asia-pacific/1063976.stm.

62. Emil P. Bolongaita Jr., "The Philippines in 1999: Balancing Restive De-

mocracy and Recovering Economy," *Asian Survey* 40, no. 1 (January–February 2000): 68; Mel C. Labrador, "The Philippines in 2000: In Search of a Silver Lining," *Asian Survey* 41, no. 1 (January–February 2001): 221–229.

63. See the interviews in Jose Torres Jr., *Into the Mountain: Hostaged by the Abu Sayyaf* (Quezon City, Philippines: Claretian Publications, 2001), 39–40.

64. Abu Sayyaf spokesman, quoted in ibid., 156.

65. Ellen Nakashima, "Bali Blast Linked to Another in 2000," *Washington Post Online*, March 11, 2003.

66. Labrador, "The Philippines in 2000," 224–226.

67. *Juetang* is essentially a numbers game played mostly by the poor, similar to the numbers games in the United States. For the personal relations between Singson and Estrada, see Emma Batha, "A Tale of Betrayal and Revenge," *BBC New Online*, January 19, 2001, http://news.bbc.co.uk/2/hi/asia-pacific/1057819.stm.

68. For the charges, see Tatad, *A Nation on Fire*, 111–128. See also "Estrada: The Charges," *BBC News Online*, July 10, 2001, http://news.bbc.co.uk/2/hi/asia-pacific/1430835.stm.

69. Tatad, *A Nation on Fire*, 51.

70. Labrador, "The Philippines in 2000," 223–224.

71. See the gentle critique of Estrada and harsh criticism of his opponents by one of his former allies, former senator Tatad, *A Nation on Fire*, 2. Tatad calls Estrada's removal a "coup" at the behest of "mob rule." For a harsher critique of Estrada and limited praise of the uprising, see Ben Reid, "The Philippine Democratic Uprising and the Contradictions of Neoliberalism: EDSA II," *Third World Quarterly* 22, no. 5 (2001): 777–793. See also Patricio N. Abinales, "Coalition Politics in the Philippines," *Current History* 100, no. 645 (April 2001): 154–161.

72. The U.S. State Department noted that during the insurgencies in 2000 there were "serious human rights abuses by both sides." Specifically, members of the security forces were guilty of "extrajudicial killings, disappearances, torture, and arbitrary arrest and detention." The Philippine Commission on Human Rights, which had been set up in the 1987 Constitution, opined that the PNP was the worst abuser of human rights in 2000. U.S. Department of State, Bureau of Democracy, Human Rights, and Labor, "Philippines: Country Reports on Human Rights Practices—2000," February 23, 2001, http://www.state.gov/g/drl/rls/hrrpt/2000/eap/764.htm

73. "PMGA's Speech during the National Intelligence Summit, Heroes Hall, Malacanang (06 March 2002)," http://www.ops.gov.ph/speeches2002/speech-2002mar06.htm.

74. President Arroyo mentioned this problem specifically in her speech. Ibid.

75. Efren Danao, "Senate Panel Finds Proof of AFP-Sayyaf Collusion in Basilan," *Philippine Star Online*, August 16, 2002; John Unson, "Faisal's Wife Willing to Name 'Padrinos' in Military and Police," *Philippine Star Online*, August 30, 2002.

76. Communication from Clamor.

77. "PMGA's Speech."

78. Communication from Clamor. For more on extraregional international support in the fight against terrorism through training aid and intelligence sharing, see John Aglionby, "Manila Asks UK to Help Rout Rebels," *Guardian Online*, January 28, 2002, http://www.guardian.co.uk/international/story/0,640407,00.html; Government of the Philippines, "GMA Bares Jordanian King's Offer to Provide Intelligence Info in Fight against Terrorists," http://www.gov.ph; Jeannette Andrade, "Israelis Here to Help Drive vs. Terrorists," *Sunday Manila Times Online*, April 21, 2002; Max de Leon, "Israel Offers RP Help in Improving Intelligence Gathering," *Manila Times Online*, December 9, 2002.

BEST PRACTICES

Balancing Democracy and Effectiveness

Steven C. Boraz and Thomas C. Bruneau

Intelligence reform will undoubtedly continue to be an extremely important issue, and sometime dilemma, for every democratic nation. For those countries that are (or will be) on the path toward democratic consolidation, restructuring intelligence organizations is, as the authors have made clear throughout this book, an exceptionally difficult task, with many pitfalls and no clear road map. It is also obvious that democratic consolidation cannot occur without establishing effective democratic civilian control of the intelligence apparatus. The chapters on the U.S., British, and French intelligence communities highlight the fact that reforming intelligence can also be complex in established democracies. Moreover, the older democracies show that intelligence reform is not a one-time event but, like democracy itself, requires consistent attention, oversight, and institutional engineering if intelligence is to be effective. Just as establishing control in new democracies is a critical step in democratic consolidation, the ever-present threat of global terrorism requires that countries review their respective intelligence communities to ensure effectiveness.

ADVANCING DEMOCRATIC CONTROL AND EFFECTIVENESS

Our intent here is to aggregate some of the lessons learned in this book, as well as through our experiences, in order to provide some of the best practices for restructuring intelligence to support both democratic control and effectiveness, two of the three components of the trinity we established in the introduction. We cannot begin to capture the richness of concepts and data from the ten individual case studies but seek rather to highlight the most relevant themes for scholars and policymakers.

TABLE 13.1   SUMMARY OF CONTROL MECHANISMS
OF THE COUNTRIES EXAMINED

| Country | Level of development of control mechanism | | | | |
	Executive	Legislative	Judicial	Internal	External
United States	High	High	Medium	High	Medium to high
United Kingdom	High	Low to medium	Low	High	Medium
France	Medium	Low	Low	Medium	High
Brazil	High	Low	Medium	Medium	Medium
Taiwan	High	Low	Low	Medium	Medium
Argentina	High	Medium	Low	Medium	Medium
Romania	High	Medium	Low	Medium	High
South Africa	High	Medium	Medium	Medium	Medium
Russia	Medium	Low	Low	Medium	Low
Philippines	Medium	Low	Low	Low	Low

It seems obvious that the requirements for asserting democratic control over intelligence resemble those for establishing civilian authority over military institutions. The executive branch should provide the overarching direction for an intelligence community by defining its missions; the legislative branch should ensure adherence to organizational, management, personnel, and budgetary structures that are supported in national laws; the judiciary should ensure that intelligence operations are legal and that citizens' rights are upheld; the IC should organize so that no one agency has all the power, and it should work to instill a professional ethos; and external organizations, such as the media and NGOs, should take their watchdog role seriously. These are fundamental requirements that should be met as minimum standards for democratic control. Table 13.1 summarizes how these five control factors, as illustrated to a greater or lesser degree in each chapter, might be evaluated for each of the countries examined in this book.

Effectiveness—except by its absence, as in an intelligence failure—is all but impossible to prove. After all, intelligence is at its most effective when nobody but those directly involved are even aware of it. Yet we believe we can safely assert that effective intelligence depends on a minimal set of requirements. These include a culture that supports the legitimate role of intelligence in a democracy, civilians who are informed and engaged, an interagency process both to coordinate the different intelligence organizations and to challenge assumptions and conclusions, and a cadre of professional civilian and military intelligence officers.

Those leaders who want to exert democratic civilian control and improve the effectiveness of the intelligence apparatus must undertake several tasks that, once begun, will continue. They are not necessarily prioritized and should be pursued simultaneously. And although these recommendations might be criticized as U.S.-centric, they are so only because there is much more data available pertaining to the U.S. intelligence community from which we can draw lessons:

1. Raise public interest and pressure.

2. Increase civilian awareness and competence.

3. Institutionalize processes that support transparency and effectiveness.

4. Foster in society *and* within the intelligence community a political culture that supports the need for intelligence and encourages trust.

5. Professionalize the intelligence services.

Raise Public Interest and Pressure

An important early step in creating effective intelligence under civilian authority is to have an informed public debate about intelligence. Leaders should encourage an open discussion of intelligence policy among representatives from the executive and legislative branches; military, police, and intelligence agencies; other relevant independent government agencies; and in external stakeholders like the media, NGOs, and think tanks. Specific issues should include determining which institutions should have an oversight role and whether an intelligence community is organized properly to support decision makers. The challenge is to break through public apathy toward or fear of the intelligence community. In some older democracies, including Canada, France, Great Britain, and the United States, a fairly regular debate (which is at an abnormal peak in the wake of the 9/11 and WMD commission reports, the Intelligence Reform Act, and the continuing "war" on terrorism) is stimulated by NGOs and the media, which are periodically galvanized by intelligence failures that become public. The role of the media is crucial, and their awareness of intelligence can be encouraged in the same manner as with the public. Again, the debate can be stimulated by the politicians' commitment to establish a policy on intelligence.

A few of the newer democracies have begun to undertake this task. In Argentina, debate was stimulated by a small number of civilians who realized that democratic consolidation requires civilian control over intelligence. The Brazilian government's commitment to revise the intelligence system has generated a public discussion. The Romanian case shows how important a role the media can play in pursuing democratic control of intelligence. Even in the United States, the debate that took place following the publication of the 9/11 Commission Report had a significant impact on U.S. intelligence reform. This kind of open discussion serves numerous important functions. First, it demythologizes intelligence, thereby allowing outsiders to assess its necessity and value to the country more realistically. Second, it creates legitimate positions for civilians who want to become intelligence specialists. And third, it puts pressure on the government to be more transparent.

Increase Civilian Awareness and Competence

A second requirement is to motivate civilians, especially those in defense ministries and legislatures, to learn about intelligence so that they can control the IC and see whether it is doing its job. In virtually all authoritarian regimes, intelligence was monopolized by the military, and civilians had little role or no role whatsoever. This can even be the case in older democracies, as we have seen in France. Countries will be unable to control intelligence unless they prepare civilians well enough both to understand what intelligence is all about and to achieve some degree of cooperation, if not respect, from the intelligence professionals. This process is not easy, but it has to start somewhere. It should begin with the formal and public commitment by a government to review its intelligence functions, with the goal of establishing a new policy. In Brazil and South Africa, this was able to happen mainly because of political and institutional bargains that resulted from democratic transitions. The commitment must also open the possibility for civilian positions in intelligence. As in civil-military relations in general, civilians will not come forward if they cannot anticipate viable careers. One specific step countries can take is to open up their military intelligence training schools to civilians who might take part in oversight. Getting more civilians involved in the intelligence process supports greater transparency in any democratic system.

Civilians can also begin to learn about intelligence by reading the unclassified literature from several countries and taking advantage of cooperative training arrangements in intelligence with other nations. There are several organizations that can help with both generating the debate mentioned above and training civilians to better understand intelligence. For instance, the Naval Postgraduate School in Monterey, California, offers seminars in residence and abroad and a semester-long course on intelligence oversight. The Geneva Centre for the Democratic Control of Armed Forces (DCAF) also offers courses and publishes training materials.

Institutionalize Processes That Support Transparency and Effectiveness

Another task is to institutionalize the functions that support effective intelligence—namely, security strategy development, feedback mechanisms, and intelligence coordination. These functions should be updated in each branch of the government that has an oversight role. For instance, part of the democratic process is the routine transfer of power in the executive branch. While it is certainly the norm for a new president or prime minister to update or develop his or her security strategy upon entering office, a formalized national security structure (i.e., one that is written into policy or law) can ensure a smoother, more transparent process during executive changeovers. A legal framework that requires this step goes a long way toward providing direction to an IC. Further, a chief executive's security planning structure should include civilian intelligence or strategy coordinators —similar to the national security adviser in the United States—who can greatly enhance the national security strategy drafting process.

To promote greater effectiveness, governments should create standing committees that regularly review how well the intelligence community is doing its job of supporting national security; these committees should be formed in the appropriate branches of government where access to intelligence might be required. Such committees can substantially improve collection, analysis, and coordination, as well as deter potential abuse. A standing oversight committee can also be entrusted to review budgets and manpower decisions, provide leadership, and make organizational recommendations to the government. We are convinced that the best location for an institution such as this is in the legislature. "Select" committees, such as those in the U.S. Congress, provide legislative oversight through smaller internal organizations that can help mitigate the disclosure of secret information or its use for political purposes.

A necessary and natural tension will exist between an oversight body as described above and the executive branch, for which the intelligence services ostensibly work. For oversight to function properly, legislatures must be able to call intelligence personnel into an inquiry (a closed one if necessary to discuss classified information), and intelligence personnel must report. What we have often seen, even in established democracies, is the intelligence services or the executive branch cite national security or operational security in order to stall when there may be a question of legality or impropriety. That said, countries should ensure that inquiries are not so burdensome as to hamper the overall effectiveness of the IC—admittedly a difficult balance to achieve. Countries establishing legislative oversight would also do well to follow the Argentine approach, which provides a legal mechanism to deter the release of secret information.

Institutional changes within the IC are important as well. As noted throughout this work, particularly in the case of the United States, resource allocation for and orientation of intelligence have focused on support to military operations. Military imperatives, however, can have a negative impact on longer-term analysis. Thus it is very important that intelligence agencies ensure a proper balance between tactical (i.e., military) intelligence and strategic intelligence and set aside resources to guarantee this balance. This is not to say that supporting military requirements is necessarily harmful. When the military takes the lead in directing the IC, however, its leaders tend to have a natural bias toward supporting tactical issues. While such elements surely have their place in intelligence, tilting too far in that direction will not serve policymakers well.

As has also been shown throughout this book, one of the greatest impediments to creating an effective IC is the bureaucratic infighting that arises when multiple intelligence organizations are at work. While we fully endorse the practice of dispersing information, and thus power, to separate agencies, we urge intelligence leaders to emphasize and formalize requirements for joint or interagency operations, determine the function of each member in competitive intelligence, and ensure that one lead organization or person is empowered to speak for the IC as a unified voice to the legislative, judicial, and executive branches of government.

If countries do in fact invest power in the hands of one individual in the form of an intelligence director, they should give thought to making the position a long-term one that is out of cycle with elections of the chief executive. Many argue that an intelligence chief not selected by the sitting president or prime minister would be unable to develop the trust necessary between the top executive and his chief intelligence adviser and thus would diminish the importance of intelligence. While this is a valid argument, we believe that insulating a national intelligence director from politics is more important to national security than is a personal relationship with the chief executive. One reason is that chief executives typically rely on many more people than just one intelligence adviser to provide guidance on national security issues. Further, intelligence personnel can establish credibility with the civilians they serve by being forthright, having their facts straight, and displaying integrity beyond reproach. Finally, a longer fixed term can afford adequate time to draft and implement a strategic vision for an IC, provide continuity as political administrations turn over, and most importantly, foster the political independence and impartiality the IC needs to support national security.

Foster a Supportive Political Culture in Society and within the Intelligence Community

A fourth and broader task is to foster a political culture that supports the legitimate role of intelligence in a democracy but does not allow it to run rampant. This undertaking should be designed to increase the level of trust between the IC and the organizations created to oversee it, as well as among members of the IC itself. As civilians learn about intelligence through some of the various means noted above, they increase their credibility vis-à-vis the intelligence community and thereby become more trusted. Having civilians and intelligence personnel learn about intelligence together, for example, can help forge long-lasting personal bonds that may become the cornerstone of achieving results in a bureaucracy.

Former defense secretary James R. Schlesinger, also a former director of Central Intelligence, has made this point: "[T]o preserve secrecy, especially in a democracy, security must be part of an accepted pattern of behavior outside of government and inside."[1] The responsibility must go in both directions: democratically elected civilians have authority over the intelligence community and in turn pledge not to release classified information for personal or political reasons. Although trust cannot be legislated, the passage of laws that penalize the release of secret information would go a long way to allay concerns in the intelligence community about opening up to more civilian interface.

We are certain that establishing trust is a critical factor in support of an IC with multiple agencies. As noted above, designation of lead agencies or a single director can help balance competition among agencies. An independent oversight system outside of the executive may help to establish trust, because resources ideally would go to agencies based on need rather than favor. Trust among agencies is critical to ensure information sharing as well. In many cases we have seen, one agency with knowledge is reluctant to provide it to another for various bureaucratic reasons. But if trust exists, then information sharing, and the coordination and improved effectiveness that go with it, will follow.

Professionalize the Intelligence Services

The fifth task, professionalization, is probably the most fundamental aspect of internal control and is also crucial for effectiveness. Professionalism can be the most difficult goal to achieve in transitions to democracy, yet it is indispensable to the creation of a cadre of individuals who will form the foundation of an ethical and effective institution. This issue was highlighted by all of the authors whose chapters dealt with new democracies. The conceptualization of intelligence as a profession is particularly apt because, more than in any other single function in a democracy, its practitioners are controlled more by professional norms than by regulations. In contrast, doctors are regulated by the legal system and licensing boards, lawyers by the legal system and bar associations, politicians by the legal system and elections, and the armed forces by budgets, promotions, and myriad civilian control mechanisms. In the final analysis, internal standards have more influence on intelligence professionals than external structures that may or may not exist. Intelligence personnel are often granted the impunity to break laws abroad and have tremendous leeway even within their own country in support of national defense. Secrecy allows them to operate with an unusual amount of autonomy. They are also ensconced in a bureaucracy with other like-minded personnel, tend to develop a closed-club mentality, and are usually very suspicious of "outsiders," including at times their superiors. Thus, establishing a high standard of professionalism is of critical import to democratic control.[2]

INTELLIGENCE AS A PROFESSION

A profession can be defined in terms of three criteria: expertise, corporateness, and responsibility.[3] In the case of intelligence, the criteria are as follows. First, "expertise" is defined in line with the four intelligence functions: collection, analysis, counterintelligence, and covert action. The range of what intelligence professionals do is extremely broad, and there are few common educational requirements for intelligence professionals even among the various intelligence organizations within one country. What we find typically lacking is an educational structure, both initial and continuing, that cultivates a baseline of knowledge or certifies intelligence professionals as "experts" in, say, analysis or counterintelligence. Further, there tends to be an assumption that a good analyst will make a good counterintelligence expert. While that may be the case, there is often no formal training for the individual making the transition. Creating institutions that provide a basis for all intelligence personnel, as well as opportunities to refine skills after a certain term within the profession, could be an important step in creating expertise and can go a long way to improving effectiveness.

"Corporateness," that which unifies or characterizes individuals as intelligence professionals, is manifested in access to classified information. And unlike other professions, which feature certain limited aspects of patient or client privacy, the intelligence professional is almost totally defined by secrecy. Intelligence professionals enter their profession via security clearances, as doctors enter their profession through boards, internships, and residencies; professors by comprehensive examinations and PhD dissertations; and lawyers by law school and bar exams. In intelligence everything is compartmented; different levels of clearances, plus the "need to know," determine access. Even officers with similarly high clearances do not, and are not supposed to, discuss information unless they have "need to know," in terms of their current projects and responsibilities. Having security clearances and secretly working together on classified information and projects enhance identification among intelligence personnel as members of a unique club. A certain sense of impunity may also develop, since if nobody else knows, then how can those who don't know control those who do? Effectiveness can be enhanced in the IC realm by ensuring that standards are set and followed across all intelligence services within a country and that penalties for disclosure are meted out with equity.

Third, the "responsibility" of the intelligence professional is to serve in defense of the state. But consideration of the first two criteria (expertise in intelligence and secrecy) can result in a profession that largely governs itself according to its own definition of responsibility. In new democracies this situation is doubly serious, because the state was not previously accountable to the general population and the intelligence agents may not have been responsible even to the small group controlling the state, as in an independent security state. Who can know and who is to control? The sense of responsibility is extraordinarily important: even in stable democracies, enough incidents come to light to cause concern that IC officers are not serving the state, are serving it in limited organizational terms and not in accordance with those of the democratically elected political leadership, do not have a strong enough corporate ethic to say no when they've been told to do something illegal, or feel their illegal activity is justified because it is in support of national defense. Phillip Heymann sums up this dilemma in apt fashion: "The deepest problem of controlling domestic intelligence agencies is that they have both the capacity to hide disobedience and a justification for not taking constraints seriously."[4] Reconciling this attitude with the procedures and culture of democracy is difficult, and major efforts must be made to ensure a rigorous adherence to law. One way countries have ameliorated this dilemma is by placing legal counsel and inspectors general *within* particular intelligence agencies. Another strategy that is helpful is to institute routine training on what intelligence officials can and cannot do.

ESTABLISHING PROFESSIONALISM

Major efforts must be made in new democracies to promote and inculcate a sense of professional responsibility by making intelligence officers and agencies accountable to the state via the democratically elected leadership. One way to do this is by committing great attention and resources to recruitment and training of professionals and requiring that they remain involved in the larger polity and society. The specifics of this prescription have to be defined separately for each nation. One of the biggest obstacles to achieving this result is that governments will most easily recruit retired military men and women into civilian intelligence positions. While they may have taken off the uniform, their service attitudes and loyalty tend to remain. If new, nonmilitary personnel cannot be found, however, then can the ethic of responsibility among retired military members be changed? In most countries little explicit attention is given to promoting this ethic.[5] In the older democracies, the larger society supports responsibility to the democratic state, and political institutions are generally not under question, so there is less need to promote the responsibility ethic. In newer democracies, the need to promote it actively and explicitly is clear, as is the need to encourage an open debate on intelligence and to bring civilians into the field.[6]

It is apparent that professionalization of the intelligence apparatus is crucial to both democratic control and effectiveness. We believe it is the most important aspect for internal control and provides the best starting point for reform toward effectiveness.

Quantifying Effectiveness

There is one last issue regarding improving the effectiveness of intelligence that bears discussion: measuring intelligence.[7] There are many who believe that a set of definable and quantifiable measurements, or metrics, can be identified and analyzed for the intelligence field. We agree that it is possible to determine how many signals or images are collected, whether or not spies have been discovered, or whether a covert action succeeded in its aim; however, determining whether analysis was right or wrong can be very problematic. For example, if intelligence analysis was used by policymakers to change a course of action, it would be very difficult to determine whether the reaction from the policy change came as a result of the intelligence. In short, who can know how the future might be altered based on changes made in the present? Therefore we recommend that any use of metrics be done with caution. We believe that if democratic norms are established and coordination, professionalism, transparency, and trust exist, then a knowledgeable cadre of politicians controlling intelligence organizations will "know a good one when they see it."

FINAL THOUGHTS

All nations engage in intelligence activities on one scale or another; they must, because other countries do. No nation can afford not to know what is going on outside and inside its borders and, if necessary, counter other countries' efforts to influence its internal developments. These intelligence activities are designed to inform policy and to support operations. If no outside entity is providing policy and/or operational objectives to the IC, then intelligence has no value to anyone but its own practitioners.

In the midst of democratic consolidation, seeking to ensure democratic control over intelligence is both necessary and extremely difficult. Yet, in many countries there is still virtually no public recognition of this need. Without decisive action to support democratic controls, an authoritarian intelligence apparatus will remain a state within the state and undermine democratic consolidation. Like all else in civilmilitary relations, the many challenges require continual efforts on the part of civilians and officers to achieve the most appropriate balance of efficiency and transparency for the country. As documented throughout this book, many countries have undertaken reform of their intelligence systems and generated a public debate on the matter. Establishing democratic control over intelligence will help achieve democratic consolidation as well as create effective intelligence organizations, a twenty-first-century imperative.

NOTES

1. Quoted in Adda Bozeman, "Political Intelligence in Non-Western Societies: Suggestions for Comparative Research," in Roy Godson, ed., *Comparing Foreign Intelligence: The U.S., the USSR, the U.K. & the Third World* (Washington: Pergamon-Brassey's, 1988), 133.

2. Although Mark Lowenthal doesn't deal specifically with the issue of professionalism in new democracies, his recommendations are useful in general terms for the intelligence profession. See Mark M. Lowenthal, "Tribal Tongues: Intelligence Consumers, Intelligence Producers," *Washington Quarterly* 15 (Winter 1992): 152–168. A useful source for further discussion on the topic of professionalism is Russell Swenson and Susana Lemozy, eds., *Intelligence Professionalism in the Americas* (Washington, DC: JMIC Edition, 2003).

3. While the sociological literature on professions is huge, going back at least

to Max Weber, that which is most pertinent here is the literature on the military as a profession. The classic work is Samuel P. Huntington, *The Soldier and the State* (Cambridge, MA: Harvard University Press, 1957). The most useful additions and critiques include the following: Bengt Abrahamsson, *Military Professionalization and Political Power* (Beverly Hills, CA: Sage Publications, 1972); and Peter D. Feaver, "The Civil-Military Problematique: Huntington, Janowitz, and the Question of Civilian Control," *Armed Forces and Society* 23, no. 2 (Winter 1996): 149–177. For broader insights, see also Andrew Abbott, *The System of Professions: An Essay on the Division of Expert Labor* (Chicago: University of Chicago Press, 1988); and J. Nicholas Ziegler, "Institutions, Elites, and Technological Change in France and Germany," *World Politics* 47, no. 3 (April 1995): 341–372.

4. Philip Heymann, "Controlling Intelligence Agencies," Project on Justice in Times of Transition, Harvard University, Cambridge, MA, 2000.

5. This is precisely what Glenn P. Hastedt advocates: "Only by seeking to structure how intelligence professionals see their job can one hope to prevent abuses from occurring in the first place or ensure responsiveness." See Hastedt, *Controlling Intelligence* (Portland, OR: Frank Cass, 1991), 14.

6. The other side of recruitment is retirement of intelligence professionals. It is important for governments to ensure that their intelligence organizations develop stable career progression based on merit, including provisions for decent retirement after service. This ensures loyalty and gives professionals a viable option to leave the services if desired, rather than turn their highly specialized skills to illegal activities.

7. For example, metrics were an important topic of discussion at a RAND/Office of the Director of National Intelligence–sponsored conference held in June 2005 and attended by many leading intelligence authors and practitioners. The findings are available in Gregory F. Treverton, Seth G. Jones, Steven Boraz, and Philip Lipscy, *Toward a Theory of Intelligence: Workshop Report* (Santa Monica, CA: RAND, 2006).

SELECTED BIBLIOGRAPHY

These selections are meant to provide the broadest references for civil-military relations, intelligence, and publications with themes regarding democracy. A much more thorough bibliography was compiled by Greta E. Marlatt of the Naval Postgraduate School and is available at http://library.nps.navy.mil/home/bibs/inttoc.htm.

BOOKS, JOURNAL ARTICLES, GOVERNMENT DOCUMENTS

Abbott, Andrew. *The System of Professions: An Essay on the Division of Expert Labor.* Chicago: University of Chicago Press, 1988.

Abrahamsson, Bengt. *Military Professionalization and Political Power.* Beverly Hills, CA: Sage Publications, 1972.

Andrew, Christopher. *For the President's Eyes Only: Secret Intelligence and the American Presidency from Washington to Bush.* New York: Harper Collins, 1995.

Andrew, Christopher, and David Dilks, eds. *The Missing Dimension: Governments and Intelligence Communities in the Twentieth Century.* Urbana: University of Illinois Press, 1984.

Andrew, Christopher, and Vasili Mitrokhin. *The Sword and the Shield: The Mitrokhin Archive and the Secret History of the KGB.* New York: Basic Books, 1999.

Antunes, Priscila, and Marco A. C. Cepik. "The New Brazilian Intelligence System: An Institutional Assessment." *International Journal of Intelligence and Counterintelligence* 16, no. 3 (Summer 2003): 349–373.

Aspin-Brown Commission. "The Evolution of the U.S. Intelligence Community —An Historical Perspective." Appendix A in *Preparing for the 21st Century: An Appraisal of U.S. Intelligence*, Report of the Commission on the Roles and Capabilities of the United States Intelligence Community, March 1, 1996. Washington, DC: U.S. Government Printing Office, 1996. http://www.access.gpo.gov/intelligence/int/into22.html.

Bar-Joseph, Uri. *Intelligence Intervention in the Politics of Democratic States: The*

United States, Israel, and Britain. University Park: Pennsylvania State University Press, 1995.

Berkowitz, Bruce D., and Allan E. Goodman. *Best Truth: Intelligence and Security in the Information Age*. New Haven, CT: Yale University Press, 2000.

Best, Richard A., Jr. *Covert Action: An Effective Instrument of U.S. Policy?* CRS Report for Congress. Washington, DC: Congressional Research Service, Library of Congress, 1996.

———. *Proposals for Intelligence Reorganization, 1949–2004*. CRS Report for Congress. Washington, DC: Congressional Research Service, Library of Congress, July 29, 2004.

Born, Hans. "Democratic and Parliamentary Oversight of the Intelligence Services: Best Practices and Procedures." Geneva Centre for the Democratic Control of Armed Forces (DCAF), Working Paper Series no. 20, May 2002.

———, ed. *Parliamentary Oversight of the Security Sector: Principles, Mechanisms, and Practices*. Geneva: Geneva Centre for the Democratic Control of Armed Forces, 2003.

Born, Hans, and Ian Leigh. *Making Intelligence Accountable: Legal Standards and Best Practice for Oversight of Intelligence Agencies*. Oslo: Publishing House of the Parliament of Norway, 2005.

———, with Loch K. Johnson and Ian Leigh, eds. *Who's Watching the Spies? Establishing Intelligence Service Accountability*. Dulles, VA: Potomac Books, 2005.

Bozeman, Adda. *Strategic Intelligence and Statecraft: Selected Essays*. Washington, DC: Brassey's, 1992.

Bruneau, Thomas C. "Controlling Intelligence in New Democracies." *International Journal of Intelligence and Counterintelligence* 14, no. 3 (Fall 2001): 323–341.

———, and Scott Tollefson, eds. *Who Guards the Guardians and How: Democratic Civil-Military Relations*. Austin: University of Texas Press, 2006.

Carl, Leo D. *The CIA Insider's Dictionary of U.S. and Foreign Intelligence and Counterintelligence and Tradecraft*. Washington, DC: NIBC Press, 1996.

Chalk, Peter, and William Rosenau. *Confronting the Enemy Within*. Santa Monica, CA: RAND, 2004.

Chapman, Bert. *Researching National Security and Intelligence Policy*. Washington, DC: CQ Press, 2004.

Church Committee reports. http://www.aarclibrary.org/publib/church/reports/contents.htm.

Clarke, Richard. *Against All Enemies*. New York: Simon and Schuster, 2004.

Clegg, Stewart. *Frameworks of Power*. London: Sage, 1989.

Cogan, Charles G. *Oldest Allies, Guarded Friends: The United States and France since 1940*. Westport, CT: Praeger, 1994.

Collier, David, and Steven Levitsky. "Democracy with Adjectives: Conceptual Innovation in Comparative Research." *World Politics* 49, no. 3 (April 1997): 430–451.

Commission on the Roles and Capabilities of the United States Intelligence Community. *Preparing for the 21st Century: An Appraisal of U.S. Intelligence.* March 1, 1996. Washington, DC: U.S. Government Printing Office, 1996. http://www .access.gpo.gov/intelligence/int/into22.html.

The Commission on the Intelligence Capabilities of the United States Regarding Weapons of Mass Destruction. Washington, DC: U.S. Government Printing Office, 2005.

Dahl, Robert. *Polyarchy: Participation and Opposition.* New Haven, CT: Yale University Press, 1971.

Dandeker, Christopher. *Surveillance, Power, and Modernity: Bureaucracy and Discipline from 1700 to the Present Day.* Cambridge, UK: Polity Press, 1990.

Der Derian, James. *Antidiplomacy: Spies, Terror, Speed, and War.* Cambridge, MA: Blackwell, 1992.

Deutch, John, and Jeffrey H. Smith. "Smarter Intelligence." *Foreign Policy* (January–February 2002): 64–69.

Diamond, Larry, and Marc F. Plattner, eds. *The Global Divergences of Democracies.* Baltimore: Johns Hopkins University Press, 2001.

———. *The Global Resurgence of Democracy.* Baltimore: Johns Hopkins University Press, 1993.

Dominguez, Jorge, and Michael Shifter, eds. *Constructing Democratic Governance in Latin America.* Baltimore: Johns Hopkins University Press, 2003.

Dziak, John J. *Chekisty: A History of the KGB.* Lexington, MA: D. C. Heath, 1988.

"The Evolution of the U.S. Intelligence Community—An Historical Overview." *See* Aspin-Brown Commission.

Feaver, Peter D. "The Civil-Military Problematique: Huntington, Janowitz, and the Question of Civilian Control." *Armed Forces and Society* 23, no. 2 (Winter 1996): 149–177.

Fitch, Samuel. *The Armed Forces and Democracy in Latin America.* Baltimore: Johns Hopkins University Press, 1998.

Foley, Michael W., and Bob Edwards. "The Paradox of Civil Society." *Journal of Democracy* 7, no. 3 (1996): 9–39.

Foreign Assistance Act of 1974. Public Law 93-559, § 32, 88 *Stat.* 1795, 1804 (1974). Codified at 22 *U.S. Code* § 2422 (1988). Repealed in 1991.

Gates, Robert M. "The CIA and American Foreign Policy." *Foreign Affairs* 66, no. 2 (Winter 1987–1988): 215–230.

———. *From the Shadows: The Ultimate Insider's Story of Five Presidents and How They Won the Cold War.* New York: Simon and Schuster, 1996.

Geddes, Barbara. *Paradigms and Sand Castles: Theory Building and Research Design in Comparative Politics.* Ann Arbor: University of Michigan Press, 2003.

———. *Politician's Dilemma: Building State Capacity in Latin America.* Berkeley and Los Angeles: University of California Press, 1994.

Geneva Centre for the Democratic Control of Armed Forces (DCAF). "Intelligence Services and Democracy." DCAF Working Paper Series, no. 13, April 2002.

George, Roger Z., and Robert D. Kline. *Intelligence and the National Security Strate-*

gist: Enduring Issues and Challenges. Washington, DC: National Defense University Press, 2004.

Giddens, Anthony. *The Nation State and Violence.* Berkeley and Los Angeles: University of California Press, 1985.

Gill, Peter. "Democratic and Parliamentary Accountability of Intelligence Services after September 11th." Geneva Centre for the Democratic Control of Armed Forces (DCAF), Working Paper Series, no. 103, January 2003.

———. *Policing Politics: Security Intelligence and the Liberal Democratic State.* Portland, OR: Frank Cass, 1994.

———. *Rounding Up the Usual Suspects?* Aldershot, UK: Ashgate, 2000.

Godson, Roy. *Comparing Foreign Intelligence: The U.S., the USSR, the U.K., and the Third World.* Washington, DC: Pergamon-Brassey's, 1988.

———. *Dirty Tricks or Trump Cards: U.S. Covert Action and Counterintelligence.* Washington, DC: Brassey's, 1995.

———. *Intelligence Requirements for the 1980s: Intelligence and Policy.* Lexington, MA: Lexington Books, 1986.

———. *Intelligence Requirements for the 1990s: Collection, Analysis, Counterintelligence, and Covert Action.* Lexington, MA: Lexington Books, 1989.

Godson, Roy, and James J. Wirtz, eds. *Strategic Denial and Deception: The Twenty-First Century Challenge.* New Brunswick, NJ: Transaction Publishers, 2002.

Godson, Roy, Ernest R. May, and Gary Schmitt, eds. *U.S. Intelligence at the Crossroads: Agendas for Reform.* Washington, DC: National Strategy and Information Center, 1995.

Hall, Peter A., and Rosemary C. R. Taylor. "Political Science and the Three New Institutionalisms." *Political Studies* 44 (1996): 936–957.

Handel, Michael, ed. *Intelligence and Military Operations.* London: Frank Cass and Co., 1990.

———. *Leaders and Intelligence.* London: Frank Cass and Co., 1989.

———. *War, Strategy and Intelligence.* London: Frank Cass and Co., 1989.

Hastedt, Glenn P. *Controlling Intelligence.* Portland, OR: Frank Cass and Co., 1991.

———. "Towards the Comparative Study of Intelligence." *Conflict Quarterly* 11, no. 3 (Summer 1991): 55–72.

Herman, Michael. "Intelligence and Policy: A Comment." *Intelligence and National Security* 6, no. 1 (January 1991): 229–239.

———. *Intelligence Power in Peace and War.* Cambridge: Cambridge University Press, 1996.

———. *Intelligence Services in the Information Age.* London: Frank Cass and Co., 2001.

Heymann, Philip. "Controlling Intelligence Agencies." Cambridge, MA: Harvard University, The Project on Justice in Times of Transition, 2000.

Hibbert, Reginald. "Intelligence and Policy." *Intelligence and National Security* 5, no. 1 (January 1990): 110–128.

Higley, John, and Richard Gunther, eds. *Elites and Democratic Consolidation in Latin America and Southern Europe.* Cambridge: Cambridge University Press, 1992.

Holt, Pat M. *Secret Intelligence and Public Policy: A Dilemma of Democracy.* Washington, DC: Congressional Quarterly Press, 1995.

Hulnick, Arthur S. *Fixing the Spy Machine: Preparing American Intelligence for the Twenty-first Century.* Westport, CT: Praeger, 1999.

Huntington, Samuel P. *Political Order in Changing Societies.* New Haven, CT: Yale University Press, 1968.

———. *The Soldier and the State.* Cambridge, MA: Harvard University Press, 1957.

———. *The Third Wave: Democratization in the Late Twentieth Century.* Norman: University of Oklahoma Press, 1991.

Iraq's Weapons of Mass Destruction: The Assessment of the British Government. September 24, 2002. http://www.number10.gov.uk/output/Page271.asp.

Jervis, Robert. "Intelligence and Foreign Policy." *International Security* 11, no. 3 (Winter 1986–1987): 141–161.

———. "Reports, Politics, and Intelligence Failures: The Case of Iraq." *Journal of Strategic Studies* 29, no. 1 (January 2006).

———. "Strategic Intelligence and Effective Policy." *Studies in Intelligence* (Winter 1989).

Johnson, Loch K. *America's Secret Power: The CIA in a Democratic Society.* New York: Oxford University Press, 1989.

———. *Bombs, Bugs, Drugs, and Thugs: Intelligence and America's Quest for Security.* New York: New York University Press, 2000.

———. "Bricks and Mortar for a Theory of Intelligence." *Comparative Strategy* 22, no. 1 (January 2003): 1–28.

———. *Secret Agencies: U.S. Intelligence in a Hostile World.* New Haven, CT: Yale University Press, 1996.

———. "Preface to a Theory of Strategic Intelligence." *International Journal of Intelligence and Counterintelligence* 16, no. 4 (October–December 2003): 638–663.

Johnson, Loch K., and James J. Wirtz, eds. *Strategic Intelligence: Windows into a Secret World: An Anthology.* Los Angeles: Roxbury Publishing Co., 2004.

Kegley, Charles, and Eugene R. Wittkopf. *American Foreign Policy.* 5th ed. New York: St. Martin's Press, 1996.

Keller, William W. *The Liberals and J. Edgar Hoover: Rise and Fall of a Domestic Intelligence State.* Princeton, NJ: Princeton University Press, 1989.

Kent, Sherman. *Strategic Intelligence for American World Policy.* Princeton, NJ: Princeton University Press, 1966.

Knight, Amy. *Beria: Stalin's First Lieutenant.* Princeton, NJ: Princeton University Press, 1993.

———. *Spies without Cloaks.* Princeton, NJ: Princeton University Press, 1996.

Knott, Stephen F. "The Great Republican Transformation of Oversight." *Inter-*

national Journal of Intelligence and Counterintelligence 13, no. 1 (Spring 2000): 49–63.

———. *Secret and Sanctioned: Covert Operations and the American Presidency.* New York: Oxford University Press, 1996.

Koh, Harold H. *The National Security Constitution: Sharing Power after the Iran Contra Affair.* New Haven, CT: Yale University Press, 1990.

Kramer, Mark. "Out of Communism: Reforming the Russian Legal System." *Current History* (October 2003): 331.

———. *Oversight of Russia's Intelligence and Security Agencies: The Need for and Prospects of Democratic Control.* PONARS Policy Memo 281, Center for Strategic and International Studies, Washington, DC, October 2002.

Lahneman, William J. "Knowledge Sharing in the Intelligence Community after 9/11." *International Journal of Intelligence and Counterintelligence* 17, no. 4 (Winter 2004–2005): 614–633.

———. "Outsourcing the IC's Stovepipes?" *International Journal of Intelligence and Counterintelligence* 16, no. 4 (Winter 2003–2004): 573–593.

Laqueur, Walter. *The Uses and Limits of Intelligence.* New Brunswick, NJ: Transaction Publishers, 1993.

———. *World of Secrets: The Uses and Limits of Intelligence.* New Brunswick, NJ: Transaction Publishers, 1985.

Lijphart, Arend. *Patterns of Democracy: Government Forms and Performance in Thirty-six Countries.* New Haven, CT: Yale University Press, 1999.

Linz, Juan J., and Alfred Stepan. *Problems of Democratic Transition and Consolidation: Southern Europe, South America, and Post-Communist Europe.* Baltimore: Johns Hopkins University Press, 1996.

Lowenthal, Mark M. *Intelligence: From Secrets to Policy.* 3rd ed. Washington, DC: Congressional Quarterly Press, 2006.

———. "Tribal Tongues: Intelligence Consumers, Intelligence Producers." *Washington Quarterly* 15 (Winter 1992): 152–168.

———. *The U.S. Intelligence Community: An Annotated Bibliography.* New York: Garland Publishers, 1994.

Lustgarten, L., and Ian Leigh. *In from the Cold: National Security and Parliamentary Democracy.* Oxford, UK: Clarendon Press, 1994.

Lyon, David. *Surveillance after September 11.* Cambridge, UK: Polity Press, 2003.

———. *Surveillance Society.* Buckingham, UK: Open University Press, 2001.

Macdonald, Douglas J. *Adventures in Chaos: American Intervention for Reform in the Third World.* Cambridge, MA: Harvard University Press, 1992.

Mainwairing, Scott, and Matthew S. Shugart, eds. *Presidentialism and Democracy in Latin America.* Cambridge: Cambridge University Press, 1997.

Manget, Fred F. "Presidential Powers and Foreign Intelligence Operations." *International Journal of Intelligence and Counterintelligence* 5, no. 2 (Spring 1992): 131–148.

Migdal, Joel S. *Strong Societies and Weak States: State-Society Relations and State Capabilities in the Third World.* Princeton, NJ: Princeton University Press, 1988.

9/11 Commission. *The 9/11 Commission Report: Final Report of the National Commission on Terrorist Attacks upon the United States.* New York: W. W. Norton and Co., July 2004. http://www.gpoaccess.gov/911/.

O'Connell, Kevin M. "Thinking about Intelligence Comparatively." *Brown Journal of World Affairs* 11, no. 1 (Summer-Fall 2004): 189-199.

Odom, William E. *Fixing Intelligence: For a More Secure America.* 2nd ed. New Haven, CT: Yale University Press, 2004.

Odom, William E., et al. *Modernizing Intelligence: Structure and Change for the 21st Century.* Fairfax, VA: National Institute for Public Policy, 1997.

O'Donnell, Guillermo. "Comparative Politics and Democratic Theory." *Studies in Comparative International Development* 36, no. 1 (2001): 7-36.

————. "Delegative Democracy." *Journal of Democracy* 5, no. 1 (1994): 55-69.

Olson, James M. "The Ten Commandments of Counterintelligence." *Studies in Intelligence,* no. 11 (Fall-Winter 2001): 81-87.

Ott, Marvin C. "Partisanship and the Decline of Intelligence Oversight." *International Journal of Intelligence and Counterintelligence* 16, no. 1 (Winter 2003): 69-94.

Pion-Berlin, David, ed. *Civil-Military Relations in Latin America.* Chapel Hill: University of North Carolina Press, 2001.

Porch, Douglas. *The French Secret Services: From the Dreyfus Affair to Desert Storm.* New York: Farrar, Straus and Giroux, 1995.

Powell, Walter W., and Paul J. DiMaggio, eds. *The New Institutionalism in Organizational Analysis.* Chicago and London: University of Chicago Press, 1991.

Przeworski, Adam (series ed.), Michael E. Alvarez, Jose Antonio Cheibub, and Fernando Limongi. *Democracy and Development: Political Institutions and Well-Being in the World, 1950-1990.* Cambridge, UK: Cambridge University Press, 2000.

Przeworski, Adam, Susan Carol Stokes, and Bernard Manin, eds. *Democracy, Accountability, and Representation.* Cambridge: Cambridge University Press, 1999.

Purdum, Todd S. *A Time of Our Choosing: America's War in Iraq.* New York: Times Books, Henry Holt and Co., 2003.

Ranelagh, John. *The Agency: The Rise and Decline of the CIA.* New York: Simon and Schuster, 1987.

Richelson, Jeffrey. *A Century of Spies: Intelligence in the Twentieth Century.* New York: Oxford, University Press, 1995.

————. *The U.S. Intelligence Community.* 4th ed. Boulder, CO: Westview Press, 1999.

Richelson, Jeffrey, and Desmond Ball. *The Ties That Bind: Intelligence Cooperation Between the UK/USA Countries—the United Kingdom, the United States of America, Canada, Australia, and New Zealand.* Boston, MA: Allen & Unwin, 1985.

Rindskopf, Elizabeth R. "Intelligence Oversight in a Democracy." *Houston Journal of International Law* 11, no. 1 (1988): 21–30.

Schedler, Andreas. "Measuring Democratic Consolidation." *Studies in Comparative International Development* 36, no. 1 (Spring 2001): 66–93.

Scott, John. *Power.* Cambridge, UK: Polity Press, 2001.

Scott, W. Richard. *Institutions and Organizations.* Thousand Oaks, CA: Sage Publications, 1995.

———. *Organization: Rational, Natural, and Open Systems.* 5th ed. Upper Saddle River, NJ: Prentice Hall, 2003.

Shulsky, Abram N. *Silent Warfare: Understanding the World of Intelligence.* 2nd ed. Revised by Gary J. Schmitt. Washington, DC: Brassey's, 1993.

Shultz, Richard H., Roy Godson, and George Quester, eds. *Security Studies in the 21st Century.* Washington, DC: Brassey's, 1997.

Silverberg, Marshall. "The Separation of Powers and Control of the CIA's Covert Operations." *Texas Law Review* 68 (1990): 575–601.

Snider, L. Britt. *Sharing Secrets with Lawmakers: Congress as a User of Intelligence.* Washington, DC: Center for the Study of Intelligence, February 1997.

Steinberg, David Joel. *The Philippines: A Singular and a Plural Place.* 4th edition. Boulder, CO: Westview Press, 2000.

Stepan, Alfred. *Rethinking Military Politics: Brazil and the Southern Cone.* Princeton, NJ: Princeton University Press, 1988.

Swenson, Russell, ed. *Intelligence for Multilateral Decision and Action.* Washington, DC: JMIC, 1997.

Swenson, Russell, and Susana Lemozy, eds. *Intelligence Professionalism in the Americas.* Washington, DC: JMIC Edition, 2003.

Tilly, Charles. *The Politics of Collective Violence.* Cambridge, UK: Cambridge University Press, 2003.

Treverton, Gregory F. *Reshaping National Intelligence for an Age of Information.* Cambridge: Cambridge University Press, 2003.

Trinkunas, Harold. "Crafting Civilian Control in Emerging Democracies: Argentina and Venezuela." *Journal of Interamerican Studies and World Affairs* 42, no. 3 (Fall 2000): 77–109.

Tsypkin, Mikhail, "The Committee for Defense and State Security of the USSR Supreme Soviet." *Report on the USSR* 2, no. 19 (1990): 8–11.

Turner, Stansfield. *Secrecy and Democracy: The CIA in Transition.* Boston, MA: Houghton Mifflin, 1985.

United Kingdom. House of Commons. *Report of the Inquiry into the Circumstances Surrounding the Death of Dr. David Kelly C.M.G.* HC 247, January 2004.

———. *Review of Intelligence on Weapons of Mass Destruction.* HC 898, July 14, 2004.

———. Foreign Affairs Committee. *The Decision to Go to War in Iraq.* HC 813-I, 2003.

United Kingdom. Intelligence and Security Commission. *Iraqi Weapons of Mass*

Destruction: Intelligence and Assessments. Cm. 5972. London: Stationery Office, 2003.

U.S. Central Intelligence Agency. *A Consumer's Guide to Intelligence.* Washington, DC: CIA, Public Affairs, 1995.

———. *A Consumer's Guide to Intelligence: Gaining Knowledge and Foreknowledge of the World around Us.* Washington, DC: CIA, Public Affairs, 1999.

U.S. Central Intelligence Agency, Center for the Study of Intelligence. *The Directorate of Intelligence: Fifty Years of Informing Policy, 1952–2002.* Washington, DC: CIA, Public Affairs, 2002.

U.S. Congress. House. Committee on National Security. *H.R. 3237—The Intelligence Community Act.* Hearings, July 11, 1996. 104th Cong., 2nd sess. Washington, DC: U.S. Government Printing Office, 1997.

———. Permanent Select Committee on Intelligence. *IC21: The Intelligence Community in the 21st Century: Hearings before the Permanent Select Committee on Intelligence.* 104th Cong., 1st sess., May 22–December 19, 1995. Washington, DC: U.S. Government Printing Office, 1996.

———. Permanent Select Committee on Intelligence and Senate Select Committee on Intelligence. *Report of the Joint Inquiry into the Terrorist Attacks of September 11, 2001.* 107th Cong., 2nd sess., December 2002. S. Rep. 107-351, H. Rep. 107-792. Washington, DC: U.S. Government Printing Office, 2002. http://www.gpoaccess.gov/serialset/creports/911.html.

———. Select Committee on Intelligence. *Recommendations of the Final Report of the House Select Committee on Intelligence.* 94th Cong., 2nd sess. H. Rep. 94-833. Washington, DC: U.S. Government Printing Office, 1976.

U.S. Congress. *Joint Hearings in Executive Session as Declassified before the House Select Committee to Investigate Convert Arms Transactions with Iran and the Senate Select Committee on Secret Military Assistance to Iran and the Nicaraguan Oppositions.* 100th Cong., 1st sess. Washington, DC: U.S. Government Printing Office, 1987.

———. *Report of the Congressional Committees Investigating the Iran-Contra Affair.* 100th Cong., 1st sess. S. Rep. 216; H. Rep. 433. Washington, DC: U.S. Government Printing Office, 1987.

U.S. Congress. Senate. Commission on Protecting and Reducing Government Secrecy. *Report of the Commission on Protecting and Reducing Government Secrecy.* [Also known as the Moynihan Report.] 103rd Cong. S. Doc. 105-2. Washington, DC: U.S. Government Printing Office, 1997.

———. Select Committee on Intelligence. *Congressional Notification: Hearing before the Select Committee on Intelligence of the United States Senate.* 104th Cong., 2nd sess., September 5, 1996. Washington, DC: U.S. Government Printing Office, 1997.

———. Select Committee on Intelligence. *Counterintelligence: Hearing before the Select Committee on Intelligence of the United States Senate.* 103rd Cong., 2nd sess., May 3, 1994. Washington, DC: U.S. Government Printing Office, 1996.

————. Select Committee on Intelligence. *Findings of the Final Report of the Senate Select Committee on Intelligence and the House Permanent Select Committee on Intelligence Joint Inquiry into the Terrorist Attacks of September 11, 2001.* Washington, DC: U.S. Government Printing Office, 2002.

————. Select Committee on Intelligence. *Joint Investigation.* [Review of the activities of the U.S. Intelligence Community in connection with the September 11 terrorist attacks on the United States.] September 18–22 and October 1, 3, 8, 17, 2002. Washington, DC: U.S. Government Printing Office, 2002.

————. Select Committee on Intelligence. *Legislative Oversight of Intelligence Activities: The U.S. Experience.* Report, 103rd Cong.,2nd sess. U.S. Government Printing Office.

————. Select Committee on Intelligence. *Renewal and Reform: U.S. Intelligence in a Changing World: Hearing before the Select Committee on Intelligence of the United States Senate.* 104th Cong., 1st and 2nd sess., September 20, October 25, March 6, 19, 27, and April 24, 1996. Washington, DC: U.S. Government Printing Office, 1997.

————. Select Committee to Study Governmental Operations with Respect to Intelligence Activities. [Also known as the Church Commission.] *Foreign and Military Intelligence.* Book 1 of *Final Report of the Select Committee to Study Governmental Operations with Respect to Intelligence Activities.* 94th Cong., 2nd sess. S. Rep. 94-755, April 26, 1976. Washington, DC: U.S. Government Printing Office, 1976.

————. Select Committee to Study Governmental Operation with Respect to Intelligence Activities. [Also known as the Church Commission.] *Intelligence Activities and the Rights of Americans.* Book 2 of *Final Report of the Select Committee to Study Governmental Operations with Respect to Intelligence Activities.* 94th Cong., 2nd sess. S. Rep. 94-755, April 26, 1976. Washington, DC: U.S. Government Printing Office, 1976.

Watts, Larry L. "Conflicting Paradigms, Dissimilar Contexts: Intelligence Reform in Europe's Emerging Democracies." *Studies in Intelligence* 48, no. 1 (2004): 11–26.

————. "Control and Oversight of Security Intelligence in Romania." Geneva Centre for the Democratic Control of Armed Forces (DCAF), Working Paper Series, no. 111, 2002.

Whitaker, Reginald. *The End of Privacy: How Total Surveillance Is Becoming a Reality.* New York: New Press, 1999.

Wiarda, Howard, and Harvey Kline. *Latin American Politics and Development.* 5th ed. Boulder, CO: Westview Press, 2000.

Williams, Kieran, and Dennis Deletant. *Security Intelligence Services in New Democracies: The Czech Republic, Slovakia, and Romania.* London: Palgrave, 2001.

Winterbotham, Fredrick W. *The Ultra Secret.* London: Weidenfeld and Nicolson, 1974.

Wohlstetter, Roberta. *Pearl Harbor: Warning and Decision*. Stanford, CA: Stanford University Press, 1962.

Woodward, Bob. *Plan of Attack*. New York: Simon and Schuster, 2004.

Zegart, Amy B. *Flawed by Design: The Evolution of the CIA, JCS, and NSC*. Stanford, CA: Stanford University Press, 1999.

———. "September 11 and the Adaptation Failure of American Intelligence Agencies." *International Security* 29, no. 4 (Spring 2005): 78–111.

PERIODICALS SPECIFICALLY GEARED TOWARD INTELLIGENCE

American Intelligence Journal
Covert Action Quarterly
Defense Intelligence Journal
Intelligence and National Security
International Journal of Intelligence and Counterintelligence
Jane's Intelligence Review
Law and National Security Intelligence Report
Military Intelligence
National Security Law Report
Naval Intelligence Professionals Quarterly
Studies in Intelligence
World Intelligence Review

ABOUT THE CONTRIBUTORS

EDITORS

Thomas C. Bruneau joined the Department of National Security Affairs (NSA) at the Naval Postgraduate School (NPS) in 1987. He is now a Distinguished Professor at NPS. He earned his PhD from the University of California at Berkeley and, before coming to NPS, taught in the Department of Political Science at McGill University, Montreal. Dr. Bruneau has served both as chairman of NSA (1989–1995) and as director of the Center for Civil-Military Relations, or CCMR (2000–2004) at NPS. He has researched and written extensively on Portugal and Latin America, especially Brazil. Dr. Bruneau has published more than a dozen books in English and Portuguese as well as articles in numerous journals. His latest article on the current topic is "Controlling Intelligence in New Democracies," in *International Journal of Intelligence and Counterintelligence* 14, no. 3 (Fall 2001), 323–341.

Steven C. Boraz graduated with distinction from the Naval Postgraduate School in Monterey, California, in 1999 with a degree in National Security Affairs and has served for more than fifteen years in Naval Intelligence. His works on intelligence, naval operations and policy, and terrorism have appeared in the *International Journal of Intelligence and Counterintelligence*, *Naval Intelligence Professionals Quarterly*, *Proceedings* (magazine of the U.S. Naval Institute), and various publications from the RAND Corporation (where he served as a Federal Executive Fellow in 2004–2005). Boraz is a Naval Intelligence Officer currently assigned to Program Executive Officer Command, Control, Communications, Computers, Intelligence, and Space (PEO C4I and Space).

CONTRIBUTORS

Priscila Carlos Brandão Antunes is a doctoral candidate in the Political Science Program at the Universidade Federal de Campinas (UNICAMP) in Brazil, where she is sponsored by the FAPESP, a state government agency that promotes research in science and technology. Antunes has published *SNI & ABIN: Uma leitura da atuação dos serviços secretos brasileiros ao longo do século XX* (Rio de Janeiro: FGV, 2002) and, with Marco Cepik, "The New Brazilian Intelligence System: An Institutional Assessment," *International Journal of Intelligence and Counterintelligence* 16, no. 3 (Summer 2003).

Marco Cepik is currently an Associate Professor in the Department of Political Science, Federal University of Rio Grande do Sul (UFRGS) in Porto Alegre, Brazil. His main areas of research are international security and comparative politics. Among his recently published books is *Espionagem e democracia* (Rio de Janeiro: FGV, 2003). Cepik has published articles in English, Spanish, and Portuguese in journals in Brazil, Latin America, and the United States. He spent his sabbatical at Oxford University in 2005, working on intelligence reform issues.

Kenneth R. Dombroski is a Lecturer at CCMR. He has been on the faculty of NPS since 1999. He also teaches graduate courses in American national security policy, peacekeeping, and the role of intelligence agencies in democracies for the school's National Security Affairs Department. A retired military intelligence officer, Dr. Dombroski was a strategic intelligence officer in the Defense Intelligence Agency and deployed with the U.S. Central Command during Operation Desert Storm. During his military career he commanded an artillery battery in Germany, served as a United Nations military observer in Israel and Lebanon, and taught military history at the U.S. Army Command and General Staff College. Dr. Dombroski earned a BA in history from Loyola University, New Orleans; an MA in international studies from the University of South Carolina; and a PhD in world politics from the Catholic University of America.

Peter Gill is Professor of Politics and Security in the School of Social Science, Liverpool John Moores University, UK, where he teaches courses in criminal justice, with particular emphasis on policing, security, and intelligence. He received his degrees from the University of London and the University of Essex and is the author of *Policing Politics* (London: Cass, 1994) and *Rounding Up the Usual Suspects?* (Aldershot, UK: Ashgate, 2002). Dr. Gill is the coeditor, with Jean-Paul Brodeur and Dennis Tollborg, of *Democracy, Law, and Security: Internal Security Services in Contemporary Europe* (Aldershot, UK: Ashgate, 2003) and, with Adam Edwards, of *Transnational Organised Crime: Perspectives on Global Security* (London: Routledge, 2003). Additionally he has published articles in such journals as *Intelligence and National Security, Policing and Society, British Journal of Politics and International Relations,* and *Socio-Legal Studies.* Dr. Gill conducts seminars on aspects of the democratization of intelligence structures and is convener of the Security and Intelligence Studies Group.

Robert Jervis is Adlai E. Stevenson Professor of International Politics at Columbia University. He previously taught at Harvard and UCLA, after receiving his BA from Oberlin College in 1962 and his PhD from the University of California at Berkeley in 1968. His *System Effects: Complexity in Political Life* (Princeton, NJ: Princeton University Press, 1997) was a co-winner of the American Political Science Association's Psychology Section Best Book Award. *The Meaning of the Nuclear Revolution* (Ithaca, NY: Cornell University Press, 1989) won the Grawemeyer Award for Ideas Improving World Order. Dr. Jervis has authored or coedited more than a dozen other books and authored numerous chapters and articles. His most recent article on intelligence is "Reports, Politics, and Intelligence Failures: The Case of Iraq," *Journal of Strategic Studies* 29, no. 1 (January 2006). He serves on numerous editorial boards, is a coeditor of the Cornell Studies in Security Affairs, and currently is chair of the Historical Declassification Advisory Panel for the CIA. He is a Fellow of the American Association for the Advancement of Science and the American Academy of Arts and Sciences.

William J. Lahneman is Associate Director for Programs at the Center for International and Security Studies at Maryland (CISSM), School of Public Policy, University of Maryland, College Park. He is an adjunct faculty member at the School of Public Policy and at American University's School of International Studies. He holds a PhD in International Relations from the Johns Hopkins University's School of Advanced International Studies (SAIS), an MA in National Security Affairs from the Naval Postgraduate School, and a BS with Distinction from the United States Naval Academy. A former career U.S. naval officer, Commander Lahneman, U.S. Navy (retired) was a Surface Warfare Officer with specializations in Strategic Planning, International Negotiations, and Nuclear Propulsion. Recent publications include "Knowledge Sharing in the Intelligence Community after 9/11," *International Journal of Intelligence and Counterintelligence* (Winter 2004–2005); "Outsourcing the IC's Stovepipes?" *International Journal of Intelligence and Counterintelligence* (Winter 2003–2004); and *Military Intervention: Cases in Context for the 21st Century*, ed. (Lanham, MD: Rowman and Littlefield, 2004).

Douglas J. Macdonald has taught at Colgate University since 1987, where in the past he has served as the Director of the International Relations Program. He received his PhD from Columbia University. Dr. Macdonald's doctoral dissertation won the Helen Dwight Reid Award from the American Political Science Association for best dissertation in international relations, politics, and law for 1985–1986. It was subsequently published by Harvard University Press in 1992 as *Adventures in Chaos: American Intervention for Reform in the Third World*. He has also published articles in academic journals such as *Security Studies and International Security*, as well as contributing chapters to various edited collections. His latest contribution is "Formal Ideology and the Cold War: Toward a Framework for Empirical Analysis," in Odd Arne Westad, ed., *Reviewing the Cold War: Approaches, Interpretations, Theory* (London: Frank Cass and Co., 2000). Dr. Macdonald has been awarded Research Fellowships at the Center for International Affairs at Harvard University and the Norwegian Nobel Institute in Oslo, Norway. He is currently writing a book on the role of ideology in the origins of the cold war in Asia.

Cristiana (Cris) Matei joined the CCMR at the Naval Postgraduate School in 2003. She earned a BS in Physics from the University of Bucharest in 1996 and an MA in International Security Affairs and Civil-Military Relations from the Naval Postgraduate School in 2001. Before coming to NPS, she worked for the Romanian Ministry of Defense as a political-military analyst.

Elizabeth Rindskopf Parker became Dean of the University of the Pacific McGeorge School of Law in 2003. Her fields of expertise, in addition to the law of national security and terrorism, include international relations, public policy and trade, technology development and transfer, commerce, and litigation in the areas of civil rights and liberties. Dean Rindskopf Parker's background includes eleven years of federal service, first as general counsel of the National Security Agency (1984–1989), then as principal deputy legal adviser at the U.S. Department of State (1989–1990), and as general counsel for the Central Intelligence Agency (1990–1995). A member of the American Bar Foundation and the Council on Foreign Relations, Dean Rindskopf Parker is a frequent speaker and lecturer on national security law. Recent publications include "September 11: Responses and Responsibilities," *Judge's Journal* 42, no. 1 (2003), "Government Controls of Information and Scientific Inquiry," *Biosecurity and Bioterrorism: Biodefense, Strategy, Practice, and Science* 1, no. 2 (2003), and "Targeting Saddam and Sons: U.S. Policy against Assassinations," *IDF Law Review* (2003). Currently, she serves on several committees of the National Academy of Sciences. She was recently appointed by President George W. Bush to be a member at the Public Interest Declassification Board.

Bryan Pate is currently a law clerk for the Honorable David F. Levi, Chief Judge, United States District Court, Eastern District of California. Mr. Pate served in the United States Marine Corps as an infantry officer and an intelligence officer, deploying to the Persian Gulf with the 11th Marine Expeditionary Unit (Special Operations Capable) in 1998. He earned a BS in Earth Systems from Stanford University and a JD from Columbia Law School, where he was a James Kent Scholar.

Steven E. Phillips has been an Associate Professor of History at Towson University since 1999. He earned his PhD from Georgetown University and, before coming to Towson, worked as a historian with the United States Department of State. There he researched Sino-American relations for an upcoming volume of the Foreign Relations of the United States series. He has researched and written on Taiwan's history, cross-strait relations, and the Sino-Japanese conflict. Dr. Phillips wrote *Between Assimilation and Independence: The Taiwanese Confront Nationalist China, 1945–1950* (Stanford, CA: Stanford University Press, 2003).

Douglas Porch earned his PhD from Corpus Christi College, Cambridge University, and joined the faculty of the National Security Affairs Department in 1996, where he is now Chairman. Dr. Porch has served as Professor of Strategy at the Naval War College in Newport, Rhode Island, and is also a frequent lecturer at the United States Marine Corps University at Quantico, Virginia, and the U.S. Army War College in Carlisle, Pennsylvania. A specialist in military history, Dr. Porch has written *The French Secret Services: From the Dreyfus Affair to Desert Storm* (1995) and *The French Foreign Legion: A Complete History of the Legendary Fighting Force* (New York: Harper and Collins, 1991), which won prizes both in the United States and in France. Other works include *Wars of Empire*, which appeared in October 2000 as part of the Cassell History of Warfare series, and *The Path to Victory: The Mediterranean Theater in World War II* (New York: Farrar, Straus and Giroux, 2004).

Mikhail Tsypkin is an associate professor in the Department of National Security Affairs, Naval Postgraduate School. He served as the Salvatori Fellow in Soviet Studies at the Heritage Foundation in Washington, DC, from 1985–1987. He joined NPS in 1987, two years after completing his PhD in Political Science at Harvard University. Dr. Tsypkin has published numerous articles on Soviet and Russian military affairs. His recent publications include *Rudderless in a Storm: The Russian Navy 1992–2002* (Conflict Studies Research Center, December 2002); "The Russian Military, Politics, and Security Policy in the 1990s," in Michael H. Crutcher, ed., *The Russian Armed Forces at the Dawn of the Millennium* (Carlisle Barracks, PA: U.S. Army War College, December 2000), 23–44; and "Military Reform and Strategic Nuclear Forces of the Russian Federation," *European Security* (Spring 2000), 22–40.

INDEX

Note: United States government agencies are listed under the heading U.S.